#IRLSchoolCounseling

#IRLSchoolCounseling

AN INTRODUCTION TO THE PROFESSION

CHRISTINE J. SCHIMMEL
West Virginia University

SARAH I. SPRINGER
Monmouth University

KATHLEEN GRANT
The College of New Jersey

KARA IEVA
Rowan University

SAN DIEGO

Bassim Hamadeh, CEO and Publisher
Amy Smith, Senior Project Editor
Abbey Hastings, Production Editor
Emely Villavicencio, Senior Graphic Designer
Kylie Bartolome, Licensing Coordinator
Kim Scott/Bumpy Design, Interior Designer
Natalie Piccotti, Director of Marketing
Kassie Graves, Senior Vice President, Editorial
Jamie Giganti, Director of Academic Publishing

3970 Sorrento Valley Blvd., Ste. 500, San Diego, CA 92121

We dedicate this book to our silent contributors—our families. The time away from families to pull a project like this together cannot be measured in minutes and hours alone. Over the period of time it took to bring this book to life, we have given birth; we have had COVID; we have known severe illness; we have experienced the loss of family members. And, like everyone, we have unsteadily weathered a collective trauma. Through all of this, our families have been there for each of us in ways too numerous to count. For this, we thank Steve, Austin, Jake, Nora, Nugget, Stacy, Avery, Rylan, Dave, John, and Julia.

With love,
Chris, Sarah, Kathleen, and Kara

Brief Contents

Preface xvii
Acknowledgments xxiii
Introduction xxiv

The School Counseling Profession: Define 1

CHAPTER 1 Transformation of School Counseling 2

CHAPTER 2 The Role of the School Counselor. 26

CHAPTER 3 Navigating the Role of the School Counselor With Multiple
Community Partners. 43

The School Counseling Profession: Manage. 69

CHAPTER 4 Beliefs, Vision, and Mission: The Framework for
Comprehensive School Counseling 70

CHAPTER 5 Using Data to Locate Educational Inequities 94

CHAPTER 6 Managing Time, Teams, and Calendars 118

The School Counseling Profession: Deliver. 145

CHAPTER 7 Multi-Tiered Systems of Support—Tier 1 Interventions 146

CHAPTER 8 Multi-Tiered Systems of Support—Tier 2 Interventions. 169

CHAPTER 9 Multi-Tiered Systems of Support—Tier 3 Interventions. 188

The School Counseling Profession: Assess 215

CHAPTER 10 Assessing School Counselor and Program Impact 216

Index. 241
About the Authors. 247

Detailed Contents

Preface xvii
Acknowledgments xxiii
Introduction xxiv

The School Counseling Profession: Define 1

CHAPTER 1 **Transformation of School Counseling 2**

Learning Objectives 2
Introduction 2
#IRLSchoolCounseling 2
Bracketing Values for Ethical Practice 3
Informed School Counseling 3
  The History of the School Counseling Profession 3
  The Future of School Counseling 12
Consultation Corner: Who You Gonna Call? 13
  Consultation # 1 14
  Consultation # 2 14
  Consultation # 3 15
  Consultation # 4 15
#EduCounselor Synthesis 15
Chapter Summary 18
Reflective Practitioner Process 18
  Clinical Supervision 18
  Professional Development 19
  #PSCSelfCare: Everyday Wellness 19
Spotlight: School Counseling Advocacy 20
Learning Connections 20
  Connections to CACREP Core Curricular Areas 21
  Connection to Professional Standards 21
Comprehensive School Counseling Assignments 21
Helpful Resources 22
  Web-Based Resources 22
  Suggested Readings 22
References 23

CHAPTER 2 **The Role of the School Counselor 26**

Learning Objectives 26
Introduction 26
#IRLSchoolCounseling 27
Bracketing Values for Ethical Practice 27

Informed School Counseling 28
   Defining the School Counselor Role 29
Consultation Corner: Who You Gonna Call? 30
   Consultation #1 31
   Consultation #2 32
   Consultation #3 32
#EduCounselor Synthesis 32
Chapter Summary 34
Reflective Practitioner Process 35
   Clinical Supervision 35
   Professional Development 36
   #PSCSelfCare: Everyday Wellness 36
Spotlight: School Counseling Advocacy 37
Learning Connections 37
   Connections to CACREP Core Curricular Areas 38
   Connection to Professional Standards 38
Comprehensive School Counseling Assignments 39
Helpful Resources 39
   Web-Based Resources 39
   Suggested Readings 40
References 40

CHAPTER 3 **Navigating the Role of the School Counselor With Multiple Community Partners** **43**
Learning Objectives 43
Introduction 43
#IRLSchoolCounseling 44
Bracketing Values for Ethical Practice 45
Informed School Counseling 46
   School Counselor as Mental Health Counselor 46
   School Counselor as Mental Health Consultant 47
   School Counselor as Mental Health Collaborator 50
   School Counselor as Coordinator (or Not!) 51
Consultation Corner: Who You Gonna Call? 55
   Consultation #1 55
   Consultation #2 56
   Consultation #3 57
   Consultation #4 57
   Consultation #5 57
#EduCounselor Synthesis 58
Chapter Summary 60
Reflective Practitioner Process 60
   Clinical Supervision 61
   Professional Development 61
   #PSCSelfCare: Everyday Wellness 61

Spotlight: School Counseling Advocacy 62
Learning Connections. 63
    Connections to CACREP Core Curricular Areas 63
    Connection to Professional Standards 64
Comprehensive School Counseling Assignments. 65
Helpful Resources 65
    Web-Based Resources 65
    Suggested Readings 66
References 66

The School Counseling Profession: Manage. 69

CHAPTER 4   **Beliefs, Vision, and Mission: The Framework for
Comprehensive School Counseling. 70**

Learning Objectives 70
Introduction 70
#IRLSchoolCounseling 71
Bracketing Values for Ethical Practice 71
Informed School Counseling 72
    Program Focus 73
    Beliefs 73
    Vision Statement 76
    Mission Statement 77
    Advisory Council 79
Consultation Corner: Who You Gonna Call? 80
    Consultation #1 81
    Consultation #2 81
    Consultation #3 82
    Consultation #4 83
#EduCounselor Synthesis 83
Chapter Summary 85
Reflective Practitioner Process 85
    Clinical Supervision 85
    Professional Development 86
    #PSCSelfCare: Everyday Wellness 86
Spotlight: School Counseling Advocacy 87
Learning Connections 88
    Connections to CACREP Core Curricular Areas 89
    Connection to Professional Standards 89
Comprehensive School Counseling Assignments. 90
Helpful Resources 91
    Web-Based Resources 91
    Suggested Readings 91
References 92

CHAPTER 5 **Using Data to Locate Educational Inequities. 94**

Learning Objectives 94

Introduction 94

#IRLSchoolCounseling 95

Bracketing Values for Ethical Practice 96

Informed School Counseling 96

Types of Data 97

Locating Inequities 99

Intentional Data Collection 103

Breaking Down the Data 104

Annual Student Outcome Goals .104

Consultation Corner: Who You Gonna Call? 105

Consultation #1 105

Consultation #2 107

Consultation #3 107

#EduCounselor Synthesis 108

Chapter Summary 110

Reflective Practitioner Process 110

Clinical Supervision 110

Professional Development 111

#PSCSelfCare: Everyday Wellness 111

Spotlight: School Counseling Advocacy 112

Learning Connections 113

Connections to CACREP Core Curricular Areas 113

Connection to Professional Standards 113

Comprehensive School Counseling Assignments 114

Helpful Resources 115

Web-Based Resources 115

Suggested Readings 115

References 115

CHAPTER 6 **Managing Time, Teams, and Calendars 118**

Learning Objectives 118

Introduction 118

#IRLSchoolCounseling 118

Bracketing Values for Ethical Practice 119

Informed School Counseling 120

Annual Administrative Conference 120

Time Logs 121

Calendars 122

Action Plans 123

Lesson Planning 124

The School Counselor and Committee Work 126

Consultation Corner: Who You Gonna Call? 130
   Consultation #1 130
   Consultation #2 130
   Consultation #3 131
   Consultation #4 132
#EduCounselor Synthesis 132
Chapter Summary 134
Reflective Practitioner Process 135
   Clinical Supervision 135
   Professional Development 136
   #PSCSelf-Care: Everyday Wellness 136
Spotlight: School Counseling Advocacy 137
Learning Connections 138
   Connections to CACREP Core Curricular Areas 138
   Connection to Professional Standards .139
Comprehensive School Counseling Assignments 139
Helpful Resources 140
   Web-Based Resources 140
   Suggested Readings 141
   Mandala Coloring Book Options 141
References 142

The School Counseling Profession: Deliver 145

CHAPTER 7   **Multi-Tiered Systems of Support—Tier I Interventions** 146
Learning Objectives 146
Introduction 146
#IRLSchoolCounseling 146
Bracketing Values for Ethical Practice 147
Informed School Counseling 147
   Getting Started With Tier 1: The ASCA Student Standards 148
   Use of Screening Tools to Identify Tier 1 Needs 149
   Things to Consider 150
   Types of Tier 1 Interventions 151
Consultation Corner: Who You Gonna Call? 154
   Consultation #1 154
   Consultation #2 155
   Consultation #3 156
   Consultation #4 156
   Consultation #5 157
   Consultation #6 158
#EduCounselor Synthesis 158
Chapter Summary 161

Reflective Practitioner Process 161
    Clinical Supervision 161
    Professional Development 162
    #PSCSelfCare: Everyday Wellness 162
Spotlight: School Counseling Advocacy 163
Learning Connections 163
    Connections to CACREP Core Curricular Areas 164
    Connection to Professional Standards 164
Comprehensive School Counseling Assignments 165
Helpful Resources 165
    Web-Based Resources 165
    Suggested Readings 166
References 166

CHAPTER 8   **Multi-Tiered Systems of Support—Tier 2 Interventions** **169**
Learning Objectives 169
Introduction 169
#IRLSchoolCounseling 169
Bracketing Values for Ethical Practice 170
Informed School Counseling 170
    School Counselor Role on Intervention Teams 171
    Targeted Large Groups 172
    School-Based Small Groups 173
    Check-In/Check-Out and Mentoring 173
Consultation Corner: Who You Gonna Call? 174
    Consultation #1 174
    Consultation #2 175
    Consultation #3 175
    Consultation #4 176
    Consultation #5 176
#EduCounselor Synthesis 177
Chapter Summary 179
Reflective Practitioner Process 180
    Clinical Supervision 180
    Professional Development 180
    #PSCSelfCare: Everyday Wellness 181
Spotlight: School Counseling Advocacy 182
Learning Connections 183
    Connections to CACREP Core Curricular Areas 183
    Connection to Professional Standards 183
Comprehensive School Counseling Assignments 184
Helpful Resources 184
    Web-Based Resources 184
    Suggested Readings 184

        Mentoring Programs 185
        Suggested Readings 185
    References 185

CHAPTER 9   **Multi-Tiered Systems of Support—Tier 3 Interventions** **188**
    Learning Objectives 188
    Introduction 188
    #IRLSchoolCounseling 188
    Bracketing Values for Ethical Practice 189
    Informed School Counseling 189
        Identifying Students for Tier 3 Intervention 190
        Common Tier 3 Interventions 191
    Consultation Corner: Who You Gonna Call? 198
        Consultation #1 198
        Consultation #2 198
        Consultation #3 199
        Consultation #4 199
        Consultation #5 200
    #EduCounselor Synthesis 201
    Chapter Summary 202
    Reflective Practitioner Process 203
        Clinical Supervision 203
        Professional Development 203
        #PSCSelfCare: Everyday Wellness 204
    Spotlight: School Counseling Advocacy 205
    Learning Connections 206
        Connections to CACREP Core Curricular Areas 206
        Connection to Professional Standards 206
    Comprehensive School Counseling Assignments 208
    Helpful Resources 209
        Web-Based Resources 209
        Suggested Readings 210
    References 211

The School Counseling Profession: Assess 215

CHAPTER 10 **Assessing School Counselor and Program Impact** **216**
    Learning Objectives 216
    Introduction 216
    #IRLSchoolCounseling 217
    Bracketing Values for Ethical Practice 217
    Informed School Counseling 218
        Program Assessment 219
        Program Evaluation 220

Tech Planning Tools 223
School Counselor Performance Assessment and Appraisal 225
Consultation Corner: Who You Gonna Call? 227
Consultation #1 227
Consultation #2 228
Consultation #3 228
#EduCounselor Synthesis 229
Chapter Summary 230
Reflective Practitioner Process 231
Clinical Supervision 231
Professional Development 232
#PSCSelfCare: Everyday Wellness 232
Spotlight: School Counseling Advocacy 233
Learning Connections 235
Connections to CACREP Core Curricular Areas 235
Connection to Professional Standards 236
Comprehensive School Counseling Assignments 236
Helpful Resources 237
Web-Based Resources 237
Suggested Readings 238
Apps for Practicing Meditation 238
References 238

Index 241
About the Authors 247

ACTIVE LEARNING

This book has interactive activities available to complement your reading.

Your instructor may have customized the selection of activities available
for your unique course. Please check with your professor to verify whether
your class will access this content through the Cognella Active Learning portal
(http://active.cognella.com) or through your home learning management system.

Preface

Greetings! Thank you for all that you currently do or that you will do to support the school counseling profession. You represent a community of dedicated professionals committed to seeing students reach their greatest potential. We are excited to support you in fostering the educational and mental health needs and overall well-being of children. As counselor educators, we, Chris, Sarah, Kathleen, and Kara, share many commonalities, including a fierce passion for school counseling and a belief in the potential of all P–20 students. While we honor and teach the American School Counselor Association (ASCA, 2019) *National Model* in our classes and use the *ASCA National Model* as a framework for this text, we also acknowledge the diversity of comprehensive school counseling practices in and outside of the United States. The hashtag (#IRLSchoolCounseling) serves to connect voices around the globe and unify us as a collective school counseling community.

Context

Work began on this text as we were experiencing a global shutdown because of the COVID-19 pandemic. It was a time in history when we were collectively feeling overwhelmed, stressed, and overloaded with technology; this created both a high level of uncertainty for adults and a trickle-down impact on our P–20 children. As this project draws to its conclusion, many of the impacts of the pandemic continue. We continue to hear reports of students, and the adults who support them, struggling to regain a sense of normalcy felt before COVID-19. Many are simply trying to find their "new normal." The COVID-19 pandemic and the social justice reckoning that took place in 2020 also revealed even greater inequities in our communities and educational systems.

Alongside this uncertainty, we would be remiss if we did not also honor that our hearts have been warmed by the many reports of humanity uniting to support each other throughout the pandemic. With the evolution of technology and telehealth tools, we have learned to connect with each other in creative and sustainable ways. This has opened more opportunities for mental health advocacy and a clearer picture of the need for and value of school counselors. We are at a defining moment for the school counseling profession, and we hope that #IRLSchoolCounseling grabs hold and engages the global community in a collective pursuit toward social connectedness, educational equity, and wellness.

Book Experience

Today's students value experiential learning in the classroom (Bourgeois et al., 2016; Moody et al., 2014; Shumaker et al., 2011); they are also drawn to and often guided by information and connections found through social media platforms. This text serves to meet these priorities by exposing readers to foundational content through an engaging and experiential process. Each chapter, predicated around a real-life school counselor's social media post, walks readers through personal reflection, consultation, and information synthesis to highlight the important steps used to understand and make informed decisions in school counseling practice.

The book begins with an introductory chapter focused on school counseling as one of many programs situated in the context of a larger educational system. The following chapter introduces readers to the evolution of school counseling and highlights the historical time line that frames the way in which educators and counselors of today understand the responsibilities and training of school counselors. The diversity of voices highlighted throughout this book represents school counselors' varied experiences and the challenges they face with respect to program delivery, professionalism, and school counselor advocacy.

Unlike traditional Introduction to School Counseling textbooks where information is provided in dedicated segments (e.g., individual counseling, advocacy, ethics), this book highlights the experiences of real-life school counselors as they navigate their roles within the context of their communities. The text is divided into the four elements of the *ASCA National Model* (2019): Define, Manage, Deliver, and Assess, with the Deliver section intentionally garnering the largest portion of attention, thus aligning nicely with ASCA's recommendation that most of the school counselor's time be devoted to direct counseling services. Each chapter begins with a social media post and immediately focuses the reader's attention on ethical bracketing. This allows readers to acknowledge and set aside the impact of their own experiences and values as they learn about best practices in the profession. Reactions to the social media post from practicing school counselors around the world connect the "real-life" school counseling experience with the ideal foundational content and practice. We conclude each chapter by advocating for professional development, wellness activities, and perhaps most importantly, celebrating school counselor successes!

 ## #IRLSchoolCounseling Elements

The following is a description of embedded features in each chapter. The format is designed to highlight a variety of school counseling experiences and to engage readers in a reflective process that mirrors important ethical decision-making steps.

Learning Objectives: Each chapter contains learning objectives. These objectives draw the reader's attention to important topics contextualized throughout the school counseling literature.

#IRLSchoolCounseling: This section highlights the voices of real-life school counselors through a post pulled from a variety of social media outlets. The intent of each post is to stimulate interest in one of several themes presented throughout each chapter and to encourage readers to consider their prior learning and current emotional responses.

Bracketing Values for Ethical Practice: As a part of their ethical practice, reflective school counselors seek to develop cultural sustainability (ASCA, 2022; Ratts et al., 2016). In doing so, school counselors regularly identify personal values and biases that may interfere with their understanding of a particular situation. The "Bracketing Values" section proposes a series of questions or comments for readers to *"bracket"* to address the situation in a more objective way. *Bracketing*, a term typically used in qualitative research, refers to a process of mitigating the effects of preconceived notions on the outcome of a process (Fischer, 2009). We ask readers to practice bracketing their beliefs in relation to the #IRLSchoolCounseling post so that they recognize how prior experiences influence their initial reactions. Bracketing also encourages readers to remain open to other perspectives presented in the next sections of the chapters.

Informed School Counseling: The "Informed School Counseling" section highlights broader foundational knowledge presented thematically in relation to the post and discussed in the context of the academic literature. Readers will use this information to synthesize perspectives presented next in the consultation corner.

Consultation Corner: Who You Gonna Call? Yes, this is our fun reference to *Ghostbusters* (for those who have not seen any of the movies)! The purpose of this section is to highlight another important decision-making step: consultation. In each chapter, readers hear from at least three practicing school counselors who provide their own perspectives on the case presented in *#IRLSchoolCounseling*. These counselors represent a variety of programmatic levels, demographics, settings, and geographic locations. Oftentimes, the scenarios school counselors face are not black-and-white. Therefore, the responses/consults are meant to present a diversity of lenses and opinions from the field.

EduCounselor Synthesis: Almost simultaneously as we were constructing this text, Levy and Lemberger-Truelove (2021) were constructing their timely article on what they refer to as the "nondual" identity of school counselors. That is, school counselors can neither be seen solely as educators nor counselors; they are both. The "EduCounselor Synthesis" section of each chapter honors school counselors' identities as both counselors and educators. School counselors are expected to synthesize their knowledge about educational systems, learning, and development with their training in mental health to attend to the educational and social/emotional needs of their students. This section supports the reader with practice in merging the foundational information in the chapter ("Informed School Counseling" section) with the voices in the consultation corner to address the scenario discussed in the #IRLSchoolCounseling post. In parallel fashion, it also serves to highlight the important integration of educational and developmental knowledge with practitioners' mental health training.

Reflective Practitioner Process: School counselors engage in *clinical supervision, professional development*, and *self-care* to further develop their knowledge and skills and to help balance professional expectations with personal wellness. The "Reflective Practitioner Process" section provides advocacy for the development and maintenance of professional and personal habits that can lead to a long and rewarding career.

Clinical Supervision: The COVID-19 pandemic created an entire new world for school counselors. According to the influx of desperate social media posts surrounding these current events, school counselors appear to be reevaluating their need and interest in clinical supervision. The truth is, clinical supervision has always been a necessary part of the profession, yet, unfortunately, it continues to be an area of school counseling practice often overlooked (Bledsoe et al., 2021; Dollarhide & Miller, 2006). The intent of this section is to reinforce its value and stimulate questions in need of further inquiry.

Professional Development: The reality is that there will always be more to know as this field continues to evolve, and one textbook alone can never address all of the necessary intricacies of the profession. We recommend joining your county, state, national, and/or international association(s) for the most up-to-date conferences, webinars, and written communication that will continue to further your knowledge. There will always be unique contextual factors embedded in your specific communities (e.g., social justice, human trafficking, disaster relief). This section offers recommendations for professional development to enhance knowledge specific to the chapter topics.

#PSCSelfCare: Everyday Wellness: Compassion fatigue and counselor burnout are growing concerns in our field (Kim & Lambie, 2018; Merriman, 2015). Reflective school counselors educate and care for themselves to better meet the needs of all school members and community partners and to ensure that they keep from making decisions that could potentially harm students, themselves, others, or the profession. This includes remaining emotionally balanced and current with the latest professional knowledge. In doing so, this section highlights activities that school counselors can use in daily practice and throughout the year to address self-care.

Spotlight: School Counseling Advocacy: Taken directly from social media, this section celebrates the successes of practicing school counselors. It also presents examples of how school counselors currently market their programs to their community and colleagues.

Learning Connections: This section of each chapter highlights the integration of material with core counseling competencies. Charts are included to offer the reader a direct connection between chapter content and relevant school counseling standards.

Comprehensive School Counseling Assignments: This section provides assignments that are designed to complement the components of a comprehensive school counseling program. The suggested assignments can be used by counselor educators as stand-alone homework assignments or items that contribute to a portfolio for comprehensive review.

Helpful Resources: It is our experience that school counselors are especially hungry for resources and materials that are easily accessible and that provide practical ideas to improve their work. This brief section provides links to practical information to enhance learning and professional practice. Websites that house practical ideas for delivering school counseling programming are featured in this section.

Getting Started

Social media provides school counselors with a plethora of opportunities to stay connected to others in the field. While we are introducing #IRLSchoolCounseling to internationally connect to the profession, our goal is to provide readers with additional resources that extend their professional networks beyond this text. We encourage readers to explore the following collection of social media gatherings and use these connections as opportunities to advance their training and professional development.

Social Media Gatherings

Facebook: You can search Facebook groups online by titles. Most group administrators require you to answer questions to gain approval to join. Some examples include:

- School Counselors Connect
- School Counseling Essentials
- The School Counselor Store
- The Elementary School Counselor
- Elementary School Counselor Exchange
- Caught in the Middle School Counselors
- High School Counselor Connection

Twitter and Instagram: These resources tend to be less formal in that they seldom require administrative approval to join or follow. The following are some of the most popular hashtags frequented by professionals.

- #schoolcounseling
- #schoolcounselor
- #scchat
- #sccrowd
- #escchat
- #mscchat
- #hscchat
- #SELchat

Whether you are beginning your school counselor training or are a seasoned school counselor with years of experience, we hope you find #IRLSchoolCounseling to be a valuable resource in your development as a professional school counselor. We hope you find the material is presented in a way that helps you bridge the gap often present between training and working as a professional school counselor. And no matter the stage of your school counseling career, we thank you for the hard work you do, or will do, on behalf of all your students.

References

American School Counselor Association (ASCA). (2019). *ASCA national model: A framework for school counseling programs.* (4th ed.).

American School Counselor Association (ASCA). (2022). *ASCA ethical standards for school counselors.* https://www.schoolcounselor.org/getmedia/44f30280-ffe8-4b41-9ad8-f15909c3d164/EthicalStandards.pdf

Bledsoe, K. G, Burnham, J. J., Cook, R. M., Clark, M., & Webb, A. L. (2021). A phenomenological study of early career school counselor clinical supervision experiences. *Professional School Counseling, 25*(1), 1–10. https://doi.org/10.1177/2156759X21997143

Bourgeois, M. B., Winters, R. C., & Esters, I. G. (2016). Teaching group processes through multiple group leadership opportunities in a masters level counselor education program. *Journal of the Scholarship of Teaching and Learning, 16*(5), 1–18. https://doi.org/10.14434//josotl.v16i5.20020

Dollarhide, C. T., & Miller, G. M. (2006). Supervision for preparation and practice of school counselors: Pathways to excellence.. *Counselor Education and Supervision, 45*(4), 242–252. https://doi.org/10.1002/j.1556-6978.2006.tb00001.x

Fischer, C. T. (2009). Bracketing in qualitative research: Conceptual and practical matters. *Psychotherapy Research, 19*(4–5), 583–590. https://doi.org/10.1080/10503300902798375

Kim, N., & Lambie, G. W. (2018). Burnout and and implications for professional school counselors. *Professional Counselor, 8*(3), 277–294.

Levy, I. P., & Lemberger-Truelove, M. E. (2021). Educator–counselor: A nondual identity for school counselors. *Professional School Counseling, 24*(1), 1–7. https://doi:10.1177/2156759X211007630

Merriman, J. (2015). Enhancing counselor supervision through compassion fatigue education. *Journal of Counseling and Development, 93*(3), 370–378. https://doi.org/10.1002/jcad.12035

Moody, S., Kostohryz, K. & Vereen, L. (2014), Authentically engaged learning through live supervision: A phenomenological study. *Counselor Education and Supervision, 53*(1), 19–33. https://doi.org/10.1002/j.1556-6978.2014.00046.x

Ratts, M. J., Singh, A. A., Nassar-McMillan, S., Butler, S. K., & McCullough, J. R. (2016), Multicultural and social justice counseling competencies: Guidelines for the counseling profession. *Journal of Multicultural Counseling and Development, 44*, 28–48. https://doi.org/10.1002/jmcd.12035

Shumaker, D., Ortiz, C., & Brenninkmeyer, L. (2011). Revisiting experiential group training in counselor education: A survey of master's-level programs. *The Journal for Specialists in Group Work,* 36(2), 111–128. doi:10.1080/01933922.2011.562742

Acknowledgments

A book of this magnitude certainly does not come together without the commitment of a team of people beyond the authors listed on the cover. We would like to, as a group, acknowledge the contributions of the following individuals:

- Dr. Erin E. C. Mason, assistant professor at Georgia State University. Dr. Mason is a widely respected expert in the field of school counseling, and we knew instantly that a textbook about school counseling would not be complete without engaging Erin to pen the chapter on the history of the profession. Erin, thank you for your willingness to continue to share your expertise with our field!

- Ms. Shelby Tortorello, graduate assistant to Dr. Springer. Ms. Tortorello was a gift to this team! Pulling the social media posts together, organizing massive amounts of material into manageable folders, contacting social media contributors seeking permission to use their content, checking references, and on, and on, and on! Shelby, what can you not do?! Simply put, this book does not come together without Shelby's work ethic, organization, and the time she committed to this project from its early stages. Shelby, "thank you" barely seems enough. We are forever grateful!

- School counselors around the globe who engage on social media. The premise of this book is to position the real world of school counseling in the context of what school counselors learn in the classroom. To all our #IRLSchoolCounseling school counselors who so graciously agreed to let us use your social media posts—you rock! Keep fighting the good fight!

- School counselors around the globe who agreed to serve as professional consultants. The author team was blessed with former students, current colleagues, seasoned school counselors we all admire, and school counselor friends who agreed to reflect on the social media posts we provided and then provide their thoughts and experiences around that topic. In some ways, the material they provided to this project is the most powerful piece of this text. To all our consultants—thank you!

- Our graduate students. As we began to meet and discuss what this book should be, our discussions centered on wanting a book that would make our own graduate students in school counseling appreciate the real world of school counseling. The desire to make a very practical, useful book to guide school counselor training was always our north star. To our students—we treasure you and hope you like the final product! Now go be great advocates for all students!

Introduction
School Counselors as Leaders and Systems-Change Agents

LEARNING OBJECTIVES

#EduCounselors can

- describe how multiple systems impact student development and functioning,
- discuss the role of the school counselor in systems change as a method to support student development and the public good, and
- explain the role of transformational leadership in school counseling.

Introduction

This introductory chapter, like other chapters in this text, begins with a thought-provoking social media post. Here, we lay the foundation for the systems work that underpins counselor leadership in the schools. School counselors must contextualize their work by understanding the variety of systems that impact students' academic, social/emotional, and career development. This contextualization has become increasingly important following the social justice reckoning that followed the onset of the COVID-19 pandemic.

#IRLSchoolCounseling

The following social media post is a retweet from the account Professional School Counselors of Color (joetruss@culturallyresponsiveleadership.com), an online group aimed at school counselors who identify as Black, Latinx, Indigenous, and/or Asian. Joe Truss is an educator who focuses on dismantling White supremacy in schools.

> **Truss Leadership – Joe Truss**
> @trussleadership
>
> "If you are doing antiracist work and everybody is happy, you ain't doing antiracist work."
> @BLoveSoulPower
> Mar 15, 2021

Bracketing Values for Ethical Practice

While it is our ethical responsibility as school counselors to make systemic changes within schools to support positive outcomes for all students (ASCA, 2022), the ongoing work associated with these changes is often difficult. School counselors continuously reflect on their values, beliefs, worldviews, and cultural norms, as they can influence our work and where we choose or choose not to take action. It is important to recognize and set aside any preconceived notions, experiences, and biases to help you respond to this scenario in a culturally sustaining and ethically sound manner. Take a moment to reflect on the previous post and then consider the following questions:

- How do you respond when people around you experience discomfort? Does this change if their discomfort has to do with decisions that you are making? What types of thoughts and feelings come up for you?
- As a new member of a school community, how will you handle situations where you have to make unpopular decisions or take a position that runs counter to the prevailing school culture?
- Think about times in your life when you took a stand for something that was important to you. What helped you in this situation? What internal and external resources did you access?

Informed School Counseling
Systems Theory as a Lens for School Counseling

Twenty-first-century school counselors recognize that students are situated within multiple, overlapping, and dynamic systems that impact student growth and development. Rather than seeing students' strengths, challenges, and worldviews as a product purely of intrinsic forces, school counselors recognize that a student's environment, including their classroom, school, family, community, and historical period, impacts functioning. School counselors attempt to understand the systems in which their students reside and identify the assets and challenges that may be conferred onto individuals within that social location. School counselors, as educational leaders, advocate for change within the environment to foster optimal conditions so students can thrive.

Professionals seeking to understand this web of related systems impacting students commonly turn to systems theory to support their work. Systems theory emerged as an alternative to the dominant form of scientific thinking of the 19th and early 20th centuries, which relied on reductionism (Montuori, 2011). Reductionism is the practice of breaking down complex phenomena into the most simplistic or fundamental level (Reductionism, 2022). Systems Theory was developed to address complexity, interdependence, and wholes (Montuori, 2011). The popular systems theorist, Urie Bronfenbrenner developed his socio-ecological model of development in 1979. Bronfenbrenner's theory posits that human development is shaped by the reciprocal interactions between a person and interdependent external influences, such as family, school, community, and social, economic, and political norms (Broderick & Blewitt, 2020; Bronfenbrenner, 1979). Bronfenbrenner identified five systems that influence each person, including micro, meso, exo, macro, and chrono. Where traditional psychological theories centered behavior, thinking, and emotion primarily in the context of individual psychology, Bronfenbrenner conceptualized human thought, feeling, and behavior as a "function of a person's exposure to, and interaction with, the environment" (Bronfenbrenner, 1979 p. 9).

Bronfenbrenner conceptualized systems as dynamic and multidirectional, meaning that individuals within the system are influenced by elements of the systems and *influence* aspects of the system. Whereas the individual has agency to act upon various aspects of the system, the system is always seeking equilibrium, so individuals and institutions act in ways that maintain balance, which is often the status quo. Changes that may disrupt the equilibrium or status quo, may face significant resistance from the system.

Using Systems Theory to Conceptualize Students and Others

As school counselors gain insight into each level in Bronfenbrenner's model, they begin to better conceptualize students and understand the complexities within human life and institutions such as schools. Systems-oriented school counselors recognize that nothing happens in a vacuum but rather thoughts, feelings, and behaviors are influenced by the dynamic interactions among changing circumstances within us and around us. The following section provides a brief overview of each of Bronfenbrenner's levels: the microsystem, mesosystem, exosystem, and chronosystem, with the individual at the center, along with their genetic predispositions, unique personal characteristics, and biological components.

Microsystem

The microsystem contains the people with whom an individual comes into direct contact, such as parents, siblings, teachers, friends, and neighbors. It also includes the institutions that the individual is a part of, such as their school, place of worship, sports team, or club. The microsystem often provides a reference point from which a young person sees the world. For example, a young person who moves from a small-rural school to a large urban school would experience a drastic change in one microsystem, which would have an impact on the child's development.

Mesosystem

The mesosystem refers to the interactions and relationships among elements of the microsystem and how that impacts the individual. Mesosystem influences may include the relationship between a parent and the child's teacher, and in turn, how this interaction impacts how each interacts with the child (Brodrick & Blewitt, 2020). For example, a parent who volunteers to be the class parent provides the teacher with additional supplies and understands the cultural norms that the child's teacher expects (e.g., White female teachers often expect parents to be deferential, nonconfrontational, and pleasant). This may create a more positive relationship between teacher and parent, which will positively affect the student's relationship with the teacher.

Exosystem

The exosystem consists of elements pertaining to the larger cultural context. It includes settings that do not involve the developing youth as an active participant but influences the youth nonetheless (Bronfenbrenner, 1979). Examples include various social, economic, cultural, and political norms and practices. The exosystem includes belief systems, values, and ideologies. In the United States, White cultural values (such as individualism, rational linear thinking, and perfectionism [Okum, 2021]) are often part of the exosystem and influence the growth and development of young people. For example, when state educational authorities mandate more standardized testing for students, students have no say in the matter. However, their lives are directly impacted as teachers and school personnel feel pressure to ensure that students are successful on the assessments.

Chronosystem

Finally, the chronosystem refers to how individuals, systems, and relationships among systems change over time (Newman & Newman, 2006). This system includes social and political events that shape an individual's growth and development. Young people today are influenced by the increased documentation of police violence toward People of Color, such as the video of George Floyd's murder, along with the ensuing political and social movement of Black Lives Matter.

School counselors recognize that student development and behavior are influenced by the interactions of multiple factors across systems of the student's environment (McMahon et al., 2014). By conceptualizing human growth and functioning with a systems perspective, the sources of students' challenges transition away from a simple individualistic lens, where issues are rooted within the individual, and become more complex, nuanced, and interconnected. Therefore, a systems perspective supports the development of better interventions, as said interventions address the complexity of the individual within the larger system. Where traditional approaches to "problematic" student behavior are often individualistic and punitive (e.g., lack of attendance in school results in detentions and impacts a student's ability to graduate) a systems perspective considers how the multiple systems have influenced this behavior. In this example, a school counselor would consider each level when conceptualizing the student's presenting issue. Table I.1 provides tangible examples for each system at play in a student's experience.

TABLE I.1 BRONFENBRENNER'S SYSTEMS AND A STUDENT'S EXPERIENCE

Individual	The student has a medical condition, such as Crohn's Disease, that may influence school attendance.
Microsystem	The young person is bullied and not attending school to avoid this conflict.
Mesosystem	The student's parent had negative interactions with school officials and believes the principal is racist. This parent speaks poorly of the school, which causes the student to see the school in a negative light.
Exosystem	The school operates from White cultural values, history, and traditions so the student who identifies as Black does not feel seen or accepted.
Chronosystem	Growing up in a historical time period categorized by increased school violence, particularly seeing school shootings on the news and having trained for active shooter drills since the age of 5, a student feels extreme anxiety at school, which impacts her ability to attend school regularly.

As we reflect on the example in Table I.1, we recognize that none of the systems exist in a vacuum and that each system interacts with other systems as the individual is acting on the systems. With this knowledge, we can begin to craft more effective and just interventions, some of which may be directed at the student while others address other systemic variables, using this paradigm. In the previous example, we may ultimately learn that the student is not attending school regularly because of the racism the family has experienced, causing them to view school authority figures as threatening and intolerant of their cultural identity. This is a much more challenging problem to address than simply assigning detentions or having the student ultimately lose credit in classes that they miss. School counselors work with this issue from a systemic perspective, addressing it from multiple levels in Bronfenbrenner's model. Table I.2 presents examples of how a school counselor might work to address issues at each system level.

TABLE I.2 THE SCHOOL COUNSELOR AT WORK IN EACH OF BRONFENBRENNER'S SYSTEMS

Individual	The school counselor works with the student to develop a critical consciousness around the issues they and their family are experiencing in school. The school counselor helps the student name and process their feelings about their families' unfair treatment in school.
Microsystem	The school counselor conducts a school climate audit to examine the policies, practices, attitudes, and behaviors of the school community across the spectrum of culture.

Mesosystem	The school counselor, along with members of the school community (students, parents, teachers, administrators, and community members), develop a plan to increase community connectedness, from a cultural-competent perspective. The school acknowledges the harm it has done and creates a plan to do better, which will be regularly reviewed and assessed.
Exosystem	The school community works to understand how dominant cultural values are transmitted to students via schooling; the community endeavors to decenter whiteness.
Chronosystem	The school counselor takes into consideration the legacy of slavery, the era of Jim Crow laws, and the ongoing oppression of communities of color and the associated generational trauma when working with this student, family, and community.

Systems Theory and Cultural Considerations

A systems perspective takes each student's cultural background, cultural values, and cultural identity development into consideration when working with youth (McMahon et al., 2014). School counselors endeavor to deeply understand the experiences of their students (microlevel) and strive to gain awareness of cultural factors in the individual student. They also work to understand how culture and cultural differences impact the interactions (mesolevel) among all persons within the school, such as a teacher and a student, and how cultural forces such as racism, classism, and sexism (exolevel) impact the experiences and development of youth.

Privilege and oppression deeply shape the experiences of young people. School counselors recognize that cultural hierarchies are endemic in U.S. society and were created and are maintained as a method for those in positions of privilege to maintain power. A systems perspective helps us understand how oppression and privilege work within our society. Oppression can include racism, sexism, classism, heterosexism, and ableism, among others (Holcomb-McCoy, 2007). As we work to dismantle systemic oppression stemming from the legacy of colonialism and slavery, we also recognize that White supremacy culture permeates each level of Bronfenbrenner's model.

Historically, schools have been cultural institutions that served to maintain social hierarchy. Schools sorted students, often based on assessments, into tracks that determined what type of career a student would be able to assume. A pattern emerged based on gender, race, and socioeconomic status, with the White, male, and upper middle-class students being offered opportunities for higher education and the poorer students generally funneled into lower wage labor. In the industrial age, schools adopted practices that indoctrinated youth into practices associated with factory work, such as rigid attendance, memorization, compliance with authority (Robinson, 2006). Most schools today maintain vestiges of these practices that were developed to maintain capitalist, and classist systems of domination (such as the school bell, which was initially introduced into schools to simulate the factory work bell). Most members of a school community have "internalized the attitudes, understandings, and patterns of thoughts that allow us to function in and collaborate with systems of oppression" (Holcomb-McCoy, 2007, p. 18). Schools are often still deeply hierarchical places, which serves to maintain cultural hierarchy by teaching students that hierarchy is normal, natural, and "right." Social and cultural hierarchy is key to maintaining systems of oppression. As school counselors, we recognize that "all forms of oppression, such as racism, classism, ableism, sexism, heterosexism, clearly undermine the emotional and interpersonal well-being of students and thus potentially result in student underachievement and mental and emotional distress" (Holcomb-McCoy, 2007, p. 18). School counselors, as systems-change agents, work in community with other educational key partners, such as students, parents, teachers, and administrators, to question and dismantle harmful educational practices, policies, and beliefs.

Challenging Equilibrium

Systems theory posits that systems seek equilibrium. This tendency makes changing inequities within schools challenging. Beliefs, practices, and patterns of interaction are deeply rooted in the collective school culture and thus resistant to change. School counselors must develop not only the critical consciousness necessary to recognize how oppression/marginalization occurs within schools but also the skills and practices necessary to create systems change. The awareness and abilities required to create change in schools requires a skill set not often developed in traditional counselor education programs. Several specific strategies to bring about systemic change are discussed in the following section. Suggestions for further reading are included in the resources section.

Tools for Systems Change

Systems change work involves changing the structures and processes of an organization through specific interventions (Abercrombie et al., 2015). Systems change in schools works to shift the nature of relationships, power, policies, traditions, values, and routines with the goal of creating more equitable outcomes for all students (Atkins & Oglesby, 2019). As we have learned, systems are complex, dynamic, and interconnected. Changing systems requires different tools, skills, and attitudes versus those required for making changes to things that are more discrete and singular in nature. For example, if a high school student is bullying a peer, we often design targeted interventions to stop the bullying and endeavor to heal the bully and the target (largely individual counseling and restorative justice strategies). However, if a school has a culture of bullying, which may be subtly embedded in classroom practices, the relationships between teachers and students, the relationship between administration and teachers, the values the school overtly or covertly communicates to youth, and the parenting practices in the community, to name a few, the tools needed to create lasting change are quite different. In the later situation, strategies to consider include the following:

1. *Development of a Critical Consciousness* – Paulo Freire (2018), the Brazilian educator and philosopher who advocated for an educational pedagogy that embraced social change, indicated the first step in the development of *conscientização i*s "learning to perceive social, political, and economic contradictions, and to take action against the oppressive elements of reality" (p. 35). Critical educators are engaged in the ongoing process of examining how oppressive forces have harmed themselves and others and are active agents in designing methods to liberate themselves and others. In practical terms, a critical school counselor looks for ways the school system has harmed students. Critical educators can see how policies, norms, and structures have conferred power and privilege to certain students and community members over others and work in community with others to create more just structures.

   Critical school counselors commit to the ongoing work to undo the toxic impact of White supremacy culture in our own hearts and minds. The undoing of this culture is the work of a lifetime, and it is our ethical responsibility to commit to serious and ongoing work to grow in this area. Counselors endeavor to recognize we are all part of a system that both privileges and marginalizes. When we are not actively working to create more just and equitable schools, we are allowing the status quo to continue.

2. *Build Community* – School counselors focus on building deeply connected, collaborative, and supportive communities. We work in partnership with community members to bring about change and recognize that it takes time and effort to develop the trust and connection required to build a community. While school counselors may generally recognize the importance of community, transformational school counselors intentionally take time to build relationships and encourage others to do the same. In practice, relationship building could look like having lunch one day a week with colleagues that you don't know well, going for a walk around the campus with your administrators and getting to know them as people, and having a weekly breakfast with parents.

3. *Find Allies and Advocates* – School counselors identify community members interested and engaged in the work of systems change for more equitable outcomes. School counselors look within and beyond traditional power structures and work collaboratively, over time, to build alliances. School counselors look, especially, toward historically

marginalized populations when seeking to partner with others on behalf of systemic change, as this is a method to disrupt the status quo and invite the strengths, wisdom, and perspectives of many to collaborate to bring about change. Many communities have local groups that are advocating for change, such as affinity parent groups (i.e., parents of color, parents with children with disabilities, parent-teacher associations, etc.), civic organizations, and religious communities. School counselors partner with and amplify the work being done in these spaces to bring about change.

4. *Roll with the Resistance* – Change is hard. School counselors who engage in systems-change work will encounter significant resistance, as systems seek to maintain the status quo. Several tools school counselors use to manage the resistance include deep listening to the experiences and thoughts of others to ensure all people feel heard; allowing data to illustrate the challenges that exist, collecting data and sharing it; and being transparent in your rationale and process (Atkins & Oglesby, 2019). For example, as a school counselor, you may hear phrases like, "this is the way this has always been done" or "that won't work in our community," when advocating for change that may disrupt the status quo. Phrases like these can be discouraging responses when we are heavily invested in the process of change; however, resistance to change is often part of the change process. As school counselors, using Rogerian skills such as empathic listening and unconditional positive regard help us to listen deeply to the resistant voices to gain understanding of the thoughts and feelings behind concerns about change. A teacher of Advanced Placement (AP) classes may be concerned about removing certain policies that govern who can take AP classes, such as a teacher recommendation. You can listen deeply to the concerns of the teacher, their worry about having students with differing abilities in their class, and their fear of not being able to "produce the same high AP scores" that they have historically produced. School counselors who are committed to this type of change empathize with the challenge of letting go of this control, of taking a risk in changing how the community views you as a professional. This is a great example of where school counselor and teacher can work together to identify information and strategies that make this change less threatening (i.e., sharing data that increasing access to AP classes has not been shown to reduce AP scores; rigorous coursework is a key factor in student success in college; therefore, by expanding access to this course, you are supporting the ability for your community to thrive in higher education, providing additional training for the teacher to expand their teaching strategies in this course for more learning styles, and communicating with the community with the innovative strategies this teacher is using to increase AP access for all student).

5. *Let Go of Fear* – White supremacy culture teaches us to be afraid that we will lose everything if we disrupt the status quo. We fear that if we speak truth to power, we will lose our relationships, power, or even our jobs (Okum, 2021). We become freer and more whole as we step into our power and our work toward creating a better world for all people. School counselors recognize this dynamic in their work. It is scary to suggest that we change the ways things have "always" been done. It can be frightening to be a voice, especially a lone voice, as we all desire to be accepted in our professional spaces. Courageous leaders recognize that fear is par for the course, but they do not allow themselves to be paralyzed by the fear. Courageous leaders can be brave and afraid at the same time and often engage in activities that may feel uncomfortable or scary. School counselors who let go of fear may still feel the pounding of their heart in their chest as they prepare to say something unpopular in a meeting, but they say the controversial comment anyway. The more we practice feeling our fear and moving through it with courage, the more able we are to be courageous leaders.

6. *Find Joy* – School counselors who seek to change systems will face many obstacles and will have hard work ahead of them. Finding a sense of joy in the work helps sustain school counselors during difficult times and helps them persevere. White supremacy culture often teaches us to strive toward perfectionism, work for the future versus living in the present, and value "productivity" over all else. School counselors disrupt the status quo by taking time to find the joy and love that is all around us within schools. We can be fully present and see the beauty in every situation. Creating time every day to express appreciation, to be present, and to look for good cultivates an attitude of joy. For example, school counselors can take the time each day to express gratitude to students, teachers, and parents for the positive ways they contribute to the school community; mindfully connect with students; and find opportunities to laugh and play with others in our community. Schools are full of joyful spaces, such as a choir rehearsing, a fierce kickball game, and an intense debate in a history class. Participating in joyful activities with members of the school community will not only strengthen the school counselor's connections to others but will also help sustain us as we engage in this work.

School Counselors as Leaders

Students today live in a rapidly changing and transforming society. Not only will the youth of today have to navigate the rapid transitions inherent in the technological age, but our students are positioned to inherit some of the most challenging and pressing issues in generations, and perhaps, even in human history. Our students will live with the effects of the climate crisis (severe storms, food, and water short-ages, pandemic disease, etc.); economic inequality, which currently leaves 21% of American youth in poverty, significantly more than any other wealthy nations; and the ongoing oppression of marginalized populations, to name a few (Stanford Center on Poverty and Inequality, 2011). Students also have a profound opportunity to create change and work to mitigate the challenges and solve these problems. While schools cannot solve all global challenges, they can support the development of the skills and attitudes necessary to survive and thrive in the complex, volatile, and uncertain future.

Given the challenges the 21st-century learner will encounter in their lifetime, school counseling leadership paradigms must shift from a traditional lens to a trans-formational leadership approach. In the traditional model, leadership was exercised to support individual student success (Shields et al., 2018), whereas success is often framed as the ability to participate in the capitalist economy (Labree, 1997). This concept of leadership is often influenced by dominant cultural norms, one which sees the leader in a position of power over others and where those in positions of power think they are capable of making decisions for those who are not in positions of power (Jones & Okum, 2001).

Transformative leadership focuses on systemic and equitable change in education in the service of creating a more just, democratic, and interconnected world. This paradigm allows school counselors to move away from "fixing kids" to creating more equitable learning environments (Shields et al., 2018) that support the devel-opment of the full human potential. Transformative leadership supports the growth of individual students and models ways of being with each other rooted in collective liberation. New paradigms are necessary to break down the status quo, challenge values associated with capitalism and White supremacy, and create systemic change.

Shields (2016) proposes eight tenets of transformational leadership, which can be used to help ground leaders' thinking and guide our practice (Shields et al., 2018).

1. *A mandate for deep and equitable change.* While traditional leadership models serve to maintain the status quo, transformational leadership seeks to create a total and pervasive transformation of the conditions that create inequality. In schools, we can make changes that, ultimately, operate on a superficial level and do not fundamentally change the system. Transforma-tional leadership seeks to question, disrupt, and reconstruct many aspects of schooling. Not only are inequitable policies revised, but new mindsets are constructed. For example, as we endeavor to dismantle White suprem-acy from our schools, a superficial approach would be to simply revise the school's statement on diversity and inclusion. A deep and equitable change looks at the system as a whole and the complexities within the system. Operating from this approach, school counselors work with all key educa-tional partners and examine our implicit biases, our history, and our vision

for the future. Transformed school counselor leaders look at how our values, beliefs, policies, practices, and curriculum may reinforce the status quo, and we work with partners to create more just structures that support the growth and development of all students.

2. *The need to deconstruct knowledge frameworks that perpetuate inequality and injustice and to reconstruct them in more equitable ways.* Transformed leaders acknowledge that bias and discrimination are deeply embedded in the fabric of our society and our schools. For example, most people within the White supremacist culture develop biases about people in marginalized populations. It is the ongoing work of leaders to work with key colleagues and community partners to examine how implicit biases impact students at every level, such as curriculum and policies, and also relationships and connections, and work together to prevent future harm and promote healing. In practice, school communities often require ongoing, intentional training to gain the awareness, skills, and knowledge to support this work. Organizations like the Privilege Institute, Learning for Justice (formerly Teaching Tolerance), Project Implicit, and Teaching for Change (links found in the "Helpful Resources" section) provide resources to support all school officials in better meeting the needs of our students.

3. *The need to address the inequitable distribution of power.* Systems of marginalization and oppression thrive on power imbalances and hierarchy. People in positions of power are often able to manipulate decisions and practices to preserve their privilege and block others from having the same access to decision-making. Transformational leaders ensure that all key school partners have an equal voice within the structures of school and an equal opportunity to participate in all aspects of educational life and decision-making. In doing so, students better recognize their own power and become better prepared to participate in democratic and civic life. In practice, school counselors can work with administrators to better understand who makes important decisions in school and how. Wherever possible, students should be allowed to gain access to these spaces, and their voices should be prioritized in the conversations. Also, people from historically underrepresented populations should have a significant voice in decision-making. The democratic school movement provides further examples of student-led approaches to education (Gray & Chanoff, 1986).

4. *An emphasis on both private and public (individual and collective) good.* Where traditional school counseling leadership often focuses on individual student success, transformed leadership seeks to support the development of citizens who are prepared to participate in civic and democratic life. School is not only a place to help young people gain social mobility but also a place to help young people develop in ways where they will be assets to their family, community, and the greater world. Therefore,

transformational school counselors are framing how they work within schools around both student individual growth and success (academic, social/emotional, career) and the development of the knowledge, skills, and ability to function as a citizen within a democracy.

5. *A focus on emancipation, democracy, equity, and justice.* Transformative leaders strive to create conditions where all community partners feel welcome to participate in the life of the school, and the school is rooted in principles of democracy, justice, equity, and emancipation. The term "emancipation" refers to the active striving for freedom, freedom from political, social, or economic oppression. Emancipation not only allows people to become more fully human but also allows them to participate more fully in democracy and the struggle for equity and justice for others. In practice, school counselors recognize the ways in which the process of schooling restricts students from becoming free, such as schools that rely on a narrow curriculum. Transformed school counselors support educational practices and content designed to allow students to develop the skills, mindsets, and behaviors needed to fully participate as global citizens in the 21st century. For example, an elementary school counselor may recognize that many of the students in her school are struggling with the rigid nature of the school day. The teachers and administrators value student compliance over all else, and a "good" student is a student who is "well behaved." A transformed school counselor recognizes that many students do not like school and feel as if they can never achieve the standard that is expected of them. A practice of liberation is recognizing that the physical, social, and emotional needs of these students are not being met. The inability of many students to achieve this requirement is due in large part to a limited recess period (20 minutes of free time each day) and developmentally inappropriate expectations of normal childhood needs for movement (teachers expecting young children to sit for 90 minutes at a time). In this example, students are permitted to share why the current policies are challenging for them and work with the adults to imagine alternatives, which are informed by best-practice guidelines.

6. *An emphasis on interconnectedness, interdependence, and global awareness.* Transformed leaders seek to develop an understanding of how we are connected to others throughout our communities and the greater world. Transformed leaders embrace a systems perspective and recognize that we are all embedded within multiple, dynamic, and overlapping systems. Collective change occurs in community with others. Transformed leaders strive to develop a curiosity and understanding of how we are connected to others in our local communities and throughout the world. Transformed school counselors recognize that the thriving of individual

students is interconnected with the health of the entire community and that of the greater world. A simple example often found in schools is bullying. The bullying dynamic never occurs in isolation, it sends ripples throughout the entire school community, and impacts students' feelings of safety, acceptance, and belonging. Transformed school counselors operate from an understanding of the interconnected nature of our experiences.

7. *The necessity of balancing critique with promise.* Transformed leaders are critical thinkers who deeply understand the historical, economic, political, and cultural factors that lead to systems of inequity and oppression. Transformed school counselors are able to hold varying perspectives and experiences at once, especially experiences similar to students from marginalized communities. This critical awareness is the starting point in transforming systems. Transformed leaders balance a critical perspective with the promise of a better future, the hope that a more equitable and just system can develop through collective action. This tenet states that it is not enough to identify the conditions that make a system unequal, but that this criticism must result in action that works toward change. For example, a school counselor may recognize that the current disciplinary practices disproportionately impact students of color and can identify the historical and cultural reasons why this might exist. This school counselor is able to balance the critique of the system with the promise when they put into place a multifaceted program that addresses the underlying attitudes, biases, policies, and behaviors that maintain this system and replace them with more just and equitable mindsets, behaviors, attitudes, and practices.

8. *The call to exhibit moral courage.* Moral courage is defined as "the individual's capacity to overcome fear and stand up for [their] core values and ethical obligations" (Lachman, 2010). Morally courageous leaders "speak out, take a stand, and challenge inequity wherever they find it" (Shields et al., 2018, p. 6). The ability to stay the course, in the face of resistance, is challenging and requires skills and attitudes associated with moral courage that are not merely innate but can be developed over time. Staying the course also requires self-care to achieve maintenance over time. Transformative school counselors recognize the unjust conditions within a school, such as discriminatory disciplinary practices, policies that prevent certain students from accessing more rigorous courses, or bullying that impacts students of certain cultural identities. It takes courage to name what is happening, to shine an unflinching light on an issue that others may not want you to see. To engage with these complicated issues over time takes strength, as it is often much easier to turn away. Transformative school counselors demonstrate moral courage as they endeavor to create more just outcomes for all students.

Consultation Corner: Who You Gonna Call?

In future chapters, we ask you to bracket your feelings and experiences after reading the "Informed School Counseling" section. Then, we ask that you consider who you would call in and outside of the school building, and what you might ask them to help support your decision-making. Take a moment here to document these questions. In the chapters to come, you will read responses to the social media posts from school counselors around the globe. However, for this first chapter, we want to provide you with thoughts from the authors of the text. Here, we each provide our thoughts on schools as systems and how we have navigated systems change in our own ways.

Consultation #1

"You got to know how the system works, so you can work the system, and the system can work for you." This quote is from an episode of *21 Jump Street* that I watched when I was a teenager and has stayed with me, although shifted meanings, throughout my developmental journey as an educator and a counselor. I can't explain why the quote instilled an automatic response in me to holistically examine systems and have a wide-open lens. I carried the quote's spirit with me from undergrad as a Spanish secondary education major to my current role as a professor in higher education. Admittedly, when I think of my earlier interpretations, I assumed that as long as I understood the interconnected workings of any system (K–12 or higher ed), I could navigate the system to benefit all students and families. Within the last decade, as I continued learning, witnessing many more systems, and engaging in many critical dialogues, my lens became WIDER. I realized the interconnected systems WERE the barrier for so many and that my role in knowing the system, was to assist in dismantling the system. That also means I was helping students and families individually instead of collectively, and therefore perpetuating oppressive practices and unintentionally harming others. Engaging in anti-racist work as a school counselor is imperative as we continue to remove barriers and create opportunities and pathways for those that have been historically marginalized. Doing this work is a lifelong learning journey and I look forward to continuing to learn together.

Kara Ieva

Consultation #2

Wow—this social media post really resonates with me! As a new school counselor, I remember desperately wanting everyone in the school to like me. As a middle-class, White, female, I was socialized to believe that "good girls" are always sweet, kind, supportive, pleasing, and never rock the boat. However, as a new school counselor, I quickly learned that this type of attitude would never result in questioning the status quo and that these practices would actually create harm for some students. I had to let go of my desire to be comfortable and to be liked by everyone to be an agent of change. As the school anti-bullying specialist, I shared data with members of the school community to suggest sexist cultural values that resulted in aggressive acts toward girls and younger, less powerful boys. The football team, in particular, was a group that perpetuated harmful values and norms. While I did my best to share data from a collaborative, research-based perspective, many people, and some of them with a lot of power within the community, were upset with the overall message. It was not an easy time for me, but by then, I had done my own work around the early socialization I had received and had a strong system of allies that supported me. I was able to navigate this challenging situation and continue to advocate for systems change.

Kathleen Grant

Consultation #3

Yes, yes, yes! This post is so true and yet so hard to conceptualize as a new school counselor. One of my first jobs began when I replaced a beloved teacher, turned "guidance counselor," who had just retired at our elementary school. As I began to learn about our district, it became clear that our school demographics were changing, and I knew that our community needed a progressive school counselor who used data to advocate for change and to inform the design of culturally sustaining interventions. The problem was, not everyone in the school was ready for us to look so closely at our deficits; after all, I regularly received messages like, "We've always done things this way, and you're new here; you'll learn." On a district level, our administrators brought in researchers who highlighted our overrepresentation of children of color in special education; as faculty and school employees, we created diversity "bookclub" groups and began examining our practices more generally— to the degree that kept us comfortable, of course! The work, however, could not just be supported by self-selected individuals wanting to create deeper connections with our diverse community. We needed to have uncomfortable conversations about what wasn't being discussed! As a young female, I struggled to navigate how much to challenge antiquated and, at times, unequitable disciplinary practices, especially working in a male-dominated leadership structure. There were many dynamics to navigate in order to advocate for our students and families. I was very grateful to find wonderful mentors who helped me to find resources for our families and to make decisions about how to address certain issues. At the end of the day, however, I had to deal with the fact that decisions I made (e.g., calling Child Protective Services, addressing inappropriate behavioral referrals) did not always make my colleagues happy; in fact, we had a number of uncomfortable conversations that did not always lead to systemic change (or my popularity) but did disrupt the status quo and plant some seeds for future progress. This was obviously very disappointing in those moments, but I learned over the course of my career how important it is to me to be authentic and willing to initiate courageous conversations. The more I planted seeds, the more others (slowly and sometimes even after I left the district) joined me in advocating for change. We often don't realize the impact we make until much later, if at all, but it's still worth it! It is important for us to use our positionality as school counselors to lead the charge and use our skills to identify needs for our students AND our school communities. This is most often an uncomfortable place but one that is necessary for growth.

Sarah Springer

Consultation #4

Honestly, when I began my career as a school counselor in the early 1990s, we didn't think of schools as the complex systems they are. School counselors really did work from more of a respond-and-react state of mind. I remember working very hard to serve all students in the best way I could. I provided a ton of classroom lessons, did a lot of individual counseling, ran several small groups, and basically ignored how school, as a system, was impacting student functioning every day. I am also aware that my lack of knowledge of how our systems disadvantaged underrepresented students prevented me from being the best school counselor I could have been. When I look back, I often look back with regret that I didn't understand these concepts and I, therefore, didn't advocate for the kinds of change to which our social media poster is referring. I am excited for you, the reader, to be gaining this knowledge at this time in your training and in our history as a nation! When you know better, you do better; I am working hard to do better and I hope you will undertake this work right out of the gate, understand how these systems work, and make some "good trouble" where maybe not everyone is super happy!

Chris Schimmel

EduCounelor Synthesis

As we examine the consultant responses, it is clear that all four of us had different experiences that led us to realize how important it is to engage in anti-racist work as school counselors and school counselor educators. For Chris, her genuine, authentic, and very human realization that she had not been taught to look deeply at the complexity of systems and their impact on school communities resonates with many school counselors. How do we take a deeper dive into these issues when we don't realize they exist? This alone can cause novice and even seasoned counselors to experience shame and consequently run away from the opportunity to learn. This, just this, is also one of the greatest hurdles to overcome as we, ourselves as school counselors, have an opportunity to deepen our own awareness and then begin to ask for accountability from our community partners. Chris's response of "when you know better, you do better" is spot on. We must be willing to continually expand our knowledge and honor our community members' lived experiences.

When it comes to engaging in courageous conversations around race, inequities, and oppressive practices, many of us with privileged identities shy away from these dialogues; unfortunately, in doing so, this demonstrates the very definition of exercising our privilege. If we can look away and not engage in anti-racist practices, we become a part of the very systems that further marginalize others. The truth is, just as the post suggests, this is uncomfortable work. As we disaggregate data to examine inequities in our practices, as we review discipline records that highlight an overrepresentation of certain populations, as we review inappropriate numbers of students from historically marginalized populations in special education, as we further scrutinize student tracking and placement, we often come to a crossroad; do we move toward this data and advocate for systemic change, or do we ignore or explain it away as an "issue" with a particular set of students? These are the moments we are encouraging you to sit in the discomfort; recognize the confusion and fear that might be coming up as you consider what to do with this information. School counselors are leaders and in positions to see the larger cultural landscapes of our schools and districts. As each of the consultants suggested, learning and advocating is a journey and one that requires us to sit with ambiguity.

As Kara points out so well, the important part is for our lens to become WIDER. As we see from all the consultant responses, we all had (and still HAVE) a lot of learning to do about our own privilege, blind spots, and biases. Kathleen and my (Sarah)'s stories highlight so many of our fears of wanting to be liked, seen as competent, and appreciated. Our positionalities as counselors can have a huge impact on the way our systems either continue with the status quo or are dismantled by brave practitioners willing to sit in a space of humility. We need to acknowledge that there is a lot we don't know and be willing to continue to exercise curiosity about how we can influence our students' and their families' futures.

Chapter Summary

Twenty-first-century school counselors recognize the multiple, connected, and overlapping systems in which their students are embedded. These contextual factors are essential to understand when partnering with students and their families. School counselors, as systems-change agents, as transformational leaders, develop awareness, knowledge, and skills to reform unjust systems to promote more positive outcomes for all students.

Reflective Practitioner Process

School counselors engage in **clinical supervision, professional development,** and **self-care** to further develop their knowledge and skills and to help balance professional expectations with personal wellness. All three areas are key to ethical practice and help to mitigate counselor burnout and compassion fatigue (Atici, 2015; Lawson & Myers, 2011; Merriman, 2015; Ohrt et al., 2015).

Clinical Supervision

The *ASCA School Counselor Professional Standards and Competencies* (ASCA, 2019) direct school counselors to "consult with school counselors and other education and counseling professionals when questions of school counseling practice arise" (B-SS 5., p. 5). As a supervisee, it is important to consider the thoughts, feelings, and experiences that come up for you as you work with students, families, and colleagues and seek consultation on difficult issues. The following are some topics for consideration as you react to this chapter.

- You disaggregate your school's disciplinary data and note that Black students receive suspensions 2 times more frequently than White students. From a system's perspective, how will you begin to handle this?
- For an upcoming board of education meeting, you are asked to discuss the results from your school's climate survey, which indicates that students who identify as Black, Indigenous, and People of Color feel less safe, connected, and supported in school. The board of education consists mainly of people who identify as White. What thoughts and feelings come up for you as you approach this task? How will you approach your presentation to the board, from a system's perspective?

Professional Development

According to the *ASCA Ethical Standards for School Counselors* (ASCA, 2022), professional school counselors engage in professional development and attend training in an effort to stay current on the trends and issues that impact students (B.3.e). School counselors, novice and seasoned alike, acknowledge there is room for gaining knowledge about the variety of systems at play in schools and communities, as well as the way in which some systems disadvantage many students. Consider finding professional development opportunities on the following topics:

- Attend anti-racist school counseling seminars/webinars
- Engage in an ongoing exploration of your identity through readings, discussion groups, and personal reflection
- Join a group that is working in your community to bring about systems change

PSCSelfCare: Everyday Wellness

When designing, managing, and implementing a comprehensive school counseling program, school and community expectations can tax even the most seasoned school counselor. The *ASCA Ethical Standards for School Counselors* (ASCA, 2022) require school counselors to recognize the high levels of stress often associated with the job. Therefore, school counselors recognize that self-care must be a priority to maintain health and overall well-being (see ASCA, 2022, B.3.h).

Wellness is the cornerstone of the counseling profession and is integral in attaining human health and thriving. Not only do we support the development and maintenance of wellness in our students, but school counselors also recognize that our effectiveness in helping others depends on our personal wellness.

The Eight Dimensions of Wellness

In this chapter, we explored how multiple systems impact the functioning of the whole. Wellness is made up of various domains that interact with one another and impact the functioning of the whole person. It is our ongoing professional responsibility to continuously monitor, assess, and attend to our wellness. The eight dimensions of wellness model can help you identify areas that will support your mental health and functioning (Swarbrick, 2006). The eight dimensions are as follows (SAMHSA, 2016):

1. *Physical* – Healthy habits relating to sleep, nutrition, and physical activity. Our relationship with alcohol and other drugs is examined.
2. *Emotional* – Ability to communicate feelings, cope with life's stressors, and find joy in life.
3. *Social* – Healthy connections with friends, family, and community; having an interest in the needs of humankind.
4. *Intellectual* – Keeping our brains active through a variety of pursuits such as personal interests, creative activity, and enriching conversation with others.
5. *Occupational* – Personal satisfaction and enrichment from one's work.
6. *Spiritual* – Finding meaning, purpose, and peace in life.
7. *Financial* – An individual's relationship with money, particularly income, debt, and savings.
8. *Environmental* – Feeling safe and well in our physical environment. This can include access to clean air and water and occupying pleasant spaces that enhance our well-being.

On a piece of paper, write down each of the eight dimensions of wellness. For each dimension, reflect on the following:

1. What am I doing that is nourishing in this area?
2. What habits may I want to incorporate in this area?
3. Create three SMART (specific, measurable, attainable, realistic, and time-bound) goals based on the wellness changes you would like to make.
4. What may I need to accomplish my goals? What challenges may occur? How will I manage these challenges?
5. Who can help me be accountable when making changes?
6. How will I feel when I have achieved my goals?

Spotlight: School Counseling Advocacy

Here we spotlight the work of a school counselor educator who is well respected in the school counseling community. Dr. Ian Levy has, in many ways, spent his career devoted to implementing and researching culturally sustaining approaches to working with youth from underrepresented groups. Dr. Levy's *Hip Hop and Spoken Word Therapy* is blossoming into a widely accepted way of conducting interventions with students. His advice here is warranted and well said!

Ian P. Levy Ed.D ...

Q4: The birth of our profession was in service of White supremacy. To work against this as a **school counselor** is to expect that simply doing your job without question upholds that. Instead, collect and disaggregate data around everything. Expect **racism**.

#scchat

2/3/21

Learning Connections

Both professional school counselors in training and seasoned school counselors understand the importance of understanding the connections between the concepts commonly taught in counseling programs and the standards most associated with school counselor training. Therefore, the following table offers broad connections between the material and information in this chapter and the Council for Accreditation of Counseling and Related Educational Programs (CACREP) standards, The *ASCA School Counselor Professional Standards and Competencies* (ASCA, 2019), and the *ASCA Ethical Standards for School Counselors* (ASCA, 2022).

Connections to CACREP Core Curricular Areas

Professional Counseling Orientation and Ethical Practice	Social and Cultural Diversity	Human Growth and Development	Career Development	Counseling and Helping Relationships	Group Counseling and Group Work	Assessment and Testing	Research and Program Evaluation
X	X	X		X			

Connections to Professional Standards

CACREP	ASCA SC Competencies	Ethical Standards: SC
		A.1.c. Support all students and their development by actively working to eliminate systemic barriers or bias impeding student development.
G.2.a School counselor roles as leaders, advocates, and systems change agents in P–12 schools	B-PF 2. Demonstrate understanding of educational systems, legal issues, policies, research and trends in education	A.3.a. Provide students with a culturally responsive school counseling program that promotes academic, career and social/emotional development and equitable opportunity and achievement outcomes for all students.
G.2.d School counselor roles in school leadership and multidisciplinary teams	B-PF 6. Demonstrate understanding of the impact of cultural, social and environmental influences on student success and opportunities	A.4.c. Identify and examine gaps in college and career access and address both intentional and unintentional biases in postsecondary and career counseling.
G.3.h Skills to critically examine the connections between social, familial, emotional, and behavior problems and academic achievement	B-PF 9. Create systemic change through the implementation of a school counseling program	A.10.b. Actively work to establish a safe, equitable, affirming school environment in which all members of the school community demonstrate respect, inclusion, and acceptance.
G.3.k Strategies to promote equity in student achievement and college access	B-PA 2. Identify gaps in achievement, attendance, discipline, opportunity and resources	A.10.f. Advocate for the equitable right and access to free, appropriate public education for all youth in which students are not stigmatized or isolated based on race, gender identity, gender expression, sexual orientation, language, immigration status, juvenile justice/court involvement, housing, socioeconomic status, ability, foster care, transportation, special education, mental health and/or any other exceptionality or special need.
		A.10.g. Advocate for access to and inclusion in opportunities (e.g., Advanced Placement, International Baccalaureate, gifted and talented, honors, dual enrollment) in which students are not stigmatized, isolated or excluded based on race, gender identity, gender expression, sexual orientation, language, immigration status, juvenile justice/court involvement, housing, socioeconomic status, ability, foster care, transportation, special education, mental health and/or any other exceptionality or special need.

(Continued)

CACREP	ASCA SC Competencies	Ethical Standards: SC
		A.10.h. Actively advocate for systemic and other changes needed for equitable participation and outcomes in educational programs when disproportionality exists regarding enrollment in such programs by race, gender identity, gender expression, sexual orientation, language, immigration status, juvenile justice/court involvement, housing, socioeconomic status, ability, foster care, transportation, special education, mental health and/or any other exceptionality or special need.

Comprehensive School Counseling Assignments

The following section provides activities that allow for your continued growth as a professional school counselor. Both preservice and practicing school counselors will find it helpful to complete these activities. If you are currently in a graduate training program, your professor might assign these as part of your course.

- Write a reflection on the systems that impacted you as you moved through school.
- Select an initiative that you would like to promote within your school community to bring about change (allowing more access to AP classes, revising the curriculum to de-center whiteness, etc.). Conduct a power mapping exercise to identify your allies and strategies to work to bring about change. https://neaedjustice.org/power-mapping-101/.
- Conduct a critical analysis of your school community (current or a school you attended). How have policies, norms, and structures severed to maintain privilege for some students and oppress others? Identify targeted areas for change.

Helpful Resources
Web-Based Resources

- 3Bronfenbrenner's Ecological Systems: 5 Forces Impacting Our Lives
  - https://www.youtube.com/watch?v=g6pUQ4EDHeQ
- Privilege Institute
  - https://www.theprivilegeinstitute.com

- Learning for Justice (formerly Teaching Tolerance)
  - https://www.learningforjustice.org
- Project Implicit
  - https://implicit.harvard.edu/implicit/
- Teaching for Change
  - https://www.teachingforchange.org

References

Abercrombie, R., Harries, E., & Wharton, R. (2015). *Systems change: A guide to what it is and how to do it.* NPC. https://www.thinknpc.org/resource-hub/systems-change-a-guide-to-what-it-is-and-how-to-do-it/

American School Counselor Association (2019). *ASCA School Counselor Professional Standards & Competencies.* https://www.schoolcounselor.org/getmedia/a8d59c2c-51de-4ec3-a565-a3235f3b93c3/SC-Competencies.pdf

American School Counselor Association (ASCA). (2022). *ASCA ethical standards for school counselors.* https://www.schoolcounselor.org/getmedia/44f30280-ffe8-4b41-9ad8-f15909c3d164/EthicalStandards.pdf

Atici, M. (2015). Professional identity development of counselors-in-training in a school internship program in Turkey. *The Professional Counselor, 5*(1), 137–151. https://doi.org/10.15241/ma.5.1.137

Atkins, R., & Oglesby, A. (2019). *Interrupting racism: Equity and social justice in school counseling.* Routledge.

Broderick, P. C., & Blewitt, P. (2020). *The life span: Human development for helping professionals* (5th ed.). Pearson.

Bronfenbrenner, U. (1979). *The ecology of human development: Experiments by nature and design.* Harvard University Press

Freire, P. (2018). *Pedagogy of the oppressed: 50th-anniversary edition.* Bloomsbury.

Gray, P., & Chernoff, D. (1986). Democratic schooling: What happens to young people who have charge of their own education? *American Journal of Education, 94*(2), 182–213. https://wvu.idm.oclc.org/login?url=https://www.jstor.org/stable/1084948

Holcomb-McCoy, C. (2007). *School counseling to close the achievement gap: A social justice framework for success.* Corwin Press.

Newman, B. M., & Newman, P. R. (2006). *Development through life: A psychosocial approach* (9th ed.). Thomson-Wadsworth.

Labaree, D. F. (1997). Public goods, private goods: The American struggle over educational goals. *American Educational Research Journal, 34*(1), 39–81. https://doi.org/10.2307/1163342

Lachman, V. D. (2010). Strategies necessary for moral courage. *OJIN: The Online Journal of Issues in Nursing, 15*(3). https://ojin.nursingworld.org/MainMenuCategories/EthicsStandards/Resources/Courage-and-Distress/Strategies-and-Moral-Courage.html

Lawson, G., & Myers, J. E. (2011). Wellness, professional quality of life, and career-sustaining behaviors: What keeps us well? *Journal of Counseling and Development, 89*(2), 163–171. https://doi.org/10.1002/j.1556-6678.2011.tb00074.x

McMahon, H. G., Mason, E. C., Daluga-Guenther, N., & Ruiz, A. (2014). An ecological model of professional school counseling. *Journal of Counseling and Development, 92,* 459–471.

Merriman, J. (2015). Enhancing counselor supervision through compassion fatigue education. *Journal of Counseling and Development, 93*(1), 370–378. https://doi.org/10.1002/jcad.12035

Montuori, A. (2011). The systems approach to creativity. In M. Runco & S. Pritzker (Eds.), *Encyclopedia of creativity* (2nd ed., pp. 414–421). Academic Press.

Ohrt, J. H., Prosek, E. A., Ener, E., & Lindo, N. (2015). The effects of a group supervision intervention to promote wellness and prevent burnout. *The Journal of Humanistic Counseling, 54*(1), 41–58. https://doi.org/10.1002/j.2161-1939.2015.00063.x

Okum, T. (2021). *White supremacy culture characteristics.* White Supremacy Culture. https://www.whitesupremacyculture.info/characteristics.html

Reductionism. (2022). *Oxford reference.* https://www.oxfordreference.com

Robinson, K. (2006). *Ken Robinson: How school kills creativity* [Video]. TED Conferences. http://www.ted.com/talks/ken_robinson_says_schools_kill_creativity.htmlview/10.1093/oi/authority.20111013143903341

SAMHSA. (2016). *Creating a healthier life: A step-by-step guide to wellness.* https://store.samhsa.gov/sites/default/files/d7/priv/sma16-4958.pdf

Shields, C. M. (2016). *Transformative leadership: Primer.* Peter Lang.

Shields, C. M., Dollarhide, C. T., & Young, A. A. (2018). Transformative leadership in school counseling: An emerging paradigm for equity and excellence. *Professional School Counseling, 21*(1b), 1–11.

Stanford Center on Poverty and Inequality. (2011). *20 facts about U.S. inequality that everyone should know.* https://inequality.stanford.edu/publications/20-facts-about-us-inequality-everyone-should-know

Swarbrick, M. (2006). A wellness approach. *Psychiatric Rehabilitation Journal, 29*(4), 311–314.

PART I

The School Counseling Profession

Define

CHAPTER 1

Transformation of School Counseling

A Special Contribution by Dr. Erin C. M. Mason

LEARNING OBJECTIVES

#EduCounselors can

- identify the major historical events in the school counseling profession,
- associate the relationship between the current models of school counseling and major historical events,
- name the major professional development organizations that guide the practice of school counseling, and
- understand the evolution of the American School Counselor Association's *National Model* and its connection to accreditation, school counselor certification, and licensure.

Introduction

The school counseling profession has evolved significantly over the past century. From vocational counseling exclusively to the incorporation of mental health counseling, school counselors continue to navigate their roles amid an ever-changing societal land-scape. School counselors rely on many professional organizations to provide guidance around best practices and standards for ethical behavior and training. The following chapter provides a historical time line that leads us to current practice and highlights the advocacy still needed to ensure that school counselors are using their training to effectively meet the academic, social/emotional, and career needs of all K–12 students.

#IRLSchoolCounseling

The following is a social media post shared by an expert in the field:

 Russ Sabella
August 12, 2019

"Using the G word is like using VHS to describe the latest and greatest in video recording technology."

Bracketing Values for Ethical Practice

It is expected that school counselors continuously reflect on their values, beliefs, worldviews, and cultural norms and how each influences the ways in which they choose to take or not take action. As such, it is important to recognize and set aside any preconceived notions, experiences, and biases to help you respond to this scenario in a culturally sustaining and ethically sound manner. Take a moment to reflect on the previous post and then consider the following questions:

- What reactions come up for you when you hear school counselors referred to as the "G word" or "guidance counselors?"
- How might you feel and react if someone in an interview for a school counseling position refers to you as a "guidance counselor?"
- If you walk into a school and see that the school counselor's office is housed in the "guidance department," how do you react?

Informed School Counseling
The History of the School Counseling Profession

School counseling in the United States is young relative to other professions. Perhaps one of the most detailed accounts of the school counseling profession is that by Norm Gysbers in 2010, *Remembering the Past, Shaping the Future: A History of School Counseling*. Much of what is summarized in this chapter is drawn from this work as well as that of others who have been in a position to articulate our history. Bradley Erford (2018, p. 13) also provides a concise time line of events from 1895 to 2014 in his text. Readers are encouraged to see the full list of references and suggested readings at the end of the chapter. Older historical documents may be harder to find online. If you have connections to school counselors or professors who have been around the profession for a while, ask them if they have any of these works, and see if they'll share some of their own stories from decades past.

Like mental health counseling, school counseling is rooted in the larger field of psychology but because of the setting of schools, it has been equally influenced by education. The debate about school counselors as mental health counselors in school settings or educators with mental health expertise continues today (Lambie et al., 2019; Warren et al., 2020). Our history coupled with the contexts and setting in which school counselors work means professional identity often emerges as a tension point in various ways, both in school counseling practice and in school counselor preparation. It's complex, to say the least, but something that most school counselors are familiar with at a cellular level. Therefore, this section uses several questions to introduce key periods of history as it relates to identity, and it ends with an attempt to envision the future. The questions build on each other and grow in complexity and depth along with the evolution of our profession. These questions are as follows:

1. The First 100 Years: What Do School Counselors Do? (sources unattributed)
2. 2000 to 2020: How Are Students Different as a Result of the School Counseling Program? (Johnson & Johnson, 2000)
3. How Are Students' School Experiences More Equitable When School Counselors Advocate for Social Justice in the Building and Beyond? (J. Carver, V. Lindsay, J. Muse, & Y. Suarez, personal communication, 2020)

The First 100 Years: What Do School Counselors Do?

Originating in the early 1900s, "vocational guidance" came into being to ensure high school students were prepared for the industrialized workforce; this work was first done by teachers and administrators. Though there are others who can be credited like Jesse Davis, Frank Parsons, author of *Choosing a Vocation* (1909), is considered the most notable early founder of what would become known as the profession of "school counseling." Now you know that the term "guidance" dates back more than 100 years ago! As it has been told, the first 100 years of the school counseling profession were largely about establishing and defining itself. School counseling preceded mental health counseling, as the field emerged several decades later as a response to expanding "vocational guidance." It's important to remember that school counseling and mental health counseling had shared origins, albeit different time lines and ultimately different trajectories.

In the early 1900s and 1920s, "vocational guidance" grew but struggled under numerous names and with varied terms across the country. The National Vocational Guidance Association was founded during this time. Psychometric testing, which was popularized by the psychological and psychiatric disciplines, influenced the guidance movement in that it became more clinical and "problem-oriented" in nature (Gysbers, 2010, p. 22). Some suspect that this may have introduced deficit-based thinking into the profession, which set it on a path from which it has yet to ever recover fully. The 1930s and '40s were tumultuous as the United States recovered from the Great Depression and entered World War II. Guidance carried on but attempted to resolve a myriad of confusing terminology under the broader catch-all title of "pupil personnel services." Also, during this time, there was increasing interest in the preparation and certification of school counselors.

The "Space Race" of the 1950s, in particular, is recognized as a critical landmark in the school counseling profession. The National Defense Education Act (NDEA) of 1958 established large-scale federal funding of many more school counseling positions nationwide. During the 1950s, the Russians' launch of Sputnik was a threat to the progress of the U.S. space exploration program. School counseling at this time was called "guidance counseling" and mostly involved academic and career-related services. As a result, pressure was placed on schools to prepare more individuals in math and science careers so that the nation could be more competitive on the international space scene. If this sounds at all similar to the push for science, technology, engineering, and mathematics (STEM) careers in the 2010s, I would say it's another historic example of industry influencing the work school counselors do to prepare students for the workforce. Also notable during the 1950s was the establishment of the American School Counselor Association (ASCA) as the first division of the American Personnel and Guidance Association (APGA) in 1953. APGA would later become the American Counseling Association (ACA) in 1992. Over the years, differences of opinion would emerge and be contested between ACA and ASCA about the identity of school counselors.

In the 1960s and 1970s, the social and emotional development of students came to the forefront as the country reeled from the civil rights movement and wartime (Vietnam and Korea). Mental health issues of soldiers, families experiencing grief and loss, and racial, gender, and political tensions were prominent. As the role and function identity debate of school counselors continued, school administrators deemed them the natural choice to attend to social and emotional development. In the 1970s, early notions that school counseling might be more than just a position began to emerge as elementary school counseling came more into its own. Scholars such as Donald Dinkmeyer introduced the idea that school counseling should attend to the developmental needs of students, work that was furthered later by Don Myrick. Jerry Brown proposed in the late 1970s that school counseling include the "3 Cs" of counseling, consulting, and coordination (Brown, 1977). Having earned my master's degree in the early 1990s, I trained under these ideas.

The 1980s brought the first early models of school counseling programs by scholars such Norm Gysbers and Patricia Henderson (1988) and Curly and Sharon Johnson (2000). From here, states took the programmatic concepts put forth by these leading scholars, adapted them, and created their own state plans. As states began to intentionally define the school counseling profession for themselves, this began a time in which there was great regional scrutiny of role, function, credentialing, and supervision. Additionally, it set in motion the production of many documents outlining positions and a growing focus on political advocacy. The Council for Accreditation of Counseling and Related Educational Programs (CACREP) was established in 1981 to help define and establish training and preparation standards for graduate programs in counselor education. Graduating from a CACREP accredited program meant that students were prepared to sit for licensure exams or national certification opportunities such as those offered by the National Board for Certified Counselors. ASCA also introduced its first set of ethical standards for school counselors in 1984.

Up until this time, school counselors primarily performed a set of tasks as assigned by the building administration, which accounted for very localized assignment of duties and wide variations in school counselor functioning. The idea of a "program" brought forth a more purposeful format for organizing and providing services in three core domains of academic, career, and personal/social needs of students. The developmental nature of school counseling programs conceptualized that students had specific needs in each domain, at each school level (i.e., elementary, middle, high), and that school counseling interventions should be designed to address these needs in a systematic way.

In the 1990s, a historic document, *Sharing the Vision: The National Standards for Students* written by Chari Campbell and Carol Dahir (1997) and published by ASCA, led to greater professionalization of the field. This standards document was the first to codify what students ought to be gaining from a school counseling program in the domains of academic, career, and personal/social development. These standards would be revised in 2004. The standards-based education reform movement happening at the time drove the need for school counselors to have more objective tools for planning, delivering, and measuring their interventions. States launched legislation and large-scale efforts related to the certification and licensure of school counselors. Many, but not all states, began to drop the teaching experience requirement for obtaining a school counseling degree or certification. Today, less than a handful of states still have this requirement. During the 1990s, the identity issue resurfaced yet again with increased debate around whether school counselors provided "guidance" or "counseling," though the latter was taking precedent among leaders in the field (Gysbers, 2010).

During this time, a major movement took place that would eventually contribute to the *ASCA National Model* (ASCA, 2019a) that we know today. This movement was called the Transforming School Counseling Initiative (TSCI; Education Trust, 1996; Martin & House, 2002). TSCI focused on revising school counseling training programs to prepare school counselors for more intentional programmatic work with an emphasis on their roles as leaders, advocates, collaborators, and users of data (House & Martin, 1998). Undergirding this initiative was a belief that school counselors should act as social justice change agents who identify and help to close achievement gaps in schools, especially for marginalized groups of students facing barriers to academic and postsecondary success (Holcomb-McCoy, 2007). This shift mirrored a similar time line in the larger counseling profession. Over time, an emphasis on multicultural competencies evolved to a focus on social justice and advocacy. Examples of this shift included the growth from training and practice standards including the Multicultural Counseling Competencies in 1992 (Sue et al., 1992) to the *ACA Advocacy Competencies* in 2003 and 2010 (Lewis et al., 2018; Ratts et al., 2010), and the *ACA Multicultural and Social Justice Counseling Competencies* in 2015 (Ratts et al., 2015).

It may seem odd to use a single question to capture a 100-year period, but hopefully, after reading through the humble beginnings and somewhat cyclical nature of the profession's evolution during this time, it makes sense. During this period, school counseling seemed to be so much at the whim of what was happening around it, all the while gaining strength to define itself for its own sake. It is relevant to cite from another formative text that was written during this time. Hart and Jacobi (1992) wrote of six primary issues with school counseling: (a) lack of basic philosophy, (b) poor integration into the school system, (c) insufficient student access, (d) inadequate guidance for some students (i.e., marginalized populations), (e) lack of counselor accountability, and (f) failure to use available resources. A reckoning was needed, and it would come. The overarching question that would shape the next phase of the evolution of the profession would be one that Curly and Sharon Johnson would pose, "How are students different as a result of the [school counseling] program?" (Johnson & Johnson, 2000, p. 181).

2000 to 2020: How Are Students Different as a Result of the School Counseling Program?

Even after decades of working to establish itself as a profession and coming a long way to that end, school counseling would continue to grapple with its identity and its title in the early 2000s. Early into the new millennium, school counseling was coming into its own as states were talking with each other and the No Child Left Behind (NCLB, 2002) legislation of 2002 under the George W. Bush administration called for results-driven education reform. Curly Johnson would say, "Results are not about what counselors do. Results are about what students do" (ASCA, 2003, p. 61), which set school counseling on a path to be data-driven, a profoundly radical idea for the profession. After numerous summits with state representatives and state association presidents in the early 2000s, the *ASCA National Model*, written by Judy Bowers and Trish Hatch, was first published in 2003. The model was a culmination of the work of many leading voices (i.e., Gysbers, Johnson & Johnson, Myrick) across the country in the field at the time who sought to bring school counseling practice under a unifying framework. The model outlined four themes: leadership, advocacy, collaboration, and systemic change as core to school counseling practice. Additionally, it outlined four key components of a school counseling program: foundation, delivery system, management system, and accountability system. The *ASCA National Model* (ASCA, 2012), by its third edition, articulated "direct" and "indirect services" and how school counselors should spend their time and use data in their programs. Direct services include classroom lessons or "core curriculum," individual sessions, and responsive services, whereas indirect services include consultation, collaboration, referrals, or activities done on behalf of students (ASCA, 2012, p. 84). The model's first edition (ASCA, 2003) acknowledges all the original contributors and the states who supplied their frameworks, making it a truly valuable historic document. The *ASCA National Model*, now widely adopted and in its fourth edition (2019), has served to give school counselors a common language, a programmatic framework, and a path to accountability that relies on data-driven practices.

Social-emotional learning took greater prominence on the education stage in the 2000s as did a focus on college and career readiness and strengths-based counseling. With the early beginnings of multi-tiered systems of support, there seemed to be a gradual understanding that students' school success required the integrated partnership of all educators in the building to implement evidence-based practices (Goodman-Scott et al., 2019). The national Common Core state standards were launched in 2009 with the intent of standardizing benchmarks for measuring and testing English and math achievement across states (Dollarhide & Saginak, 2017). Interestingly, also during this time, there were significant achievements being made in the larger field of counseling. Licensure was established in all 50 states in 2009, and in 2010, ACA put forth a definition of "counseling" as part of its *2020: A Vision for the Future of Counseling*. However, ASCA was one of two divisions of ACA not to endorse the definition. Reasons cited were (a) lack of distinguishing counseling from other mental health professions, (b) lack of research to support the definition, and (c) ASCA preferred to use its own definition of school counseling (Kaplan et al., 2014, p. 369). Following these national trends, ASCA revised its 2004 National Standards for Students and in 2014 developed the *ASCA Student Standards: Mindsets & Behaviors for Student Success: K–12 College and Career Readiness for Every Student* (ASCA, 2014). Although the Common Core took hold in many states initially, over a period of years that saw unsuccessful attempts at implementation, states began to pull out of the initiative or opted to rename the standards. *ASCA Student Standards: Mindsets & Behaviors for Student Success* are still used today and mark a change in domain wording from personal/social to social/emotional.

Legislatively, the early to the mid part of the 2000s saw rights protections for undocumented students under the Deferred Action for Childhood Arrivals (DACA) and historic wins for LGBTQ individuals, including marriage equality. Another momentous landmark of the last 20 years was former first lady Michelle Obama's Reach Higher campaign from 2014 to 2016. This campaign highlighted the important role of school counselors in students' postsecondary decision-making. Multiple convenings were held across the country, bringing school counseling state and national leaders together to develop new plans for improving postsecondary access for all students and for improving the training of school counselors in postsecondary advising. Mrs. Obama was even the keynote speaker at the ASCA national conference in Orlando, Florida, in the summer of 2014! This was the first time in history that school counselors received extensive, clear, and public support from a national political figure.

In the last few years leading up to 2020, there was much attention paid to several issues impacting schools and school counseling, including STEM careers, social/emotional learning, trauma-informed practices, and social media. These were at the forefront of the profession and featured heavily at conferences and in publications. There was more appreciation for educating the whole child and understanding that academics happen in the context of students' social and emotional well-being or lack thereof (CASEL, 2017). Social media rapidly and radically changed the social context as we knew it by impacting the development of children and teens, the nature of issues they dealt with such as cyberbullying and digital predators, and device addiction and screen fatigue (Anderson & Jiang, 2018). An increase in bullying, especially cyberbullying, meant that many states began to examine policies related to bullying. This was especially publicized with the cyberbullying crime and subsequent suicide of Rutgers University student, Tyler Clementi in 2010. In 2010, I myself took graduate students to the state capitol to advocate for The Prevent School Violence Act, a bill in Illinois that added protections for LGBTQ students to current anti-bullying policies in schools; this bill was signed into law that year. Additionally, during this year, the U.S. Department of Education developed the Common Components of State Anti-Bullying Laws and Regulations (https://www.stopbullying.gov/resources/laws), and in 2011, the Anti-Bullying Bill of Rights Act was passed in the state of New Jersey that acted as a model for other states to follow. Readers are encouraged to learn more about how this law addresses harassment, intimidation, and bullying behaviors in the schools (https://www.state.nj.us/education/students/safety/behavior/hib/). Though there is no universal federal legislation related to bullying, bullying-related behaviors like harassment can often be included under other federal laws that schools must abide by like the Civil Rights Act of 1964 and Title IX (https://www.stopbullying.gov/resources/laws/federal).

As evidenced during this time, technology overall was creating waves of both inequity and innovation in educational systems. Larry Irving, who worked under President Bill Clinton's administration in the late 1990s, is often attributed to coining the phrase "the digital divide," which describes the gap between those who have access to technology (i.e., Internet, devices) and those who do not. Irving highlights that this divide is still very much an ongoing national problem, especially for education (Sanford & Irving, 2020).

By this time, the profession had all but rejected the term "guidance" as an adjective for describing a counselor, as in "guidance counselor," though it is still sometimes used to describe curriculum as in "guidance lessons," "classroom guidance," or "guidance." One issue not mentioned yet is that of student-to-school counselor ratios. Almost perennial like the identity question, ratios received some considerable play in 2017–2020 in that, in some states, it caught legislators' attention. ASCA has long touted a recommended 250:1 ratio and thus so have most in the profession. Most states' ratios have never been anywhere near this number and the logic of lowering the caseload for school counselors so that students can receive more attention makes sense. However, the ratio recommendation dates to a 1959 suggestion made by a Harvard chemist who studied only 75 high-achieving American high schools (Barshay, 2020). Savitz-Romer (2019), a former school counselor, writes in *Fulfilling the Promise, Reimagining School Counseling to Advance Student Success*, a valuable account of the profession's history while continuing to articulate the predicament in which the profession finds itself. She calls into question the usefulness of only focusing on ratios, given the variation of school populations and student needs, and argues that education must rethink the organizational frameworks in which school counselors work; this includes protecting their time for the tasks that lead most directly to positive student outcomes. Likewise, recently, ASCA has called for research to investigate the effectiveness of the 250:1 ratio.

In 2018, ASCA officially split from ACA and became an independent association. Shortly thereafter, ASCA began to develop its own accreditation process under the Council for the Accreditation of Educator Preparation (CAEP), which has now become an official pathway for school counseling graduate programs in 2020. Pay close attention to the language here. CAEP is an accrediting body for educator preparation. CACREP is an accrediting body for counselor preparation. Once again, this raises the question about the role of the school counselor. Are we educators? Are we counselors? Or, are we both? The CAEP created some confusion and discord for graduate school counseling programs as CACREP has existed since the 1980s and had been accrediting many school counseling programs for years, often viewed as the "gold standard" in counseling accreditation. Accreditation is a complex and often controversial topic about which there are wide-ranging opinions.

2020

And then there is 2020. A year that will go down in history all on its own. The year 2020 consisted of two pandemics, one for COVID-19 and one for racial injustice, all during a very tumultuous election year in the United States. The combination of these two pandemics hit Americans especially hard, and the divide in the United States is a palpable reality. And yet, as they always have, educators carry on, including school counselors, doing their best to figure out how to use the skills they possess to support students. The challenges are vastly different but the commitment to creativity and flexibility are the same.

In March of 2020, stay-at-home orders went into effect in the United States, and most K–12 schools, colleges, and universities scrambled quickly to pivot to fully online instruction. By April 2020, the unemployment rate was at its highest since the Depression era, 14.7% (Long & Dam, 2020). The virus raged on during spring and summer and by fall, the COVID-19 deaths continued to rise in the United States (Times, 2020). The public health crisis further highlighted racial, ethnic, and socio-economic gaps such as those in health care, housing, job security, food security, technology access, and mental and behavioral health access that have historically plagued the country (Singu et al., 2020).

On May 25, a Minnesota man, George Floyd, was killed when a police officer held his knee on Floyd's neck for more than 9 minutes while nearby officers failed to intervene. His cry was, "I can't breathe." It was the beginning of an uprising of historic proportions (CNN, 2020). Floyd's murder was a prominent death during the pandemic, as were those of Breonna Taylor, Ahmaud Arbery, and Rayshard Brooks. These murders called attention to many, many other murders, a history of police brutality, oppression, racism, and White supremacy in America. Intertwined with the COVID-19 pandemic, protests erupted across the country, and the nation was embroiled in social unrest.

In July 2020, the country mourned the death of longtime Congressional Representative John Lewis of Maryland who died of cancer at the age of 80. Representative Lewis was a great and humble civil rights leader, the youngest at the March on Washington in 1963, and one of the original 13 Freedom Riders. In 1965, at the young age of 25, Lewis led protesters in a voting rights march across the Edmund Pettus Bridge in Selma, Alabama, on what would become known as Bloody Sunday (Seelye, 2020). Even at the end of his days, Lewis stood with Black Lives Matter protesters in honor of George Floyd and the many lives taken by violent acts of racism. His legacy lives on in the movements for social justice as one person devoted to making "good trouble."

Yet another supreme legacy was lost just two months later when Supreme Court Justice Ruth Bader Ginsberg died of cancer, at the age of 87. Justice Ginsberg served for 27 years on the Supreme Court as a champion for the rights of marginalized groups—namely, women. Prior to this, her law career included working as a professor at Rutgers and Columbia then many years with the American Civil Liberties Union, founding the Women's Rights Project and arguing sex discrimination cases. As the primary liberal voice in the court, there was a chance for Republicans to gain the seat and have a more dominant contingent. On her deathbed, Ginsberg stated her final wish was that she not be replaced until a new president had been elected (Totenberg, 2020). Ginsberg's legacy will be her sharp intellect and her characteristic dissent.

The compounded effect of these two pandemics, enormous death and loss, and an antagonistic election season make it all feel exponentially challenging. Specifically, for anyone in the Black community, for those who are immunocompromised, or those who lack health care, employment, live in poverty, are elderly, disabled, or otherwise marginalized by these recent events, life can be nothing less than extraordinarily hard. This extends of course to the students, families, and school employees with whom school counselors work, and for school counselors themselves. The year 2020 was a perfect storm of crises, and many are searching for meaning (Ramsden, 2020).

School counselors, professionally, are charged with supporting students and families as they navigate these challenging times, all while personally experiencing the sociopolitical climate themselves. The silver lining of school counseling is that it is inherently important and relevant work, even when it is hard because it serves the greater good. For school counselors during the pandemics, the challenges have been many and will continue to be as our country is forced to embrace the unknown health and political unrest that lies ahead. The very physical format by which school counselors are doing their work is different. They may be working in their buildings with masks on, virtually from home, or perhaps some combination of the two, switching gears every few days or as their districts mandate. Health-compromised school counselors must take extra precautions, wear more protective gear, or fill out copious amounts of paperwork to be approved to work from home. While delivering their school counseling programs, they may engage in additional tasks such as contacting students who are attending virtually but not logging in or who are having technical issues, advocating to administration for camera optional policies for virtual learning, or reporting abuse or neglect concerns based on teacher reports of something witnessed in the online environment.

The Future of School Counseling

How Are Students' School Experiences More Equitable When School Counselors Advocate for Social Justice in the Building and Beyond? (J. Carver, V. Lindsay, J. Muse, & Y. Suarez, personal communication, 2020)

School counseling, as a profession, stands at a crossroads, a time for change unlike any it has met before. From here on out you will set the course for the next phase of the profession. From here, school counseling must be more equity focused, which means being equally committed to supporting students and examining the policies and the systems of the schools they attend. School counselors will need to engage all students (and in some cases staff) in healthy racial identity development. Mental health awareness, assessment, intervention, and referral will take higher priority. The academic, career, and postsecondary domains will be less clear in the foreseeable future, so school counselors will need to be vigilant as far as advocacy for every student and be aware of new ethical challenges as they arise.

The history that has come before you has largely been written by White scholars; at its inception, mostly White men, then White men and women, and then some others who represent minority groups, many of whom are cited in this chapter. School counseling, in this way, is like the larger professions of education and counseling. ASCA maintains membership demographics and, as of July 2020, it reported its membership as 76% White and 85% female; this is similar to teacher demographics. All of those who influenced the history of school counseling and wrote about it were deeply committed to the profession and made lasting and valuable contributions. The past is important to understand because it helps to explain why the present is what it is. However, the future is aspirational; school counseling can take lessons from the past and the strengths of the present, and create something new we might only imagine.

The training and preparation for school counselors will likely shift and hopefully be proactive to meet the demands of the present and the call of the future. Graduate programs that seek to earn or maintain CACREP accreditation will need to have 60 credit hours, and in likely more states, graduation from a CACREP program will be required for professional counselor licensure. This may mean for school counselors who choose to also seek professional counselor licensure that they will have portability if they move states and may be able to practice outside of schools. ACA began an interstate compact plan toward portability in 2019 (Meyers, 2020). School counselor certification (also called licensure in some states for added confusion!)

often follows national movements, meaning the *ASCA National Model*, such that states models, certification tests, or evaluation tools are updated to reflect the language of the national model. ASCA's introduction of the CAEP accreditation poses an interesting new variable into the mix for school counselor preparation. It is likely the identity question that the school counseling profession has grappled with for so long will continue to be in play.

Time is of the essence, and society is calling for us to reexamine our purpose. Our lack of diversity within the profession is problematic, given the growing rate of diversity among the students we serve. What we need within our ranks is more of the following: school counselors of color, multilingual school counselors, male school counselors, those who identify as LGBTQ+, those who are gender nonconforming, those with disabilities, and dominant culture school counselors who are anti-racist, social justice, and equity focused. By choosing to pursue a degree in school counseling, you have become part of a large and dynamic professional community that believes in and commits to the worth of every student. My hope is that you will define for yourself what that worth really means and consider how far you will go to keep your commitment.

Four of my current students are credited with the final question for this history section. They had taken the Introduction to School Counseling course with me the previous semester, their first in the program. Because of the timing of the course, we processed together a lot of what happened during the summer of 2020. I knew that I couldn't come up with the question myself, and they were the future of school counseling that needed to be heard. We reviewed the first two questions, and I asked them, "What question do you think it will be your job to answer as future school counselors?" They shared ideas and discussed how much the program emphasized the need for counselors to advocate on many fronts. I gave them a few days, and they came back with the question that serves as the header for this section. So, their question is your question and one for all of us who are in the profession currently. These four students are the class of 2022. They are all students of color, two females, two males, each embracing a few other identities. I'll end by telling you what I told them at the end of their first semester, "You may not think you know much yet, but you will learn everything you need to. Your future students are already out there waiting for you to be their counselor. There's no time to waste. Keep going."

Consultation Corner: Who You Gonna Call?

After reading the "Informed School Counseling" section and the history of our profession, think about what else comes up for you about the "counseling/guidance" discussion presented in the social media post. What further questions might you have? Let's see what current professional school counselors from around the world have to say about this.

Consultation # 1

Hi, my name is Rachel, and I am a PK to eighth-grade Catholic school counselor in a small suburban town in New Jersey. While yes, using the term "guidance counselor" is very old-fashioned, what a great opportunity for current school counselors to advocate for themselves! There are many times I find myself correcting others to the proper term and educating them on how much our role has changed over the years. As an example, I advocated for having the proper title of "school counselor" on our school website and in our advertising material (I work in a pre–K to eighth-grade Catholic School) and was pleased to see how just by that adjustment it affected how I was introduced by my school administration during parent nights and during conferences.

(Rachel Sole, elementary school counselor, New Jersey)

Consultation # 2

Early in my career, I didn't see the harm in people referring to me as a "guidance counselor" or referring to my comprehensive school counseling program as the "guidance" department. I had the mindset that it didn't really matter what we were called as long as we were effective at our jobs and people respected what we did. However, the more time I have spent as a school counselor, the more my perspective on this matter has changed. Using the term "guidance" in our titles is at best an inaccurate depiction of our roles and for some school counselors, an offensive term which belittles and diminishes the work we do for the students, families, and communities we serve. It is an antiquated term with a very narrow scope. It implies that our only role is to guide students through the challenges associated with school and help them become academically successful. Although this IS one crucial aspect of our jobs, it does not even come close to encompassing all that we do. School counselors are responsible for a multitude of things, including helping develop social skills, running student support groups, teaching lessons, closing skill gaps, crisis intervention and de-escalation, referring students and families to community mental health services, connecting families with financial aid resources, making referrals of abuse and neglect, and teaching students skills to survive in an abusive environment; these are just some of the responsibilities of a school counselor, and to imply that our only role is to focus on "guidance" is simply not an accurate description of what we do. Many emerging school counselors will find that several people still use the term "guidance" when referring to school counseling services. In my experience, the best way to change this is to work together with your administrators and those within your school who support you and your counseling program to start changing this terminology, while also changing peoples' understandings of the roles and responsibilities of all school counselors.

(Lucas Ziems, middle school counselor, West Virginia)

Consultation # 3

Hi, my name is Kristina Weiss, and I am a middle school counselor working in a suburban K–8 building. I agree that the title "guidance counselor" is antiquated. In 1958, the NDEA set forth orders for school counseling services to primarily focus on career and college readiness. Their main role was to "guide" their students in pursuit of postsecondary education. This role shifted, however, in the late '90s with the emergence of ASCA and a push towards providing services beyond career and college readiness. School counselors today are mental health providers within the school. School counselors are providing social and emotional learning, advocating for diverse student needs, and challenging systemic inequities that impact our marginalized populations. With such a large shift in our professional role, it is up to us to educate others on the role of the school counselor and politely correct them if they use the "G" word.

(Kristina Weiss, middle school counselor, New Jersey)

Consultation # 4

Hey Russ, my name is Alicia Oglesby, and I am a high school counselor in Prince George's County, Maryland. This is a common issue that I, too, want to eradicate. Language evolves and terms change over time. The terms we use for groups of people matter. The words we choose to describe educators of all sorts are a direct reflection of their roles in contemporary society. Frankly, professional school counselors who have been educated and trained in the last decade quite often find the use of "guidance counselor" to be offensive. A somewhat extreme analogy would be the use of the word "Negro" to describe Black people. While our profession is not an obvious part of our physical identity, the comparison illustrates how the words we choose justifiably change over time. The current title is school counselor and we deserve to be called by the correct term.

(Alicia Oglesby, high school counselor, Maryland)

#EduCounselor Synthesis

The use of the "G" word is an important point of discussion within the school counseling field. As you may experience in practice, many school districts still regularly refer to school counselors as "guidance" counselors. In the "Informed School Counseling" section of this chapter and echoed by our consultant, Kristina, you learned that our history stemmed from vocational guidance, evolved to college and career readiness, and now current training and expectations focus on efforts to address students' growing mental health concerns. This is also historically noted in the shift in credits needed to complete school counselor training. At one time, school counselors needed only 30 credits to graduate and practice, with this number increasing to 48 credits and many states dropping an accompanying mandatory teaching certification. As discussed earlier, school counseling programs are transitioning to 60 credit requirements (CACREP, 2018) which is yet another signal to the field that school counselors are prepared to take on many of the short-term mental health needs and responsibilities of their school populations. While you are learning about and experiencing these shifts in graduate school, it is important to note that current practitioners trained in the earlier years of school counseling as well as administrators who may be drawing exclusively from their own experiences are not aware of the evolution and mental health training requirements of contemporary school counselors. This has likely led to the continued usage of antiquated terms and even more concerning, the underutilization of school counselors' mental health skills. This is especially relevant, as the mental health needs of students and families will continue to rise long after the immediate concerns surrounding the coinciding health and racial pandemics. For these reasons, it is important that school districts understand and leverage the full range of capabilities of school counselors. As you read previously, this is still an issue in our field and may be compounded by states who attach funding to the job description of "guidance counselor." As such, do not be surprised to see and hear the word "guidance" when you walk into your first school counseling interviews. From online job postings to the "guidance department" label secured on the walls of many schools, the "G word" still regularly appears to be a "semantic" battle that many school counselors begin their careers feeling compelled to address. The question comes in as to if, how, and when a new school counselor should advocate for this change in language; after all, a shift in phraseology, suggested by our consultants, may dually result in the more appropriate usage of counselors' skills. The answer to this is tricky. Guided by our *American Counseling Association Advocacy Competencies* (2018), school counselors must always look to advocate for AND on behalf of their students. This includes school counselors promoting their appropriate roles and responsibilities, all while learning to navigate multiple and often "politicized" systems in a professional way. Professionalism is key, and directly confronting some members of the school community who use incorrect language or suggest inappropriate roles for school counselors (e.g., dress code monitor) could negatively affect the way you and your program are perceived. School counselors must address these issues strategically as a result.

As counselor educators, we often find that this conversation first surfaces as early as faculty-led group supervision field placement classes. In our experiences, students and beginning school counselors generally find it immediately uncomfortable to see this language in the school and even promoted by many of their site supervisors and colleagues. As we share in our field placement classes, much thought and self-awareness are needed around this dilemma. Think about the initial questions you were asked to consider in this chapter after reading the post. Looking back on them now, what feelings and thoughts come up for you when you see a need for school counselor advocacy? When school counselors are dysregulated and uncalculated in their responses, they can inadvertently hurt their programs and reputations. We encourage you to consider that schools, like many other systems, can take time to evolve, and it is common to hear a "we've always done it this way" stance from school and community partners. Just as you are taught to do with clients in your skills classes, it is important that school counselors make every effort to foster strong working relationships with community partners to develop trust and reliability. Timing and language are important to consider when addressing areas about your school counseling program that you desire to change. Let's look further at how colleagues in the field consider this dilemma.

After reading Rachel, Lucas, Kristina, and Alicia's responses, each of them readily acknowledges the need to shift their communities' understanding of the name, roles, and responsibilities of school counselors. Lucas specifically discussed a desire to target administrators in advocacy efforts. Rachel suggested that using the correct language on the program website and through advertising materials was one way that helped educate the community and get administrators on board. A similar nonconfrontational way to communicate a shift in language may be to respond to an individual's "guidance counselor" language by using the correct terminology with them directly. Consider this dialogue:

> *Principal:* It seems like the guidance counselors might be the right people to work with students struggling with test anxiety.

> *School Counselor:* I agree, Principal Nash; we as school counselors can certainly run small counseling groups that target the anxiety many of our students experience as they prepare for state testing

Alicia likened the outdated "guidance" terminology to other historically antiquated terms that feel offensive. Lucas shared further concerns that school counselors who allow this language to continue might be substantiating the inaccuracies of the roles and responsibilities currently placed on school counselors. The bottom line is, this is not just a semantic argument, which many community partners and practicing counselors may, themselves, believe. As you will learn about in future chapters of this text, school counselors are often using their energy to navigate the ways in which others define their roles, rather than spending this time implementing comprehensive school counseling programs. The need to engage the community in advocacy efforts is clear; school counselors, however, must be strategic in the ways in which they initiate this dialogue. Many counselors affiliated with school counselor–specific Facebook, Twitter, and Instagram pages regularly offer tips and suggestions for advocacy efforts that consistently showcase appropriate academic, social/emotional, and career-related counseling initiatives. You may also find resources in the ASCA SCENE thread on the ASCA website and in the ACA *Counseling Today* publication. We encourage you to begin locating resources early in your careers and regularly practice the professional language needed to support your programs. Furthermore, as you will hear consistently throughout this text, we ask you to regularly consider how you are and will continue to articulate the important roles and responsibilities of school counselors and how through a variety of initiatives you will address discrepancies in language and usage of school counselors in practice.

Chapter Summary

This chapter outlines the history of the school counseling profession from its inception to current practice. As you read, over the years, our history reflects the social and political events of the time and continues to affect the ways in which school counselors are currently perceived. It is important for beginning school counselors to understand these origins to ensure that their advocacy efforts focus on the trends of today. Specifically, appropriate language, a mental health focus, and socially just practices reflect current school counseling priorities, and it is incumbent upon beginning school counselors to adopt these as professional values and aspirations.

Reflective Practitioner Process

School counselors engage in **clinical supervision, professional development**, and **self-care** to further develop their knowledge and skills and to help balance professional expectations with personal wellness. All three areas are key to ethical practice and help to mitigate counselor burnout and compassion fatigue (Atici, 2015; Lawson & Myers, 2011; Merriman, 2015; Ohrt et al., 2015).

Clinical Supervision

The *ASCA School Counselor Professional Standards & Competencies* (ASCA, 2019) direct school counselors to "consult with school counselors and other education and counseling professionals when questions of school counseling practice arise" (B-SS 5., p. 5). As a supervisee, it is important to consider the thoughts, feelings, and experiences that come up for you as you work with students, families, and colleagues and seek consultation on difficult issues. The following are some topics for consideration as you react to this chapter.

- What is your new perspective on the term "guidance counselor" or the usage of the "G word?"
- How might you approach an individual when they refer to you as a "guidance counselor?" How might you address any fears associated with correcting or confronting more seasoned colleagues?
- Imagine that you are asked to speak at Back to School Night. How might you define and discuss the role of the school counselor with parents to help them differentiate from potential preconceived ideas about "guidance counselors" that may have formed when they were in school?

Professional Development

According to the *ASCA Ethical Standards for School Counselors* (ASCA, 2022), professional school counselors engage in professional development and attend trainings in an effort to stay current on the trends and issues that impact students (B.3.e). Relative to the contents of this chapter, consider finding professional development on the following topics:

- Attend a local, state, or national school counseling conference for orientation to the profession.
- Join your state or national school counselor association for access to monthly newsletters, magazines, and journals that serve as professional development for the profession.

#PSCSelfCare: Everyday Wellness

When designing, managing, and implementing a comprehensive school counseling program, school and community expectations can tax even the most seasoned school counselor. The *ASCA Ethical Standards for School Counselors* (ASCA, 2022) require school counselors to recognize the high levels of stress often associated with the job. Therefore, school counselors recognize that self-care must be a priority to maintain health and overall well-being (see ASCA, 2022, B.3.h).

Life as a Pie

As you learned in this chapter, the school counseling profession continues to evolve. As such, school counselors have an ethical responsibility to self-assess their own emotional and physical health to ensure professional effectiveness (ASCA, 2022, B.3.h). One way to self-monitor is to create boundaries to ensure work/life balance. This is especially true in deciding where and when to advocate for things like your job title and roles and responsibilities. To start, let's examine how you currently allocate your time and reflect on whether this is working for you. For this activity, you will need a blank piece of paper and a pen/pencil.

1. Place a small circle in the center to represent you, and label it with your name. Then draw a larger circle on the outside (toward the edge of the paper).
2. Thinking of your life as a pie, divide the slices, and label them to show the various activities that you are engaged in on a regular basis. Some of the "pie slices" may include work, learning, family and other relationships, contributions to others, fun and leisure, physical and emotional self-care, and spiritual well-being.
3. Reflect on your current life by considering the following questions.
   - In looking at your pie slices, what are the areas you most value? Are my priorities and/or values reflected in this allocation of time?
   - If I had one month left to live, how might this pie look different?

- How much of my time is spent caring for others? For myself?
- Are there areas of my life that need my attention?

Spotlight: School Counseling Advocacy

Future professional school counselors below take advantage of National School Counselor Week as a time to promote the changing landscape of the profession. Each year, during the first week of February, school counselors celebrate and advocate for the profession to continue to educate community partners about the evolving role we play in schools. Begin to think about creative ways in which you want to advocate for our profession.

Jennifer Grimaldi
@Wtpscounseling

Future school counselors right here at **Rowan!**
@RowanCED @karaieva24 #Rowanproud #NSCW2020
#BuildingBetterHumans

Image 1.1

Feb 5

Learning Connections

Both professional school counselors in training and seasoned school counselors understand the importance of understanding the connections between the concepts commonly taught in counseling programs and the standards most associated with school counselor training. Therefore, the following table offers broad connections between the material and information in this chapter and the CACREP (2016) standards, the *ASCA School Counselor Professional Standards & Competencies* (ASCA, 2019b), and the *ASCA Ethical Standards for School Counselors* (ASCA, 2022).

Connections to CACREP Core Curricular Areas

Professional Counseling Orientation and Ethical Practice	Social and Cultural Diversity	Human Growth and Development	Career Development	Counseling and Helping Relationships	Group Counseling and Group Work	Assessment and Testing	Research and Program Evaluation
X	X						

Connection to Professional Standards

CACREP	ASCA Competencies	Ethical Standards: SC
1.a: History and philosophy of the counseling profession and its specialty areas	B-PF 8: Demonstrate advocacy for a school counseling program.	
1.d: The role and process of the professional counselor advocating on behalf of the profession	B-PF 2.d.: Explain the history of school counseling to create a context for the current state of the profession and school counseling programs.	B.3.b: Maintain membership in school counselor professional organizations to stay up to date with current research and to maintain professional competence in current school counseling issues and topics.
G.1.a: History of development of school counseling	B-PF 7.h: Serve as a leader in the school and community to support student success.	
G.2.a: School counselor roles as leaders, advocates, and systems change agents in P-12 schools	B-PF 8.a: Model school counselor advocacy competencies to promote school counseling program development and student success.	

Comprehensive School Counseling Assignments

The following section provides activities that allow for your continued growth as a professional school counselor. Both preservice and practicing school counselors may find it helpful to complete these activities. If you are currently in a graduate training program, your professor might assign these as part of your course.

1. State Certification and Licensure Awareness:
   a. Take out your course sequence for your master's program that lists all the requirements. Keep that to the side.
   b. Visit Department of Education websites, and locate information related to school counselor certification. What are the specific requirements for your state or other states in which you might like to work?
   c. Visit your state licensing board (e.g., Licensed Professional Counselor, Licensed Mental Health Counselor). Look at the specific requirements.
      Are there courses that you are missing that you would need to take to achieve licensure in that state? Are there gaps in the coursework between the requirements for school counselor certification and professional counselor licensure? How might this information guide your future goals and plans?

2. Back to School Night Brochure: Design a brochure for families to be given out about the appropriate role of the school counselor.

Helpful Resources
Web-Based Resources

- The ASCA Scene:
  - https://scene.schoolcounselor.org/home
- The American Counseling Association's Advocacy Competencies:
  - https://www.counseling.org/docs/default-source/competencies/aca-advocacy-competencies-updated-may-2020.pdf?sfvrsn=f410212c_4
- The ASCA Twitter page graphic, "Guidance Counselors or School Counselors:"
  - https://twitter.com/ASCAtweets/status/1131619594144288768/photo/1

Suggested Readings

- Article outlining Advocacy competencies for professional school counselors:
  - Trusty, J., & Brown, D. (2005). Advocacy competencies for professional school counsleors. *Professional School Counseling, 8*(3), 259–265. https://www.schoolcounselor-ca.org/files/Advocacy/Advocacy%20Competencies%20for%20School%20Counselors.pdf
- Text highlighting the transformation of the school counseling profession:

- Hart, P., & Jacobi, M. J. (1992). *From gatekeeper to advocate: Transforming the role of the school counselor.* College Board.
- Text highlighting the role of the school counselor in closing achievement gaps:
  - Holcomb-McCoy, C. (2007). *School counseling to close the achievement gap: A social justice framework for success.* Corwin Press.
- Text highlighting the history of the emerging role of the school counselor:
  - House, R. M., & Martin, P. J. (1998). Advocating for better futures for all students: A new vision for school counselors. *Education, 119*(2), 284.
- Text highlighting the history of the school counseling profession by Dr. Norm Gysbers, one of the prominent figures in the field:
  - Gysbers, N. C. (2010). School counseling principles: *Remembering the past, shaping the future, a history of school counseling.* American School Counselor Association.

References

American Counseling Association (ACA). (2018). *American Counseling Association advocacy competencies.* https://www.counseling.org/docs/default-source/competencies/aca-advocacy-competencies-updated-may-2020.pdf?sfvrsn=f410212c_4

American School Counselor Association (ASCA). (2003). *ASCA national model: A framework for school counseling programs* (2nd ed.).

American School Counselor Association (ASCA). (2012). *ASCA national model: A framework for school counseling programs* (3rd ed.).

American School Counselor Association (ASCA). (2014). *ASCA student standards: Mindsets & behaviors for student success: K–12 college and career readiness for every student.*

American School Counselor Association (ASCA). (2019a). *ASCA national model: A framework for school counseling programs.* (4th ed.).

American School Counselor Association (ASCA). (2019b). *ASCA school counselor professional standards & competencies.* https://www.schoolcounselor.org/asca/media/asca/home/SCCompetencies.pdf

American School Counselor Association (ASCA). (2022). *ASCA ethical standards for school counselors.* https://www.schoolcounselor.org/getmedia/44f30280-ffe8-4b41-9ad8-f15909c3d164/EthicalStandards.pdf

Anderson, M., & Jiang, J. (2018). Teens' social media habits and experiences. *Pew Research Center: Internet, Science & Tech.* https://www.pewresearch.org/internet/2018/11/28/teens-social-media-habits-and-experiences/

Atici, M. (2015). Professional identity development of counselors-in-training in a school internship program in Turkey. *The Professional Counselor, 5*(1), 137–151. https://doi.org/10.15241/ma.5.1.137

Barshay, J. (2020). *Lowest student-to-school-counselor ratio since 1986.* The Hechinger Report. https://hechingerreport.org/lowest-student-to-school-counselor-ratio-since-1986/

Brown, J. A. (1977). *Organizing and evaluating elementary school guidance services: Why, what, and how.* Brooks/Cole.

Campbell, C. A., & Dahir, C. A. (1997). *Sharing the vision: The national standards for school counseling programs.* American School Counselor Association Press.

CNN, E. C. M. (2020, August 9). *How George Floyd's death ignited a racial reckoning that shows no signs of slowing down.* CNN. Retrieved October 1, 2020, from https://www.cnn.com/2020/08/09/us/george-floyd-protests-different-why/index.html

Collaborative for Academic, Social and Emotional Learning (CASEL). (2017). *Competencies.* https://casel.org/what-is-sel/

Council for Accreditation of Counseling and Related Educational Programs (CACREP). (2016). *2016 CACREP standards.* http://www.cacrep.org/wp-content/uploads/2017/08/2016-Standards-with-citations.pdf

Council for Accreditation of Counseling and Related Educational Programs (CACREP). (2018). *CACREP board of directors delays on implementation of 60 semester credit hour requirement.* http://www.cacrep.org/wp-content/uploads/2018/02/CACREP-Special-Announcement-48-to-60.pdf

Dollarhide, C. T., & Saginak, K. A. (2017). *Comprehensive school counseling programs: K–12 delivery systems in action* (3rd ed.). Pearson.

Gysbers, N. C. (2010). *Remembering the past, shaping the future.* American School Counselor Association.

Gysbers, N. C., & Henderson, P. (1988). *Developing and managing your school guidance program.* American Association for Counseling and Development. https://books.google.com/books?id=fM1XAAAAYAAJ

Education Trust. (1996). *National initiative to transform school counseling* [Brochure].

Erford, B. T. (2018). *Transforming the school counseling profession* (5th ed.). Pearson.

Goodman-Scott, E., Betters-Bubon, J., & Donohue, P. (2019). *The school counselor's guide to multi-tiered systems of support.* Routledge.

Hart, P., & Jacobi, M. J. (1992). *From gatekeeper to advocate: Transforming the role of the school counselor.* College Board.

Holcomb-McCoy, C. (2007). *School counseling to close the achievement gap: A social justice framework for success.* Corwin.

House, R. M., & Martin, P. J. (1998). Advocating for better futures for all students: A new vision for school counselors. *Education, 119*(2), 284.

Johnson, C. D., & Johnson, S. K. (2000). *Results-based student support programs: Leadership academy workbook.* Professional Update.

Kaplan, D. M., Tarvydas, V. M., & Gladding, S. T. (2014). 20/20: A vision for the future of counseling: The new consensus definition of counseling. *Journal of Counseling & Development, 92*(3), 366–372.

Lawson, G., & Myers, J. E. (2011). Wellness, professional quality of life, and career-sustaining behaviors: What keeps us well? *Journal of Counseling and Development, 89*(2), 163–171. https://doi.org/10.1002/j.1556-6678.2011.tb00074.x

Lambie, G. W., Stickl Haugen, J., Borland, J. R., & Campbell, L. O. (2019). Who took "counseling" out of the role of professional school counselors in the United States? *Journal of School-Based Counseling Policy and Evaluation, 1*(3), 51–61. https://doi.org/10.25774/7kjb-bt85

Lewis, J. A., Arnold, M. S., House, R., & Toporek, R. L. (2018). *American Counseling Association advocacy competencies.* https://www.counseling.org/docs/default-source/competencies/aca-advocacy-competencis-updated-may-2020.pdf?sfvrsn=f410212c_4

Long, H., & Dam, A. V. (2020, May 8). U.S. unemployment rate soars to 14.7 percent, the worst since the Depression era. *Washington Post.* Retrieved October 1, 2020, from https://www.washingtonpost.com/business/2020/05/08/april-2020-jobs-report/

Martin, P. J., & House. R. M. (2002). *Transforming school counseling in the transforming school counseling initiative.* The Education Trust.

Merriman, J. (2015). Enhancing counselor supervision through compassion fatigue education. *Journal of Counseling and Development, 93*(1), 370–378. https://doi.org/10.1002/jcad.12035

Meyers, L. (2020). *Interstate compact plan provides hope for licensure portability.* Counseling Today. https://ct.counseling.org/2020/04/interstate-compact-plan-provides-hope-for-licensure-prtability/.

No Child Left Behind Act of 2001, Pub. L. No. 107–110 (2002). https://www2.ed.gov/nclb/overview/intro/execsumm.pdf

Ohrt, J. H., Prosek, E. A., Ener, E., & Lindo, N. (2015). The effects of a group supervision intervention to promote wellness and prevent burnout. *The Journal of Humanistic Counseling, 54*(1), 41–58. https://doi.org/10.1002/j.2161-1939.2015.00063.x

Parsons, F. (1909). *Choosing a vocation.* Houghton Mifflin.

Ramsden, P. (2020, June 15). *How the pandemic changed social media and George Floyd's death created a collective conscience.* The Conversation. Retrieved October 1, 2020, from http://theconversation.com/how-the-pandemic-changed-social-media-and-george-floyds-death-created-a-collective-conscience-140104

Ratts, M. J., Toporek, R. L., & Lewis, J. A. (2010). *ACA advocacy competencies: A social justice framework for counselors.* American Counseling Association.

Ratts, M. J., Singh, A. A., Nassar-McMillan, S., Butler, S. K., & McCullough, J. R. (2015). *Multicultural and social justice counseling competencies.* https://www.counseling.org/docs/default-source/competencies/multicultural-and-social-justice-counseling-competencies.pdf?sfvrsn=14

Sanford, S., & Irving, L. (2020, July). *The digital divide is causing an educational crisis.* CNN. https://www.cnn.com/2020/07/31/opinions/digital-divide-kids-education-wellness/index.html

Savitz-Romer, M. (2019). *Fulfilling the promise: Reimagining school counseling to advance student success.* Harvard Education Press.

Seelye, K. Q. (2020, August 4). John Lewis, towering figure of civil rights era, dies at 80. *The New York Times.* https://www.nytimes.com/2020/07/17/us/john-lewis-dead.html

Singu, S., Acharya, A., Challagundla, K., & Byrareddy, S. N. (2020). Impact of social determinants of health on the emerging COVID-19 pandemic in the United States. *Frontiers in Public Health, 8.* https://doi.org/10.3389/fpubh.2020.00406

Sue, D. W., Arredondo, P., & McDavis, R. J. (1992). Multicultural counseling competencies and standards: A call to the profession. *Journal of Counseling & Development, 70*(4), 477–486. https://doi.org/10.1002/j.1556-6676.1992.tb01642.x

Times, T. N. Y. (2020, July 20). Covid in the U.S.: Latest map and case count. *The New York Times.* https://www.nytimes.com/interactive/2020/us/coronavirus-us-cases.html

Totenberg, N. (2020, September 18). *Justice Ruth Bader Ginsburg, champion of gender equality, dies at 87.* NPR.org. Retrieved October 5, 2020, from https://www.npr.org/2020/09/18/100306972/justice-ruth-bader-ginsburg-champion-of-gender-equality-dies-at-87

Warren, J. M., Jones, S., & Unger, D. (2020). Strengthening professional school counseling: Recommendations for preparation. *Professional Issues in Counseling,* VI, 61–76. https://www.shsu.edu/academics/counseloreducation/piic/journals/2020/

Credit

CHAPTER 2

The Role of the School Counselor

LEARNING OBJECTIVES

#EduCounselors can

- identify various professional organizations that support the identity and roles of professional school counselors,

- recognize multiple lenses through which school counselors define their roles,

- define the differences between appropriate and inappropriate school counseling duties, and

- learn to navigate school and community partner requests in a professional manner.

Introduction

The role of the school counselor is framed within the context of the *American School Counselor Association (ASCA) National Model: A Framework for School Counseling Programs* (2019a). The *ASCA National Model* is used to create, implement, and assess a comprehensive school counseling program. The first section of the model, *Define*, draws upon three sets of standards, including the *ASCA Student Standards: Mindsets & Behaviors for Student Success, ASCA Ethical Standards for School Counselors*, and *ASCA School Counselor Professional Standards & Competencies*. This chapter explores the role of the school counselor, within the context of the three sets of standards as well as our broader professional organizations such as the American Counseling Association (ACA) and the International School Counselor Association (ISCA).

While these professional standards guide our practice, school counselors collaborate with key partners within a school community to develop a comprehensive school counseling program, which then guides the daily actions of school counselors. It is crucial that school counselors acknowledge their preservice mental health and educator training backgrounds and then be able to articulate their knowledge and skill sets to a variety of school and community partners. Advocacy efforts must continue for the collective school community to appropriately define various aspects of the role and use school counselors effectively as leaders, mental health providers, and educators.

As mentioned in Chapter 1, the field of school counseling has a history of role ambiguity. While there are currently clear guidelines that inform our work, such as the *ASCA National Model* and other standards, school counselors today often experience challenges when defining their role within a school and community. This chapter explores the challenges often faced by school counselors when asked to perform tasks and activities that may fall outside of the scope of what is appropriate for a school counselor.

#IRLSchoolCounseling

The following is a social media post from one of the many school counseling groups on Facebook, *Caught in the Middle School Counselors*. Caught in the *Middle School Counselor Exchange* is a Facebook group primarily hosting topics posed by middle school counselors.

> Anonymous ▶ Caught In The Middle School Counselors
> Nov 18, 2019 at 9:21 PM
>
> My administration asked me and my other counselor to begin doing lunch duty for 20 minutes each day. I am a team player and will do as I am asked. I did share my perspective that it is not an appropriate use of our time and that it puts us in a disciplinary role and I hope it will only be for the remainder of this year. I hate doing lunch duty and it has only been a few days! Last Friday they were throwing food and taking things off of each others trays. I was barking in the microphone at them and just generally being grumpy about the whole thing. Any suggestions for shifting my perspective on this?

Bracketing Values for Ethical Practice

It is expected that school counselors continuously reflect on their values, beliefs, worldviews, and cultural norms and how each influences the ways in which they choose to take or not take action. As such, it is important to recognize and set aside any preconceived notions, experiences, and biases to help you respond to this scenario in a culturally sustaining and ethically sound manner. Take a moment to reflect on the previous post and then consider the following questions:

- What is your gut response to school counselors supervising lunch duty?
- What initial feelings do you experience toward Laura's reaction?

- What initial feelings do you experience toward Laura's administration?
- Consider a time that you have been asked to do something that did not align with either your beliefs or expected roles (e.g., think personal life, think school life, think work life). How might those experiences influence your reaction to Laura's situation?

After considering your answers to these questions, separate out those thoughts and place them on hold while you digest the following foundational information needed to answer this social media post.

Informed School Counseling

Since the inception of the profession of school counseling, there has been confusion and inconsistency about the appropriate role of the school counselor. As the evolution of the field from the traditional reactive "guidance" counselor to the prevention and early intervention-minded school counselor continues, practitioners are often caught in between generational differences and district "past practice." The nature of the development of school counseling as a profession has therefore led to role confusion surrounding what duties truly lie within the scope of the school counselor's abilities and training (Burnham & Jackson, 2000; Zyromski et al., 2019). A frequent struggle over the question "What do school counselors do?" continues to plague the profession (Beale, 2004; Robertson et al., 2016) as school leaders, administrators, teachers, and parents frequently view the school counselor's role differently. Equally concerning are the discrepancies that continue to exist among practicing school counselors, regarding their roles and how they should allocate their time (Kolbert et al., 2016).

Much has been written about how the appropriate roles, functions, and duties of the school counselor contribute meaningfully to the academic mission and success of all students (Cholewa et al., 2015; Clark & Amatea, 2004; Dahir, 2001; Goodman-Scott et al., 2018; House & Hayes, 2002; King-White, 2019). When looking for guidance around the definition of their role and the appropriate activities therein, school counselors consult professional organizations to support their advocacy efforts with school partners. According to the ASCA (n.d.), "School counselors are certified/licensed educators who improve student success for ALL students by implementing a comprehensive school counseling program." Further, the *ASCA National Model* defines appropriate and inappropriate duties of school counselors (see ASCA, 2019a, xiv and ASCA, 2020).

The ACA provides guidance to professional school counselors by offering a series of school counseling issue briefs (2020) on areas in which school counselors should be working. Topics such as bullying, equity issues in schools, college readiness, human trafficking, and dealing with school shootings are covered by the ACA in their efforts to support the appropriate work of school counselors as mental health experts in the school setting.

School counselors around the globe look to the ISCA to help determine their appropriate role. ISCA provides guidance and resources for school counselors and outlines appropriate activities delivered through the following: the school counseling curriculum (systematic school-wide curriculum), responsive services to students (individual and small-group counseling), individual student supports (personal goals and future plans), and system supports (administer and manage the comprehensive school counseling program; ISCA, 2020).

Defining the School Counselor Role

School counselors support the academic, social/emotional, and career success of all students, guided by each school's comprehensive school counseling program. School counselors engage in a range of activities and multi-tiered interventions such as individual and small-group counseling; the development and implementation of a preventative, developmental, and culturally relevant counseling curriculum; and ongoing consultation and collaboration with all partners within a school community. Finally, school counselors recognize that institutional and social factors impact students differently across cultural identities, serving to privilege certain students and marginalize others. Effective school counselors must be skilled at identifying factors that impact student success and work in community with others to create systems change.

The next section highlights the guiding documents which inform school counseling practice, as included in the first component of the *ASCA National Model*: *Define*. These include the *ASCA Student Standards: Mindsets & Behaviors for Student Success*, *ASCA Ethical Standards for School Counselors*, and *ASCA School Counselor Professional Standards & Competencies*. By exploring these standards, we gain a better understanding of the role of school counselors in developing, implementing, and assessing school counseling programs.

ASCA Student Standards: Mindsets & Behaviors for Student Success

Today's school counselors are increasingly called upon to navigate complex student issues as they assist in the academic, social/emotional, and career achievement of all students. Some of these issues include violence, substance abuse, pregnancy, values conflicts, family separation, and racism, to name a few (Dahir, 2004; Musheno & Talbert, 2002). Additionally, school counselors recognize how student behaviors and mindsets impact human thriving and well-being. Comprehensive school counseling programs support students who are dealing with challenges and adversity and provide a framework for healthy development for all students. ASCA provides a set of standards that describes the knowledge, attitudes, and skills that students need to help them prepare to thrive in all aspects of life—emotionally, socially, academically, and as citizens and workers. The *ASCA Student Standards* guide the practice of school counseling broadly and are discussed in many of the chapters in this text. The *ASCA Student Standards: Mindsets & Behaviors for Student Success* (ASCA, 2021) can be found on the ASCA website.

ASCA School Counselor Professional Standards & Competencies

Like the mindsets for student success, the *ASCA School Counselor Professional Standards & Competencies* (ASCA, 2019b) focus on attitudes and behaviors that all school counselors should strive to cultivate. They outline both the personal beliefs that school counselors hold as they attempt to meet the needs of all PK–12 students and the skills needed to design, implement, and assess a comprehensive school counseling program. This set of standards should be used by school counselors to assess their own mindsets and behaviors and to guide their professional development. These standards and competencies also direct school counselors to adhere to the *ASCA Ethical Standards for School Counselors.*

ASCA Ethical Standards for School Counselors

The profession of counseling has long been guided by ethical standards for counselors that often depend on the counselor's affiliation with their identified professional development organization. For school counselors, the *ASCA Ethical Standards for School Counselors* (ASCA, 2022) "specifies the obligation to the principles of ethical behavior necessary to maintain the highest standards of integrity, leadership, and professionalism" (ASCA, 2022). According to these ethical standards,

> School counselors have unique qualifications and skills to implement a comprehensive school counseling program that addresses pre-K–12 students' academic, career and social/ emotional development needs. School counselors are leaders, advocates, collaborators, and consultants who create systemic change to ensure equitable educational outcomes through the school counseling program. School counselors demonstrate the belief that all students have the ability to learn by advocating for and contributing to an education system that provides optimal learning environments for all students. (ASCA, 2022)

The *ASCA Ethical Standards for School Counselors* serve as a guide for ethical practice and highlight the responsibilities school counselors have to their students, caregivers, and school. The standards highlight the unique ethical responsibilities of school counselor administrators and supervisors. The *ASCA Ethical Standards for School Counselors* provide school counselors with a specific framework from which to practice. Frequent reflection on the standards, along with peer consultation, support school counselors at every stage of professional development in ensuring ethical behavior. The *ASCA Ethical Standards for School Counselors* can be found on the ASCA website.

Consultation Corner: Who You Gonna Call?

After bracketing your thoughts and reading the "Informed School Counseling" section, who would you call in and outside of the school building, and what might you ask them to support your decision-making? Take a moment to document these questions. Now that you have considered your questions for consultation, let's see what professional school counselors from around the world have to say about this case.

Consultation #1

Hi, my name is Heidi, and I am an elementary school counselor in a predominantly low socioeconomic status urban school setting. As a part-time counselor in a building with very high needs (e.g., parental incarceration, violence in the home, poverty), I have 650 students on my caseload; I am always looking for opportunities to connect with my students in any way possible. I hear your frustration about having to do lunch duty. It can feel very overwhelming to be taken away from the individual, small-group, and developmental counseling initiatives we are taught to provide and perhaps enjoy implementing most. I was asked to do lunch and playground duty, myself, and here is my perspective. While initially, I felt a bit annoyed to be expected to do this, given my already limited time with the kids, call me crazy, but by the end of the school year, I actually ended up enjoying it! This was a time for me to watch kids in more of their natural contexts. I could especially keep a close eye on my highest needs students to see how they were interacting with their peers outside of their classrooms. This was all data that I was collecting and recording as advocacy with my principal for more time needed with students in the future! In fact, this also became a time for me to note strengths I didn't realize my students had (i.e., organizing teams for kickball, helping friends solve an issue during a peer argument, leading their peers in cleaning up a spill at the table). These were cool opportunities to catch students "doing good" for the school. I've even thought of creating a small group of leaders whom I identify making positive choices at lunch to help me reinforce the school culture when I'm not there. Additionally, I was able to reinforce shared language that we had talked about in my developmental counseling lessons. For instance, when a student came to an adult with a problem, I asked "Is this a big butterfly problem where you need adult help, or is this a small caterpillar problem that can be worked out on your own?" I was shocked to see kids applying what we'd learned, even if they had to be reminded. I also liked working in the lunchroom and at recess because I could model healthy student responses for other adults in the room. I know that this is a very chaotic time, and it tests the nerves of all of the adults, just as you described. I would often model for and, in a professional way of course, directly help my noncounseling colleagues learn language that supported their connections with the kids. Many of them were grateful that I was there, too, and I got a chance to show them our skills as counselors directly. Good advocacy! Yes, at times I had to skirt around being a disciplinarian. I tried my best to offer feedback and support kids in making healthy choices. This meant using my counseling skills at lunch tables or on the playground. If students' choices were not good, I was also there directly to talk to them about their reactions to the natural consequences (e.g., principal's office) and to follow up later in supporting them toward healthier goals. Truthfully, there were days I wished I could be running small lunch groups instead, but in all, I ended up realizing that this was one of the most meaningful ways that I could connect with students.

(Heidi Roselle, former elementary school counselor, California)

Consultation #2

Hi, my name is Sam, and I'm a middle school counselor in rural Appalachia. I work with two other school counselors, and we are, essentially, the first and last line of mental health defense for kids. My time with them is critical for both assessment and intervention. When I started at my current school, I had lunch duty every day for 3 years. I used my use of time data to have it removed from my list of responsibilities. However, I found that my connection and relationship with kids decreased as did my knowledge of what was going on with kids. After 2 years, I volunteered for lunch duty because I was missing a critical time to connect with kids who wouldn't typically come to my office. We are a positive behavioral interventions and supports school, so when kids misbehave, I talk to them about expectations and have them identify how they need to modify their behavior to meet expectations.

(Sam Springer, middle school counselor, New Jersey)

Consultation #3

Hi, my name is Daisy, and I am a high school counselor working in an upper middle-class suburban 9–12 high school. Prior to lunch duty, my team of six counselors met to eat lunch together and discuss professional and personal issues. Once our lunch was over, we all went into lunch duty together; we were the only people covering lunch aside from a school resource officer. We each were placed at a different station with an assigned task for what to monitor in relation to students' behavior. Overall, it was a great experience because we were able to do check-ins or give out information requested by students. And then...there were times when there was fighting in the lunchroom. We were the only people trained in restraint techniques, and therefore, we were the ones responsible for separating students. This came with mixed emotions from both the students and us (I often got shoved up against a wall when trying to stop fights). Most students felt bad that we were getting pushed but at times it caused tension among the students who felt as though we were getting involved in something we should have stayed out of. The school resource officer often had to step in.

(Daisy Diaz, high school counselor, Florida)

#EduCounselor Synthesis

Having read "Informed School Counseling" and the perspectives of other school counselors, how are you now making sense of Laura's dilemma? School counselors are challenged daily to navigate both professional and personal expectations; oftentimes, they face having to walk the fine line between helping students make good choices and supporting their emotional reactions to receiving behavioral consequences. Ideally, schools have assistant principals to oversee disciplinary practices. Sadly, at times, the school counselor is called upon to assume all or part of this role. For example, it is expected in some states that school counselors "investigate" bullying behaviors, potentially compromising the safe environments they work so hard to cultivate. It is no wonder why most school counselors have strong initial reactions when asked to perform duties that might result in less positive connections with students.

In the initial #IRLSchoolCounseling post, it seems like Laura felt torn between professional beliefs about the role of the school counselor and personal beliefs about "being a team player." Reconciling personal and professional beliefs about one's role as a school counselor is particularly important and is pointed out frequently throughout this book. Despite this challenge, Laura's willingness to consult other professionals and modify personal perspectives to serve the school is both insightful and admirable. Laura's initial reactions prompted strong feelings toward performing lunch duty. Choosing to ignore the principal's request may have put Laura at risk of being labeled as insubordinate, which could damage career aspirations and negatively impact how administrators and other school partners view school counseling more broadly. Laura, instead, chose to consult colleagues before reacting, which is aligned with the *ASCA Ethical Standards for School Counselors* (ASCA, 2022) B.3.j. "Apply an ethical decision-making model and seek consultation and supervision from colleagues and other professionals who are knowledgeable of the profession's practices when ethical questions arise," and B.2.a "Develop and maintain professional relationships and systems of communication with faculty, staff and administrators to support students." Likewise, Laura's desire to change perspective to preserve the relationship and support students in alternative ways is evidence of attention to professionalism.

School counselors are leaders in schools (Bowers et al., 2017; Goodman-Scott & Grothaus, 2017; Lopez & Mason, 2017) and exhibit leadership by modeling the introspection, collaboration, and communication skills they hope to instill in their students. Openness to feedback and flexibility are traits that administrators often look for when initially hiring school personnel (Glenn et al., 2015). Laura's ability to identify feelings, seek consultation, and approach this situation with a different attitude suggests the resourcefulness and self-awareness needed to be successful in the field (Bowers et al., 2017; Mullen et al., 2016; Mullen et al., 2017).

As discussed in the introduction of this chapter, ASCA (2019a) distinctly defines the appropriate and inappropriate duties for school counselors; lunch duty potentially falls into the inappropriate duties category of *performing disciplinary actions or assignment discipline consequences*, as well as *supervising classrooms or common areas*. Laura's fear that performing lunch duty may position the school counselor role with students as a disciplinarian is valid and in line with Sandy's response about how the school expected school counselors to use their training in restraint to mitigate conflict during recess duty. Both school counselors were worried about how students might struggle to connect with the counselor after seeing them in these roles. However, as suggested by Heidi, Sam, and even Daisy, there are, in fact, alternative ways in which Laura might be able to still serve students in meaningful ways while performing these duties.

All three consultants discussed the value of using less structured time of the day to connect differently with students. Understanding student behavior and social-ization patterns outside of the classroom setting is important as school counselors identify student strengths. Heidi talked about lunch duty as an opportunity to col-lect more data points surrounding high-needs students. School counselors collect different types of data as members and leaders of Multi-tiered Systems of Support (Goodman-Scott et al., 2019) teams and specifically use this data to inform their school counseling practices (Carey & Dimmitt, 2012; Young & Kaffenberger, 2015; Ziomek-Daigle et al., 2016). Heidi also discussed opportunities to reinforce school-wide language and initiatives during this time (e.g., reinforcing conflict resolution skills). The implementation of school-wide interventions aids in the facilitation of equitable student support, positively contributing to school culture (Goodman-Scott & Grothaus, 2017; Sink, 2016). Heidi went on to suggest how to use these times to find students making good choices and to use these opportunities to encourage and recognize leadership attributes. After all, appropriate peer models are import-ant for students as they develop their identities (Ja & Jose, 2017; Rageliene, 2016). Additionally, finding opportunities to highlight students' strengths can reinforce untapped leadership skills while ultimately supporting the overall culture of the school. As Heidi shared, school counselors who are present during student conflicts (which often happen during less structured times of the day) have opportunities to engage in "teachable moments." It is here that school counselors help students learn to communicate and problem solve more effectively with peers and discuss feelings associated with natural consequences. When the school counselor-prin-cipal relationship is strong, the pair can work together; the principal provides the consequences (e.g., detention for hitting a peer), and the school counselor helps to process students' feelings while engaging them in future goal setting to mitigate these behaviors (Randick et al., 2019).

Chapter Summary

Let's refer to the social media post, which highlights a common, controversial dilemma faced by school counselors and the need for professional advocacy. Laura's case reflects the challenge school counselors continue to face about the definition of their roles. They are often faced with responding to an administrator who may ask them to perform duties outside the scope of the profession. Despite clear and consistent articulation of the school counseling role through professional organiza-tions, best practice guidelines, competencies, and ethical standards, the practice of school counseling varies significantly within the United States and around the world. As leaders in their buildings, successful school counselors model creative problem solving and advocate for ways to support all students across a variety of assumed roles. As evidenced by the *#IRLSchoolCounseling* case and commentary, those who exercise flexibility, adaptability, and develop strong collaborative relationships with all school and community partners can often use their positionalities to navigate through administrative duties while concurrently impacting students' experiences in very positive ways.

Reflective Practitioner Process

School counselors engage in **clinical supervision**, **professional development**, and **self-care** to further develop their knowledge and skills and to help balance professional expectations with personal wellness. All three areas are key to ethical practice and help to mitigate counselor burnout and compassion fatigue (Atici, 2015; Lawson & Myers, 2011; Merriman, 2015; Ohrt et al., 2015).

Clinical Supervision

The *ASCA School Counselor Professional Standards & Competencies* (ASCA, 2019b) direct school counselors to "consult with school counselors and other education and counseling professionals when questions of school counseling practice arise" (B-SS 5., p. 5). As a supervisee, it is important to consider the thoughts, feelings, and experiences that come up for you as you work with students, families, and colleagues and seek consultation on difficult issues. The following are some topics for consideration as you react to this chapter.

- When I am tasked with processing emotional reactions after students receive behavioral consequences, how do I support the student and the district's discipline policy at the same time? What if I disagree with the student's consequences?
- School counselors often witness student conflict (e.g., verbal, and physical) directly. Questions you might discuss include the following: Can I break up a fight? What is the school and district policy for putting my hands on students?
- If my district has asked that I present the consequences to students, how do I feel about handing out consequences personally, and how do I navigate them professionally? Or, how do I advocate to remove myself from discipline-related assignments?
- As we work with students during internship, can small pockets of interactions with students around discipline issues count as direct or indirect service, and if so, how do I document it? Also, what about documenting lunch/recess duty?

Professional Development

According to the *ASCA Ethical Standards for School Counselors* (ASCA, 2022), professional school counselors engage in professional development and attend trainings to stay current on the trends and issues that impact students (B.3.e). Relative to the contents of this chapter, consider finding professional development on the following topics:

- State and District Discipline Policies for Educators
- Student Restraint Training (e.g., Crisis Prevention Institute)
- Effective Communication with Supervisors (e.g., Transactional Analysis)

#PSCSelfCare: Everyday Wellness

When designing, managing, and implementing a comprehensive school counseling program, school and community expectations can tax even the most seasoned school counselor. The *ASCA Ethical Standards for School Counselors* (ASCA, 2022) require school counselors to recognize the high levels of stress often associated with the job. Therefore, school counselors recognize that self-care must be a priority to maintain health and overall well-being (see ASCA, 2022, B.3.h).

Supporting Your Decision-Making Bandwidth: H (Hungry), A (Angry), L (Lonely), T (Tired)

Multiple counseling and developmental theorists encourage working with clients from the perspective of helping them to address their basic needs (e.g., Maslow, Adler, Glasser). School counselors, highly susceptible to compassion fatigue and burnout, must learn to focus first and foremost on caring for themselves; counselors ensure that they put on their "oxygen" masks before supporting others. This includes cultivating a healthy lifestyle and intentionally addressing their own wellness.

Individuals in recovery use the acronym **HALT** as a reminder to continually address their basic needs to maintain sobriety. As school counselors, it is important to work to ensure that you do not become **H**ungry, **A**ngry, **L**onely, or **T**ired.

A few tips for school counselors may include (1) taking time for a lunch break during the workday, (2) taking time to eat healthy foods, (3) addressing emotional triggers (e.g., anger, resentment), (4) managing conflicts that create negative energy, and (5) attending supervision sessions and engaging in personal counseling throughout their careers.

It is quite common to hear a school counselor say, "I didn't even have lunch today!" Make planning breaks for lunch and a snack a priority. Consider learning about meal preparation, and always go to work with nutritious foods that can provide the sustenance you need during the day. School counselors can work 24 hours a day, 7 days a week, and still not meet the needs of all students and families. Intentionally taking a break each day during lunch to stop working, breathe, and recharge is a powerful tool to increase effectiveness and protect against burnout.

Make professional contact with other *school counselors* a priority. Many school counselors work independently in schools, and it is important to find an outlet to collaborate and consult with colleagues. The work of a school counselor can be exhausting, especially if we are working in isolation. Connection and collaboration with other school counselors and supportive educators will make the work more enjoyable and successful.

Spotlight: School Counseling Advocacy

In the following social media post, Erin presented what school counselors do to help promote student success to all members of the school community. Think about how you might use social media to promote your own counseling program and communicate with school and community members.

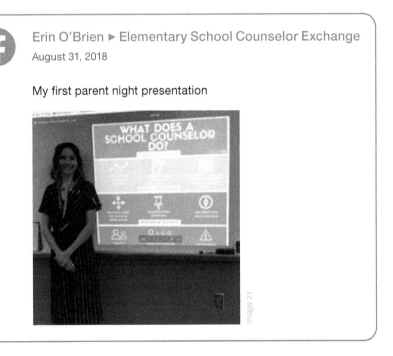

Learning Connections

Both professional school counselors in training and seasoned school counselors understand the importance of understanding the connections between the concepts commonly taught in counseling programs and the standards most associated with school counselor training. Therefore, the table that follows offers broad connections between the material and information in this chapter and the Council for Accreditation of Counseling and Related Educational Programs (CACREP,

2016) standards, the *ASCA School Counselor Professional Standards & Competencies* (ASCA, 2019b), and the *ASCA Ethical Standards for School Counselors* (ASCA, 2022).

Connections to CACREP Core Curricular Areas

Professional Counseling Orientation and Ethical Practice	Social and Cultural Diversity	Human Growth and Development	Career Development	Counseling and Helping Relationships	Group Counseling And Group Work	Assessment and Testing	Research and Program Evaluation
X				X			

Connection to Professional Standards

CACREP	ASCA Competencies	Ethical Standards: SC
1.d: Models of school-based collaboration and consultation	M.6: School counselors are leaders in the school, district, state and nation.	A.3.b: Collaborate with administration, teachers, staff and stakeholders for equitable school improvement goals.
2.a: School counselor roles as leaders, advocates, and systems change agents in P–12 schools	B-SS 6: Collaborate with families, teachers, administrators, other school staff and education stakeholders for student achievement and success.	A.3.g: Share data outcomes with stakeholders.
2.d: School counselor roles in school leadership and multidisciplinary teams	B-PA 7: Establish agreement with the principal and other administrators about the school counseling program.	A.6.a: Collaborate with all relevant stakeholders, including students, school faculty/staff and parents/guardians, when students need assistance, including when early warning signs of student distress are identified.
3.l: Techniques to foster collaboration and teamwork within schools	B-PF 7: Demonstrate leadership through the development and implementation of a comprehensive school counseling program.	A.14.e: Use multiple data points, both quantitative and qualitative whenever possible, to provide students and families with complete and accurate information to promote students' well-being.

Comprehensive School Counseling Assignments

The following section provides activities that allow for your continued growth as a professional school counselor. Both preservice and practicing school counselors may find it helpful to complete these activities. If you are currently in a graduate training program, your professor might assign these as part of your course.

1. **Social Media Introduction** – Create a brief video/visual social media post with the hashtag #IRLSchoolCounseling to introduce yourself to the community.
   a. Graduate Student: Include your name (last name optional), what program you attend, if you are currently in a clinical experience and what level, what led you to the school counseling profession, and what you are excited about learning.
   b. Practicing School Counselor: Include your name (last name optional), how many years you have as a practicing school counselor, where you are located geographically, what programmatic level you currently serve, your caseload, the population you serve, and what excites you about the school counseling profession.
2. **Interview a School Counselor From Around the Globe** – Ask about specific duties they are assigned. Refer to the interview protocol provided on the active learning platform for broader questions you can ask to get acquainted with the profession or to find out what school counselors do in various school settings.
3. **Reflective Journal** – Write a reflective journal (could be video/presentation/artistic expression) where you discuss why you wanted to pursue a career as a school counselor. Address the following: Who is/are a role model(s) that has/have influenced your interest in school counseling? What qualities do you feel an "exceptional" professional school counselor must have? What do you see as your role as a school counselor?

Helpful Resources
Web-Based Resources

- The Role of the School Counselor (ASCA):
  - https://www.schoolcounselor.org/asca/media/asca/Careers-Roles/RoleStatement.pdf
- Appropriate Versus Inappropriate School Counselor Duties (ASCA):
  - https://www.schoolcounselor.org/asca/media/asca/home/appropriate-activities-of-school-counselors.pdf

- *ASCA School Counselor Professional Standards & Competencies*:
  - https://www.schoolcounselor.org/asca/media/asca/home/SCCompetencies.pdf

Suggested Readings

- ASCA Position Statements:
  - ASCA provides a comprehensive set of documents outlining the organizations positions on a variety of issues. The ASCA position statements can be accessed here:
    - https://www.schoolcounselor.org/asca/media/asca/PositionStatements/PositionStatements.pdf
- ACA's Strategies for School Counselors Self-Care:
  - https://www.counseling.org/docs/default-source/school-counseling/selfcare_strategiesforcounselors.pdf?sfvrsn=9306572c_2

References

American Counseling Association (ACA). (2020). *School counselor connection: School counseling issue briefs.* https://www.counseling.org/membership/aca-and-you/school-counselors/school-counselor

American School Counselor Association (ASCA). (n.d.). *The role of the school counselor.* https://www.schoolcounselor.org/getmedia/ee8b2e1b-d021-4575-982c-c84402cb2cd2/Role-Statement.pdf

American School Counselor Association (ASCA). (2019a). *ASCA national model: A framework for school counseling programs* (4th ed.).

American School Counselor Association (ASCA). (2019b). *ASCA school counselor professional standards & competencies.* https://www.schoolcounselor.org/asca/media/asca/home/SCCompetencies.pdf

American School Counselor Association (ASCA). (2020). *Appropriate and inappropriate activities for school counselors.* https://www.schoolcounselor.org/asca/media/asca/home/appropriate-activities-of-school-counselors.pdf

American School Counselor Association (ACA). (2021). *ASCA student standards: Mindsets & behaviors for student success.*

American School Counselor Association (ASCA). (2022). *ASCA ethical standards for school counselors.* https://www.schoolcounselor.org/getmedia/44f30280-ffe8-4b41-9ad8-f15909c3d164/EthicalStandards.pdf

Atici, M. (2015). Professional identity development of counselors-in-training in a school internship program in Turkey. *The Professional Counselor, 5*(1), 137–151. https://doi.org/10.15241/ma.5.1.137

Beale, A. V. (2004). Questioning whether you have a contemporary school counseling program. *The Clearing House, 78*(2), 73–76. https://doi.org/10.3200/TCHS.78.2.73-77

Bowers, H., Lemberger-Truelove, M. E., & Brigman, G. (2017). A social-emotional leadership framework for school counselors. *School Counseling Leadership in Practice, 21*(1b), 1–10. https://doi.org/10.1177/2156759X18773004

Burnham, J. J., & Jackson, C. M. (2000). School counselor roles: Discrepancies between actual practice and existing models. *Professional School Counseling, 4*(1), 41–49. https://eric.ed.gov/?id=EJ629043

Carey, J., & Dimmitt, C. (2012). School counseling and student outcomes: Summary of six statewide studies. *Professional School Counseling, 16*(2), 146–153. https://doi.org/10.1177/2156759X0001600204

Cholewa, B., Burkhardt, C. K., & Hull, M. F. (2015). Are school counselors impacting under-represented students' thinking about postsecondary education? A nationally representative study. *Professional School Counseling, 19*(1), 144–154. https://doi.org/10.5330/1096-2409-19.1.144

Clark, M. A., & Amatea, E. S. (2004). Teacher perceptions and expectations of school counselor contributions: Implications for program planning and training. *Professional School Counseling, 8*(2), 132–140. https://www.jstor.org/stable/42732615

Council for Accreditation of Counseling and Related Educational Programs (CACREP). (2016). *2016 CACREP standards.* http://www.cacrep.org/wp-content/uploads/2017/08/2016-Standards-with-citations.pdf

Dahir, C. (2001). The national standards for school counseling programs: Development and implementation. *Professional School Counseling, 4*(5), 320–327. https://www.jstor.org/stable/42732275

Dahir, C. (2004). Supporting a nation of learners: The development of the national standards for school counseling programs. *Journal of Counseling and Development, 82*(3), 344–353. https://doi.org/10.1002/j.1556-6678.2004.tb00320.x

Glenn, M., Leppma, M., & Thorne, K. (2015). Clinical supervisors' perceptions of counselor characteristics associated with effective and well-balanced practices. *Journal of Applied Rehabilitation Counseling, 46*(4), 29–36. https://doi.org/10.1891/0047-2220.46.4.29

Goodman-Scott, E., & Grothaus, T. (2017). School counselors' roles in RAMP and PBIS a phenomenological investigation. *Professional School Counseling, 21*(1), 130–141. https://doi.org/10.5330/1096-2409-21.1.130

Goodman-Scott, E., Sink, C. A., Cholewa, B. E., & Burgess, M. (2018). An ecological view of school counselor ratios and student academic outcomes: A national investigation. *Journal of Counseling & Development, 96*(4), 388–398. https://doi.org/10.1002/jcad.12221

Goodman-Scott, E., Betters-Bubon, J., & Donohue, P. (2019). *The school counselor's guide to multi-tiered systems of support.* Routledge.

House, R. M., & Hayes, R. L. (2002). School counselors: Becoming key players in school reform. *Professional School Counseling, 5*(4), 249–256. https://eric.ed.gov/?id=EJ655189

International School Counselor Association (ISCA). (2020). *Delivering a comprehensive counseling program.* https://iscainfo.com/page-18154

Ja, N. M., & Jose, P. E. (2017). "I can't take hold of some kind of a life": The role of social connectedness and confidence in engaging "lost" adolescents with their lives. *Journal of Youth and Adolescents, 46*(9), 2028–2046. https://doi.org/10.1007/s10964-017-0656-x

King-White, D. L. (2019). The role of school counselors in supporting mental health models in schools. *Journal of School Counseling, 17*(1–23), 1–24. https://eric.ed.gov/?id=EJ1210764

Kolbert, J. B., Williams, R. L., Morgan, L. M., Crothers, L. M., & Hughes, T. L. (2016). *Introduction to professional school counseling.* Routledge. https://doi.org/10.4324/9781315797441

Lawson, G., & Myers, J. E. (2011). Wellness, professional quality of life, and career-sustaining behaviors: What keeps us well? *Journal of Counseling and Development, 89*(2), 163–171. https://doi.org/10.1002/j.1556-6678.2011.tb00074.x

Lopez, C. J., & Mason, E. C. M. (2017). School counselors as curricular leaders. *Professional School Counseling, 21*(1b), 1–12. https://doi.org/10.1177/2156759X18773277

Merriman, J. (2015). Enhancing counselor supervision through compassion fatigue education. *Journal of Counseling and Development, 93*(1), 370–378. https://doi.org/10.1002/jcad.12035

Mullen, P. R., Gutierrez, D., & Newhart, S. (2017). School counselors' emotional intelligence and its relationship to leadership. *Professional School Counseling, 21*(1b), 1–12. https://doi.org/10.1177/2156759X18772989

Mullen, P. R., Lambie, G. W., Griffith, C., & Sherrell, R. (2016). School counselors' general self-efficacy, ethical and legal self-efficacy, and ethical and legal knowledge. *Ethics & Behavior, 26*(5), 415–430. https://doi.org/10.1080/10508422.2015.1033627

Musheno, S., & Talbert, M. (2002). The transformed school counselor in action. *Theory into Practice, 41*(3), 186–191. https://doi.org/10.1207/s15430421tip4103_7

Ohrt, J. H., Prosek, E. A., Ener, E., & Lindo, N. (2015). The effects of a group supervision intervention to promote wellness and prevent burnout. *The Journal of Humanistic Counseling, 54*(1), 41–58. https://doi.org/10.1002/j.2161-1939.2015.00063.x

Rageliene, T. (2016). Links of adolescents' identity development and relationship with peers: A systemic literature review. *Journal of the Canadian Academy of Child and Adolescent Psychiatry, 25*(2), 97–105. https://www.ncbi.nlm.nih.gov/pmc/articles/PMC4879949/?tool=pmcentrez&report=abstract

Randick, N. M., Dermer, S., & Michel, R. E. (2019). Exploring the job duties that impact school counselor wellness: The role of RAMP, supervision, and support. *Professional School Counseling, 22*(1), 1–11. https://doi.org/10.1177/2156759X18820331

Robertson, D. L., Llyod-Hazlett, J., & Zambrano, E. (2016). Program directors' perceptions of school counselor roles. *Journal of Professional Counseling, Practice, Theory, & Research, 43*(2), 1–13. https://doi.org/10.1080/15566382.2016.12033952

Sink, C. (2016). Incorporating a multi-tiered system of supports into school counselor preparation. *The Professional Counselor, 6*(3), 203–219. https://doi.org/10.15241/cs.6.3.203

Young, A., & Kaffenberger, C. (2015). School counseling professional development: Assessing the use of data to inform school counseling services. *Professional School Counseling, 19*(1), 46–56. https://doi.org/10.5330/1096-2409-19.1.46

Ziomek-Daigle, J., Goodman-Scott, E., Cavin, J., & Donohue, P. (2016). Integrating a multi-tiered system of supports with comprehensive school counseling programs. *The Professional Counselor, 6*(3), 220–232. https://doi.org/10.15241/jzd.6.3.220

Zyromski, B., Hudson, T. D., Baker, E., & Granello, D. H. (2019). Guidance counselors or school counselors: How the name of the profession influences perceptions of competence. *Professional School Counseling, 22*(1), 1–10. https://doi.org/10.1177/2156759X19855654

Credit

CHAPTER 3

Navigating the Role of the School Counselor With Multiple Community Partners

LEARNING OBJECTIVES

#EduCounselors can

- recognize the unique position of the school counselor as mental health expert in the school,
- describe the various approaches to school-based counselor consultation,
- identify the difference between confidentiality and privileged communication as it relates to how the school counselor communicates with building colleagues and partners, and
- clarify the differences between Family Educational Rights and Privacy Act and Health Insurance Portability and Accountability Act in relation to the sharing of information in a school setting.

Introduction

School counselors are trained to develop, implement, and assess comprehensive school counseling programs, which are designed to support the academic, social/ emotional, and career success of all students. School counselors use a wide variety of interventions to achieve the goals outlined in comprehensive school counseling programs. These include traditional mental health counseling interventions, such as individual and small-group counseling and research-based interventions that are informed by educational best practices; each relies on a deep understanding of how students learn and thrive in school settings. School counselors also bring a systems lens, where they endeavor to understand how the interactions among all school community members, the school climate, the students' developmental stage, and societal factors such as systemic racism and oppression impact students' academic growth and wellness. Therefore, school counselors have a unique knowledge and skill set.

While school counselors undergo a rigorous training program and are well equipped to fulfill the responsibilities defined under the *American School Counselor Association (ASCA) National Model* (ASCA, 2019a), school counselors may experience challenges due to their unique role within schools. Teachers and administrators often do not receive training on the role of the school counselor and how to effectively work together to advance student success. This disconnect can create challenges, especially when school counselors and other key partners have different visions for their work. Additionally, teachers and administrators may view school counselors with skepticism if they do not have prior professional experience as a teacher. These challenges can sometimes lead school counselors to feel tension between the role they have been trained for and the expectations from their colleagues. When tension is great, school counselors may even feel isolated from colleagues and struggle to identify allies with whom they can consult and collaborate.

School counselors must have a clearly defined identity and advocate for their role to be aligned with best practices in the school counseling field (e.g., ASCA, American Counseling Association (ACA), International School Counselor Association, Council for Accreditation of Counseling and Related Educational Programs (CACREP)). This chapter explores the role of the school counselor with respect to indirect student services, specifically as a consultant and collaborator, and direct student services as a counselor. The chapter offers guidance and advice on how school counselors manage this information based on a variety of ethical and legal responsibilities and how school counselors negotiate these challenges while balancing the priorities of their profession and their school districts. In doing so, the chapter highlights the differences between confidentiality and privileged communication (and when those concepts must be set aside), privacy laws (Family Educational Rights and Privacy Act (FERPA) vs. Health Insurance Portability and Accountability Act (HIPAA)), and the appropriate roles and settings in which school counselors share information about students with interested partners.

#IRLSchoolCounseling

The following is a social media post from one of the many school counseling groups on Facebook, *Elementary School Counselor Exchange*. This Facebook group primarily hosts topics posed by elementary school counselors.

Had a hard conversation with a teacher. 2 weeks ago she pushed hard to learn what I was talking abt with a kid. I did reveal she was upset about a micro aggression made. Teacher said kid was a liar and denied making the comment. Last week, a group of 3 students made comments about unwanted touching. One was in tears. Not inappropriate or abusive touching but like- hand on wrist, hand on chest to move the kid. One kid has had violence in her family and said she doesn't like any kind of touching. And then another kid yesterday: he said she was trying to stop him from walking and pulled him by the hood hurting his neck. This kid told his mom who emailed me and principal. It was not an injury, but the kid was upset about the action. We decided I would talk with the teacher- sort of a heads up- this is what several people are saying. It did NOT go well. She was very upset and I'm sure felt betrayed by the kids. She also said the kid with the hood was a liar. I worked hard to not be accusatory and I hope she knows I'm not her supervisor. I do think she's a caring teacher, who I like, and who might just need to be careful about comments/actions that come across the wrong way. But she denied it ALL and I'm thinking the whole thing was pointless and now she feels angry and upset and I feel bad too. Just hoping you all can relate. Or if you think I should not have had this conversation at all, please let me know how you would have handled it.

Bracketing Values for Ethical Practice

It is expected that school counselors continuously reflect on their values, beliefs, worldviews, and cultural norms and how each influences the ways in which they choose to take or not take action. As such, it is important to recognize and set aside any preconceived notions, experiences, and biases to help you respond to this scenario in a culturally sustaining and ethically sound manner. Take a moment to reflect on the previous post and then consider the following questions:

- How do you feel about sharing information with teachers?
- How have you reacted in the past when someone has pushed you for information that you were not sure you should share?
- How do you currently handle confrontation when it comes to colleagues and administrators? How do power imbalances impact your behavior?
- How might you feel and choose to act when you know something is "right" or "ethical," but a colleague is or might be upset with you for taking a stand?

Informed School Counseling

The *ASCA National Model for School Counseling* (ASCA, 2019a), delineates the various ways in which school counselors deliver services to support student growth, development, and achievement. These activities fall into two categories, direct student services, which include instruction, appraisal and advisement, and counseling, and indirect student services, which include consultation, collaboration, and referrals. This chapter highlights the school counselor's role in delivering indirect student services and provides a brief introduction to the school counselor's role as a mental health counselor. The following scenario provides an example of a school counselor working as a collaborator, consultant, and counselor. Consider this example as you read through this section:

> A fifth-grade teacher, Ms. Robinson, emails you with concerns about her student, Daniel. She states that Daniel is highly disorganized, and it is impacting his ability to succeed academically. You set up a meeting with Ms. Robinson to gain more information and to provide strategies to support Daniel (consultation). You work with Daniel individually to support the development of new organizational skills (counseling). You contact Daniel's parents to better understand his strengths and what has worked for him in the past; together, you work to develop a plan to help Daniel organize his materials each evening for school the next morning (collaboration).
>
> You then circle back to the classroom teacher to check in on Daniel's morning routine so that each of the educational partners is on the same page in terms of implementing the counseling plan (consultation). At the next team meeting, you share your experiences and facilitate a group dialogue with other student support teachers (e.g., learning consultant, reading specialist) and administrators to help devise a time line to monitor Daniel's progress (collaboration).

As you can see from this example, school counselors can wear several hats at once as they work to address student needs. Each day, school counselors practice flexibility as they deliver their comprehensive counseling programs. While learning about each of these roles more specifically in the following sections, consider which comes most naturally to you. A successful school counselor develops competency as a leader, advocate, counselor, and consultant, and it is important to consider how you can continue to develop skills in all these areas.

School Counselor as Mental Health Counselor

The *ASCA Ethical Standards for School Counselors* (ASCA, 2022) suggest that school counselors "provide culturally responsive counseling to students in a brief context and support students and families/guardians in obtaining outside services if students need long-term clinical/mental health counseling" (A.1.e). Going further, Stone

(2017) specifically identifies the provision of individual and small-group counseling as an "appropriate" duty (para. 17), while also identifying "providing therapy or long-term counseling in schools to address psychological disorders" as an "inappropriate duty" (para. 18). The struggle for many professional school counselors is to comply with our ethical guidelines while also addressing the growing mental health needs of students.

According to the Centers for Disease Control and Prevention (CDC, 2020b), one in six children ages 2–8 are diagnosed with a mental, behavioral, or developmental health condition. A review of the statistics over the last 10 years also suggests that children experience comorbidity at increasingly higher rates such as the fact that three in four children ages 3–17 years are diagnosed with depression while also having a diagnosis of anxiety (73.8%) and almost one in two children with depression also have diagnosable behavior problems (47.2%). Additionally, the CDC (2020a) cites suicide as the second leading cause of death for people 10–34 years of age in most recent reports. Combined with the lack of access to mental health treatment for children and adolescents, especially in rural areas (CDC, 2018), school counselors find themselves on the front lines when a student's mental health issues interfere with their ability to succeed in school.

Additionally, as we mentioned in a previous chapter, it is likely that many of these mental health challenges will persist over the next several years as a direct result of the COVID-19 pandemic and the simultaneous experiences of racial unrest. Greater stressors such as social isolation, family economic changes, increase in anxiety, inability to adapt to remote learning, and grief and loss of both people and preferred activities will likely impact student mental health for years to come. Because school counselors are often the point people for assisting students with both the academic and mental health needs of students (Ieva et al., 2021), it is imperative that they remain aware of these trends and consistently assess how these issues impact students' success. In Chapter 9, we dive more deeply into the school counselor's role as mental health counselor and provide more information on the extent to which school counselors engage in providing counseling to students.

School Counselor as Mental Health Consultant

To successfully meet the needs of all students, school counselors consult with others who interact with students on a regular basis (ASCA, 2022, B.2.q). According to Henderson and Thompson (2011), consultation is "a process in which the consultant works with the consultee with the goal of bringing about positive change" (p. 529). Oftentimes, student behavior (e.g., emotional dysregulation, lack of engagement) is a symptom of a larger concern, which may be connected to additional social, emotional, or mental health issues (Erchul & Martens, 2010). In the case of school counselors, this typically involves the school counselor as the professional consultant; a teacher, parent, or administrator as the consultee; and a student(s) as the client/client system

(Hill, 2014). What is the best way for school counselors to share their expertise and support their students? That depends on the goal of consultation. Typically, consultation processes can be categorized by one of two styles: a collaborative-process model or an expert-driven model. In a collaborative-process driven model, the school counselor (as consultant), works with others, or consultees (i.e., parents, teachers, administrators), as co-experts or partners to seek solutions. In the expert-driven model, the school counselor (as consultant), is viewed as the expert who suggests ideas on the best way to approach problem-solving (Perera-Diltz et al., 2011). Broadly, the specific models of consultation often referred to in school counseling literature include behavioral, family systems, and solution-focused consultation (SFC; Davis, 2005; Kolbert et al., 2016; Perera-Diltz et al., 2011).

Behavioral Consultation (BC)/Conjoint Behavioral Consultation (CBC)

Derived from learning theory rooted in the work of Skinner, Bandura, and Meichenbaum, the goal of BC is to work collaboratively with school and community partners (e.g., parent, teacher, administrator) to produce change in the student. However, student outcomes are not always simply improved by working solely with the student. BC or CBC recognizes that student outcomes may improve as a result of working to evoke change in the parent or teacher as well. Additionally, the school counselor may identify a change in the classroom or school setting that can impact student behavior. Given that many problematic student behaviors often begin in the home, BC or CBC aims to engage parents and families in the problem-solving process; parents/caregivers work in tandem with teachers and school staff to develop strategies to address problem behaviors. Behavioral approaches to consultation are viewed as family partnership models that involve "child-focused approaches where families and professionals cooperate, coordinate, and collaborate to enhance opportunities and success for children and adolescents across social, emotional, behavioral, and academic domains" (Sheridan et al., 2013, p. 718).

Family Systems Consultation

A family systems or systems approach to consultation views the issues and solutions to student issues as not solely lying within the student but rather the result of interactions between the student and the teacher, or between the teacher and parents. In other words, school counselors who approach consultation through a systems lens view a student's issues at school as often the result of ineffective interaction patterns either with teachers or families (Davis, 2005). As such, if those ineffective patterns can be identified at school or at home, school counselors can work with the adults within the system (generally parents and teachers) to teach new, more effective ways of communication and connection with the youth, which will yield positive changes in the youth. Conversely, from a family systems perspective, school counselors recognize that a positive change in the classroom can be undone at home without the support and encouragement of the family to support the change in behavior at home (Herman-Turner & Benoit, 2019). Family systems interventions are often a first-line treatment for students with externalizing disorders and oppositional tendencies (Zhang & Slesnick, 2018).

Solution-Focused Consultation (SFC)

Based on principles of solution-focused counseling theory, solution-focused consultation (SFC) draws on the idea that individuals (students, teachers, parents) possess the resources to meet their goals. SFC deemphasizes the problem or the diagnosis and instead focuses energy on the future and creating solutions based on client strengths and past successes. In other words, "What has worked in the past when this issue was not an issue?" In this approach, the consultant is viewed as a facilitator, a collaborator, and a coach who works with the consultee to develop solutions (Kahn, 2000; Sabella, 2018). Additionally, a basic premise of the approach is that the ability to change a behavior must not solely rely on the client. For example, a school counselor using SFC to assist a teacher with a student who is struggling with attention issues might approach the situation as follows: Instead of focusing on the student potentially having a diagnosis of attention deficit hyperactivity disorder, using a strength-based approach, the school counselor would work with the teacher to uncover times in which the student has been able to attend better. In addition, the school counselor may then ask the teacher, "Do you notice a time of day or certain activities that lead to this increased level of attentiveness by the student?," and "Can you (the teacher) recall what behavior you (the teacher) are doing at those times when you have seen increased attentiveness on the part of the student in the classroom?"

The school counselor in this case is building on multiple assumptions held true in SFC. The first being that there is significant value in identifying times in which the student IS able to attend with little or no prompting from the teacher and that if the teacher and counselor work together to identify those times, they can begin to build on those behaviors. The second assumption in play in this scenario is that this small change on the part of the teacher or the parent (i.e., the ability to recognize when attending is NOT a problem) "will cause rippling effects throughout the entire system, including the students' behaviors" (Khan, 2000, p. 249). As a result, the teacher, and even the parent, will begin to see the student for their engagement and contributions, as opposed to their deficits.

Additional Models of Consultation

Like other aspects of school counseling, consultation models and concepts have progressed over the last few years. We encourage you to explore additional models of consultation that have been historically written about in school counseling literature. Literature on these models, including collaborative-dependent, collaborative-interdependent, triadic-dependent, and collaborative-dependent serve to help school counselors achieve a better understanding of the specific roles each team member assumes in the broader models of consultation (Erford, 2011).

Although the foci and philosophy of each consultation model may differ, common processes exist (Erchul & Martens, 2010; Kurpius et al.,1993) among consultation models. These processes are (a) entry/joining, a rapport-building phase where consultants establish a collaborative environment; (b) problem-identification, where the consultant facilitates definition and assessment of the goal or problem by the consultee; (c) intervention planning, where the consultant facilitates identification of strategies to influence or resolve a problem; (d) implementation of intervention and regrouping, where the strategies are tested and the consultant and the consultee reflect on the process, and (e) evaluation, termination, and follow-up, where the outcome of the consultation is assessed and future assessment contacts are negotiated.

School Counselor as Mental Health Collaborator

As mentioned earlier, school counselors use various roles and skills to assist school and community partners in meeting the needs of all students. Collaboration is another way school counselors work with other school personnel to ensure the success of every student academically, social/emotionally, and as it relates to career success. Collaboration is the process of working with all partners, both inside and outside the school system, to develop and implement educational programs that support students (Mathieson, 2017). During the collaboration process, collaborators must trust, respect, be open, listen, and maintain communication (Dixon et al., 2008). Stone (2005) describes the art and ethics of collaboration as cultivating relationships with school and community partners, similar to an *"ambassador"* (p. 9) to best support the instructional process for students. There are many colleagues with whom school counselors collaborate; some of these colleagues include mental health counselors, teachers, families, administration, and outside services. School counselors often collaborate with the other school counseling colleagues in their districts as well to develop social/emotional curricula and calendars for classroom lessons for the academic year. Engaging in this collaboration can reduce the individual workload while offering pathways for articulation across all grade levels and schools within each district.

Another way you might collaborate with other support staff (e.g., nurse, school social worker, school psychologist, student assistance coordinator) is to attend regularly scheduled meetings, often referred to as *Student Assistant Teams, Multidisciplinary teams* (MDTs), or *Multi-Tiered Systems of Support Teams* (MTSS). At these meetings, a variety of professionals meet to discuss and address issues with which a single student or a group of students may be struggling. Collectively, the team works toward a plan to support students. Another example of collaboration is when a school counselor works with a community mental health counselor in partnership with a student at your school. Following a parental release of information, both the school counselor and mental health counselor collaborate on treatment plans that can be enacted in both the school and home settings for student success.

Ultimately, school counselors build relationships with a variety of professionals throughout the year, so when it is time to collaborate, there is already a mutually established trusting partnership that can serve to assist students.

School Counselor as Coordinator (or Not!)

We begin this small section by saying that coordination is a bit of a controversial topic in the school counselor literature. ASCA (2019a) stipulates appropriate and inappropriate duties for school counselors, and coordination of building-based teams lands on the inappropriate side. As authors, we agree that, while school counselors should be involved as collaborators and consultants, the clerical duties often associated with coordination should be managed by building administrators and support staff. However, our goal in this text is to provide readers with a realistic view of the roles school counselors often play in their schools, so we feel that it is necessary to mention that this is a role many practitioners are asked to negotiate, regardless of whether it represents best practice. While school counselors are often involved with team-based collaboration (e.g., MTSS, MDTs), some school counselors are also unfortunately asked to serve as leaders in their schools by coordinating a multitude of these collaborative services. In the role of coordinator, school counselors manage a wide variety of indirect services to help their students succeed. These do, however, include both collaboration and consultation efforts. For instance, counselors often serve as a liaison between teachers, parents, support personnel, and community resources to facilitate success for both individual students and/or the entire school (Fitch & Marshall, 2004). Examples of coordination include everything from assisting parents in obtaining needed services for their children through a referral and follow-up process to working with a local mental health agency to provide school-wide programming on the dangers of vaping. School counselors who understand their appropriate roles should advocate to provide collaboration and consultation on these teams exclusively, if possible.

Confidentiality/Privileged Communication

In all areas of school counselor practice, it is essential that school counselors understand the requirements and limitations of information sharing. When school counselors consider sharing information exchanged between the counselor and students, as well as sharing information about students, two terms frequently arise: confidentiality and privileged communication. Confidentiality refers to the school counselor's ethical and legal obligation to keep information obtained during a counseling relationship with a student contained within that relationship (ASCA, 2018). According to ASCA's (2018) position statement on confidentiality and the school counselor, "It is the school counselors' responsibility to fully respect the right to privacy of those with whom they enter a counseling relationship and to provide an atmosphere of trust and confidence" (ASCA, 2018, para. 2).

Privileged communication on the other hand refers to the privilege of privacy that is given to a client. According to Remley and Herlihy (2020), "privileged communication means that a judge cannot order information that has been recognized by law as privileged to be revealed in court" (p. 107). In a seminal federal court case, the ACA (n.d.) notes that in a U.S. Supreme Court decision, *Jaffee v. Redmond* (APA, n.d.), communications between psychotherapists and their clients were established as privileged and, therefore, protected from forced disclosure in cases involving federal court. However, in matters involving state statutes and codes, the granting of privileged communication in cases of counseling and therapy varies. Therefore, school counselors research state laws and statutes for guidance on how these concepts are applied in their respective states.

In spite of ASCA's mandate for school counselors to work diligently to protect student rights to privacy and in the absence of state laws and statutes that provide the protection of privileged communication, there are times when it is required to share student information that is determined to be private and confidential in nature. In other words, there are limits to confidentiality that are driven by the school counselor's obligation to report certain pieces of information in cases of suspected abuse and neglect. Generally, limits of confidentiality apply to the following:

- Any cases of suspected child abuse or neglect; all states mandate the reporting of suspected child abuse (Stone, 2018). See Table 3.1 for a list of categories of child abuse and mistreatment that should be reported under the obligation of the school counselor as a mandated reporter
- Any intention to harm an individual or society including threats of harm to self, suicidal intention or ideation, harm to other students or individuals
- Any cases of suspected elderly abuse or neglect
- Court orders for school documents and records

TABLE 3.1 **FOUR TYPES OF CHILD MALTREATMENT**

Neglect	Failure to provide for a child's basic needs
	Physical Neglect – lack of appropriate supervision or failure to provide necessary food, shelter, or medical care
	Educational Neglect – failure to educate a child or attend to special education needs
	Emotional Neglect – inattention to a child's emotional needs or exposure to domestic violence
Physical Abuse	Physical injury (ranging from minor bruises to severe fractures or death) as a result of punching, beating, kicking, biting, shaking, throwing, stabbing, strangling, hitting (with a hand, stick, strap, or another object), burning, or otherwise harming a child. Such injury is considered abuse regardless of whether the caretaker intended to hurt the child

Sexual Abuse	Includes activities by parents or caretakers such as fondling a child's genitals, penetration, incest, rape, sodomy, indecent exposure, and commercial exploitation through prostitution or the production of pornographic materials
Emotional Abuse	Includes any pattern of behavior that impairs a child's emotional development or sense of self-worth. This may include constant criticism, threats, or rejection, as well as withholding love, support, or guidance

(Fortson et al., 2016, p. 8)

The *ASCA Ethical Standards for School Counselors* (ASCA, 2022) provide guidance around the ways in which school counselors approach the breaking of confidentiality. School counselors recognize that it is not always possible to maintain confidentiality; they explain the limits of confidentiality to students in developmentally appropriate ways and across a variety of platforms. School counselors also recognize that the primary obligation of confidentiality is to the student but balance that obligation with the understanding that parents/caregivers reserve the right to be the guiding voice in the child's life (ASCA, 2022). The ASCA guidelines state that when a breach of confidentiality is necessary, school counselors:

> Collaborate with and involve students to the extent possible and use the most appropriate and least intrusive method to breach confidentiality if such action is warranted. The child's developmental age and the circumstances requiring the breach are considered and, as appropriate, students are engaged in a discussion about the method and timing of the breach. Consultation with professional peers and/or supervision is recommended. (ASCA, 2022, A.2.h)

As such, school counselors account for students' developmental levels and act accordingly. Considerations for a breach should apply a student's developmental age as well as their chronological age in attempting to honor the student's rights to make decisions (Remley & Herlihy, 2020). Welfel (2002) notes that "generally, the more mature the minor, the greater the measure of confidentiality that a young person is given in counseling" (p.102). In other words, the younger the student, the more control parents have over decisions governing their children. Additionally, elementary school counselors tend to consult with teachers concerning student problems more frequently compared to high school counselors and have much more contact with parents and teachers than school counselors at other programmatic levels, making the sharing of information more frequently necessary (Hardesty & Dillard, 1994; Nugent, 1990).

FERPA Versus HIPAA

FERPA, established in 1974, is a federal law that governs and provides guidance for the access and sharing of student educational records (U.S. Department of Education, 2018). The law applies to all schools (pre-K–12), school districts, and postsecondary institutions that receive federal monies from the U.S. Department of Education. A nonpublic school that does not receive federal funding is exempt from the law.

FERPA defines educational records as any record pertaining to a student's attendance, behavior, academics, testing and assessment, and school activities (Erford, 2011; USDE, 2018). Even if a school designates student records as health records, special education records, confidential records, or assigns some other designation to a student record for the sake of storage and ease of access, all these records are considered part of the educational record and are thereby covered under FERPA. As such, FERPA gives parents and "eligible" students (students who have reached the age of 18) the right to review and inspect applicable student records. FERPA also gives parents and eligible students the right to request that a student record be corrected in the case where they believe the record is inaccurate. FERPA requires that schools obtain written permission to release any information from a student record except when the following person/entity requests access:

- School officials with a legitimate educational interest
- Other schools to which a student transfers
- Designated officials for evaluation and audit
- Appropriate persons connected to a student's financial aid
- Organizations conducting studies for the school
- Accrediting organizations
- Court order or a subpoena
- Appropriate officials in the case of a health or safety emergency
- State and local authorities such as juvenile justice (USDE, 2018)

What is important for the professional school counselor to be attuned to when it comes to FERPA? First, school counselors must understand the obligations required of schools when it comes to student records. School counselors assist schools in protecting the privacy of students and student records and advocate for students when there is a concern that the school is in violation of the law. Second, school counselors are cautious about creating content that is added to a student record. School counselors are also aware of an exception for "personal notes." It is recommended that school counselors keep two distinct sets of notes: counseling and personal. Counseling notes that reference times and days of counseling sessions or interactions, nature of interactions, goals for counseling sessions, etc., are considered counseling notes and become part of the student's educational record. However, school counselors often keep personal or "sole possession notes." These notes refer to personal notes made by the school counselor to jog the memory or provide an extension to the work done with a student. These notes remain in the sole possession of the maker. It is important to remember that these notes should stay in the sole possession of the maker and if shared, they are no longer personal and become part of the official student record.

Established in 1996, HIPAA provides oversight and guidance to health-care providers regarding the protection and sharing of an individual's health records. Issued by the Department of Health and Human Services, HIPAA's *Standards for Privacy of Individually Identifiable Health Information* ("Privacy Rule") establishes a set of national standards for the protection of certain health information (Office of Civil Rights, 2013). Often, schools receive information from outside providers about medical issues, diagnoses, and other medical information covered by HIPAA. However, schools may enter that information into the educational record. School counselors must be aware of school district policies in terms of what information is designated as covered by HIPAA and/or FERPA and advocate that student information only be shared with those individuals who legally and ethically have rights. Collaboration with the school nurse may be especially helpful in this area. Furthermore, it is important to note with respect to HIPAA that school counselors are aware of and adhere to all school board policies, federal laws, and state laws that govern the protection of student records. This includes health information and any information documented as a part of student special services (i.e., HIPAA, FERPA, Individuals with Disabilities Education Act; ASCA, 2018).

In summary, school counselors serve in multiple appropriate roles (counselor, consultant, and collaborator) as they deliver school counseling programs. Each role requires a unique set of skills and yet all require building and maintaining relationships with school and community partners to better support students. As school counselors transition from role to role, there are multiple laws and professional ethical codes school counselors evoke to ensure the safety of both student information and student mental health.

Consultation Corner: Who You Gonna Call?

After bracketing your thoughts and reading the "Informed School Counseling" section, who would you call in and outside of the school building, and what might you ask them to support your decision-making? Take a moment to document these questions. Now that you have considered your questions for consultation, let's see what professional school counselors from around the world have to say about this case.

Consultation #1

I think you did the right thing in having the conversation. These situations are clearly important to your students and their families, and could ultimately affect their learning. One thing that helps me guide conversations like this is asking the students and/or parents what is the outcome they are seeking. If they have a reasonable expectation for the outcome, I then ask how would they like me to support them. I try to give options like: would you like to speak to the teacher about it on your own, would you like to talk to your teacher about it together, or would you like me or an administrator to speak to the teacher for you? If they prefer to not participate in the conversation, I ask: would you like me to use your name, or would you rather be anonymous?

It sounds like this teacher quickly became very defensive, which makes me curious. I wonder where that defensiveness is coming from? Maybe there's something deeper going on for her personally or professionally you could try to support her with. Although, it may be difficult for him/her to accept support if he's/she's still angry.

(Loren Riedel, elementary school counselor, Texas)

Consultation #2

Hi, my name is Nicole Cartwright, and I am an elementary school counselor in a suburban district with urban-like qualities. A large percentage of the students qualify for free or reduced lunch and are of African American and Latino descent. I currently have a caseload of 569 students and am the only school counselor in the school. I would also like to mention that I have extensive experience as a high school counselor, within the same district, with a caseload of over 250 students. Likewise, I have ten years of teaching experience within a middle school in the same district. There are a couple of ways that I would have approached these situations.

First, I would not have disclosed the information that the student had disclosed to me. If the teacher asked, then I would explain to the teacher that I could not disclose the information because of confidentiality. Second, once I finished speaking to the teacher, I would speak to the student again and encourage them to speak to their teacher to ensure that they learn how to properly advocate for themselves. In doing so, I would role play with the student various scenarios to adequately prepare them. Third, I would consult with a colleague or director of guidance, to see if they would agree with my handling of the situation or to see if they may have any other suggestions that may be helpful. Lastly, I would have the student and the teacher meet with me in my office and I would mediate the conversation.

Regarding the incident with the teacher and the unwanted touching of students, I would not have addressed that matter directly with the teacher. I have had situations similar to this one. Since the parent emailed the counselor and the principal, I would have met with the principal to ensure that the parent receives a timely response and suggest that they explain in the email that they would be addressing the matter with the teacher directly. Teachers are our colleagues and we should not get involved in matters that could involve disciplining other colleagues. Although the intention of giving a teacher a "heads up" is kind, we should remember to establish appropriate boundaries.

(Nicole Cartwright, elementary school counselor, New Jersey)

Consultation #3

I've been in similar situations as you—multiple students disclose to me, the school counselor, issues that they are having with a particular teacher. In your case, you cited three examples of students having a problem with one of your teachers. When there appears to be a pattern where the teacher is the common denominator, I ask for the students' permission to share what was reported in my office along with asking what the students would like to see happen. If I do receive permission, I talk to the teacher without revealing the specific student's name (although the teacher probably has some idea who the student(s) is/are).

Before I talk with a teacher in this type of situation, I keep in mind that he/she may not be receptive to what I have to say. I start off with positive comments (you mentioned that he/she is a caring teacher) and then say that a student or a parent contacted me about an issue. Then, I would definitely listen to what the teacher has to say and emphasize that the purpose of the meeting is to give a "heads up" on being careful about comments/actions. If more complaints about the teacher come from students, I would ask the students to write a statement and give it to administration.

(Rudy Escobar, middle school counselor, Virginia)

Consultation #4

Hi, my name is LeTishia Little, I currently work as a middle school counselor in an urban area for a charter school. I can relate to having difficult conversations with the teachers about how students felt. I often remind myself and the staff that our population has experienced some difficult times, and some (if not most) have experienced some form of trauma. With that reminder, it is imperative to be mindful of tone, wording, and movement when addressing these scholars. For the protection of all parties' staff and scholars, we have a no hands-on policy. I would have addressed the teacher as well as a heads up and worked with the teacher to work through looking at each of these incidences can be all about perception, and if you look at it through the lens of a scholar who may have had a preexisting traumatic experience, this action can come off as aggressive. In my experience, a restorative circle has even been conducted between the scholar and the teacher to address the feelings of the scholar and how to navigate, in the future, boundaries and expectations.

(LeTishia Little, middle school counselor, New Jersey)

Consultation #5

Hey there, I'm Jeff, and let me say that is an incredibly tough spot to be in. While the circumstances were different, I was also in a place that blurred the lines between an admin duty and "other duties as assigned." In my small school, I tend to take on a bit more of an admin-like role than you may see at larger schools due to the need and the limited number of admin on campus. While I think we all have a role to play on the team and should pitch in where we can, your specific circumstance seems like one I would be extra cautious with. Both circumstances could easily end up in litigation, and you don't want to be the one acting outside of your credential or license in court. The other angle to look at it from is that you are also there to support the teachers as a school counselor. This experience may have severely limited your ability to support this teacher (and potentially others when they find out about the "heads up"). It's the same reason we are not to deal in discipline—it changes the dynamic of the relationship and reduces our overall effectiveness.

In your circumstance, I would have likely offered to help with the conversation, but I would have asked that an admin be present and lead the conversation. I would have preferred to act more as the conflict mediator versus the admin in the scenario. Easier said than done sometimes.

(Jeff Ream, high school counselor, California)

#EduCounselor Synthesis

Having read the "Informed School Counseling" section and the perspectives of other school counselors, think about how you are making sense of the initial post. The "Informed School Counseling" section discusses the many relationships school counselors encounter daily. As suggested, in addition to their clinical work, school counselors often act as a bridge in these relationships, most often between teachers and students, parents and teachers, and administration and teachers/students. In these roles, they must learn to navigate relationships as both a consultant and liaison. Consultation is an essential part of school counseling practice, especially in schools where school counselors have large caseloads (Cholewa et al., 2020). Many school counselors, especially those whose roles are not clearly defined, struggle to negotiate these responsibilities and at times, find it difficult to maintain confidentiality and objectivity as they help to mediate conflicts between interested parties. In fact, school counselor consultation, while one of the most common activities (Perera-Diltz et al., 2011) might also be a skill set school counselors in training feel least prepared to initiate (Goodman-Scott, 2015). It is therefore not surprising that our consultants had a lot to say about the initial post and the consultative challenge presented by this school counselor. As a reminder from this chapter, school counselors should draw on their state's legal and organizations' ethical codes for clarity around the sharing of information between colleagues.

In our opening scenario, the counselor clearly feels uncertain about how they can support the student while also cultivating and maintaining a trusting relationship with a colleague. As reiterated by our consultants, this is an all too familiar situation for many school counselors. Without a clearly defined role in the school, the counselor can be left with split-second decisions that can result in negative consequences for relationships with students, colleagues, and administrators. One example of this role confusion occurs when school counselors are placed in the role of disciplinarians (for students and even teachers). The role of school counselor as disciplinarian is something that, while often not intended, comes up by virtue of school counselors' unique intermediary positions within the school setting. Understanding the role of confidentiality as it relates to FERPA and HIPAA laws in a school setting and developing skills to navigate the sharing of information with others takes time, trust, and an investment in providing education to the school community. Let's examine the advice provided by our consultants.

Loren and Rudy recommended finding out what the student or parent needed from the school counselor in disclosing information. On this same line, it might be equally beneficial to ask a teacher the same question who shares information with you about a student or parent. While it might be easy for school counselors to jump into the rescuer or "fix-it" role, it is important to remember our clinical training, particularly the basic listening skills school counseling students learned in most graduate programs (e.g., paraphrasing, reflection of feeling/meaning). Sometimes educational partners want to be heard or need to vent out frustrations or confusion, and once they do, with some good reflections on the part of the counselor, they are able to gain more of their own clarity on the situation. Learning about what the individual is looking for from their consultation with the school counselor may help to circumvent situations in which the school counselor might inadvertently feel as though they need to act outside of their appropriate role (e.g., supervisory position over a colleague). Loren also demonstrated curiosity as far as the teacher's reaction in this scenario. Using our basic listening skills to further understand a collegaue's purpose in sharing information and what might be triggering their reactions may help to address the situation in a more productive way.

Clarification around the school counselor's role as far as confidentiality is equally important as discussed in the "Informed School Counseling" section of this chapter and reiterated by Jeff's and Nicole's responses. Whether we are noting that only certain information can be shared due to confidentiality or requesting that an administrator share parent concerns with the teacher directly, it is important that the school counselor and the school community delineate the boundaries around how and with whom the school counselor mediates situations. Several of the consultants recommended that the school counselor advocate for consultation with a director of school counseling or another administrator and/or request to help *mediate r*ather than lead confrontational discussions between parents and administrators and teachers and students. Attention to FERPA and HIPAA laws is particularly important here and should be considered before any information is shared.

LeTishia recommended that psychoeducation be provided to the teacher around potential trauma to help provide an additional perspective. LeTishia and Nicole also suggested empowering the student to speak directly with the teacher with guidance from the school counselor. It is common for school counselors to role-play scenarios with students or even attend the meetings between other professionals to help both sides feel heard. Rudy also suggested a self-advocacy intervention whereby the student could share concerns about the physical altercation directly with the administration in a more indirect way (i.e., letter writing). School counselors can work with students in these efforts.

The author of our post talked about wanting to give the teacher a "heads up" regarding the situation. Our consultants shared different views about this. Nicole appeared cautious about how that might position the counselor's role. Others provided some examples of how the school counselor could address this directly with the teacher. In reviewing this situation, it is important to consider that on one hand, speaking directly to the teacher could help to foster more trust in the collegial relationship, and on the other hand, it could also end up resulting in what feels like a punitive conversation, as appears to be the case in this scenario. School counselors need to have strong relationships with teachers to truly be able to support all students in the school (Bryan & Henry, 2012). This is especially important for educators working with our struggling students who may be a part of special education or receiving 504 support. Aligned with the solution-focused BC model, Rudy suggested that the school counselor speak with the teacher by leading with the teacher's strengths as a caring individual. The sandwich technique (i.e., positive comment, critical feedback, positive comment) is one way in which conflict resolution situations (Care Academy, 2018) could be addressed in this scenario.

Chapter Summary

The focus of this chapter includes a discussion around the many school counselor roles navigated when serving multiple school and community partners. Understanding the many hats that school counselors wear daily informs the development of a comprehensive school counseling program. It is incumbent upon school counselors to familiarize themselves with FERPA and HIPAA laws and how confidentiality and the sharing of information on a "need to know" basis is handled within their respective schools. School counselors must be intentional with the information they do share and continue to advocate for their appropriate roles with all interested parties in order to ensure that they are practicing ethically and cultivating relationships that best serve their students and school communities.

Reflective Practitioner Process

School counselors engage in **clinical supervision, professional development,** and **self-care** to further develop their knowledge and skills and to help balance professional expectations with personal wellness. All three areas are key to ethical practice and help to mitigate counselor burnout and compassion fatigue (Atici, 2015; Lawson & Myers, 2011; Merriman, 2015; Ohrt et al., 2015).

Clinical Supervision

The *ASCA School Counselor Professional Standards and Competencies* (ASCA, 2019b) direct school counselors to "consult with school counselors and other education and counseling professionals when questions of school counseling practice arise" (B-SS 5., p. 5). As a supervisee, it is important to consider the thoughts, feelings, and experiences that come up for you as you work with students, families, and colleagues and seek consultation on difficult issues. The following are some topics for consideration as you react to this chapter.

- How might working with other colleagues in schools affect your professional relationships?
- How might you handle conflict with school and community partners with whom you have a personal relationship?

Professional Development

According to the *ASCA Ethical Standards for School Counselors* (ASCA, 2022), professional school counselors engage in professional development and attend trainings to stay current on the trends and issues that impact students (B.3.e). Relative to the contents of this chapter, consider finding professional development on the following topics:

- Child and Family Services and Mandating Reporting (specific to your state and local district)
- FERPA Law
- Administrator and School Counselor Partnerships
- Community Mental Health Resources (specific to your state and local district)

#PSCSelfCare: Everyday Wellness

When designing, managing, and implementing a comprehensive school counseling program, school and community expectations can tax even the most seasoned school counselor. The *ASCA Ethical Standards for School Counselors* (ASCA, 2022) require school counselors to recognize the high levels of stress often associated with the job. Therefore, school counselors recognize that self-care must be a priority to maintain health and overall well-being (see ASCA, 2022, B.3.h).

Gratitude Journal—It's the Little Things

Any day above ground is a good day. Before you complain about anything, be thankful for your life and the things that are still going well.

—Germany Kent

Life comes with a series of ups and downs. On dark days, it can be hard to see through the clouds and appreciate all that we have. It is in those moments that practicing gratitude becomes especially helpful. Practicing gratitude is not just about feeling appreciative when things are going well. It is about reflecting and acknowledging what you have, instead of focusing on what's missing.

Research shows that practicing gratitude deepens relationships, increases happiness, and improves physical and mental health (Harvard Health Publishing, 2019). When you begin to focus on things to appreciate, it can have powerful effects on your mood and the way you see your life. Gratitude helps you savor the good things in life—big and small—and gives you the ability to weather any storm.

Next, you will find a series of questions to help you reflect on your gratitude (University of Texas at Austin, 2017). Feel free to journal, draw visuals, or create digital collages to help you with your process.

1. What are three things you are grateful for today?
2. What made you laugh today?
3. What is your favorite movie of all time? Why? And who were you with when you first saw it?
4. One thing I appreciate about myself is _____.
5. Draw three things that brought you joy today.
6. What is a specific childhood memory that makes you smile?
7. Write down the name of someone who made you smile or laugh this week. Who was it? Why did they make you smile or laugh?
8. In reflecting on your past, who has taught you something? What was it?
9. Write down three to five things you enjoy doing that get you through your day.
10. What are ways you outwardly express gratitude?

Spotlight: School Counseling Advocacy

Here, we provide an example of a school counselor using the Calendly software to efficiently collaborate and consult with community partners (e.g., parents). The roles of the school counselor are not always confined to the traditional school day hours; using technology allows, many families, especially historically marginalized parents, greater accessibility to the school counselor.

Missy Smith, Elementary Counselo
@CounselingSmith

I added office hour time slots to my website so that parents may schedule meetings with me for consultation or student check-ins. I used Calendly, which is a free service and super user friendly. How are you scheduling?

#scchat #schoolcounseling

Image 3.1

Learning Connections

Both professional school counselors in training and seasoned school counselors recognize the importance of understanding the connections between the concepts commonly taught in counseling programs and the standards most associated with school counselor training. Therefore, the following table below offers broad connections between the material and information in this chapter and the CACREP standards (CACREP, 2016), the *ASCA School Counselor Professional Standards and Competencies* (ASCA, 2019), and the *ASCA Ethical Standards for School Counselors* (ASCA, 2022).

Connections to CACREP Core Curricular Areas

Professional Counseling Orientation and Ethical Practice	Social and Cultural Diversity	Human Growth And Development	Career Development	Counseling and Helping Relationships	Group Counseling and Group Work	Assessment and Testing	Research and Program Evaluation
X		X		X			

Connection to Professional Standards

CACREP	ASCA Competencies	Ethical Standards: SC
F.1.b: The multiple professional roles and functions of counselors across specialty areas, and their relationships with human service and integrated behavioral health care systems, including interagency and interorganizational, collaboration, and consultation	B-PF 2: Demonstrate understanding of educational systems, legal issues, policies, research, and trends in education.	A.2.f: Keep information confidential unless legal requirements demand confidential information be revealed or a breach is required to prevent serious and foreseeable harm to the student or others. Serious and foreseeable harm is different for each minor in schools and is determined by a student's developmental and chronological age, the setting, parental/guardian rights and the nature of the harm. School counselors consult with appropriate professionals when in doubt as to the validity of an exception.
F.1.i: Ethical standards of professional counseling organizations and credentialing bodies, and applications of ethical and legal considerations in professional counseling; and G.2.m: legal and ethical considerations specific to school counseling	B-PF 3: Apply legal and ethical principles of the school counseling profession.	A.6.a: Collaborate with all relevant stakeholders, including students, school faculty/staff and parents/guardians, when students need assistance, including when early warning signs of student distress are identified.
F.3.g: Systemic and environmental factors that affect human development, functioning, and behavior; and G.3.f: characteristics, risk factors, and warning signs of students at risk for mental health and behavioral disorders	B-SS 4: Make referrals to appropriate school and community resources.	A.6.c: Connect students with services provided through the local school district and community agencies and remain aware of state laws and local district policies related to students with special needs, including limits to confidentiality and notification to authorities as appropriate.
F.5.b: Theories, models, and strategies. For understanding and practicing consultation; and G.2.a: school counselor roles in consultation with families, P–12, and postsecondary school personnel and community agencies	B-SS 5: Consult to support student achievement and success.	A.6.f: Attempt to establish a collaborative relationship with outside service providers to best serve students. Request a release of information signed by the student and/or parents/guardians before attempting to collaborate with the student's external provider.
F.7.a: Procedures for identifying trauma and abuse for reporting abuse	B-SS 6: Collaborate with families, teachers, administrators, other school staff and education stakeholder for student achievement and success.	

Comprehensive School Counseling Assignments

The following section provides activities that allow for your continued growth as a professional school counselor. Both preservice and practicing school counselors may find it helpful to complete these activities. If you are currently in a graduate training program, your professor might assign these as part of your course.

1. **Consultation Approach Comparison** – Compare and contract at least four different consultation approaches (independent-triadic, dependent-triadic, BC, CBC, etc.). Reflect on similarities, differences, and the various elements involved in the approaches. After reflecting on at least four, reflect on what approach you feel might fit you best.

2. **Mandated Reporting Practice** – When reporting to your state's child and family services (name varies between states), school counselors must share specific information to initiate a potential investigation. Look up your state's process and gather the forms that indicate what information you would need. This may feel like an overwhelming process, but it is important to remember that we are mandated reporters, and our goal is to connect students and families with the resources they need. Once you locate the process and sample forms required for reporting in your state, consider developing a mock student situation that would require you filing a report. Then, pair up with a fellow student and practice making that call to child services.

Once you have practiced, reflect with the following questions.

1. Did you have an emotional response to this activity? Did you have any physical response to this activity (e.g., shaking voice, fidgeting)?
2. In thinking about reporting future cases in your role as a school counselor, what might be your greatest challenge? What kinds of support (e.g., emotional, logistical, legal) will you need to navigate the first time you have to make a report?
3. What might you need to do to set boundaries so that you do not take these emotionally taxing situations home with you?

Helpful Resources
Web-Based Resources

Missouri Professional School Counselors and Counselor Educators (2017). *Professional school counselor consultation guide: A professional school counselor's guide to consulting and collaborating.*

- http://www.missouricareereducation.org/doc/consult/CollabConsult.pdf

Suggested Readings

- Text to guide understanding of the school counselor's role in special education:
  - Trolley, B., Haas, H., & Patti, D. C. (2009). *The school counselor's guide to special education.* Corwin Press.
- For further information on FERPA and HIPPA:
  - U.S. Department of Health and Human Services (n.d.). *FERPA and HIPAA.* https://www.hhs.gov/hipaa/for-professionals/faq/ferpa-and-hipaa/index.html

References

American School Counselor Association (ASCA). (2018). *The school counselor and confidentiality.* https://www.schoolcounselor.org/asca/media/asca/PositionStatements/PS_Confidentiality.pdf

American School Counselor Association (ASCA). (2019a). *ASCA national model: A framework for school counseling programs* (4th ed.).

American School Counselor Association (ASCA). (2019b). *ASCA school counselor professional standards & competencies.* https://www.schoolcounselor.org/asca/media/asca/home/SCCompetencies.pdf

American School Counselor Association (ASCA). (2022). *ASCA ethical standards for school counselors.* https://www.schoolcounselor.org/getmedia/44f30280-ffe8-4b41-9ad8-f15909c3d164/EthicalStandards.pdf

American Psychological Association (APA). (n.d.). *Jaffee v. Redmond, 518 U.S. 1.* American Psychological Association. Retrieved August 23, 2022, from https://www.apa.org/about/offices/ogc/amicus/jaffee

Atici, M. (2015). Professional identity development of counselors-in-training in a school internship program in Turkey. *The Professional Counselor, 5*(1), 137–151. https://doi.org/10.15241/MA.5.1.137

Bryan, J., & Henry, L. (2012). A model for building school-family-community partnerships: Principles and process. *Journal of Counseling and Development, 90*(4), 408–420. https://doi.org/10.1002/j.1556-6676.2012.00052.x

Council for Accreditation of Counseling and Related Educational Programs (CACREP). (2016). *2016 CACREP standards.* http://www.cacrep.org/wp-content/uploads/2017/08/2016-Standards-with-citations.pdf

Care Academy. (2018, October 11). *How to give constructive criticism.* https://blog.careacademy.com/how-to-give-constructive-criticism

Centers for Disease Control and Prevention (CDC). (2018). *Providing access to mental health services for children in rural areas.* https://www.cdc.gov/ruralhealth/child-health/policy-brief.html

Centers for Disease Control and Prevention (CDC). (2020a). *Preventing suicide.* https://www.cdc.gov/violenceprevention/suicide/fastfact.html

Centers for Disease Control and Prevention (CDC). (2020b). *Data and statistics on children's mental health.* https://www.cdc.gov/childrensmentalhealth/data.html

Cholewa, B., Goodman-Scott, E., Warren, J. M., & Hull, M. F. (2020). School counselor consultation preparation: A national study. *Counselor Education and Supervision*, 59(1), 46–58. https://doi.org/10.1002/ceas.12165

Davis, K. (2005). School-based consultation. In C. Sink (Ed.), *Contemporary school counseling: Theory, research, and practice* (pp. 295–326). Houghton Mifflin.

Dixon, A. L., Devoss, J. A., & Davis, E. S. (2008). Strengthening links between the levels: School counselor collaboration for successful student transitions. *Journal of School Counseling*, 6(21), 1–33. https://files.eric.ed.gov/fulltext/EJ894792.pdf

Erchul, W. P., & Martens, B. K. (2010). *School consultation: Conceptual and empirical bases of practice* (3rd ed.). Springer. https://doi.org/10.1007/978-1-4419-5747-4

Erford, B. T. (2011). *Transforming the school counseling profession* (3rd ed.). Pearson Education.

Fitch, T. J., & Marshall, J. L. (2004). What counselors do in high-achieving schools: A study on the role of the school counselor. *Professional School Counseling*, 7(3), 172–177. https://www.jstor.org/stable/42732559

Fortson, B. L., Klevens, J., Merrick, M. T., Gilbert, L. K., & Alexander, S. P. (2016). *Preventing child abuse and neglect: A technical package for policy, norm, and programmatic activities.* National Center for Injury Prevention and Control, Centers for Disease Control and Prevention. https://doi.org/10.15620/cdc.38864

Goodman-Scott, E. (2015). School counselors' perceptions of their academic preparedness and job activities. *Counselor Education and Supervision*, 54(1), 57–67. https://doi.org/10.1002/j.1556-6978.2015.00070.x

Hardesty, P. H., & Dillard, J. M. (1994). The role of elementary school counselors compared with their middle and secondary school counterparts. *Elementary School Guidance & Counseling*, 29(2), 83–91. https://www.jstor.org/stable/42871149

Harvard Health Publishing. (2019). *Giving thanks can make you happier.* https://www.health.harvard.edu/healthbeat/giving-thanks-can-make-you-happier

Henderson, D. A., & Thompson, C. L. (2011). *Consultation. In counseling children* (8th ed.). Brooks/Cole.

Herman-Turner, K. M., & Benoit, E. N. (2019). Working with families. In A. Vernon, & C. J. Schimmel, *Counseling children and adolescents* (5th ed., pp. 493–527). Cognella.

Hill, A. (2014). *Theories of consultation for school counselors.* Prezi. https://prezi.com/sah9yoaue1zx/theories-of-consultation-for-school-counselors/

Ieva, K. P., Beasley, J., & Steen, S. (2021). Equipping school counselors for antiracist healing engagement: Challenging group counseling preparation and connected curricula. *Teaching and Supervision in Counseling*, 3(2). https://doi.org/10.7290/tsc030207

Kahn, B. B. (2000). A model of solution-focused consultation for school counselors. *Professional School Counseling*, 3(4), 248. https://search.proquest.com/openview/8c50bd893290553aceb78fb4e50cdf56/1?pq-origsite=gscholar&cbl=11185

Kolbert, J. B., Williams, R. L., Morgan, L. M., Crothers, L. M., & Hughes, T. L. (2016). *Introduction to professional school counseling: Advocacy, leadership, and intervention.* Routledge.

Kurpius, D. J., Fuqua, D. R., & Rozecki, T. (1993). The consulting process: A multidimensional approach. *Journal of Counseling & Development*, 71(6), 601–606. https://doi.org/10.1002/j.1556-6676.1993.tb02249.x

Lawson, G., & Myers, J. E. (2011). Wellness, professional quality of life, and career-sustaining behaviors: What keeps us well? *Journal of Counseling and Development*, 89(2), 163–171. https://doi.org/10.1002/j.1556-6678.2011.tb00074.x

Mathieson, B. (2017). Lessons in collaboration in school counseling. *ASCA Newsletter.* https://www.schoolcounselor.org/newsletters/october-2017/lessons-in-collaboration-in-school-counseling

Merriman, J. (2015). Enhancing counselor supervision through compassion fatigue education. *Journal of Counseling and Development, 93*(3), 370–378. https://doi.org/10.1002/jcad.12035

Nugent, F. (1990). *An introduction to the profession of counseling.* Merrill.

Office of Civil Rights (OCR). (2013). *Summary of the HIPAA privacy rule.* https://www.hhs.gov/hipaa/for-professionals/privacy/laws-regulations/index.html

Ohrt, J. H., Prosek, E. A., Ener, E., Lindo, N. (2015). The effects of a group supervision intervention to promote wellness and prevent burnout. *The Journal of Humanistic Counseling, 54*(1), 41–58. https://doi.org/10.1002/j.2161-1939.2015.00063.x

Perera-Diltz, D., Moe, J. L., & Mason, K. L. (2011). An exploratory study in school counselor consultation engagement. *Journal of School Counseling, 9*(13). https://eric.ed.gov/?id=EJ933179

Remley, T. P., & Herlihy, B. P. (2020). *Ethical, legal, and professional issues in school counseling* (6th ed.). Pearson Education.

Sabella, R. (2018). Solution-focused brief counseling. In A. Vernon & C. J. Schimmel, *Counseling children & adolescents* (5th ed., pp. 147–184). Cognella.

Sheridan, S. M., Ryoo, J. H., Garbacz, S. A., Kunz, G. M., & Chumney, F. L. (2013). The efficacy of conjoint behavioral consultation on parents and children in the home setting: Results of a randomized controlled trial. *Journal of School Psychology, 51*(6), 717–733. https://doi.org/10.1016/j.jsp.2013.09.003

Stone, C. (2005). *School counseling principles: Ethics and law.* American School Counselor Association.

Stone, C. (2017, September). Appropriate vs. inappropriate duties. *ASCA School Counselor.* https://www.schoolcounselor.org/magazine/blogs/september-october-2017/appropriate-vs-inappropriate-duties

Stone, C. (2018, July 1). *Suicide and child abuse reporting. ASCA school counselor.* https://www.schoolcounselor.org/magazine/blogs/july-august-2018/suicide-and-child-abuse-reporting

Welfel, E. R. (2002). *Ethics in counseling and psychotherapy: Standards, research, and emerging issues* (2nd ed.). Brooks/Cole.

University of Texas at Austin, Counseling and Mental Health Center. (2017). *Gratitude journal.* https://cmhc.utexas.edu/pdf/UTCMHC_GratitudeJournal_2017.pdf

U.S. Department of Education (USDE). (2018). *Family educational rights and privacy act (FERPA).* https://www2.ed.gov/policy/gen/guid/fpco/ferpa/index.html

Zhang, J., & Slesnick, N. (2018). The effects of a family systems intervention on co-occurring internalizing and externalizing behaviors of children with substance abusing mothers: A latent transition analysis. *Journal of Marital and Family Therapy, 44*(4), 687–701. http://dx.doi.org.ezproxy.monmouth.edu/10.1111/jmft.12277

Credit

PART II

The School Counseling Profession

Manage

CHAPTER 4

Beliefs, Vision, and Mission

The Framework for Comprehensive School Counseling

LEARNING OBJECTIVES

#EduCounselors can

- identify the foundational tools school counselors develop to manage and direct an inclusive and equitable comprehensive school counseling program,

- recognize important elements of well-written school counseling program vision and mission statements, and

- understand the appropriate role of the school counseling program advisory council in supporting the program vision and mission.

Introduction

When asked why a new professional is considering a career in school counseling, a common response often includes a desire to help children and adolescents overcome personal and academic challenges. However, all our actions within a school should stem from our collective vision and mission, as articulated in our comprehensive school counseling program. Our collective beliefs and values guide our decisions, specifically the interventions we choose to use to support our students' academic, social/emotional, and career development.

School counselors recognize that certain traditional educational practices support unequal student outcomes, such as the persistent opportunity gap and the school-to-prison pipeline. A well-designed, equitable, and culturally informed comprehensive school counseling program contributes to more just outcomes for all students. In developing the plan, school counselors must consider their own values, worldviews, and experiences with privilege and oppression. Additionally, we must look at the values, policies, and practices that make up the school culture and assess to see if they serve to maintain unfair systems or if they support collective growth and liberation. After a thorough examination of these beliefs, school counselors work collaboratively with key school partners to develop materials that articulate these values and use their leadership skills to promote a program that equitably addresses the needs of the entire school community.

#IRLSchoolCounseling

The following is a social media post captured from one of the many school counseling groups on Facebook. *Caught in the Middle School Counselors* is a community of school counselors whose work is geared toward serving middle school students.

> My goal is to start implementing the ASCA model into my program … problem is that I'm the only counselor in my building and I have 574 students. I spend too much time on responsive type situations, only push in to 8th grade FCS classes 3× a quarter for career lessons and 7th grade health classes once a semester for a coping skills lesson. … I don't currently run small groups. I do a few school wide initiatives (career speakers every Friday and a college awareness week … both for all grade levels) … I just feel like I'm not running my program aligned enough to the model to create things like a mission statement or the annual agreement! It's so hard being the only counselor and saying things like "the goal of the counseling program" when I'm one person. Anyone else in this boat? Where do I start?! It seemed so easy when I was learning how to do all of this in grad school! haha

Bracketing Values for Ethical Practice

It is expected that school counselors continuously reflect on their values, beliefs, worldviews, and cultural norms and how each influences the ways in which they choose to take or not take action. As such, it is important to recognize and set aside any preconceived notions, experiences, and biases to help you respond to this scenario in a culturally sustaining and ethically sound manner. Take a moment to reflect on the previous post and then consider the following questions:

- How do you feel about this school counselor providing responsive "random acts of guidance" rather than proactive services?
- This school counselor wants to implement the *ASCA National Model* with fidelity, but there are obstacles that prevent them from achieving their goal. What is your reaction to hearing that the realities of school counselor practice in some schools may be different from the ideal comprehensive model taught in graduate school? How do you manage/cope when you pre-plan something, only to find yourself having to adjust and change course?
- What are some ways in your personal and professional life that you find yourself more responsive than proactive?

- When faced with an obstacle such as our school counselor in this post, what is your go-to response? Do you just give in and go with the flow, or do you challenge yourself to think creatively and offer broader ideas that serve the needs of more students? How will you challenge yourself to think "outside of the box" to creatively address issues that come up in your practice?

Informed School Counseling

School counselors hold important leadership responsibilities in schools and must develop the skills needed to advocate for systemic change. Leadership looks different across a variety of contexts, but one important commonality includes the need for leaders to recognize and operationalize their beliefs. School counselor leadership should specifically include an examination of these beliefs as they relate to school and community partner interactions and program development (Young & Kneale, 2013). In other words, leaders who understand their beliefs and take time to reflect on their implicit biases have the potential to drive the direction of the school counseling program; this includes connecting the vision and mission of the school district with the values of the program and ensuring that personal values are not reflected in the program's focus.

Successful school counselor leadership often starts with a strong collaborative relationship with building administrators. When these partnerships work in tandem, school counseling outcome goals are aligned with district priorities, and there is mutual respect and advocacy for the skill sets each brings to the table. For school counselors to be able to address systemic inequities and advocate for change, they must come to the table with a clear direction, informed by a combination of best school counseling practice, district priorities, and collaboration with a variety of interested partners. This begins by identifying the focus of the program and its beliefs and articulating these in the form of vision and mission statements. Leaders who prioritize these areas and leverage the strengths of school and community members' voices are on their way to creating a culturally sustaining school counseling program.

School counselor literature is ripe with many terms associated with diversity and equity, including cultural competence and cultural responsiveness. While there are no perfect terms, each of these respectively implies an ending point and a reactive stance toward inclusive practice (Grothaus et al., 2020). In this chapter, we discuss *culturally sustaining* school counseling as an ongoing intentional practice by which school counselors recognize and leverage school and community partner strengths to build an inclusive community. Furthermore, culturally sustaining school counseling programs reject the idea that all students must fit in with the mainstream, dominant culture and, rather, acknowledge individual diversity as important and beneficial to the collective whole. The following sections examine the important tools school counselor leaders prioritize as they manage their programs and move toward equity and inclusive practice.

Program Focus

To address lamenting the importance of direction in one's life, the famous motivational speaker, Zig Zigler once wrote, "Lack of direction, not lack of time, is the problem. We all have 24-hour days." Finding direction for a comprehensive school counseling program is critical to ensuring that the program serves all students in an equitable and consistent fashion. Writing to an educational leadership audience, Savitz-Romer et al. (2020) echo this importance as they advocate for principals to recognize the school counselor's expertise in developing a vision for the school counseling program that reflects the goals of the school. Similarly, the *ASCA National Model* (ASCA, 2019a) connects leadership to program direction as it states, "Without (school counselor) leadership, the school counseling program is disconnected to the overall mission of the school" (p. 32). As such, school counselors are charged with developing a strong foundation for a comprehensive school counseling program that marries the values of the district with the priorities of inclusive school counseling practice. This foundation is referred to as the program focus; it includes the school counselor's beliefs, vision, and mission for the program and is shared with school and community partners in the form of clearly articulated statements that reflect the heart of the program (ASCA, 2019a; Grothaus et al., 2020).

In each chapter of this text, we ask you to consider how the intersection of your cultural identity, values, and worldview influences your perceptions of the work school counselors do. In this chapter, you must now consider how those positions influence the development of your beliefs, vision, and mission for a school counseling program. First, we start with a discussion of school counselor beliefs.

Beliefs

A seminal question guides the development of comprehensive school counseling programs; that is, what do you believe about the way students learn and about the way they experience school? Historically, educational leaders have subscribed to the practice of supporting student development by focusing on the teaching of specific competencies to "fix kids," as if they were broken and in need of repair. However, leaders in the field are shifting to a new perspective—a perspective that includes viewing student development with an equity lens and a "broader asset-based approach that includes a focus on adult beliefs and mindsets and the systems and policies necessary to create equitable learning environments that support holistic student success" (The Education Trust, 2021, p. 15). Put simply, leaders now acknowledge that it is the *system* that needs examining and "fixing," rather than the kids! An effective, efficient, culturally sustaining school counseling program begins with school counselors taking a leadership role in identifying their professional school counseling beliefs, articulating these to school and community partners in the form of public statements, and then implementing school counseling programs aligned with these beliefs. Additionally, school counselors listen to input from students to ensure that the beliefs of the program align with what students report they need to succeed.

School counselors recognize that the *ASCA Ethical Standards for School Counselors* (2022) support the examination of these professional beliefs as a process to help guide the development and implementation of school counseling programs (ASCA, 2019a; Grothaus et al., 2020). At the same time, these ethical standards also remind school counselors of the need to "respect students' and families' values, beliefs and cultural background, as well as students' sexual orientation, gender identity and gender expression, and exercise great care to avoid imposing personal biases, beliefs or values rooted in one's religion, culture or ethnicity" (A.1.h.). Transformational school counselors not only respect the cultural identities of their students and families but also recognize how culture impacts every interaction in school, from what is taught (curriculum), to how it is taught (pedagogy), to what behavior is seen as "normal," just to name a few examples. We also acknowledge the detrimental mental health and educational outcomes associated with the legacy of colonialism, slavery, and the ongoing effects of White supremacy and how these forces serve to privilege certain people and oppress others. As mental health leaders in the educational context, it is especially important for school counselors to model intentionality both as it relates to program planning and the bracketing of personal values.

To that end, school counselors understand and articulate that "beliefs matter" (ASCA, 2019a, p. 29) and that those beliefs in turn influence behaviors (Grothaus et al., 2020). School counselors who fail to engage in a reflective process to identify their professional beliefs are in danger of not only imposing their own personal values but also reinforcing systemic biases inherent in school policy and practices (Shields et al., 2017). According to the Wisconsin Department of Public Instruction, "Before school teams and individuals begin to identify strategies and develop systems to support students whose behavior interferes with their learning or the learning of others, adults must first examine their own biases and beliefs about student behavior in addition to examining the social norms of the school community" (Wisconsin Department of Public Instruction, 2021, p. 1). In other words, developing your beliefs statements should not be viewed as a "check the box" exercise. School counselors must intentionally examine their professional and personal values and consider the influence of both in the creation and direction of their programs. To begin the process of exploring one's beliefs, the *ASCA School Counselor Professional Standards & Competencies* (ASCA, 2019b) provide seven school counselor beliefs for direction. These school counselor beliefs are outlined in Table 4.1.

TABLE 4.1 **ASCA SCHOOL COUNSELOR PROFESSIONAL STANDARDS & COMPETENCIES MINDSETS**

M 1	Every student can learn, and every student can succeed.
M 2	Every student should have access to and opportunity for a high-quality education.
M 3	Every student should graduate from high school prepared for postsecondary opportunities.

M 4	Every student should have access to a school counseling program.
M 5	Effective school counseling is a collaborative process involving school counselors, students, families, teachers, administrators, other school staff and education stakeholders.
M 6	School counselors are leaders in the school, district, state, and nation.
M 7	School counseling programs promote and enhance student academic, career and social/emotional outcomes.

(ASCA, 2019b)

Successful school counselors consider these mindsets as they reflect on their beliefs and the future direction of their programs.

As clarity around these beliefs emerge, school counselors look to take the pulse of their departments and district schools. Do members of the counseling department share similar professional beliefs? How does the department proceed should a difference in beliefs exist? How do counseling colleagues in the same department challenge each other when personal values and the presence of bias impact students, collegues, and/or the direction of the program (e.g., disagreements around how systemic racism should be discussed in school or how we support youth wishing to transition their gender identity). These are critical questions that must be addressed to unite the counseling program and support the health of all students. In cases where personal beliefs and biases prohibit the delivery of an inclusive program, it is imperative that schools "explore and examine implicit biases and the impact on practice and interaction with students; apply learning to program practice and development" (ASCA, 2022, B.3.f). This may include recognizing and addressing systemic practices that marginalize students or confronting colleagues whose personal values and subsequent behaviors result in an unsafe school climate. While not always comfortable, leaders engage in these courageous conversations to ensure that the foundation of their school counseling programs is based on equity and access. Stone (2020) perhaps said it best: "School counselors have to be committed to the ethics of our profession, which implore us to advantage each and every student in our charge" (p. 7).

As school counselors engage in this process, the counseling department as a whole works to develop collective beliefs statements to be shared widely throughout the school and the community. These statements should include the articulation of professional priorities that level the playing field for all students. School counselors pay particular attention to their use of inclusive language, which ultimately forms the basis for the program's vision and mission; as the foundation for any program, it is important to ensure that both are transparently communicated to all school and community partners. To assist in this process, Grothaus et al. (2020) provide the following sentence stems to consider when crafting or adapting your program's beliefs statement:

● With regard to our commitment to personal and professional growth, I/we believe. ...

- With regard to our school counseling program's commitment to equitable, inclusive, culturally sustaining services, I/we believe. ...
- Regarding placement in rigorous coursework, I/we believe. ...
- Considering access to our school counselor(s) and program services, I/we believe. ...
- Regarding our school climate, I/we believe. ...
- With regard to school-family-community collaboration, I/we believe. ...

Once these beliefs are articulated and publicized, they serve as the foundation for nearly every decision that is made about the program; they guide not only the management but also the delivery and the assessment of effective school counseling programs. Finally, inclusive belief statements position school counselors to question policies that are in direct conflict with the belief statements or that negatively impact students and school counseling programming.

Vision Statement

> *A vision is not just a picture of what could be; it is an appeal to our better selves, a call to become something more.*
>
> Rosabeth Moss Kanter

Vision statements are short, concise, simple statements that outline what an organization would like to ultimately achieve. They also give purpose to the existence of an organization (Wright, 2020). While they are most commonly associated with companies, we are all familiar with such as Nike and McDonald's, vision statements are not reserved for use in business alone; they are planning tools often used in nonprofit and government agencies and schools. According to Ray (2018), "A vision statement is a document that states the current and future objectives of an organization. The vision statement is intended as a guide to help the organization make decisions that align with its philosophy and declared set of goals. It can be thought of as a roadmap to where the company wants to be within a certain timeframe" ("What Is a Vision Statement" section, para. 1). In the world of the school counselor, the program vision statement "communicates what school counselors hope to see for students five to 15 years in the future" (ASCA, 2019a, p. 30).

As a critical piece of the school counseling program focus, vision statements are bold and aspirational and, in our view, unapologetically ambitious. They guide what we value and want for our students. Effective leaders create visions that identify goals and a path by which to get there (Young & Kneale, 2013).

According to ASCA (2019a), effective vision statements contain the following elements:

- a clear picture of success for all students,
- a description of a future in which student outcomes are achieved,

- a statement of the best outcomes for all students that extend 5–15 years out from high school or beyond, and
- language that aligns with the school and district vision statements, when applicable.

School counselors are firm in their commitment to vision statements that lay the foundation for programs that do not oppress or marginalize students. Once the vision is adopted and advertised, the tone is set for school counselors to respond to actions or policies that do not align with the vision.

Like all pieces of your program focus, vision statements are not intended to simply be the product of an exercise in comprehensive school counseling program planning and management. Leadership, advocacy, and systemic change are central themes involved in developing a vision statement for a school counseling program (Young & Kneale, 2013). Strong leaders have vision, and strong vision allows the school counselor to advocate for student success; communicating a clear vision to the school and community promotes the elimination of barriers to student success (ASCA, 2019a). The following are two examples of school counseling program vision statements published on their school's respective websites:

> The students at North Forsyth High School are inspired learners who use their gifts to impact those around them to make a difference in their school, community, and world. All students will participate in a rigorous curriculum that prepares them to be college and career ready and meet their personal potential. Support from the comprehensive school counseling program will enable students to meet the challenges of the future while fostering a healthy school climate that values diversity, knowledge, and achievement.
>
> *North Forsyth High School, n.d., Cumming, Georgia; RAMP 2017*
> *(https://www.forsyth.k12.ga.us/Page/50641)*

> Our Vision as school counselors at Wildlight Elementary School is to deliver a comprehensive developmental counseling program that addresses social, emotional, and academic needs of all students. Through collaboration, advocacy, and leadership, we are professional student advocates who provide support to maximize achievement and student potential. Our goal is to implement a multi-tiered system of supports to ensure students have access to the resources and skills needed to become universally competitive life-long learners.
>
> *Wildlight Elementary School, n.d., Yulee, Florida*
> *(https://www.nassau.k12.fl.us/Page/2519)*

Mission Statement

Merriam-Webster defines a mission statement as something that states the purpose or goal of a business or organization (Merriam-Webster, 2021). According to

Patrick Hull (2013), writing for *Forbes*, an effective mission statement answers the following questions:

- What do we do?
- How do we do it?
- Whom do we do it for?
- What value are we bringing?

While these questions may have been written for consumption in the business world, these same questions are vital for the development of a comprehensive school counseling mission statement. Notably, when giving thought to the nature of the questions posed by Hull, a mission statement is different from a vision statement in that it conveys action. School counseling program mission statements are concise; they clearly connect to the school and the district mission statements, and they outline the desired outcomes for all students (ASCA, 2019a; Kolbert, 2016). According to ASCA (2019a), the elements of an effective mission statement include

- a clear focus for the school counseling program to reach the vision;
- a description of the program's overarching purpose;
- language that aligns the program's mission with both the school and the district's mission;
- an emphasis on equity, access, inclusion, and success for all students; and
- language that indicates long-range results desired for all students.

A search for school counseling mission statements reveals a wide variety of approaches by various schools. Next, we provide examples of well-written school counseling program missions statements:

> The mission of Witch Hazel Elementary School's school counseling department is to advocate for all learners through creating an equitable and accessible school environment by collaborating with stakeholders to remove barriers. Through participation in the data-driven school counseling program, all students—regardless of their race, ethnicity, ability, gender, socio-economic status, or sexual orientation—will develop long-term self-directed, realistic, and responsible decision-making skills, as well as grow consistent attitudes and behaviors that will help them to achieve their future goals.
>
> *Witch Hazel Elementary School, n.d., Hillsboro, Oregon; RAMP 2020*
> *(https://www.hsd.k12.or.us/Page/6003)*

> The mission of the Gateway Professional School Counselors is to provide a comprehensive developmental counseling program for all students K–12. Professional school counselors provide equitable access to maximize academic achievement, to foster personal and social growth, and to facilitate career development in partnership with parents, guardians and all other

members of the school community. We are key stakeholders in a collaborative effort to provide a safe and supportive environment academically, physically, and emotionally. Advocacy, leadership, collaboration, and systematic change are the framework of the Gateway School District School Counseling Program. Our mission is to inspire all students to develop their individual potential to become life-long learners who are college and career ready citizens in our diverse and changing world.

Gateway High School, n.d., Monroeville, Pennsylvania; RAMP 2012)
(https://www.gatewayk12.org/departments/counseling)

Advisory Council

Throughout this chapter, we have framed the tools associated with the school counseling program as similar to the tools used in business and industry to chart corporate direction. We want to acknowledge this as a means to help readers see the parallels between the two entities. However, we also want to note that there is much concern in education around its direction toward corporatization. In other words, many educators are concerned about the growing trends to apply corporate models to address educational systemic issues, as these models are often rooted in for-profit capitalism and lack focus on social justice initiatives. Indulge us as we continue that pattern in a discussion about the school counseling advisory council. In large, corporate industries, CEOs and CFOs are often required to answer to a body of interested parties known as the company's board of directors. Boards of directors exist to pull together a panel of people who represent diverse perspectives and the interests of shareholders. Similar to answering to a board of directors, school counselors turn to their program advisory councils to both guide the vision and mission of the program and share program impact, success, and obstacles with a diverse set of school and community partners. Advisory councils ideally mirror the community while also offering a diverse perspective to help guide, continuously reflect, and improve the counseling program.

One way in which the advisory council can mirror the community is to recognize that schools are a microcosm of the larger society. As mentioned in the first two chapters of this text, one of the monumental events that took place in the summer of 2020 centered around the death of George Floyd. The racial unrest that followed has compelled the school counseling profession to become increasingly more aware of the need to dismantle racist practices often embedded and perpetuated in school systems. Sweeney (2020) notes that when advocating for social justice in schools, counselors use the advisory council as one of the important groups to engage in dialogue around race-based stress and trauma impacting their communities.

A first step in creating the school counseling program advisory council is to engage in a reflective process to identify members. Remember, diversity of membership is the greatest asset for program advocacy. Begin by asking the following:

- How can I create a group of diverse perspectives? Who is represented on the council? (i.e., Does the membership represent multiple identities and multiple roles in the community?)
- Who is absent from the advisory council?
- In creating a diverse group of perspectives, how will I create norms? (e.g., What safeguards need to be in place to ensure that members do not feel the need to speak on behalf of a given identity?)
- How will I manage conflict?
- What will be this group's goal with regards to supporting student success and assisting in removing barriers?
- What happens when the principal and superintendent want to place someone with power on the council?

As suggested in these questions, a good way to think about the development of the advisory council is to keep in mind the tenets of group work. Leadership style, member selection, norms, participant roles, management of conflict, goal setting, and accountability are all important considerations in the formation, implementation, and assessment of the advisory council's success.

Finally, once the advisory council is formed and the commitment by all members is solidified, school counselors must establish timelines and dates for meetings. The *ASCA National Model* (ASCA, 2019a) recommends that advisory councils meet at least twice a year (once in the fall and once in the spring) and that school counselors provide meeting agendas and document activities in the form of meeting minutes (Griffith & Kuranz, n.d). For the council to be a meaningful and productive experience, we urge you to consider establishing meeting times and frequencies that best assist you in engaging your specific members of the council. This may mean polling members to learn about their schedules and interests. Implementing a comprehensive school counseling program that supports all students; eliminates barriers to student success by addressing systemic issues, such as racism and other oppressive practices; and accepts and affirms students of all races and identities takes intentionality with respect to educating and engaging school and community partners. This may not be possible in only two meetings each year. Additionally, the advisory council should be aware of other program factors. Factors such as program success, resource needs, data resulting from recent initiatives, and overall needs of the program should be on advisory council agendas as well. That is a lot of information to dispense if only meeting a couple of times each year! School counselors must clearly prioritize their time and initiatives to successfully plan a program that includes school and community input and meets the needs of the student population.

Consultation Corner: Who You Gonna Call?

After bracketing your thoughts and reading the "Informed School Counseling" section, who would you call in and outside of the school building, and what might you ask them to support your decision-making? Take a moment to document these questions. Now that you have considered your questions for consultation, let's see what professional school counselors from around the world have to say about this case.

Consultation #1

Hello, my name is Alexandra, and I am an elementary school counselor in a predominantly low socioeconomic status urban school setting where the needs of our students are very high. Our students' basic needs are not always met at home, so they are often left for the school to fulfill. While I am one of two school counselors in a school of almost 700 students, I too spend much of my time responding to crises, some days more than others. I think first, it is important to remember that our job as school counselors is unique in the aspect that no day is the same and there is much beauty in that. With that said, some days you may respond to crisis calls for much of the day and that is okay in my opinion, when you are working at a high-needs school, it is almost inevitable. I think it makes you a better counselor and can shape the focus of your groups and individual sessions. For example, after seeing that student in crisis a few times, you may add them into a small group with other students who also need help regulating their emotions. The next time you see that student in crisis, you can help them use the tools you taught them during group in action. I think this is an amazing part of being a school counselor. You do not only get to help them develop coping strategies in a session or small group, but you can also help them use what they have learned in an actual crisis because you are there with them. On another note, it is important to be kind to yourself and know that you cannot do all things right away, especially when there is only one of you in a school of such large size. I would take it year by year. It sounds like you have several whole school initiatives, so maybe this coming year you focus on putting out a needs assessment to determine what small groups would be most beneficial and if you only have time for three or four groups all year, that is okay. The needs assessment in general will help you be more proactive rather than reactive, in turn, less crisis calls because those kids who are often in crisis were identified on the needs assessment day one, so you are already seeing them individually or in a small group. You cannot expect yourself to have the perfect comprehensive school counseling program in one year. It is something you build over time. Trust me, I am very proud of all the accomplishments I made this year as a first-year school counselor, but I know my comprehensive school counseling program is far from perfect. We can always grow and learn new ways to make our school counseling programs better, but the important part is that even with the uncertainty of our day-to-day jobs, we start trying.

(Alexandra West, elementary school counselor, Maryland)

Consultation #2

The other major step I took this year was forming my school counseling advisory council. As you probably know, this is a component of having an ASCA-aligned program. While I admit I was extremely intimidated in creating this forum, and it was stressful to plan, I am so grateful I did it, as it laid the groundwork for building my capacity in an amazing way. I invited administrators, teachers, parents, students, and other community stakeholders to participate in a meeting at which I educated them on what school counselors can do for our students and how powerful being intentional and proactive can be. I shared goals I cocreated with my principal and how we would accomplish them. The participants were able to provide feedback, which gave them a sense of ownership over the counseling interventions, and some volunteered to take on tasks! I gained a set of advocates through this process who felt like they were a part of the counseling "program," and I didn't have to feel like I was doing everything alone. By educating them on the purpose of my interventions, and my goals in doing the activities I was doing, they could see a method to my madness, so to speak. So many counselors (myself included) are running around daily putting out fires, while worried that staff and parents don't understand how much we do, and yet it's often hard for us to promote ourselves and earn the time to do our proactive interventions we know could benefit students. This group allowed me to expand my team and my reach. I would recommend starting this process, however small, to gain feedback on your "program" and gain buy-in and support! You truly can't do this job well on your own!

(Alexandra Todd, elementary school counselor, California)

Consultation #3

Hi, my name is Dr. Bobby Gueh, and I've had the opportunity to be an elementary, middle, and currently a high school counselor. My first 5 years in counseling were at the middle school level. First, let me say to be a middle school counselor, you should get an award every year just by making it to the end of the year, and on top of that, you are the "only". I would say start by doing a review of the ASCA model, you can even use the *ASCA Student Standards: Mindsets & Behaviors for Student Success* guide and do a cross-analysis of what those standards are, and all that you are actually doing. I would guess with confidence that despite not having some components like a mission statement or participation agreement, you will find that most of what you are doing, by yourself, fits a lot of those standards, and you just have to find time to organize what you are doing and relate it to the ASCA model. I've been a counselor for almost 20 years, and I have worked in departments that were strong ASCA model departments, and some that struggle a bit. But the main difference was just the organization and realizing that you are already doing a lot of the work and standards. I would encourage you to reach out to your district-level leaders for the counselors and consider getting an intern every year who can help you with the heavy lifting, and give you some time to work on more program planning tasks. Also, use the summer to do some of those ASCA planning, like coming up with your mission statement, participation agreement, and even planning your advisory council. Those are things that I typically organize over the summer, and we are ready to go when the year starts.

(Bobby Gueh, high school counselor, Georgia)

Consultation #4

Hi, I am Amy, and I am a high school counselor at a career technical school. My first school counseling position was at a charter school; I was the first and only school counselor. It was challenging to implement the ASCA model into my program, with the other responsibilities I had on my plate. So, I created an outline of all of my duties and how effective it was with the students. I arranged a meeting with my principal to present my framework and suggested how active my role would be to use the ASCA model in the school counseling program. After I met with my principal, she was very impressed with my ideas and supported me in improving my role and the students' needs. I believe that one must advocate for themselves to strengthen their better position to increase their engagement with their students and the school community. I also suggest reaching out to other school counselors for support and creating a network of school counselors, who may be the only school counselors.

(Amy Lombardo, high school counselor, New Jersey)

#EduCounselor Synthesis

The author of the post expresses concerns shared by many school counselors. They have a larger than ideal caseload, and they do not feel as though they are able to realistically provide the type and quantity of direct services that align with the *ASCA National Model*. As referenced in earlier chapters, balancing the ideal role of the school counselor with the realities of individual job descriptions can be challenging. One strategy the author identifies as an opportunity to address these gaps is through the identification and articulation of a clear program mission. Before creating this, however, it is important for school counselors to know what they believe about students and how students navigate their schooling experiences. The author of the post expresses great intentions to move their program forward by wanting to create a mission statement and engage in an annual administrative conference (see Chapter 6) with their building administrator. Examining their beliefs first—a process they have likely been doing since their graduate studies—can help them to develop vision and mission statements that speak directly to their program's values. This intentional process will assist in informing conversations with their building administrator at an upcoming annual meeting and allow them to lead these conversations with a strong understanding of their beliefs and goals for future programming. The key here, echoed by our consultants, is to be okay with not doing everything at once. Programs are not built in a day, and the clearer your beliefs and the more you understand the priorities of the school district, the more valuable your vision and mission may be to the overall success of your program.

Examining our consultants' responses, we see that they provide validation and several good suggestions for how the author might address their concerns. Alexandra noted that even with a smaller caseload, it is easy to spend most of the time on responsive services. This can occur more when there are higher needs in the school and fewer resources available for students outside of the school. In fact, sometimes, the school counselor is the only mental health provider to support families at all. When this is the case, school counselors may develop a vision and mission for their school counseling program that is focused on areas such as fostering community partnerships, identifying grants, and advocating for more in-school mental health providers and out-of-school pro bono or lower cost options. Identifying what your community needs (e.g., people, resources, services) and drawing on your advocacy skills is important.

Alexandra T., Amy, and Bobby all discussed the importance of bringing school and community voices into the development of the school counseling program (e.g., advisory council). Each specifically referenced collaboration with administrators. This is valuable as far as creating a vision and mission for the program and helping to articulate the mental health needs of the district. As mentioned earlier in this chapter, one suggestion is to examine the vision and mission of the school and school district and connect the proposed school counseling statements to the goals and objectives outlined therein. Administrators will especially appreciate these efforts because it assists them in advocating for more resources with their superiors (e.g., superintendent, board of education).

When developing these tools (i.e., beliefs statements, vision, mission), school counselors do not need to reinvent the wheel. There are many examples of vision and mission statements from which to draw on (see a few examples in our previous section), and as alluded to by Amy, reaching out to other counselors who are eager to share their processes and resources can be particularly helpful. Another way to involve school and community partners includes Alexandra T.'s suggestion to concentrate on the development of an advisory council, something the author, themselves, noted; this group should include school personnel, families, and community partners, and possibly even students. Using the advisory council as a vehicle to share observations and needs assessment data with the community might help to garner more advocacy as school counselors work to build their programs. This is a good time to show how the responsive services that the author is already providing suggest a need for prevention services in the future. For instance, the author of the post discusses their career lessons. Perhaps feedback from these lessons suggests student anxiety around college essay writing. This data could help them advocate for the need to provide future psychoeducation lessons, perhaps as a push-in collaboration with the English teachers.

As far as the limited time expressed by the author in the post, this is something that feels all too familiar for many practicing school counselors. Bobby suggested that it can be helpful to make a list of what you are already doing and connect these with the national model and standards. This is a great way to spearhead conversations with school and community members; not only can articulating these national standards further expose school and community partners to the appropriate role of the school counselor, but it may also exhibit your intentionality in terms of the interventions you provide and the goals you share for the program moving forward. Gathering this information to bring to an advisory council may be a great way to slowly build your program in a stepwise fashion. As previously suggested, Alexandra and Alex remind the author that a comprehensive school counseling program is not built overnight. Adding in a new initiative slowly each year and as Bobby suggested, even leveraging an intern to support you in the design and articulation of new interventions can be particularly useful.

Chapter Summary

School counselors often struggle to reconcile creating the "graduate school version" of a comprehensive school counseling program with the "real-world version" of their program. The first step in developing and managing a sustainable program that meets the needs of all students and addresses district priorities and systemic challenges is to create and articulate the tools needed to lay a solid foundation for the direction of the program. To that end, school counselors serve as leaders when they work in collaboration with other key school and community partners to develop and clearly articulate the program focus—the beliefs, the vision, and the mission of the school counseling program. These are the critical tools associated with managing a culturally sustaining school counseling program that serves all students. School counselors garner support and resources for their programs by working with a school counseling program advisory council. Sharing program goals and results with a diverse group of school and community members ensures that school counselors receive important community feedback to better assist them in continuing to advocate for their programs.

Reflective Practitioner Process

School counselors engage in **clinical supervision**, **professional development**, and **self-care** to further develop their knowledge and skills and to help balance professional expectations with personal wellness. All three areas are key to ethical practice and help to mitigate counselor burnout and compassion fatigue (Atici, 2015; Lawson & Myers, 2011; Merriman, 2015; Ohrt et al., 2015).

Clinical Supervision

The *ASCA School Counselor Professional Standards & Competencies* (ASCA, 2019b) direct school counselors to "consult with school counselors and other education and counseling professionals when questions of school counseling practice arise" (B-SS 5., p. 5). As a supervisee, it is important to consider the thoughts, feelings, and experiences that come up for you as you work with students, families, and colleagues and seek consultation on difficult issues. The following are some topics for consideration as you react to this chapter.

- What feelings come up as you consider developing the initial tools (beliefs, vision, mission) associated with managing a school counseling program?
- How do you begin the process of developing school counseling vision, mission, and beliefs if you are the only school counselor in your school?
- What school and community partners are the priority for sharing these statements? How do you share these tools broadly?
- Upon entering a position with an established counseling team whose belief, vision, and mission statements are dated (developed 5 years or more ago), you notice some values are absent from the statements. How do you approach a discussion with your colleagues?

Professional Development

According to the *ASCA Ethical Standards for School Counselors* (ASCA, 2022), professional school counselors engage in professional development and attend trainings in an effort to stay current on the trends and issues that impact students (B.3.e). Relative to the contents of this chapter, consider finding professional development on the following topics:

- Implicit Bias Training
- ASCA U Specialist: Culturally Sustaining School Counseling Specialist
- ASCA U Specialist: School Counseling Leader Specialist
- Decolonizing Education and Counseling materials and practices

#PSCSelfCare: Everyday Wellness

When designing, managing, and implementing a comprehensive school counseling program, school and community expectations can tax even the most seasoned school counselor. The *ASCA Ethical Standards for School Counselors* (ASCA, 2022) require school counselors to recognize the high levels of stress often associated with the job. Therefore, school counselors recognize that self-care must be a priority to maintain health and overall well-being (see ASCA, 2022, B.3.h).

Sleep Assessment and Reflection

We know there are a variety of factors that influence getting quality sleep. However, we also know sleep is one of the most powerful tools to support your overall well-being. Consider the many physical and emotional benefits of getting enough sleep. They include

- boosting your immune system,
- strengthening your heart,

- reducing stress,
- supporting better hormone balance,
- increased energy,
- stronger memory, and
- quicker learning (Calm, n.d.).

There are small changes that we can make to increase our chances of getting the sleep our brains and bodies need to optimally function. According to the Sleep Foundation (2020), here are a few things you can do to improve sleep:

1. Turn off all technology (i.e., television, phone, screens, etc.) at least 30 minutes before bedtime. These devices emit blue light that your brain easily confuses for sunlight, which sends your body a signal that it is time to be awake. This is often called "sleep hygiene."
2. Transform your bedroom into a dark, quiet, and cool oasis with curtains that blackout any light and a noise machine to help you relax. Also, consider lowering your bedroom temperature to the low or mid-60s to optimize sleep
3. Go to bed and wake up at the same time every day. Consistent sleep schedules train your brain to both wake up and go to sleep.
4. Set a sleep schedule that allows you to get the necessary 7–9 hours of sleep adults need each night.
5. Get a bedtime routine going! Make sure that routine includes relaxing activities that calm you and inform your brain that it is time to chill out! Consider taking a warm bath or listening to calming music.
6. No coffee (within 5 hours of bedtime) or alcohol (within 3 hours of bedtime) late into the evening!
7. Get some sun in the morning! Just 15–30 minutes outside in the sun can help wake you up and reset your circadian rhythm.

Over the next few days or even a week, commit to improving sleep behaviors. Try this: select one or two of the activities recommended by the Sleep Foundation and commit to them for the time frame you select. Make your goal achievable; that is, do not commit to doing all seven activities for 6 months! Start small and then document your results. Hold yourself accountable by sharing your goals with a friend. Take just 5 minutes a day to write down any mental or physical shifts you see in your well-being.

Spotlight: School Counseling Advocacy

Here, we highlight a school counselor who celebrates the result of their collaborative effort to develop school counseling belief, vision, and mission statements. This school counselor, having garnered the support and input needed to develop the program's management tools, felt compelled to use social media to further connect school and community partners to the work of the school counseling program!

Park Hill South Counseling
@CounselorsPHS

After months of valuable feedback and input from our
teachers/staff, students, parents, community, and
stakeholders. ... we're EXCITED to publish our department's
Vision, Mission, and Beliefs!

#parkhillproud #moedchat #scchat #studentimpact #corevalues
@DrShariSevier ©myMSCA

Feb 21, 2022

Learning Connections

Both professional school counselors in training and seasoned school counselors
understand the importance of understanding the connections between the concepts
commonly taught in counseling programs and the standards most associated with

school counselor training. Therefore, the following table offers broad connections between the material and information in this chapter and the Council for Accreditation of Counseling and Related Educational Programs (CACREP, 2016) standards, The *ASCA School Counselor Professional Standards and Competencies* (ASCA, 2019b), and the *ASCA Ethical Standards for School Counselors* (ASCA, 2022).

Connections to CACREP Core Curricular Areas

Professional Counseling Orientation and Ethical Practice	Social and Cultural Diversity	Human Growth and Development	Career Development	Counseling and Helping Relationships	Group Counseling and Group Work	Assessment and Testing	Research and Program Evaluation
X	X						

Connection to Professional Standards

CACREP	ASCA SC Professional Competencies	Ethical Standards: SC
F.1.e: Advocacy process needed to address institutional and social barriers that impede access, success, equity, and success for clients	B-PF 7: Demonstrate leadership through the development and implementation of a school counseling program.	A.1.h: Respect students' and families' values, beliefs and cultural background, as well as students' sexual orientation, gender identity and gender expression, and exercise great care to avoid imposing personal biases, beliefs or values rooted in one's religion, culture or ethnicity.
F.1.i: Ethical standards of professional counseling organizations and credentialing bodies, and applications of ethical and legal considerations in professional counseling; and G.2.m: legal and ethical considerations specific to school counseling	B-PF 9: Create systemic change through the implementation of a school counseling program.	A.3.a: Provide students with a culturally responsive school counseling program that promotes academic, career and social/emotional development and equitable opportunity and achievement outcomes for all students.
F.2.g: Strategies for identifying and eliminating barriers, prejudices, and processes of intentional and unintentional oppression and discrimination	B-SS 6: Collaborate with families, teachers, administrators, other school staff and education stakeholder for student achievement and success.	A.10.b: Actively work to establish a safe, equitable, affirming school environment in which all members of the school community demonstrate respect, inclusion and acceptance.
G.1.d: Models of school counseling programs	B-PA 1: Create School counseling program beliefs, vision, and mission statements aligned with the school and district.	B.2.b: Design and deliver comprehensive school counseling programs that are integral to the school's academic mission informed by analysis of student data, based on the ASCA National Model.

(Conintued)

CACREP	ASCA SC Professional Competencies	Ethical Standards: SC
G.2.1: School counselor roles as leaders, advocates, and systemic change agents in P-12 schools	B-PA 8: Establish and convene and advisory council for the school counseling program.	B.2.d: Exercise leadership to create systemic change to create a safe and supportive environment and equitable outcomes for all students.
G.2.i: Qualities and effective styles for effective leadership in schools		

Comprehensive School Counseling Assignments

The following section provides activities that allow for your continued growth as a professional school counselor. Both preservice and practicing school counselors may find it helpful to complete these activities. If you are currently in a graduate training program, your professor might assign these as part of your course.

1. **Identifying Your Professional Values** – As a school counselor, you are a leader in your building. School leaders must often make hard decisions and advocate for what they believe to be in the best interest of children and adolescents. This includes garnering support from school and community partners who bring their own perspectives and experiences with mental health into the conversation. When faced with hard conversations in the past, consider what values you lean on to help you walk into a brave space. For instance, if you are about to give someone difficult feedback, how do you motivate yourself to have this courageous dialogue? What values propel you to engage in these conversations? When you are struggling to advocate for something important, which values motivate you to keep going even when these conversations create discomfort? Using Brené Brown's *Dare to Lead* list of values (see helpful resources section), identify ***two to three professional values*** that "keep you in the game." While many of these values may resonate with you, it is important that you consider which two to three allow you to stay in a brave space. After you have chosen these two to three values, write down what these mean to you and provide an example of how you have leaned on each to support you in standing up for your beliefs.

2. **Personal Beliefs Statement** – Now that you have identified important values that help you walk into difficult conversations, think about your role as a school counselor. Create an "I believe" statement about your future school counseling program. Consider turning your answers to the following questions posed by Grothaus et al. (2020) into statements, *I believe. ...*

- How are you committed to grow personally and professionally?
- How are you (and the future program you create) committed to equitable, inclusive, and culturally sustaining practices?
- How do you believe students will access school counseling services?
- What do you believe about school climate?
- What do you believe about school-family-community partnerships?
- How do you see school counselors as advocates for students?

  Reflection Question: Based on your answers, how can your school counseling beliefs statement influence your decisions, intervention choices, attitudes, and interactions with school and community partners? How might these impact the way you view your role and the choices you make for your school counseling program?

3. **Create a Mock Advisory Council**

After learning about the advisory council and its purpose, start thinking about the school and community partners you would want in this group and the steps you will need to take to ensure that you include a diverse set of voices around the table. Use the following to create your aspirational advisory council of six to eight individuals.

- Think about the school district you attended as a child and the resources you knew about in your community.
  - Create a list of possible representatives you might invite to the advisory council. What is your rationale for inviting these particular people?
  - Based on this same school district and the beliefs statement you previously created, list the top three topics you might want to discuss with your advisory council.
  - What data might you want to collect related to the topics you identify in bullet #2 that will help you justify your concerns and advocate for your program's needs?

Helpful Resources
Web-Based Resources

- Simon Sinek Ted Talk – *How Great Leaders Inspire Action*:
  - https://www.ted.com/talks/simon_sinek_how_great_leaders_inspire_action?language=en

Suggested Readings

- Helpful guide to assist in aligning comprehensive school counseling programs to the *ASCA National Model*:

- ▪ American School Counselor Association. (2019). *ASCA national model implementation guide.* (2nd ed.).
- ● Critical text for anyone wishing to implement a culturally sustaining school counseling program:
  - ▪ Grothaus, T., Johnsons, K. F., & Edirmanasinghe, N. (2020). *Culturally sustaining school counseling.* American School Counselor Association.
- ● Complete guide to school counselor leadership that includes reflective activities for school counselors who want to better understand school counselor leadership and their leadership style:
  - ▪ Young, A., & Kneale, M. M. (2013). *School counselor leadership: An essential practice.* American School Counselor Association.

References

American School Counselor Association (ASCA). (2019a). *ASCA national model: A framework for school counseling programs.* (4th ed.).

American School Counselor Association (ASCA). (2019b). *ASCA school counselor professional standards and competencies.* https://www.schoolcounselor.org/getmedia/a8d59c2c-51de-4ec3-a565-a3235f3b93c3/SC-Competencies.pdf

American School Counselor Association (ASCA). (2022). *ASCA ethical standards for school counselors.* https://www.schoolcounselor.org/getmedia/44f30280-ffe8-4b41-9ad8-f15909c3d164/EthicalStandards.pdf

Atici, M. (2015). Professional identity development of counselors-in-training in a school internship program in Turkey. *The Professional Counselor,* 5(1), 137–151. https://doi.org/10.15241/MA.5.1.137

Council for Accreditation of Counseling and Related Educational Programs (CACREP). (2016). *2016 CACREP standards.* http://www.cacrep.org/wp-content/uploads/2017/08/2016-Standards-with-citations.pdf

Calm. (n.d.). *Sleep: A better sleep guidebook.* https://static1.squarespace.com/static/57b5ef68c-534a5cc06edc769/t/5d9611fffb61de027b11317f/1570116113717/IntentionsJournal_Sleep.pdf

The Education Trust. (2021). Social/emotional and academic development through an equity lens. *ASCA School Counselor.* https://www.ascaschoolcounselor-digital.org/ascaschool-counselor/january_february_2021/MobilePagedArticle.action?articleId=1653296#articleId1653296

Gateway School District. (n.d.). *School counseling mission statement.* https://www.gatewayk12.org/departments/counseling

Griffith, K., & Kuranz, M. (n.d.). *6: Advisory council 5 points* [Webinar]. American School Counselor Association. https://videos.schoolcounselor.org/ramp-scoring-rubric-webinar-section-6-advisory-council

Grothaus, T., Johnsons, K. F., & Edirmanasinghe, N. (2020). *Culturally sustaining school counseling.* American School Counselor Association.

Hull, P. (2013, January 13). Answer 4 questions to get a great mission statement. *Forbes.* https://www.forbes.com/sites/patrickhull/2013/01/10/answer-4-questions-to-get-a-great-mission-statement/?sh=5e9e6b8b67f5

Kolbert, J. B., Williams, R. L., Morgan, L. M., Crothers, L. M., & Hughes, T. L. (2016). *Introduction to professional school counseling: Advocacy, leadership, and intervention.* Routledge.

Lawson, G., & Myers, J. E. (2011). Wellness, professional quality of life, and career-sustaining behaviors: What keeps us well? *Journal of Counseling and Development, 89*(2), 163–171. https://doi.org/10.1002/j.1556-6678.2011.tb00074.x

Merriman, J. (2015). Enhancing counselor supervision through compassion fatigue education. *Journal of Counseling and Development, 93*(3), 370–378. https://doi.org/10.1002/jcad.12035

Merriam-Webster. (2021). Mission statement. In *Merriam-Webster.com dictionary.* https://www.merriam-webster.com/dictionary/mission%20statement

North Forsyth High. (2020, March 13). *Mission, vision, & ASCA/RAMP.* NFHS. https://www.forsyth.k12.ga.us/Page/50641

Ohrt, J. H., Prosek, E. A., Ener, E., & Lindo, N. (2015). The effects of a group supervision intervention to promote wellness and prevent burnout. *The Journal of Humanistic Counseling, 54*(1), 41–58. https://doi.org/10.1002/j.2161-1939.2015.00063.x

Ray, S. (2018, May 16). *A guide to writing the perfect vision statement (with examples).* Project Manager. https://www.projectmanager.com/blog/guide-writing-perfect-vision-statement-examples#:~:text=What%20Is%20a%20Vision%20Statement,and%20declared%20set%20of%20goals

Savitz-Romer, M., Colletta, L., & Duarte, D. (2020, March). *Five strategies for advising students.* https://www.nassp.org/publication/principal-leadership/volume-20/principal-leadership-march-2020/leadership-for-a-strong-school-counseling-program-march-2020/

Shields, C. M., Dollarhide, C. T., & Young, A. A. (2017). Transformative leadership in school counseling: An emerging paradigm for equity and excellence. *Professional School Counseling, 21*(1b). https://doi.org/https://doi.org/10.1177/2156759X18773581

Sleep Foundation. (2020). *Mental health and sleep.* https://www.sleepfoundation.org/mental-health

Stone, C. (2020). Change must happen: The ASCA ethical standards guide the way. *ASCA School Counselor, 57*(6), 6–9.

Sweeney, D. (2020, July 1). *Stand up, stand together.* American School Counselor Association. https://www.schoolcounselor.org/Magazines/July-August-2020/Stand-Up,-Stand-Together

Wisconsin Department of Public Instruction. (2021). *Inclusive strategies to address behavioral needs for students with IEPs.* https://dpi.wi.gov/sites/default/files/imce/sped/pdf/pbis-behavior-bias-adult-practice-2a.pdf

Wildlight Elementary School. (n.d.). *WES school counselor vision statement.* https://www.nassau.k12.fl.us/site/default.aspx?PageType=3&ModuleInstanceID=5426&ViewID=C9E0416E-F0E7-4626-AA7B-C14D59F72F85&RenderLoc=0&FlexDataID=5256&PageID=2519

Witch Hazel Elementary School. (n.d.). *Witch Hazel Elementary School mission statement.* https://www.hsd.k12.or.us/Page/6003

Wright, T. (2020, June 25). *How to write a good vision statement, step-by-step and with examples.* Cascade. https://www.cascade.app/blog/write-good-vision-statement

Young, A., & Kneale, M. M. (2013). *School counselor leadership: The essential practice.* American School Counselor Association.

Credit

CHAPTER 5

Using Data to Locate Educational Inequities

LEARNING OBJECTIVES

#EduCounselors can

- summarize the assortment of school-based documents used by school counselors to align school counseling programs with school goals and plans

- define and identify ways to gather the primary types of school data: participation, mindsets and behaviors, and outcome,

- identify existing data sources and data collection tools used to inform school counseling programs and examine educational inequities, and

- identify ways in which school counselors use data to create action plans for interventions that align with the *ASCA Student Standards: Mindsets & Behaviors for Student Success.*

Introduction

As referenced in Chapter 1, an issue that nearly cost the school counseling profession its foothold in the early 1970s was the inability of school counselors to use data as a basis for making decisions about the programs and activities they offered their students (Aubrey, 1973). This led to difficulties proving that school counselors made a difference in student lives. For school counselors to be able to show that their services make a difference, they must first be able to use data to locate the primary issues facing students in their schools. School counselors who fail to find gaps in student success via school data will also fail to prove that their interventions contribute to the solutions schools are seeking. Additionally, data collection has proved challenging for many school counselors because locating and analyzing data is not often at the top of the "why I wanted to be a school counselor" list! The modern-day professional school counselor recognizes the importance of developing skills around collecting and analyzing data to inform their comprehensive school counseling programs. In this chapter, we offer ideas about how school counselors can begin to locate the issues in their schools by using relevant school reports and data. We also present information about the various kinds of data school counselors often examine and the tools with which they use to collect this information.

#IRLSchoolCounseling

The following is a social media post from one of the many school counseling groups on Facebook. *High School Counselor Connection* is a platform where school counselors frequently use the hashtag #scchat to connect with professionals around the globe:

Matthew Shervington
18 hrs

Hoping someone can give me some insight on data collecting. I am a huge advocate for the importance of data, not only to guide your practice but to advocate for my position to administration and/or parents.

Traditionally I have gathered data through online options such as Google Forms or Naviance Surveys. I've been able to do this for the entirety of my caseload and/or an entire class. When using this method, I often feel as if the data is very <u>accurate</u> but it unfortunately usually requires a series of follow-ups ensure that students have complete their Google Form/Naviance Survey.

On the other <u>hand</u> during my string of meeting with juniors this past month I went to a traditional pen- and-paper survey following the meetings. Using this method there was no need for follow-ups because | students were very willing to complete the survey on paper instead of having to take out a Chromebook and click on a link and/or log into an account to do the survey. Unfortunately, with this method I don't know if the data is as accurate because I feel like students feel intimidated knowing I have "immediate" access to their survey.

Has anyone faced a similar problem and if so, what are some of your workarounds/solutions to get students to complete pre- or post-intervention surveys with less resistance while also working to ensure better accuracy?

Thank You

Matthew Shervington-Jackson, "High School Counselor Connection Facebook Post." Copyright © 2019 by Matthew Shervington-Jackson. Reprinted with permission.

Bracketing Values for Ethical Practice

It is expected that school counselors continuously reflect on their values, beliefs, worldviews, and cultural norms and how each influences the ways in which they choose to take or not take action. As such, it is important to recognize and set aside any preconceived notions, experiences, and biases to help you respond to this scenario in a culturally sustaining and ethically sound manner. Take a moment to reflect on the previous post and then consider the following questions:

- What comes to mind when you see the words "data" and "school counselor" in the same sentence? What previous experiences shape your reaction to the word data?
- How do you feel about Matthew's dilemma as he decides which type of survey to administer? What are your feelings about taking surveys? How might that influence your interest in collecting data through surveys?
- Social desirability bias refers to when students respond to questions in the ways they think the counselor might want rather than reflecting their true thoughts or feelings. Matthew is concerned about the impact of social desirability bias in his data collection. Imagine Matthew finds out that he needs to report these results to his district for his summative evaluation. How might you feel about balancing the district's desire for greater student participation with your interest in obtaining the most accurate results?
- How do you feel about maintaining student anonymity when asking students to complete surveys? Should Matthew choose online tools that ensure that students' information cannot be identified? If so, how come?

 ## Informed School Counseling

Why is data so important to comprehensive school counseling programs? The answer: It's the foundation! School counselors must be able to collect and analyze data to demonstrate the impact our programs have on students and the community and to inform our practices (ASCA, 2019c; Dahir & Stone, 2003; Hatch & Hartline, 2021; Springer et al., 2018). As mentioned in the introduction to this chapter, when school counselors have historically neglected to use data as the foundation for their school counseling programs, the consequences have been damaging to the profession. According to Young and Kaffenberger (2011), the acknowledgment of the power of data to inform school counseling programs is one of the most significant outcomes of education reform and a transformational event in the profession (ASCA, 2019c; The Education Trust, 1999).

The *ASCA School Counselor Professional Standards & Competencies* (ASCA, 2019a) call on school counselors to develop annual student outcome goals and action plans based on student data. To that end, school counselors must recognize the various kinds of data they collect and how to locate this data within their schools. School counselors then strategize how to analyze data to find problem areas or inequities. Finally, school counselors use data to plan activities and interventions to address student/school issues in supporting the successful growth of all students' academic, social/emotional, and career development (ASCA, 2019a, B-PA 4.). Let us begin by examining the kinds of data that school counselors track.

Types of Data

The *ASCA National Model* provides guidance regarding the kinds of data school counselors collect (ASCA, 2019c). It is imperative that school counselors be able to delineate between the three primary kinds of data that are collected as part of building and maintaining a comprehensive school counseling program; participation, mindsets and behaviors, and outcome data are key metrics in the school counseling program (Kaffenberger & Young, 2019). While some counselors may feel that understanding the three kinds of data is confusing (we did as young counselors!), making sense of the kinds of data does not have to be overly difficult. Provided here are simple definitions of each kind of data.

Participation Data

Participation refers to the number of students/persons served during program delivery. It also refers to the number of activities offered during program delivery (ASCA, 2019c). Collecting participation data is important, as it provides evidence of the numerous activities school counselors offer and who they serve; however, participation data does not provide evidence of how students change as a result of an activity (Kolbert et al., 2016). Examples of participation data include the following:

1. Fifty-seven fourth graders participated in career awareness developmental lessons.
2. One hundred and fifty 12th-grade students completed a postsecondary workshop offered by local colleges and universities.
3. Ten small group counseling groups were offered to seventh graders in the fall semester.
4. The school counseling team provided 45 developmental classroom lessons to third graders in the previous school year.
5. One hundred and sixty-five eighth-grade students completed the pre-educational planning tool.
6. Eighty-seven parents and caregivers of middle school students attended a workshop on how to better understand the adolescent developmental stage and strategies for effective parenting.
7. Twenty high school teachers were trained on strategies to support students experiencing emotional dysregulation in the classroom.

Mindsets and Behaviors

Previously we introduced you to the *ASCA Student Standards: Mindsets & Behaviors for Student Success* (ASCA, 2021). School counselors seek to understand students' perceptions of how they are different because of content delivery. According to

ASCA (2019c), school counselors are interested in answering the question, "What did students learn through participation in school counseling activities?" (p. 35). Here, we provide examples of data based on the *ASCA Student Standards: Mindsets & Behaviors for Student Success* (ASCA, 2020) that include a designation indicating if they address a mindset (M) or a behavior (B):

1. Following six classroom lessons on diversity and acceptance, 91% of 11th graders view understanding the experiences of classmates who are different from them as important (M-2).
2. After attending five events during college and career week, 89% of 5th graders report that they value postsecondary education (M-6).
3. A survey of students following a classroom unit on growth mindset revealed that 85% of 10th graders recognized the difference between growth mindset and fixed mindset (M-3; M-4).
4. At the conclusion of a lesson on decision-making, 72% of 9th graders recognize three healthy strategies to employ when at a party with drugs or alcohol (B-SMS 1; B-SS 5).
5. Following four lessons on successful organizational strategies, 88% of second-grade students could pack a backpack with items needed to complete homework (B-LS 3).
6. Following a virtual lesson on personal safety, 78% of sixth graders indicate that they know how to reach out for help when home alone (B-SMS 9).

Outcome Data

ASCA (2019c) defines outcome data as the metrics used to evaluate attendance, academics, and discipline. In other words, outcome data is collected to answer the question, "How did the learning affect students' achievement, attendance, or discipline?" (p. 36); the term "learning" refers to gains made because of interventions and activities based on the *ASCA Student Standards: Mindsets & Behaviors for Student Success* (ASCA, 2021). While participation and mindsets and behavior data are important to assess specific activities provided by the school counselor. Outcome data is the metric that will most likely influence school and community partners as they evaluate the quality of the school counseling program (Kolbert et al., 2016). In other words, school and community colleagues, especially administrators, are often most interested in how the school counseling program contributes to improving students' attendance, achievement, or helps in reducing discipline issues because these are likely tied to school/district goals or initiatives. Note that outcome data is obtained from a variety of sources often easily accessible to school counselors via state and local school information databases. We provide examples of outcome data next alongside the area to which they connect:

1. High school dropout rates (achievement)
2. Elementary school promotion rates (achievement)
3. Number of days absent in K–8 school (attendance)

4. Standardized test scores – all grades (achievement)
5. Discipline referrals – all grades (discipline)
6. Percentage of students enrolling in college (achievement)
7. Middle school course failure rates (achievement)
8. Elementary loss of instructional time (discipline)

Here are some tips you can use to help make sense of the three types of data. Participation data is data that you as the school counselor actively and systematically collect and track. In other words, school counselors actively count and keep records of students served and activities offered.

ASCA Student Standards: Mindsets & Behaviors for Student Success data are thoughtfully and deliberately collected by school counselors. Oftentimes, school counselors create pre- and posttests or surveys to assess student acquisition of the standards. The important question is, "What do students/participants perceive they learned or gained from this intervention or series of interventions?"

Finally, outcome data refers to data that is most often collected by the school or school district as a part of normal operations. Outcome data most frequently refers to the data metrics that administrators are most interested in: attendance, academics, and behavior/discipline. Other examples of outcome data include graduation rates, dropout rates, college-going rates, state test scores, numbers of suspensions and expulsions, and data related to student course selection and enrollment (i.e., numbers of students taking International Baccalaureate, Advanced Placement, or Dual Credit courses). While collecting and analyzing data related to participation in the school counseling program and student beliefs about how they benefited from a certain aspect of the school counseling program is important, outcome data is typically most valuable to building level administrators, district leaders, and school and community partners in general (Young & Miller-Kneale, 2013). But school counselors take note, while outcome data typically refers to the common ways we measure student growth in schools, we also recognize that we are evolving in terms of which student outcomes matter most. Schools are gathering less traditional metrics, such as students' feelings of safety in school or baseline mental health functioning. School counselors must pay attention to the ***variables that matter*** to key school and community partners and look for quantitative and qualitative ways to measure student growth.

Locating Inequities

As discussed earlier, school counselors use data to track **who** is participating in school counseling programming, **what** they learn, and **how** the programming impacts major education outcomes, such as achievement. School counselors also use data to identify inequities and then design interventions to address them. Data can highlight gaps in student opportunities, access, and achievement, among others.

To locate inequities, school counselors must first identify the critical questions pertaining to student success, wellness, and thriving. We may wonder about our school's ability to educate all students (Holcomb-McCoy, 2007). How is academic success defined within our school? Do certain students, or groups of students, have difficulty achieving that standard? If academic success is defined by a 3.0 or higher grade point average (GPA), we can identify inequities by disaggregating GPA data (data that has been broken down by particular population, such as race or socioeconomic status) to see if a particular group or groups of students are not meeting the standard.

School counselors recognize that student success is influenced by a wide array of factors, such as the school culture and climate, the quality of instruction, and sociocultural factors, such as poverty and racism that often negatively impact our children's ability to learn and grow. We can collect both qualitative and quantitative data to gain insight into our students' experiences in and out of school. For example, school culture data could include how safe and respected students feel in school, data on the quality of relationships within a school, and experiences of having students' identities affirmed. *The School Data Culture Report* is one tool we have to assess these factors; however, school counselors also consider these factors when collecting, analyzing, and communicating data using all other tools.

As Atkins and Oglesby (2019) state, the process of locating inequities cannot be done in a vacuum and requires an ongoing dialogue with students and their families. Schools cannot assume that we know best or understand better than those we seek to serve. Therefore, when we have used the data to illuminate a theme within our school, we must engage with school and community partners, primarily students and their families, to help make sense of the data. For example, when one author (KG) was a school counselor, they used data (a summary of all reported bullying cases in an academic year, disaggregated) to reveal that students who identified as transgender were experiencing high rates of bullying. If KG had stopped there, they might have created a Tier 1 intervention to address bullying for all students in the school. However, when KG conducted one-on-one meetings to further explore these incidents with the impacted students, it appeared that the bullying was happing *to* students who identified as transgender *by* students who identified as transgender. These interviews illuminated cases of internalized oppression these students were experiencing, as well as a deep pain about their identity that they turned outward and against others who held a similar identity. In this case, the intervention that would best support these students looked quite different and involved Tier 2 and 3 approaches directed at this population specifically.

Once you have a firm grasp on the kinds of data school counselors collect and track, you likely ask yourself, "Where do I even begin to know where to look at the data?," or "Do I just have to look at ALL data?" Or maybe you simply ask, "Where do I even start?" Young and Kaffenberger (2019) offer a simple approach to begin the process. Their Design, Ask, Track, and Analyze, or *DATA*, approach recommends beginning by asking, "What is your goal?" (p. 14). This section offers common approaches to getting started in the quest to identify obstacles that frequently prevent all students from finding success and achieving their goals.

Existing School Data

Step one in starting your data journey is to locate data that will help you answer the "what is your goal" question. School counselors support student success across three domains: social/emotional, academic, and career. A comprehensive school counseling program defines what success looks like for its student population. One of the first things school counselors can do is to locate existing school data to answer this question. They often do so by using school-based data technology. School counselors rely on technology tools to help them collect, organize, and analyze the data they gather. In this section, we introduce several technology tools frequently used by school counselors. It is important to know that we do not endorse any of the tools or products that we mention in this section. Additionally, we do not stand to benefit financially from use of any of the products. We simply offer them as tools that many school counselors report makes their data collection more efficient.

School Information Systems (SIS)

All schools use some type of information system to track and collect school data. It is important to find out what information system your school uses, to what pieces of data that system has access, and where your school is "holding" data around the big issues in need of improvement. Many school counselors may find it helpful to track activities via the school's preferred SIS system. Some state and local school districts may use a regionally implemented system that is not well-known. However, frequently used SIS include nationally recognized software programs such as Real-Time, Genesis, and Powerschool. Powerschool (powerschool.com), for example, offers a wide variety of data tracking options for school personnel at the local as well as district levels. Powerschool can help school counselors manage data such as attendance, discipline, testing, report cards, and transcripts (Powerschool Eschool Plus SIS, https://www.powerschool.com/solutions/student-information-system/eschoolplus-sis/). Powerschool.com claims that the Eschool Plus SIS program can assist in efforts to track and improve student achievement.

While the aforementioned tools assist in gathering data on the big three areas of attendance, academics, and behavior, we would be remiss if we failed to encourage school counselors to be attentive to data around postsecondary and college planning. Naviance and ACT DISCOVER Career Planning Programs are two options for school counselors targeting data collection around students' career and postsecondary interests. Founded in 2002 in Washington, DC, Naviance is a web-based platform that assists students in their college research, career assessments, and course planning, and they offer surveys to help students connect learning to postsecondary plans (Deslonde & Becerra, 2018; Hobsons, 2018). ACT DISCOVER is a comprehensive career guidance system. This computer-based platform, based on evolving career theories, allows schools and students to store and track information about students and their career interests. Students (grade five to adult) can complete career interest inventories, acquire information about a wide variety of careers, and find information about colleges and financial aid (ACT, 2006).

School Improvement/Strategic Plans (SIP)

The SIP is a document created collaboratively each year by school leaders and school leadership teams. SIPs identify the goals and strategies that are center stage in the school's attempt to raise student achievement and increase graduation rates (Learning & Teaching, n.d.). Data found in the SIP is based on academic, attendance, and other data accumulated from the previous school year. The school counseling program supports the overall mission of the school; therefore, school counselors examine the mission, vision, and goals of the school as they relate to attendance, achievement, and discipline to determine how the school counseling program assists in meeting the goals outlined in the SIP (ASCA, 2019c). Once school counselors review their school's SIP, they work with administrators to determine their view of how the school counseling program can assist the school in meeting school, district, and state-level goals. It is important for school counselors to advocate for SIP goals that reflect identified inequities based on race, socioeconomic status, or other categories of identity. School counselors can play a role in identifying strategies to be included in the SIP (Atkins & Oglesby, 2019). SIPs and strategic plans are public knowledge and can often be found easily by asking school support staff at the building level for a hard copy.

In most states where there is a single governing body over schools such as a department of education, the department's website likely hosts access to SIPs, as well as a wealth of school and state-based data. In the "Helpful Resources" section of this chapter, you will find several links to examples of state-based websites that house school data. School counselors need only to become familiar with state-specific data management and publication formats to have easy access to a great deal of data.

School Data Summary

Once school counselors examine existing viable sources to gather as much school data as possible, it becomes necessary to find a way to view the data in a manageable way. Preparing a school data summary is one way for school counselors to view a snapshot of the existing data in its entirety. To ease the burden of deciding on an organizational approach to a school data summary, ASCA has created a template that is easily accessible to school counselors (schoolcounselor.org). This template allows users to methodically examine school demographics alongside attendance, achievement, and discipline (ASCA, 2019b). A school data summary or report is a synthesis of data that includes metrics on the standard data points with which school counselors are most concerned (attendance, academics, behavior), but the summary goes further by asking the school counselor to disaggregate that data by parsing out the numbers based on race, disability, socioeconomic status, etc. Finally, the data summary template provided by ASCA encourages the completer to include data from the 2 years prior, the previous year, and the current school year, allowing for a more robust picture of how the school data has evolved over time (ASCA, 2019b).

Intentional Data Collection

But wait—there's more of the story to be told! School improvement plans and school data summaries often fail to tell the whole story of student needs. School counselors embark on an intentional process to understand, more specifically, the needs of students in their respective schools. While a school data summary may reveal trends, for example, that English language learners, as a group, miss school more frequently than students whose first language is English, the data may not reveal why that is. There are myriad ways in which to get at the why. Here we discuss two of the most common approaches that complement existing data: needs assessments and focus groups.

Needs Assessments

Needs assessments are commonly conducted as surveys distributed to an entire school or a subset within the school. They often ask Likert-style questions (e.g., scaling 1–5) to gain information about a particular need. In this example, students might be asked to respond to the following statements about their school climate and provide feedback on a range of responses:

"Adults working at this school treat all students respectfully."

1 = strongly disagree, 2 = disagree, 3 = not sure, 4 = agree, 5 = strongly agree

"People of different cultural backgrounds, races, or ethnicities get along well at this school."

1 = strongly disagree, 2 = disagree, 3 = not sure, 4 = agree, 5 = strongly agree

Platforms such as Survey Monkey, JotForm, and NearPond are digital survey tools worth exploring to assist in the collection of survey data, including qualitative responses from students (Tierney, 2020). Again, looking simply at existing outcome data, such as attendance rates, fails to tell school counselors why students in their school are absent or locate the challenges related to students getting to school. By surveying students via a needs assessment, school counselors can begin to focus interventions around the issues that students report; school counselors can begin to understand the needs that exist around school attendance.

Focus Groups

Much can be gained by bringing students or other school and community partners together in small groups and encouraging discussion around issues in which school counselors are interested. Focus groups, using the previous example, might involve selecting several students for whom attendance is an issue, bringing them into a safe environment, and encouraging them to share thoughts around why getting to school can prove difficult for students. Further, focus groups then allow for discussions around what focus group members believe would help improve attendance. Student and school/community input on school counselor interventions is valuable to designing the comprehensive school counseling program.

Breaking Down the Data

Why does the school data summary break down school data by student identities? It is important for school counselors to not simply look at a single piece of data and take that data at its face value. To avoid this trap, school counselors engage in the process of disaggregating their school data; that is, they "break down" the data and examine it based on a variety of student features (e.g., race, gender, ability status; Kolbert et al., 2016). For example, a school, at first glance, may appear to be meeting its attendance goals as outlined in its school's strategic plan. Perhaps the school's average daily attendance rate is 85%. However, the skillful, data-savvy school counselor examines the data more closely to determine who exactly is missing school. Upon examination, it is determined that students who identify as Black have lower attendance rates (75%) than students who identify as White (90%). School counselors can work together with students who identify as Black and their families to better understand the barriers to greater school attendance (perhaps they have to stay home to care for a younger sibling, have issues accessing transportation, are experiencing racism in school, etc.) and tailor interventions to support students.

There are different tools the data-savvy school counselors can use to disaggregate data. Microsoft Excel is a useful application that can be used to examine specific groups of students who might be at greater risk. For example, users can enter demographic data alongside outcome data (e.g., eighth-grade students by name, their ethnicity, socioeconomic status, attendance) and then use the "sort" function in Excel to break down that data according to the indicator for which they are interested. Google forms and documents are also common tools used by school counselors to parse out and graph sets of data among different subsets of students.

Annual Student Outcome Goals

Now that a school counselor has located appropriate areas for improvement, it is time to develop annual student outcome goals. But first, heed this warning: It would be impossible for the school counseling program to address all the issues that are likely to make themselves known following a thorough review of all data. According to ASCA (2019b), student outcome goals are developed after examining the data and targeting the area on which the comprehensive school counseling program will focus. Additionally, these goals are typically written as SMART goals meaning they follow the following format: they are **S**pecific, **M**easurable, **A**ttainable, **R**elevant, and **T**ime based (Doran, 1981). Hatch and Hartline (2021) liken the identifying of these areas and the resulting goals to shining a flashlight on the target areas for which the program will focus its energies (see more on this in Chapter 10!). Annual student outcome goals drive the comprehensive school counseling program throughout the year, and while the school counseling program most certainly offers programming around issues other than those identified by the student outcome goals, the primary goal of the program for the year is to address the outcome metrics reflected in the student outcome goals.

Consultation Corner: Who You Gonna Call?

Thinking back to Mathew S.'s post and now having read the Informed School Counseling section, who would you call in and outside of the school building to help you with his dilemma? What might you ask them to support your decision-making? Take a moment to document these questions. Now that you have considered your questions for consultation, let's see what professional school counselors from around the world have to say about this case.

Consultation #1

Hello Matthew,

While I am an elementary school counselor, it is my opinion that the collection of data through pre-/postintervention is universal, regardless of grade level. The best way that I have learned to collect data, specific to pre-/postinterventions, is through Office 365 Forms or Google Forms. When I began my career 12 years ago, I would do paper/pencil, but the overwhelming amount of time spent hand grading 300+ surveys/assessments was time-consuming and left little time for more important work. Currently, my state department of education uses Office 365 Forms, but my county purchased Chromebooks for all students, thus the use of Google Forms at times. Regardless, both essentially do the same thing. From your post, it sounds as though you have some familiarity with Google Forms.

You stated, "I feel like" in your post. One thing that I have learned through years of data collection is that if I am saying "I feel like" about something, I probably need to be collecting data on that very thing itself. Do you have data to show the percent of survey completion with technology versus paper/pencil? Have you polled your students (either formally or informally) to see which they prefer? Moving from "I feel" to "the data shows" may be your first area of focus.

Notwithstanding, it sounds as though your biggest struggle is getting students to complete the surveys. Correct? For me, the most effective way to get students to complete pre-/postsurveys electronically is for me to physically go into the classrooms and administer them myself. I also find this helpful because I can explain certain questions or terms that students may not understand on their own, or even with teacher assistance. There is an inherent risk in asking teachers to proctor surveys or having students complete them on their own (like not doing them at all or being confused about certain questions and putting random answers to get it done).

On my website, I post hyperlinks for each respective assessment/survey I want students to complete. Then, after working with teachers to schedule times to go into classrooms, I administer those surveys much faster with whole classrooms. I ask each student to open their Chromebook (or for middle/high school students, they can do them on their cell phones. Using a QR-code generator that links to the forms is also very helpful when using cell phones too). I then instruct them on how to get to my school counselor website on the school web page where the links are posted. I then read each question aloud (this also helps with students who may have certain accommodations). I also find it helpful to have the teacher present so that he/she can help remediate any issues that students have with technology or can answer more individual questions that students may have.

One mistake I learned is making sure I duplicate each assessment/survey if I am using it in a pre/post manner. When I put the hyperlinks on my website, I need to make sure that each hyperlink connects to the correct survey. For example, one year I gave students a preassessment and then came back at the end of the year to give the postassessment. Unfortunately, in the end-of-the-year madness, I had forgotten to change the hyperlink to the posttest, so all the answers went back into the pretest form! As a result, it was difficult to go back and decipher which was pre and which was post. It is much easier to duplicate the forms when I make them and then REMEMBER to change the link on my web page prior to giving the assessment to students.

On another note, I also create specific fields in the forms/quizzes that include "first name" and "last name." Most forms or quizzes will automatically insert the person's email address once completed, but my elementary students do not have access to their individual Gmail accounts. There is also no way to track if they are completing the quizzes on their cell phones. This, of course, can all be managed in the settings for each individual form. Creating the "first name" and "last name" fields has been enormously helpful when I download the data into Excel (or Google Sheets) to easily and quickly filter or sort. If, for example, I created a quiz linked to social-emotional learning, I can easily download that data into Excel, sort from highest to lowest scores, and filter out a specific grade level or group to see where I may need to target my interventions.

I can understand if you are thinking, "But I don't have time to get into every classroom to give these myself. I am too busy juggling 100 other things!" To that, I ask, what is data worth to you? For me, data is king. It is the very foundation of my comprehensive school counseling program. Data informs all decisions I make based on a multi-tiered systems of support model. From system-wide Tier 1 interventions to Tier 3 intensive/individualized interventions. For me, I am willing to prioritize working time into my schedule to get into classrooms to ensure giving these are done.

(Matthew Tolliver, elementary school counselor, West Virginia)

Consultation #2

Hi, my name is Kristina Weiss, and I am a middle school counselor working in a suburban K–8 building. Within my building, I have found greater success with students taking surveys on paper rather than online. When the surveys are emailed to students, they often do not check their accounts or, as you mentioned, a few rounds of follow-ups are needed. One successful way I have discovered is teaming up with a teacher in the building. Teachers have allowed me to use their class time to administer surveys or elicit student feedback. Additionally, some staff members have given out the surveys as an "exit ticket" before the students leave or asked students to complete the survey once they have finished a test. After using this method, I have received more responses and more accurate results. I think students like the anonymity of it, and it also gives me a chance to collaborate with my staff and advertise our role as school counselors.

(Kristina Weiss, middle school counselor, New Jersey)

Consultation #3

Hi, my name is Joey, I'm a high school counselor at a specialized high school in a major city and an adjunct instructor of school counseling. Matthew! As I read your post, I found myself agreeing out loud because I feel like I have been in a similar situation. I, too, rely very heavily on survey data for things like needs assessments, developing the curriculum for classroom lessons, and putting together my class meetings. Depending on how much time you have to gather data, and what kind of access your school allows to technology, you might try the following: (1) For some of my developmental classroom lessons, I try to reserve the computer lab or the classroom section of the library with the Chromebook cart, so my students have access to technology immediately following my lesson. I tend to build in time for survey completion, AND the added benefit is if students have questions about a particular prompt, you're right there to address anything which might feel unclear. (2) You can initially send the survey to all students, then after identifying the students you need to follow up with, I might group them into small-lunch bunch groups, reserve the Chromebook for your office or conference space, and meet with students for a check-in while providing the time and technology to complete the survey. In the same way group counseling is more time efficient and effective, this provides more face time, a check-in, and the completion of your data. (3) My department has worked very closely with the Parent Association to purchase some gift cards for some of our students' favorite lunch spots in the neighborhood. In the call for survey participation, we might raffle off a gift card, and I've noticed that participation increases!

(Joseph Feola, high school counselor, New York)

#EduCounselor Synthesis

From the onset of his post, Matthew S. certainly believes in the use of data to learn about the program and to market it to school and community partners. This is a strong stance that will undoubtedly help to advocate for the program. Many people (not just school counselors!) fear the word "data" because they immediately think of statistics. If this is you, we hope that you can hang in there while we challenge this assumption! The goal of this chapter remains to demystify this notion and to help us look at data as our ally, rather than our enemy. Matthew S. brings a positive attitude into this conversation and is looking to use available resources to help begin collecting data with the most amount of accuracy. Many times, we have access to resources that we don't know about or are not sure how to use to help us. In these moments, reaching out to others to learn about their data collection efforts is key. Additionally, connecting with your school's technology and administrative personnel can be incredibly helpful in supporting you with easily accessible (and free!) resources.

In this case, Matthew S. is drawing on technology options provided by the school (Google & Naviance) to help gather data. There is not a one-size-fits-all answer for the use of technology tools for data collection. Readers may look to Deslonde and Becerra (2018) and Mason et al. (2019) for more examples. Matthew S. is also acknowledging the advantages and disadvantages of paper and pencil surveys previously used with the upperclassman. Matthew is worried about important research challenges associated with response bias. Specifically, there could be worry about social desirability bias, or the tendency to give the answer students believe the school counselor *wants* to hear, or acquiescence bias where people are more likely to agree to an answer rather than state their true feelings. Both can skew data collection efforts and potentially paint a rosier picture of your students' needs. Matthew S. understandably wants the most accurate information possible and is seeking advice about how others have navigated this challenge.

As we examine our consultants' responses, we see that each of them holds a belief that data collection is important to the role and function of the school counselor. They also validated the challenges of collecting survey data in terms of time constraints and logistical obstacles within each individual school system. Navigating the school day and students' schedules from elementary to high school can be challenging but is clearly not insurmountable. Matthew T. asked, "what is data worth to you?" This is an important question that will likely be molded into your counseling philosophy. Consider how you will discuss data during school counseling interviews and when you meet with various school and community partners like administrators, teachers, and parents after you are hired. All three consultants specifically noted the value of collaborating with others in the school. How might you cultivate these relationships so that you can garner support for your data collection efforts?

Kristina talked about teachers using their classroom downtime, either at the end of an assessment or right before students leave for the day, while Matthew T.

and Joey discussed scheduling classroom time or the technology lab to allow for students to use computers or Chromebooks. Regardless, all three consultants and Matthew S. alluded to the importance of partnerships and creative problem-solving. These "soft skills" are essential for school counselors to develop and cultivate (Young & Bryan, 2015; Young et al., 2015) to interact with the community in productive ways. Imagine if you could model the appropriate use of data for educators who might also have negative attitudes toward data collection. This can facilitate more partnerships, allow for future advocacy efforts, and perhaps, most importantly, foster more community trust in showing that what you do as a school counselor makes a difference in the lives of students.

One of the things that the consultants discussed openly, and perhaps differed slightly on, was use of time and delivery methods for survey collection. This is common, as each school and relationship school counselors have within the confines of their buildings is different. Some teachers will welcome the opportunity to partner in data collection. Others might feel more protective of their time or do not appreciate its benefit. Scheduling outside technology space or using time during developmental counseling lessons represent ways to navigate such challenges. Kristina and Matthew T. referenced the benefits of perceived anonymity in survey data collection. Many researchers would argue that true anonymity is very difficult or potentially impossible to gain (Adinoff et al., 2013). A level of confidentiality in the data collection process, however, may in fact help students to feel more confident in sharing sensitive information about the program or their own needs (Bjarnason & Adalbjarnardottir, 2000). This has the potential to yield more accurate data; however, not knowing which students are struggling specifically can limit school counselors' abilities to target certain populations, such as Joey suggested in identifying students to further assess. As two of the consultants pointed out, there may also be benefits to remaining in the room to clarify instructions or answer questions; as you assess the needs of your school, you will likely have a better idea of what is best for your students. Collecting data around survey administration itself, as suggested by Matthew T., may be a good way to determine exactly what you need to do. Providing short answers or open-ended questions on surveys might help students feel more comfortable sharing information.

Finally, it cannot be overstated how important it is to use your resources! Joey and Matthew T. both discussed using Google Forms, Excel, Naviance, and Office 365 to collect and organize data. These were all available to them and may be to you in your future practice as well. Talking with your building administrator about other school-based data collection efforts can not only provide you with current tools already in place but can also help you learn about outcome data efforts that can be paired with school counseling data collection initiatives. Using the parent network to advocate for survey incentives, as Joey suggests, or writing a grant proposal for other school counseling specific data collection programs or school counseling specific research conferences like the National Evidenced-Based School Counseling

Conference (https://www.ebscc.org/) might serve the dual purpose of providing you with more access and/or training and greater visibility for your program. Ultimately, your goal for collecting data is to inform your program and be able to develop action plans and create initiatives that address the outcomes of both your school counseling program and your district.

Chapter Summary

School counselors use multiple data touch points to inform their practices. Additionally, they use many different technological tools to collect, organize, and disaggregate data to tailor specific program interventions. In synthesizing the data, it is important to view the nuances inherent within the data as it relates to education equity; examining the data at its face value may in fact result in a misleading story. While data provides a foundation and starting point, school counselors must always assess how they can continue to gather additional information from school and community partners to ensure that they are reaching ALL students with a comprehensive school counseling program.

Reflective Practitioner Process

School counselors engage in **clinical supervision, professional development**, and **self-care** to further develop their knowledge and skills and to help balance professional expectations with personal wellness. All three areas are key to ethical practice and help to mitigate counselor burnout and compassion fatigue (Atici, 2015; Lawson & Myers, 2011; Merriman, 2015; Ohrt et al., 2015).

Clinical Supervision

The *ASCA School Counselor Professional Standards and Competencies* (ASCA, 2019a) direct school counselors to "consult with school counselors and other education and counseling professionals when questions of school counseling practice arise" (B-SS 5., p. 5). As a supervisee, it is important to consider the thoughts, feelings, and experiences that come up for you as you work with students, families, and colleagues and seek consultation on difficult issues. The following are some topics for consideration as you react to this chapter.

- Which part of the data process (collecting, interpreting, planning, communicating) are considered direct service hours? Which parts of the process are considered indirect service hours?
- What happens if I don't understand what the data are saying or what they mean? What might I do?
- How do I proceed if there is some data missing?

Professional Development

According to the *ASCA Ethical Standards for School Counselors* (ASCA, 2022), professional school counselors engage in professional development and attend trainings to stay current on the trends and issues that impact students (B.3.e). Relative to the contents of this chapter, consider finding professional development on the following topics:

- Data Collection (e.g., strategies, bias)
- Technology use in Data Collection (e.g., survey platforms, development implementation)
- Data Organization platforms
- Consider attending the Evidence-Based School Counseling Conference (https://www.ebscc.org/)

#PSCSelfCare: Everyday Wellness

When designing, managing, and implementing a comprehensive school counseling program, school and community expectations can tax even the most seasoned school counselor. The *ASCA Ethical Standards for School Counselors* (ASCA, 2022) require school counselors to recognize the high levels of stress often associated with the job. Therefore, school counselors recognize that self-care must be a priority to maintain health and overall wellbeing (see ASCA, 2022, B.3.h).

Getting Rid of the Noise: A Social Media Cleanse

Mental noise represents extraneous sounds that can cloud one's ability to focus. Without recognizing the impact of this noise, people may struggle to remain calm and productive. It is therefore important to employ strategies to help quiet the mind and recharge. Counselors are tasked with monitoring their own wellness in order to operate at their full capacity. Given that many individuals use multiple social media platforms to engage personally and professionally, removing yourself for some time can provide the "quiet brain space" for reflection.

Social media cleanses can prove beneficial. They may (a) reduce feelings of anxiety, (b) provide more time for people and activities you enjoy, (c) increase productivity, (d) decrease the feeling of missing out (FOMO), (e) increase overall sleep performance (Hanley et al. 2019; Scott & Woods, 2018; Woods & Scott, 2016). We challenge you to perform a **social media cleanse**. The time frame is up to you. We recommend a full three days or up to a week for maximum benefit. Additionally, incorporate this into your wellness routine at least once per month. To begin, follow these steps:

1. Choose the time that you are committing to engage in the cleanse. You might consider posting publicly on social media that you are stepping away for a certain length of time. This provides accountability, garners support from your network, and models wellness for others.
2. Turn off notifications for all social media on your electronic devices.

3. Reduce the urge to look. This may look different from one person to the next; it could be removing the app from the first page of your phone or placing your phone in a space that is less accessible.

4. Make a list of activities that will replace the time spent on social media. This might include simple activities such as sitting in silence or taking a nap.

After engaging in the cleanse, reflect on the following questions to highlight your experience:

1. What was the experience like for you? Was it easy or challenging? Did that change over time? In examining the ease or challenge, consider why that was.

2. How do you feel physically? Emotionally?

3. Would you engage in this again? Why or why not?

4. If you were to recommend this to a future student or colleague, what information might you share to highlight the benefits?

Spotlight: School Counseling Advocacy

In the following social media post shared on Twitter, ASCA'S 2020 *School Counselor of the Year* demonstrates the use of ASCA's School Data Profile Template to examine school demographics and develop program goals.

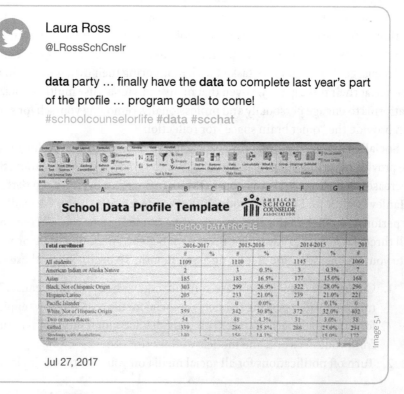

Laura Ross, "Laura Ross Tweet." Copyright © 2017 by Laura Ross. Reprinted with permission.

Learning Connections

Both professional school counselors in training and seasoned school counselors understand the importance of understanding the connections between the concepts commonly taught in counseling programs and the standards most associated with school counselor training. Therefore, the following table offers broad connections between the material and information in this chapter and the Council for Accreditation of Counseling and Related Educational Programs (CACREP, 2016) standards, The *ASCA School Counselor Professional Standards and Competencies* (ASCA, 2019a), and the *ASCA Ethical Standards for School Counselors* (ASCA, 2022).

Connections to CACREP Core Curricular Areas

Professional Counseling Orientation and Ethical Practice	Social and Cultural Diversity	Human Growth and Development	Career Development	Counseling and Helping Relationships	Group Counseling and Group Work	Assessment and Testing	Research and Program Evaluation
X	X		X			X	X

Connection to Professional Standards

CACREP	ASCA SC Professional Competencies	Ethical Standards: SC
1.e: Assessments specific to P–12 education	M.5: Effective school counseling is a collaborative process involving school counselors, students, families, teachers, administrators, other school staff and education stakeholders.	A.3.d: Review and use school and student data to assess and address needs, including but not limited to data on strengths and disparities that may exist related to gender, race, ethnicity, socioeconomic status, disability and/or other relevant classifications.
3.a: Design and evaluation of school counseling programs	B-PF 5. Use ASCA Mindsets & Behaviors for Student Success to inform the implementation of a school counseling program.	
3.m: Use of accountability data to inform decision-making	B-PA 3. Develop annual student outcome goals based on student data.	A.3.f: Collect and analyze participation, ASCA Mindsets & Behaviors and outcome data to determine the progress and effectiveness of the school counseling program.

(Continued)

CACREP	ASCA SC Professional Competencies	Ethical Standards: SC
3.n: Use of data to advocate for programs and students	B-SS 1. Design and implement instruction aligned to ASCA Mindsets & Behaviors for Student Success in large-group, classroom.	A.3.c. Use data collection tools adhering to confidentiality standards expressed in A.2.
	B-PF 2.i: Use current trends in technology to promote student success.	
	B-PF 9.b: Use data to identify how school, district and state educational policies, procedures and practices support and/or impede student success.	

Comprehensive School Counseling Assignments

The following section provides activities that allow for your continued growth as a professional school counselor. Both preservice and practicing school counselors may find it helpful to complete these activities.

1. **Getting Friendly With School Data:** As mentioned, a first step in the data gathering process is reviewing school data. Using your state's department of education website, choose a school and review three previous years of data.
   a. What trends are evident across the time period?
   b. How does the school compare to other district and state data?
   c. What data are missing? What more might you want to know?
   d. What data would be helpful to plan your school counseling program?
2. **Student Outcome Goals:** Based on the data of the school you chose in #1.:
   a. What do you notice about the data and how might you explain it?
   b. Using the SMART goal format, develop three student outcome goals for the school counseling program based on the following:
      i. Achievement
      ii. Attendance
      iii. Discipline
3. **Consumer Reports:** In attempting to choose data collection platforms, you will need to perform an analysis to present to financial decision-makers in your schools. Let's practice. Choose two data collection technology tools/platforms (e.g., Powerschool, Genesis, Realtime) and provide a product analysis in which you compare, contrast, and give an overall summary for the preferred program. Here are some items to consider:

    a. Ease of use/user-friendly
    b. Confidentiality/ethical guidelines
    c. Integration to an SIS
    d. Effectiveness of comprehensive school counseling program planning
    e. Applicable for individual student planning
    f. Organization of results

Helpful Resources
Web-Based Resources

Several states in the United States provide web-based platforms through which they communicate school performance indicators to school and community partners. We provide two examples here for your review:

- Zoom WV:
  - https://zoomwv.k12.wv.us/Dashboard/dashboard/28116
- WV Balanced Scorecard Dashboard:
  - https://wveis.k12.wv.us/essa/dashboard.html
- For more information on how to disaggregate data, check out the following:
  - Forum Guide to Collecting and Using Disaggregated Data on Racial/Ethnic Subgroups https://nces.ed.gov/forum/pdf/Disaggregated_Data_PPT.pdf
- For assistance in developing SMART goals, check out the following:
  - Template for Developing a School Counseling Program Goal in SMART-Goal Format https://www.schoolcounselor.org/asca/media/asca/ASCA%20National%20Model%20Templates/SMART-Goal.pdf

Suggested Readings

Young, A., & Kaffenberger, C. (2018). *Data as easy as 1–2–3*. https://www.schoolcounselor.org/newsletters/october-2018/data-as-easy-as-1-2-3?st=CO

References

ACT. (2006). *Research support for DISCOVER assessment components*.

American School Counselor Association (ASCA). (2019a). *ASCA school counselor professional standards & competencies*. https://www.schoolcounselor.org/asca/media/asca/home/SCCompetencies.pdf

American School Counselor Association (ASCA). (2019b). *ASCA national model implementation guide: Manage & assess*. (2nd ed.).

American School Counselor Association (ASCA). (2019c). *ASCA national model: A framework for school counseling programs*. (4th ed.).

American School Counselor Association (ASCA). (2021). *ASCA student standards: Mindsets & behaviors for student success.* https://www.schoolcounselor.org/getmedia/7428a787-a452-4abb-afec-d78ec77870cd/Mindsets-Behaviors.pdf

American School Counselor Association (ASCA). (2022). *ASCA ethical standards for school counselors.* https://www.schoolcounselor.org/getmedia/44f30280-ffe8-4b41-9ad8-f15909c3d164/EthicalStandards.pdf.

Adinoff, B., Conley, R. R., Taylor, S. F., & Chezem, L. L. (2013). Protecting confidentiality in human research. *The American Journal of Psychiatry, 170*(5), 466–470. https://doi.org/10.1176/appi.ajp.2012.12050595

Atici, M. (2015). Professional identity development of counselors-in-training in a school internship program in Turkey. *The Professional Counselor, 5*(1), 137–151. https://doi.org/10.15241/ma.5.1.137

Atkins, R., & Oglesby, A. (2019). *Interrupting racism: Equity and social justice in school counseling.* Routledge.

Aubrey, R. F. (1973). Organizational victimization of school counselors. *The School Counselor, 20*(5), 346–354.

Bjarnason, T., & Adalbjarnardottir, S. (2000). Anonymity and confidentiality in school surveys on alcohol, tobacco, and cannabis use. *Journal of Drug Issues, 30*(2), 335–344. https://doi.org/10.1177/002204260003000206

Council for Accreditation of Counseling and Related Educational Programs (CACREP). (2016). *2016 CACREP standards.* http://www.cacrep.org/wp-content/uploads/2017/08/2016-Standards-with-citations.pdf

Dahir, C. A., & Stone, C. B. (2003). Accountability: A M.E.A.S.U.R.E of the impact school counselors have on student achievement. *Professional School Counseling, 6*(3), 214–221. https://www.researchgate.net/publication/234603382_Accountability_A_MEASURE_of_the_Impact_School_Counselors_Have_on_Student_Achievement

Deslonde, V., & Becerra, M. (2018). The technology acceptance model (TAM): Exploring school counselors' acceptance and use of Naviance. *The Professional Counselor, 8*(4), 369–382. https://doi.org/10.15241/vd.8.4.369

Doran, G. T. (1981). There's a SMART way to write management's goals and objectives. *Management Review, 70*(11), 35–36. https://community.mis.temple.edu/mis-0855002fall2015/files/2015/10/S.M.A.R.T-Way-Management-Review.pdf

The Education Trust. (1999). *National center for transforming school counseling at The Education Trust.* http://www2.edtrust.org/EdTrust/Transforming+ School+Counseling/main

Hanley, S. M., Watt, S. E., & Coventry, W. (2019) Taking a break: The effect of taking a vacation from Facebook and Instagram on subjective well-being. *PLoS ONE, 1*(6), Article e0217743. https://doi:10.1371/journal.pone.0217743

Hatch, T., & Hartline, J. (2021). *The use of data in school counseling: Hatching results for students, programs, and the profession* (2nd ed.). Corwin.

Hobsons (2018). College, career and life readiness (CCLR) framework: Build mindsets and skillsets for student success. (Naviance). https://www3.naviance.com/content/cclr-framework#:~:text=The%20College%2C%20Career%20and%20Life,career%20and%20life%20readiness%20initiatives

Holcomb-McCoy, C. (2007). *School counseling to close the achievement gap: A social justice framework for success.* Corwin Press.

Kaffenberger, C., & Young, A. (2019). *Making data work* (3rd ed.). American School Counselor Association.

Kolbert, J. B., Morgan, L. M., Crothers, L. M., & Hughes, T. L. (2016). *Introduction to professional school counseling: Advocacy, leadership, and intervention.* Routledge.

Lawson, G., & Myers, J. E. (2011). Wellness, professional quality of life, and career-sustaining behaviors: What keeps us well? *Journal of Counseling and Development, 89*(2), 163–171. https://doi.org/10.1002/j.1556-6678.2011.tb00074.x

Learning & Teaching. (n.d.) *School improvement plans.* https://www.isd742.org/domain/560

Mason, E. C. M., Griffith, C., & Belser, C. T. (2019). School counselors' use of technology for program management. *Professional School Counseling, 22*(1), 1–10. https://doi.org/10.1177/2156759X19870794

Merriman, J. (2015). Enhancing counselor supervision through compassion fatigue education. *Journal of Counseling and Development, 93*(1), 370–378. https://doi.org/10.1002/jcad.12035

Ohrt, J. H., Prosek, E. A., Ener, E., & Lindo, N. (2015). The effects of a group supervision intervention to promote wellness and prevent burnout. *The Journal of Humanistic Counseling, 54*(1), 41–58. doi:10.1002/j.2161-1939.2015.00063.x

Scott, H., & Woods, H. C. (2018). Fear of missing out and sleep: Cognitive behavioural factors in adolescents' nighttime social media use. *Journal of Adolescence, 68*(1), 61–65. https://doi.org/10.1016/j.adolescence.2018.07.009

Springer, S. I., Land, C. W., Moss, L. J., & Cinotti, D. (2018). Collecting school counseling group work data: Initiating consensual qualitative research through practitioner–researcher partnerships. *The Journal for Specialists in Group Work, 43*(2), 128–143. https://doi.org/10.1080/01933922.2018.1431346

Tierney, K. (2020, January 3). *How school counselors use data to help students succeed.* JotForm Education. https://www.jotform.com/blog/how-school-counselors-use-data/

Woods, H. C., & Scott, H. (2016) #Sleepyteens: Social media use in adolescence is associated with poor sleep quality, anxiety, depression and low self-esteem. *Journal of Adolescence, 51*(1), 41–49. https://doi.org/10.1016/j.adolescence.2016.05.008

Young, A., & Bryan, J. (2015). The school counselor leadership survey: Instrument development and exploratory factor analysis. *Professional School Counseling, 19*(1), 1–15. https://doi.org/10.5330/1096-2409-19.1.1

Young, A., Dollarhide, C. T, & Baughman, A. (2015). The voices of school counselors: Essential characteristics of school counselor leaders. *Professional School Counseling, 19*(1), 36–45. https://doi.org/10.5330/1096-2409-19.1.36

Young, A., & Kaffenberger, C. (2011). The beliefs and practices of school counselors who use data to implement comprehensive school counseling programs. *Professional School Counseling, 15*(2), 67–76. https://doi.org/10.5330/PSC.n.2011-15.67

Young, A., & Miller-Kneale, M. (2013). *School counselor leadership: The essential practice.* American School Counselor Association.

Credits

CHAPTER 6

Managing Time, Teams, and Calendars

LEARNING OBJECTIVES

#EduCounselors can

- understand the appropriate role of the school counselor in committee work that supports student success,
- recognize the value and importance of school counselors tracking their time,
- recognize the topics and content to be discussed at an annual conference with school administrators, and
- understand the value in using calendars to plan both annual and weekly events offered by the school counseling program.

Introduction

As you are learning, a comprehensive school counseling program is multifaceted and complex! To effectively deliver the program to all students, school counselors must have a clearly defined path for their work. The more clearly we articulate how we spend our time, the more efficient we are in delivering services, and the better able we are to communicate our appropriate role. This allows school counselors to better measure how our work impacts students. This chapter explores the variety of tools school counselors use to manage their comprehensive school counseling program, including use-of-time logs and calendars. Additionally, this chapter explores how school counselors balance their participation in committees and on teams while maintaining strong professional boundaries.

#IRLSchoolCounseling

The following is a social media post from one of the many school counseling groups on Facebook. *Elementary School Counselor Exchange* is a Facebook group primarily hosting topics posed by elementary school counselors.

Question: at your school, who is in charge/oversees/
coordinates the SST process? (I.e. Students referred for
behavior/academics who might potentially be eligible for
an IEP once evaluated) I am the School counselor and SST
Coordinator at my school, but in the SST Manual for my
district it states that the Assistant Principal should be the
SST Coordinator, though the counselor can also participate
at varied capacities (I.e. For FABs and BIPs). My concern is
that this takes up a major chunk of my time and I hardly have
time for actual counseling responsibilities (individual, group, or
classroom lessons). When I vocalized this to my principal, she
stated that the needs of the school dictate how the roles and
responsibilities will be assigned (and I am at a low SES, high-
need school). I want to be a team player, but I also want to
be fair to myself and not veer away from my true passion and
professional goals (by doing less administrative support and
having more contact with and access to the kids). I am hoping
for some ideas on how this is managed at your school so that
perhaps I can propose something similar at my own school.
Thanks in advance!

Bracketing Values for Ethical Practice

It is expected that school counselors continuously reflect on their values, beliefs,
worldviews, and cultural norms and how each influences the ways in which they
choose to take or not take action. As such, it is important to recognize and set aside
any preconceived notions, experiences, and biases to help you respond to this scenario
in a culturally sustaining and ethically sound manner. Take a moment to reflect on
the previous post and then consider the following questions:

- What is your reaction when you hear that the principal has designated
  coordination of a team/committee to the school counselor?
- How do you feel about leading discussions related to student academic,
  behavioral, and social/emotional progress in schools? What excites and/or
  concerns you about leading these types of discussions?
- How do you feel about engaging in tough conversations with your principal about the allocation of your time each day?
- Consider a scenario where there is a need to initiate a conversation with
  your superior related to your job duties. What thoughts and feelings sur-
  face when you consider this conversation?

Informed School Counseling

In Chapter 5, we shared information regarding the importance of using data to locate the salient issues in schools; issues for which school counselors direct the work of their comprehensive school counseling programs. We also provided information on the kinds of data that are used to locate educational inequities. The advocacy for implementing a school counseling program and the appropriate use of the school counselor's time, however, does not end with the collection of participation, mindsets and behaviors, and outcome data exclusively. Here, we examine other critical pieces of data, including those that come from school counselors' participation in building-based teams and committees.

Annual Administrative Conference

According to the American School Counselor Association (ASCA, 2019b), the annual administrative conference is a discussion between school counselors and the appropriate administrators who oversee the school counseling program. Erford (2011) notes that formal meetings such as this "enhance communication among counselors and building leaders because they provide an opportunity not only to share information, but also to build rapport" (p. 123). Grothaus and colleagues (2020) further emphasize the importance of the annual conference as an opportunity to advocate for and collaborate on plans for the school to continue to grow as a "culturally sustaining learning community" (p. 70), in which the school counselor makes the case for "moving forward toward greater inclusivity and equity" (p. 70). Rutledge (2020) encourages school counselors to use the annual conference as a time to talk with administrators about the school counselor's focus and goals related to social justice and dismantling inequitable practices and policies. Additionally, the annual conference provides a time for the school counselor to make the case that an effective school counseling program that is serving the needs of all students, especially those students historically underserved, leads to enhanced success for school leadership.

Both the *ASCA National Model* (ASCA, 2019b) and the *ASCA National Model Implementation Guide* (ASCA, 2019a) offer templates that can be used to ensure that important items are discussed during the annual conference. In general, agenda items include the following:

1. School counseling data (participation, mindsets and behaviors, outcome; see Chapter 5)
2. Priorities for the school counseling program based on this data
3. Goals for the school counseling program that align with school goals and strategic plans
4. School counselor use of time spent in direct and indirect student services (highlighting any inappropriate activities in which the school counselor engages)
5. Ratios and caseloads

6. Advisory council meeting dates and membership
7. Professional development opportunities
8. School counselor involvement on committees and teams not directly related to the school counseling program
9. Budgetary items such as supplies and materials needed to support the program
10. Priorities and practices that support or hinder the school counselor from engaging in social justice advocacy and eliminating policies and practices that hurt marginalized students

Once consensus and agreement are firmly in place regarding the priorities for the school counseling program, school counselors begin the work of developing activities, events, and interventions agreed upon at the annual conference. Intentional use-of-time logs and calendars assists school counselors in staying on track to accomplish the tasks they prioritize.

Time Logs

The ASCA recommends that 80% of the school counselor's time be spent in direct and indirect services to students (ASCA, 2019b). This begs a seminal question in the development of a school counseling program, "Where are school counselors currently spending their time?" This question can only be answered when school counselors keep track of and monitor the amount of time spent on activities. In doing so, school counselors can examine this data in collaboration with school and community partners (e.g., administrators, parents, board of education) to further outline their role in the school. Simply put, time logs are advocacy tools and, in conjunction with participation, mindsets and behaviors, and outcome data, provide an important selling point for the future of the school counseling program.

While the appropriate and inappropriate duties often assigned to the school counselor are outlined in Chapter 2, the following is an abbreviated list of just a few of the direct and indirect services that make up the prescribed 80% of direct service to students:

Direct (in-person between school counselor and students):

- Individual, short-term, goal-oriented counseling
- Group counseling
- Classroom instruction
- Student advising
- Student appraisal

Indirect (on behalf of students):

- Collaboration with other school and community partners
- Consultation with teachers, caregivers, parents on behalf of the student(s)
- Referrals to outside resources on behalf of student(s)

It is important for school counselors to track the realistic allocation of direct and indirect activities in which they engage. Tracking activities helps to paint a picture of how the school counselor's time is spent across a variety of interventions and duties. If need be, the tracking of time spent in direct and indirect services provides important data that can be used for advocacy purposes in instances where school counselors find themselves performing inappropriate tasks.

Just as there are a variety of platforms by which school counseling training programs insist students track their time in practicums and internships (e.g., Time-2Track, Tevera, Supervision Assist, etc.), so too are there a multitude of ways in which school counselors can track their time in practice. We would be foolish to attempt to prescribe or recommend a time tracking system that works for everyone. The key is that school counselors find a time tracking system, technology, strategy, or approach that works best for them. The fourth edition of the *ASCA National Model* (ASCA, 2019b) along with the accompanying *ASCA National Model Implementation Guide* (ASCA, 2019a) provides the "Use-of-Time Calculator" (ASCA, 2019b, p. 64–65) and online template as one option for tracking time. However, some school counselors prefer to use platforms such as SCUTA, Google Forms, or Excel spreadsheets to create a time tracking tool that suits their needs. Additionally, some states and school districts dictate a particular time tracking tool that school counselors are required to use. Regardless of the tool or strategy you use, ensuring that the tool can delineate between direct and indirect activities, as well as appropriate and inappropriate duties, is important. In the helpful resources section of this chapter, we provide links to a variety of tools to help you think about a time tracking system that works for you.

Irrespective of the tool you choose to use to track time, *it is imperative that you maintain a time log!* Your advocacy efforts are greatly diminished in the absence of any data on how your time is spent. Data generated by tracking time allows the school counselor to determine if any groups are being underserved. While time logs help us account for our daily activities, calendars help us structure our time across an academic year, with both an annual and weekly focus.

Calendars

Developing program calendars and publishing them is an essential aspect of the school counseling program; calendars demonstrate that a school counseling program is systematic, sequenced, and organized in its efforts to deliver services (Erford, 2011). The *ASCA National Model* (ASCA, 2019b) recommends school counselors develop both annual and weekly calendars. From this, school counselors can more intentionally plan daily calendars with specific activities.

Annual Calendars

Once school counselors have a clear understanding of their program goals, they may begin to use the multi-tiered system of supports (MTSS) framework (see Chapters 7–9) to plan, organize, and disseminate details like when, where, and how activities and interventions will take place over the course of the academic year. Annual calendars often include important events such as classroom lessons, back-to-school nights, school open houses, parent/teacher conferences, college and financial aid workshops, small-group counseling initiatives, and program planning events.

Similar to our advice on time tracking tools, there are many technological tools, platforms, and strategies school counselors use to develop professional, easy-to-follow, appealing annual calendars. Tools such as Calendy, Google Calendars, and ASCA's own calendar template make developing calendars easy and attractive. Again, we encourage you to explore the many options available, including tools that other school counselors have developed and offer on sites such as Teachers Pay Teachers. The key is to develop an annual calendar that aligns with program priorities and items agreed upon in the annual administrative conference.

Weekly Calendars

Effective school counselors create weekly calendars to guide their work and prevent them from getting drawn into unnecessary activities and tasks that are not the priority for the program that week. Of note here is that weekly calendars allow for some level of flexibility while also guiding the work in an intentional way; crises do arise and need attention, but in the absence of crises, the weekly calendar allows school counselors to stay on track with priorities. Weekly calendars help to support the MTSS framework and may include interventions at all three tiers: classroom lessons and whole school activities, small-group counseling, individual student check-ins, consultation, and committee and team meetings. Upon establishing calendars for the year, and even more specifically, the week, school counselors begin to plan, design, and implement a plan of action to cover the *ASCA Student Standards: Mindsets and Behaviors for Student Success* (ASCA, 2021).

Action Plans

It is critical for school counselors to plan specific activities tied to the *ASCA Student Standards* (ASCA, 2021) when choosing activities aimed at meeting program goals. The *ASCA National Model* (ASCA, 2019b) encourages school counselors to use two specific kinds of action plans to assist in the prioritizing of program activities around the student standards: classroom and small-group action plans and closing-the-gap action plans/results reports (we address the results piece in Chapter 10). While some school counselors may see the utility of using action plans solely as a function of applying to ASCA's RAMP (Recognized ASCA Model Program) designation, the use of action plans is commonly considered best practice for aligning school counseling programs with school improvement plans. Templates for both closing-the-gap and classroom action plans are easily accessed using the ASCA website. However, content common to both action plans includes

- participants identified for activities based on school data,
- description of activities to be delivered,
- setting for each activity,
- *ASCA Student Standards* for each activity, and
- timing of activities.

Classroom and small-group action plans are used to broadly deliver the *ASCA Student Standards* (ASCA, 2021) to all students across the school counseling curriculum. Closing-the-gap action plans also target the delivery of the *ASCA Student Standards* but target only those mindsets and behaviors that help close educational gaps for students who are marginalized in the areas of attendance, academics, and behavior. In other words, "closing the gap," refers to the intentional work that should be done to "deliver researched-based interventions to help close achievement, attainment, information, attendance, discipline, resource, and opportunity gaps" (ASCA, 2022 A.3.e) and level the playing field for all students. With action plans now in place, the process of planning classroom lessons and small-group sessions begins.

Lesson Planning

Now that you met with your administrator; outlined the priorities for the year; developed annual and weekly calendars that include the lessons, interventions, and activities on which you will focus; and outlined appropriate action plans for the program, it is time to put pen to paper and begin to plan classroom lessons and small-group sessions.

Classroom Lessons

Many school counselors who come from education backgrounds are familiar with the key elements of a well-thought-out lesson plan. According to Lewis (2019), the key components of a comprehensive lesson plan include lesson objectives that are tied to student standards, engaging strategies to grab students' attention, strategy to deliver the content, lesson conclusion, and a strategy to encourage student independent learning. Additionally, many classroom teachers and counselors value adding a materials list to any lesson plan. A general rule we use to guide novice school counselors in the development of lesson plans is to include all information that would be needed in the event that you could not go into the class and present the lesson; what would your replacement need in terms of materials, information, resources, and activities to complete the lesson in your absence?

The *ASCA National Model* (ASCA, 2019b) especially recommends that school counselors include the following in all lesson plans:

- The *ASCA Student Standards* to be covered
- Learning objectives
- Materials
- Evidence base (identify any evidence available to support the lesson)

- Procedure
- Evaluation plan
- Follow up

Templates for the ASCA recommended lesson plan are available through the ASCA website. However, a simple Internet search will yield additional ideas and formats for planning classroom lessons. Programs that are specifically interested in achieving ASCA's RAMP designation should consider using the ASCA template exclusively.

Small-Group Counseling

The literature on small-group counseling in schools is rich with experts who emphasize the need to plan small-group counseling interventions (Corey, 2016; Jacobs et al., 2022; Springer et al., 2022). When planning small-group interventions, it is not necessary to create activities from scratch. Many school counselors share ideas and small-group plans on websites such as Pinterest, Facebook, and private blogs. Springer et al. (2022) provide session plans for students in K–12 on topics around grief, social skills, decision-making, and anxiety. The key is that small-group counseling requires the same thought and planning as classroom interventions. In your absence, your small-group plans should be easily interpreted by a school counselor colleague who could, if appropriate, step in in your absence and lead a productive group counseling session. More information about direct services and their alignment with the MTSS framework is discussed in the "Deliver" section of this text. Additionally, many school counselor training programs offer a standalone course in leading small groups. However, oftentimes, these courses fail to differentiate the skills needed to run small groups in schools from the skills required to lead small groups in clinical settings (Springer & Schimmel, 2016). Running small groups in schools is an essential part of a comprehensive school counseling program, and school counselors must feel comfortable leading groups at all developmental levels. Continued professional development to enhance your group leading skills is critical if you do not feel competent upon completion of your graduate-level training.

Many of the essential skills needed to run small groups in schools are equally useful when helping to facilitate school-based committees or serving in leadership roles on school teams. School counselors are in a unique position when taught effective group leading skills and to facilitate productive, time-efficient adult committee meetings. However, just because the school counselor possesses these skills does not suggest that school counselors should lead, facilitate, plan, and organize all (or any!) school-based teams and committees. In fact, coordinating such teams is listed on ASCA's inappropriate school counseling duties list. And, given that school counselors will likely participate on such teams, it is important for them to be mindful to set boundaries so that committee work doesn't interfere with designing and managing a comprehensive school counseling program that serves all students.

The School Counselor and Committee Work

Many preservice school counselors enter the profession expecting that most of their time is spent solely on the activities commonly considered "direct." While direct activities are at the heart of a school counselor's role, it is important to recognize that school counselors also do the valuable work of collaborating, consulting, and serving on teams and committees that directly impact student growth and development. Many of these indirect services occur through MTSS and, according to ASCA (2018), represent important areas of decision-making in which school counselors should be involved. While a detailed explanation of MTSS and its alignment with comprehensive school counseling programs is beyond the scope of this text, we briefly highlight the leadership role school counselors often assume that fall into the category of indirect service to students. More information about MTSS can be found in the resources section of this chapter.

The school counseling advisory council, discussed in Chapter 4, is an example of one type of group that school counselors lead to both gather and share data about their programs. In many school districts, administrators assign leadership of other building-based committees to the school counselor as well. For instance, school counselors often encounter school policies that state that Response to Intervention (RTI) and Section 504 teams are the responsibility of the administrator OR the administrator's designee. In many cases, especially at the elementary level where there is only one administrator, principals look to the school counselor to not only participate in but coordinate these groups. Despite guidance from ASCA (2016) and an acknowledgment that the coordination of Individualized Education Plans (IEP) and 504 action plans represent an inappropriate duty for school counselors, the reality is that some school counselors are asked to coordinate these committees.

While some school counselors may feel that leadership on such teams takes valuable time away from essential responsibilities, we encourage you to view participation as a potential opportunity. Data gathered from these committees can be used to both advocate for more direct services for students and gain a deeper understanding of the needs of their school's population. However, as in the case with the author of our social media post, many practitioners share similar frustrations around the amount of time this work demands. As mentioned earlier, keeping detailed time logs is especially important in providing administrators with a clear picture of the school counselor's schedule; in some cases, these logs may in fact assist the counselor with advocating to reduce such administrative duties like coordination.

RTI

Over the past 15 years, many school districts have chosen to organize academic and behavioral support services within an MTSS framework; one of the most prevalent initiatives to help struggling learners within this framework is the RTI approach (Ziomek-Daigle et al., 2016). RTI is designed to provide early identification and support to students with behavior or learning needs. The process begins with universal screening of all students within a general education setting. Learners who struggle are given increasing intensities of research-based interventions. The RTI approach includes ongoing assessment to measure the effectiveness of the interventions and the degree to which the intervention supported growth in student achievement or behavior.

The RTI team is often composed of a variety of educational professionals, all with different expertise in terms of student growth and development. Team members often include professionals such as general education teachers, special education teachers, school counselors, reading/math specialists, learning consultants, and behaviorists. The RTI team may go by a variety of names (e.g., Student Study Team, Student Assistance Team, Intervention & Referral Services, School Based Assistance Team) depending on the state or school district. Simply stated, the RTI team is a group of individuals who come together to brainstorm ways to support students who are struggling. The outcome of these meetings includes the formulation of action plans that outline researched-based interventions completed by a variety of persons who are in contact with the student (e.g., the classroom teacher, bus operator, school counselor). Data is collected, progress is monitored over time, and the team then reconvenes to discuss how students are responding to these interventions.

RTI, a framework that resulted from the No Child Left Behind Act (Klein, 2015), is based on early intervention, evidence-based practices, and accountability (Crockett & Gillespie, 2007; Ziomek-Daigle et al., 2016) and organized in a three-tiered model. Interventions change with each tier based on the intensity needed to support academic or behavior challenges. For instance, with a student who is struggling academically, Tier 1 interventions are often implemented in the classroom by the classroom teacher; Tier 2 interventions may include additional classroom-based services or out-of-classroom remediation from a specialist educator two to three times per week. Tier 3 represents the most intense level of intervention and might include direct instruction via a student support teacher four to five times per week. If students are not responding to intervention by the Tier 3 level, as evidenced in data collected after each intervention, the team may refer students for evaluation via the school's process for special education services. It is important to note that the RTI system can be used across the spectrum of student needs: academic, behavior, social, and emotional. In this model, all students are receiving the targeted support they need as part of an integrated, evidence-based, and data-driven system, and the goal is to meet the needs of all students within the RTI system. Special education referrals and interventions may also occur as part of an RTI. More discussion around school counseling tiered support is found in the "Deliver" section of this text.

Interdisciplinary members on an RTI team often vary by school and student needs, and often, certain team members may transition in and out of meetings. For example, parents and guardians should be a part of this process but may not attend every meeting. As a member of the RTI team, school counselors learn about students and their engagement within the regular education curriculum and, at times, provide school counseling interventions (e.g., test anxiety support) to address specific student needs. School counselors, as team members, may provide consultation and intervention; however, school counselors are sometimes tasked with a leadership role, which consists of setting up meetings, collecting data from a variety of sources, connecting with families, and monitoring the action plans for some students. The administrative tasks (e.g., mailing out notices, coordinating meeting times, ensuring attendance by all members, gathering updates from all participants) typically fall outside of the scope of the role of a school counselor, according to the *ASCA National Model* (ASCA, 2019b), yet school counselors may be asked to take on these responsibilities. As you will hear in the "EduCounselor" section, some of the consultants provide suggestions for negotiating these responsibilities.

Section 504 Team

Section 504 of the Rehabilitation Act of 1973 ensures that students with an identified mental or physical impairment that substantially limits one or more major life activities receive appropriate accommodations. The goal of 504 plans is to prevent any discrimination based on a disability and ensure that students with disabilities have equal access to education. Section 504 plans are administered within the context of *general education.* For example, consider a student with a documented medical diagnosis of diabetes. This student may have to leave class at several points in the school day to go to the nurse's office to test their blood sugar, compromising their ability to access their education, as they are frequently missing class due to the nature of the illness. A 504 plan would provide accommodations for this student to ensure that they have the same access to education as their peers without this disability, such as class notes from the sections of class that they miss and additional time with the teacher to review any missed material. Section 504 plans are legally binding documents that protect the rights of students with disabilities. Each school has a multidisciplinary 504 team composed of educational partners such as general education teachers, special education teachers, school administrators, school nurses, and the student's parent, for example, whose task it is to review documentation of disability, academic records, feedback from teachers to design a plan to support positive student outcomes. This plan should be reviewed at regular intervals to assess if the interventions are working. School counselors can consult with the 504 team within the scope of our professional practice and may provide short-term, goal-focused individual or small-group counseling (ASCA, 2016). In some districts, school counselors will be tasked with coordinating the 504 team or participating as a member. Whether coordinating the 504 team or not, school counselors should familiarize themselves with Section 504 of the Rehabilitation Act of 1973 (and the 2008 amendment) and understand the legal implications for creating and implementing these plans.

IEP

The 504 plans differ from IEPs, which are part of *special education* programs and protect and support students in different ways. A student is eligible for an IEP when they have one or more of the conditions outlined in the Individuals with Disabilities in Education Act (IDEA; i.e., specific learning disability, autism spectrum disorder) and this condition adversely impacts their ability to succeed in school. An IEP details the support and services the child will receive, along with learning goals and strategies to assess the student. The IEP team must include specific members of the school staff, and generally should not include the school counselor. More information regarding the qualifications under IDEA and Section 504 for students with hidden disabilities can be found on the U.S. Department of Education Office of Civil Rights web page provided in the resources section.

School Climate and Culture Team

School counselors recognize the profound impact school climate and culture have on student social, emotional, and academic outcomes. School districts are increasingly required to create committees to examine the nature of the unique school climate and culture and create interventions to improve it. Such teams often include representation from a range of key school and community partners, such as students, parents, school counselors, teachers, administrators, support staff, and community members. Teams use a variety of qualitative (i.e., surveys, bullying reports) and quantitative (focus groups) measures to examine the quality of the school climate. Teams work together to design interventions based on needs identified in the data. It is critical that school climate and culture teams examine the experiences of students from varying cultural backgrounds, compared to the norm, to identify and correct systematic patterns of marginalization or inequity. In New Jersey, members of the School Safety Team must, by law, collect data regularly on school climate, identify patterns of bullying within schools, and design interventions to address the identified issues. An example of this might be advocating for implementation of the Peaceful School Bus program if data suggests that bullying behaviors are occurring regularly on school buses.

Crisis Team

While prevention is at the heart of the counseling profession, crises, such as the loss of a student or teacher, a natural disaster, or a suicide completion, unfortunately, will occur at some point within all school communities. Many members of a school community will likely be emotionally impacted by a crisis. Therefore, it is imperative that clear, comprehensive protocols have been established prior to events such as the ones outlined. For example, a crisis plan contains separate planned interventions for each type of crisis, and each subplan includes the steps each member of the leadership team takes in the event of the crisis. These plans often provide details down to the exact communication that will be sent out to various school and community partners, the nature of community meetings that will be held, and the resources that will be mobilized to support the community. The crisis team is often responsible for the creation of crisis plans, and ongoing training of themselves and others to prepare for future crises. With our training in mental health, human development, and trauma, school counselors are essential members of the crisis team (ASCA, 2019d).

Consultation Corner: Who You Gonna Call?

After bracketing your thoughts and reading the "Informed School Counseling" section, who would you call in and outside of the school building, and what might you ask them to support your decision-making? Take a moment to document these questions. Now that you have considered your questions for consultation, let's see what professional school counselors from around the world have to say about this case.

Consultation #1

My assistant principal is formally in charge of coordination of the paperwork, signatures, filing completed packets with central office, etc., but I am grateful that at my campus it is largely a shared workload. My campus is a similar population, and we recently prioritized our academic RTI process in a major way. We collect and track regular data on evidence-based, small-group interventions to ensure kids are making progress. Every 9 weeks, an RTI committee of our admins, myself, a special education teacher, the diagnostician, and the RTI lead teacher (interventionist) set aside a day to meet with every teacher for a check-in on their tier III RTI students (5–20 minutes, depending on the number of students to be discussed). The committee discusses the students' data, their progress, and the teacher's observations. As a committee, we often decide to refer students for special education evaluations within those meetings. Since we are all together with the data in front of us, we can quickly and easily fill out the necessary paperwork and delegate who needs to collect any further information.

It is a very long and fast-paced day to meet with every teacher. Depending on the size of your campus, it may be better to break it up into two days. We also hire a substitute for the day to travel from class to class and cover the teacher while they sit in on their RTI meeting so they don't give up their conference time. Although it might seem like a lot for the school counselor to give up entire days, I think it saves time in the long run, and everyone is on the same page making strong referrals. This is only possible if you have the RTI systems and infrastructure in place, however.

If you're not able to take coordinating off your plate entirely, this system may help you streamline and delegate some of the responsibilities so you can spend more time on your counseling program. Keep advocating for yourself and your role as counselor!

(Loren Riedel, elementary school counselor, Texas)

Consultation #2

One thing I find extremely helpful when advocating for my use of time is the annual administrative conference at the beginning of the year. I typically come prepared with as many components from the *ASCA National Model* for the current year (student outcome goals, closing-the-gap action plan, small-group and classroom counseling plans, etc.) as I can. I use all these documents to outline how my time will be spent during the year and to educate them about which responsibilities are considered direct services and which are considered indirect services. I'm fortunate to have worked with the same administrative team for 6 years, so these meetings run like clockwork now! During the first few years, their questions would be along the lines of, "Can you do this or that?" Now, they usually ask, "How can we support you with all the work you do?" It has helped me define my role and better support the students and staff at my school!

(Amanda George, elementary school counselor, Virginia)

Consultation #3

Hello there,

My name is AJ, and I'm a school counselor at a Bay Area K–8 where I am also the SST (Student Support Team) coordinator. I agree that this piece of my job can take an inordinate amount of my time, and certain pieces seem very administrative. Moreover, I don't think that most of us got into school counseling because we really loved paperwork! However, I have found it useful to attend these meetings because it keeps me on the front lines in terms of which students are struggling and it gives me time to be able to collaborate with important stakeholders. Something that has helped me to be able to balance the collaborative work of SSTs with direct interventions like lessons or individual counseling is to build a clear schedule at the beginning of the year with times for all the activities I would like to have in my program. When I set up my program at the beginning of the year, I'll build in time for lessons, time for counseling, time for workshops, etc. That way when I need to schedule an SST, I make sure it works around my lessons so that I still get to have face time with the students. I also try to build my schedule so that I group similar activities together. For example, I try to schedule all of our SSTs for Tuesdays and lessons for Wednesdays, or I block off all lunch/recess times for individual/group counseling. Obviously, emergencies or special situations come up that necessitate flexibility (e.g., we will have to schedule a meeting for a different day, or I might have to respond to an emergency and cancel a lesson), but I find that building my schedule in this way up front allows me to be most efficient. When I have all my meetings on just a few days, I can save the rest of the week for other types of interventions and programs.

I've been able to balance my schedule this way, but if this is not possible for you, it might be worthwhile to do a use-of-time assessment. For a couple of weeks, you can track how long you spend on various tasks, and then you can use that data to advocate to your admin for a shift of responsibilities. For example, if you show that you are spending 3 hours a week just scheduling meetings (and with some families I feel like coordinating one meeting can take a full 24 hours!) you could then suggest that perhaps someone like a school secretary could take over just this piece. It seems wasteful to be paying a school counseling professional to schedule a meeting when you could be using that time to teach an entire class lesson on anxiety.

(AJ Holdsambeck, elementary school counselor, California)

Consultation #4

Hi, I'm Jeff, and I too (along with my co-counselor) are the SST coordinators at our school. I am at the high school level, and I think that it is more common in the upper grades for the school counselor to be the coordinator than in lower grades. My elementary school colleagues are not the SST coordinator (a teacher takes that role on) but are a vital part of the process. This works at these levels because the students generally only have one teacher. Because my high school has six-plus teachers and other stakeholders, the role falls de facto to us in the school counseling office.

We have worked on a system, which is not quite where we want it yet, that reduces the total amount of work put on us. The referral process, when followed, requires the requesting teacher(s) to find the bulk of the data to bring to the initial meeting. The SST coordinator is also paid a stipend for the role, though it works out to well under minimum wage when you count up all the hours.

To answer your question, if we were going straight by the *ASCA National Model* expectations, school counselors would not be the SST coordinator (nor the test coordinator). However, in a realistic setting for most school counselors, it may fall into your role. I would suggest that instead of working on the role being removed from you, because you will still likely attend those meetings anyway, work on the process and who the tasks are assigned to. Delegate the different bits to some stakeholders. Many people can do a cume review, a secretary can make phone calls to set up a meeting, a teacher can review grades over the prior grading periods, etc. By doing that, you reduce the overall load and can capture some of your time back to put into other areas of your school counseling program.

(Jeff Ream, high school counselor, California)

 # #EduCounselor Synthesis

Acronyms, acronyms, acronyms! Every state and every district seem to refer to building-based school groups differently. While this may feel overwhelming, the key is to learn about the function of commonly organized building-based groups so that you have an idea of how school counselors traditionally operate within them. You'll learn the lingo when you get hired!

The author of the post, like many other school counselors who have shared their experiences, is struggling with their role as defined by building administrators. According to the *ASCA School Counselor Professional Standards and Competencies* (ASCA, 2019c, p. 2), school counselors "assess and report program results to the school community (B-PA-5), make referrals to appropriate school and community resources (B-SS-4), and collaborate with families, teachers, administrators, and other school staff and education stakeholders for student achievement and success (B-SS-6)." In the informed school counselor section of this chapter, we discussed a few of these building-based teams and their roles in supporting students and educators. As discussed, while not supported as an appropriate school counselor duty by ASCA, coordination of these groups is commonly assigned to school counselors; the perspectives taken around its place in a school counseling program, however, may lead you to dread this part of your day or appreciate its value in learning more about the needs of students in your building. Whether this is the school counseling advisory council or the RTI team discussed in our post, school counselors should be involved with and on the front lines of efforts that support struggling students. Additionally, given that school counselors are trained in process group facilitation skills, their position as leaders in the school creates a strong case for their abilities to help facilitate successful small groups; thus, leadership within these adult groups is one way in which school counselors can indirectly serve students. The parameters around what this role looks like in the context of a comprehensive school counseling program, however, are variable and can and should be discussed in the annual administrative meeting. Our post suggests that the author discussed coordination with their principal but perhaps did not process what coordination could look like in relation to their other duties. As suggested in the "Informed School Counseling" section, bringing time logs into the meeting as an advocacy tool may be especially important in preparing for this conversation.

The author speaks about their professional goals aligning more with direct service interventions like individual and small-group counseling. You may feel similarly as you conceptualize your role in the school. As we have seen with other consultant responses across chapters, school counselors' attitudes toward indirect service (and unfortunately, sometimes inappropriate duties) often make a big difference in the way they use their time and the way they frame future conversations with administrators. If you are given the assigned role of coordinator for a building-based team, we encourage you to consider how this role can help you collect meaningful data, collaborate with a variety of school and community partners, and use your group leadership skills to facilitate dialogue that supports student success. Another way to view an assigned coordination duty is to consider how facilitating these groups may in fact help get you closer to your professional goals by allowing you the information to advocate for the creation of more future (appropriate!) counseling interventions.

As we draw our attention to the consultant responses, look for ways that they advocate for their time and maintain open lines of communication with school and community partners.

It appears that each of the consultants plays a role on their RTI teams. Whether they share the load or coordinate it themselves, they agree that learning to negotiate the amount of time spent is important. AJ talks about the value found in creating a calendar early to help set up the counseling program for the year. In doing so, AJ can fit the building-based team meetings into a schedule that already includes direct counseling interventions. Amanda suggests that the annual administrative conference is an important time to bring time logs and other ASCA model tools and components to building administrators so that they can discuss together the best use of the counselor's time specific to coordination and other administrative duties. Completing the calendar that AJ suggested in preparation for the annual conference, as discussed earlier in this chapter, might be especially useful in helping administrators understand your intentions and program goals for the year.

It is also important to consider that as a coordinator and facilitator, school counselors may have more to say about how information is gathered, when you will meet and the structure of the meetings, and who will perform different responsibilities. This cannot be overstated and may allow you as the counselor more opportunities to fit these meetings and the associated time needed to coordinate them into your schedule. Loren and Jeff outline different processes for their meetings, and we encourage you to research how other school counselors lead or participate on their teams so that you can reference specific strategies from other schools in your advocacy efforts. Jeff suggests that team members each pitch in to gather information and complete paperwork. Creating detailed forms that ask attendees to prepare information ahead of the meeting time might cut down on the counselor's time, encourage member accountability, and help meetings to be more productive overall. An example of forms created for an RTI team at the former elementary school of one of our text authors is available for you to see in the engagement platform.

Identifying the structure of each meeting is often part of leadership and particularly important as far as the counselor's time. Loren outlines one type of structure and presents the option of hiring a rotating substitute teacher to free up educators to attend meetings. One of the authors advocated for a similar structure at their own school to help bring a diversity of voices to the table. It also encourages the group to meet for an extended period on a given day. At Jeff's school, additional money is set aside as a stipend for the coordinators. Financial supports like this or hiring a rotating substitute teacher may not be available to all schools, and creativity in the way meetings are structured is needed. In addition to these suggestions, we have seen coordination occur during teacher preparation periods and outside of traditional school hours, as stipulated by union contracts (often referred to as "extra duty contracts"). Regardless of the type of building-based group and how meetings are structured and scheduled, both Loren and AJ echo the value of having concentrated time spent collaborating with school and community partners and using the information collected to help plan for the future of the school counseling program.

Chapter Summary

School counselors engage in many activities that help to advocate for the implementation of comprehensive school counseling programs. These activities include keeping time logs and sharing these with district administrators. When school counselors fail to track their time, they often have little leverage to advocate against performing noncounseling duties and administrative roles. Building-based team membership represents important opportunities in which school counselors collaborate and consult with school and community partners in the collection of individual student and school-wide climate data; however, the administrative coordination of these teams often results in time-intensive, noncounseling tasks that take the counselor away from direct service. Presenting this information to administrators, in formal meetings such as the annual administrative conference is a form of advocacy. Sharing this information allows for improved communication between school counselors and administrators and the potential for the reassessment of school counseling duties, if needed. Additionally, presenting a multitude of data (e.g., interventions, time logs) provides an opportunity to cocreate weekly and yearly calendars that include appropriate consultation with school and community partners and meaningful direct service with students and families.

Reflective Practitioner Process

School counselors engage in **clinical supervision**, **professional development**, and **self-care** to further develop their knowledge and skills and to help balance professional expectations with personal wellness. All three areas are key to ethical practice and help to mitigate counselor burnout and compassion fatigue (Atici, 2015; Lawson & Myers, 2011; Merriman, 2015; Ohrt et al., 2015).

Clinical Supervision

The *ASCA School Counselor Professional Standards and Competencies* (ASCA, 2019c) directs school counselors to "consult with school counselors and other education and counseling professionals when questions of school counseling practice arise" (B-SS 5., p. 5). As a supervisee, it is important to consider the thoughts, feelings, and experiences that come up for you as you work with students, families, and colleagues and seek consultation on difficult issues. The following are some topics for consideration as you react to this chapter.

- Given the importance of tracking your time as a school counselor, reflect on your current time management skills. What strategies and tools do you use in your personal life that you might apply to your professional role?
- The author of our post discussed her passion for counseling and her vision for conducting direct services with students as a school counselor. Our consultants referenced the fact that most school counselors do not go into the field because they enjoy doing paperwork. The way counselors carry themselves when faced with disappointment (e.g., indirect/administrative services) can often impact how others in the building experience their role. Reflect on the beliefs, vision, and mission statements you considered earlier in this text. How might you reframe your thinking if asked to engage in administrative duties?

- Many school partners look to the school counselor for leadership. As such, your performance and the trust built with others are "graded" not only on your counseling skills but on the way you manage your time, your written and oral expression, and your willingness to collaborate with educational teams. Organizational skills are especially important for school counselors and help your program stay on track. Think about your strengths and areas of growth specific to planning and organizing documents. Is this something that excites you or that you are good at but do not love?
    - Think about your reactions to coordinating the types of days our consultants discussed. What skill sets will you need to address for yourself personally so that, if asked to coordinate, you will feel prepared to take it on willingly and confidently? Many school partners gain or lose faith in school counselors based on their responsiveness, collaboration, and follow-through.

Professional Development

According to the ASCA *Ethical Standards for School Counselors* (ASCA, 2022), professional school counselors engage in professional development and attend trainings to stay current on the trends and issues that impact students (B.3.e). Relative to the contents of this chapter, consider finding professional development on the following topics:

- Technology tools that track time spent on counseling duties
- Training: Section 504; MTSS; state-specific anti-bullying laws and initiatives
- Lesson planning templates and RAMP program examples

#PSCSelf-Care: Everyday Wellness

When designing, managing, and implementing a comprehensive school counseling program, school and community expectations can tax even the most seasoned school counselor. The *ASCA Ethical Standards for School Counselors* (ASCA, 2022) require school counselors to recognize the high levels of stress often associated with the job. Therefore, school counselors recognize that self-care must be a priority to maintain health and overall well-being (see ASCA, 2022, B.3.h).

The Mandala

Commonly used by tantric Buddhists, mandalas are tools used to aid in meditation. Mandalas are visual meditations that can restore harmony, balance, and well-being to mind, body, and spirit. According to blogger Sara Roizen (2020), self-care mandalas "naturally shift our focus inwards." Basic mandalas are circular images that one colors or even creates. Figure 6.1 represents an example of a mandala used to help lessen outside distractions while you narrow your focus on the mandala's form.

According to Art Therapy Blog (n.d.), there are several steps you can take to generate the most benefit from your mandala work:

1. Choose or create a mandala that is appealing to you.
2. Decide which materials you will need (i.e., markers, colored pencil, pens, etc.). There are no "rules" for the types of materials you can choose. Do not limit yourself; choose something you are comfortable using!

FIGURE 6.1 **BASIC MANDALA**

3. Choose a good location in which to work on your mandala. Try to find a place that has limited distractions.
4. Allow your feelings and emotions to inspire the colors and choices you make!
5. Finally, when completed, allow yourself to notice your choice of colors and, if you created your own mandala from scratch, notice any patterns or designs you were led to create. Then, consider writing any notes you feel are important regarding the choices you made.

You do not have to be an artist to use mandalas for self-care and to promote well-being. If creating your own mandala seems like too daunting of a task, do not fear! A simple web search for mandala coloring books yields many options for sale! In the "Helpful Resources" section, we include titles of a few of the mandala coloring book options but encourage you to find one that speaks to your interests.

Spotlight: School Counseling Advocacy

Here we spotlight the work of a school counselor who, after having collected program data, used food to draw attention to the work and the impact of the school counselor—and they did this during National School Counseling Week! National School Counseling Week and donuts, who wouldn't want to hear about the good things happening as a result of the school counseling program? Collecting data on the use of time, the impact of programming, and the ability to devote the necessary time to serving students is all for not when school counselors fail to take opportunities to share this data with school and community partners either in a way similar to our spotlight school counselor shared or during committee meetings!

Diego Castro
@CounselorDiego

We DONUT know what I would do without you! Happy
National School Counseling Week!

Yesterday the staff was informed about our school counseling
program **data** with some donuts and coffee!

#scchat #advocate #nscw

Feb 4

Learning Connections

Both professional school counselors in training and seasoned school counselors
understand the importance of understanding the connections between the concepts
commonly taught in counseling programs and the standards most associated with
school counselor training. Therefore, the following table offers broad connections
between the material and information in this chapter and the Council for Accreditation of Counseling and Related Educational Programs (CACREP, 2016) standards,
the *ASCA School Counselor Professional Standards and Competencies* (ASCA, 2019c),
and the *ASCA Ethical Standards for School Counselors* (ASCA, 2022).

Connections to CACREP Core Curricular Areas

Professional Counseling Orientation and Ethical Practice	Social and Cultural Diversity	Human Growth and Development	Career Development	Counseling and Helping Relationships	Group Counseling and Group Work	Assessment and Testing	Research and Program Evaluation
					X		X

Diego Castro, "Diego Castro Tweet." Copyright © 2022 by Diego Castro. Reprinted with permission.

Connection to Professional Standards

CACREP	ASCA SC Professional Competencies	Ethical Standards: SC
G.2.a. School counselor roles as leaders, advocates, and systems change agents in P-12 schools	B-PF 7. Demonstrate leadership through the development and implementation of a school counseling program.	A.3.b: Collaborate with administration, teachers, staff and stakeholders for equitable school improvement goals.
G.2.d. School counselor roles in school leadership and multidisciplinary teams	B-PF 9. Create systemic change through the implementation of a school counseling program.	A.3.a: Provide students with a culturally responsive school counseling program that promotes academic, career and social/emotional development and equitable opportunity and achievement outcomes for all students.
G.2.f. Competencies to advocate for school counseling roles	B-SS 6. Collaborate with families, teachers, administrators, other school staff and education stakeholders for student achievement and success.	A.3.e: Deliver research-based interventions to help close achievement, attainment, information, attendance, discipline, resource and opportunity gaps.
G.3.b. Design and evaluation of school counseling programs	B-PA 2. Identify gaps in achievement, attendance, discipline, opportunity and resources.	B.2.a. Develop and maintain professional relationships and systems of communication with faculty, staff and administrators to support students.
G.3.c. Core curriculum design, lesson plan development, classroom management strategies, and differentiated instructional strategies	B-PA 6. Use time appropriately according to national recommendations and student/school data.	B.2.b. Design and deliver comprehensive school counseling programs that are integral to the school's academic mission, informed by analysis of student data, based on the ASCA National Model.
	B-PA 7. Establish agreement with the principal and other administrators about the school counseling program.	B.2.c. Advocate for a school counseling program free of nonschool-counseling assignments identified by "The ASCA National Model: A Framework for School Counseling Programs."

Comprehensive School Counseling Assignments

The following section provides activities that allow for your continued growth as a professional school counselor. Both preservice and practicing school counselors may find it helpful to complete these activities. If you are currently in a graduate training program, your professor might assign these as part of your course.

1. **Annual Calendar.** Research practicing school counselors' websites to learn about school-wide initiatives, speakers, and other activities planned throughout the year. Create an "ideal" annual calendar based on your hypothesized mission and vision for your program. Consider including

activities for holidays and other weekly or daily observances (e.g., Anti-bullying Week, Red Ribbon Week, Pride Week, National School Counseling Week)

2. **Time Management Tools Inventory.** Research technology tools school counselors use to log their time (hint: look up Dr. Russell Sabella's work). Write a one- to two-page letter to your administrator (Home School Association/Parent Teacher Association (HSA)/PTA) advocating for why you believe this tool is useful to your practice.

   a. If the tool you have chosen costs money, write a one- to two-page letter to your HSA/PTA asking for grant funding for this tool by discussing how school counselors can use it to share information with the school community (hint: check out practicing school counselors' websites to see how they are using tools in their practices).

3. **Role-Play Annual Administrative Conference.** Create a list of data points you would want to share to advocate for your school counseling program (e.g., time logs, monthly lesson topics). Identify one (hypothetical) challenge you are having with your time. Create a wish list of materials/speakers, etc., you would want to bring to your school next year. After preparing this plan for your annual conference, role-play this annual conference with a colleague. Practice discussing your allocation of time and the vision you have for future interventions.

Helpful Resources
Web-Based Resources

School counselors often do not need to reinvent the wheel when it comes to identifying effective and efficient ways to track their time. Here we provide examples of only a few tools often used by school counselors.

- SCUTA
  - https://counselorapp.com/
- My Hours
  - https://myhours.com/
- Toggl Track
  - https://toggl.com/
- Review of Time Tracking Apps by Miss Daisy's Counseling Corner
  - http://missdaisyscounselingcorner.blogspot.com/2017/04/reviewing-time-tracking-apps.html

- For information regarding eligibility for 504 accommodations for students IDEA: https://www2.ed.gov/about/offices/list/ocr/docs/edlite-FAPE504.html504
  - U.S. Department of Education Office of Civil Rights
- For Individuals with Hidden Disabilities:
  - https://www2.ed.gov/about/offices/list/ocr/docs/hq5269.html

Suggested Readings

- Goodman-Scott, E., Betters-Bubon, J., Olsen, J., & Donohue, P. (2020) *Making MTSS work*. ASCA.
- Hall, J. G. (2015). The school counselor and special education: Aligning training with practice. *The Professional Counselor*, 5(1), 217–224. https://doi.org/10.15241/JGH.5.2.217
- Trolley, B. C., Haas, H. S., & Patti, D. C. (2009) *The school counselor's guide to special education*. Corwin.
- Goodman-Scott, E., Betters-Bubon, J., & Donohue, P. (2019). *The school counselor's guide to multi-tiered systems of support*. Routledge.
- Ciofalo, J. E. *School safety team training*. http://www.hibsterpd.com/wp-content/uploads/2017/03/School-Safety-Team-Training.pdf
- American School Counselor Association (ASCA). (2020). *Tech tools for school counselors*. https://videos.schoolcounselor.org/tech-tools-for-school-counselors
- American School Counselor Association (ASCA). (2019). *Using evidence-based practices in school counseling*. https://videos.schoolcounselor.org/using-evidence-based-practices-in-school-counseling
- Sabella, R. (2021). *Time elapsed analysis & reporting system (T.E.A.R.S.)*. SchoolCounselor.com. https://schoolcounselor.com/tears/
- Davies, J. (2017, April 14). *Reviewing time tracking apps*. Miss Daisy's Counseling Corner. http://missdaisyscounselingcorner.blogspot.com/2017/04/reviewing-time-tracking-apps.html
- U.S. Department of Education. (2020). *Protecting students with disabilities*. Office for Civil Rights. https://www2.ed.gov/about/offices/list/ocr/504faq.html

Mandala Coloring Book Options

- Yakubouskaya, Viktorya. (2019). *Mandala coloring book for adult relaxation: Coloring pages for meditation and happiness*. Independently Published.
- Berry, Sally. (2021). *300 coloring mandala designs for adult relaxation: World's most amazing selection of stress relieving and relaxing mandalas*. Independently Published.

References

Art Therapy Blog. (n.d.). *Healing with mandala art therapy–a multicultural idea worth exploring.* http://www.arttherapyblog.com/art-therapy-ideas/healing-with-mandala-art-a-multi-cultural-idea-worth-exploring/#.YEUbv2hKjIU

American School Counselor Association (ASCA). (2016). *The school counselor and students with disabilities.* https://www.schoolcounselor.org/Standards-Positions/Position-Statements/ASCA-Position-Statements/The-School-Counselor-and-Students-with-Disabilitie

American School Counselor Association (ASCA). (2018). *The school counselor and multitiered system of supports.* https://www.schoolcounselor.org/Standards-Positions/Position-Statements/ASCA-Position-Statements/The-School-Counselor-and-Multitiered-System-of-Sup

American School Counselor Association (ASCA). (2019a). *ASCA national model implementation guide: Manage & assess.*

American School Counselor Association (ASCA). (2019b). *ASCA national model: A framework for school counseling programs.* (4th ed.).

American School Counselor Association (ASCA). (2019c). *ASCA school counselor professional standards & competencies.* https://www.schoolcounselor.org/asca/media/asca/home/SCCompetencies.pdf

American School Counselor Association (ASCA). (2019d). *The school counselor and safe schools and crisis response.* https://www.schoolcounselor.org/Standards-Positions/Position-Statements/ASCA-Position-Statements/The-School-Counselor-and-Safe-Schools-and-Crisis-R

American School Counselor Association (ASCA). (2021). *ASCA student standards: Mindsets and behaviors for student success.* https://www.schoolcounselor.org/asca/media/asca/home/MindsetsBehaviors.pdf

American School Counselor Association (ASCA). (2022). *ASCA ethical standards for school counselors.* https://www.schoolcounselor.org/getmedia/44f30280-ffe8-4b41-9ad8-f15909c3d164/EthicalStandards.pdf

Atici, M. (2015). Professional identity development of counselors-in-training in a school internship program in Turkey. *The Professional Counselor, 5*(1), 137–151. https://doi.org/10.15241/MA.5.1.137

Corey, G. (2016). *Theory & practice of group counseling.* Cengage Learning.

Council for Accreditation of Counseling and Related Educational Programs (CACREP). (2016). *2016 CACREP standards.* http://www.cacrep.org/wp-content/uploads/2017/08/2016-Standards-with-citations.pdf

Crockett, J. B., Gillespie, D. N. (2007). Getting ready for RTI: A principal's guide to response to intervention. *ERS Spectrum, 25*(4), 1–9. https://eric.ed.gov/?id=EJ795670

Erford, B. T. (2011). *Transforming the school counseling profession* (3rd ed.). Pearson Education.

Grothaus, T., Johnsons, K. F., & Edirmanasinghe, N. (2020). *Culturally sustaining school counseling.* American School Counselor Association.

Klein, A. (2020, December 7). *No child left behind: An overview.* Education Week. https://www.edweek.org/policy-politics/no-child-left-behind-an-overview/2015/04

Lawson, G., & Myers, J. E. (2011). Wellness, professional quality of life, and career-sustaining behaviors: What keeps us well? *Journal of Counseling and Development, 89*(2), 163–171. https://doi.org/10.1002/j.1556-6678.2011.tb00074.x

Lewis, B. (2019, October 9). *8 components of a well-written lesson plan*. ThoughtCo. https://www.thoughtco.com/components-of-a-well-written-lesson-plan-2081871

Merriman, J. (2015). Enhancing counselor supervision through compassion fatigue education. *Journal of Counseling and Development, 93*(3), 370–378. https://doi.org/10.1002/jcad.12035

Ohrt, J. H., Prosek, E. A., Ener, E., Lindo, N. (2015). The effects of a group supervision intervention to promote wellness and prevent burnout. *The Journal of Humanistic Counseling, 54*(1), 41–58. https://doi.org/10.1002/j.2161-1939.2015.00063.x

Roizen, S. (2020, October 23). *Easy care mandalas*. Art Therapy Spot. https://arttherapyspot.com/2020/10/23/simple-self-care-mandalas/#:~:text=One%20way%20to%20turn%20self,energy%20into%20the%20mandala%20form

Rutledge, M. L. (2020). Change is gonna come. *ASCA School Counselor*, pp. 10–13. https://www.ascaschoolcounselor-digital.org/ascaschoolcounselor/july_august_2020/MobilePagedArticle.action?articleId=1601128#articleId1601128

Springer, S. I., Moss, L. J., & Schimmel, C. J. (Eds.). (2022). *A school counselor's guide to small groups: Coordination, leadership, and assessment* (2nd ed.). Cognella.

Springer, S. I., & Schimmel, C. J. (2016). Creative strategies to foster pre-service school counselor group leader self-efficacy. *The Journal for Specialists in Group Work, 41*(1), 2–18. https://doi.org/10.1080/01933922.2015.1111486

Ziomek-Daigle, J., Goodman-Scott, E., Cavin, J., & Donohue, P. (2016). Integrating a multitiered system of supports with comprehensive school counseling programs. *The Professional Counselor, 6*(3), 220–232. https://doi.org/10.15241/jzd.6.3.220

PART III

The School Counseling Profession

Deliver

CHAPTER 7

Multi-Tiered Systems of Support—Tier I Interventions

Introduction

As discussed earlier in the text, the multi-tiered systems of support (MTSS) is a framework for organizing and delivering a comprehensive school counseling program (CSCP). MTSS interventions are designed to be both prevention and evidence based, and support student growth across the academic, social, emotional, and behavioral spectrums (Sugai, et al., 2019). Tier 1 provides the foundational support for students, with curriculum and interventions designed to equip students with the attitudes and skills to succeed in school (Mason & Lopez-Perry, 2019). Tier 1 often consists of the core school counseling curriculum, universal mental health screening (UMHS), and positive behavioral support systems. In an MTSS framework, all students receive Tier 1 interventions, often in the form of social/emotional learning, school-wide positive behavior programs, and proactive classroom lessons. Tier 1 supports are typically sufficient in serving the needs of approximately 80% of students. Additionally, school counselors contribute to student appraisal and advisement and crisis response planning that involves educating the whole school on a variety of topics.

#IRLSchoolCounseling

The following is a social media post from one of the many school counseling groups on Facebook. *Caught in the Middle School Counselors* is a Facebook group primarily hosting topics posed by middle school counselors.

I have had a crazy amount of students this year who are unmotivated and do not care about school. Not turning work in … even work that they are doing during class time. How do you all instill "intrinsic motivation" in students who have the attitude that middle school grades don't matter. Very little support or follow-through at home. Teachers and I are at a loss with some of these students. … We are dealing with way more students than normal with this attitude. I swear my entire 6th grade could be on a behavior reward chart! LOL

I would love to hear your thoughts and see any resources you may have in regards to this.

Bracketing Values for Ethical Practice

It is expected that school counselors continuously reflect on their values, beliefs, worldviews, and cultural norms and how each influences the ways in which they choose to take or not take action. As such, it is important to recognize and set aside any preconceived notions, experiences, and biases to help you respond to this scenario in a culturally sustaining and ethically sound manner. Take a moment to reflect on the previous post and then consider the following questions:

- Describe a student who is unmotivated. How do they behave? What are your immediate reactions to them?
- Think about your reactions to certain terminology that people use to describe children and adolescents (e.g., entitled, soft, bratty). Based on your previous experiences, which specific terms evoke reactions or strong emotions for you and why?
- What are your immediate thoughts about the origins of behavioral problems in school?

After considering your answers to these questions, separate out those thoughts and place them on hold while you digest the following foundational information needed to respond to this social media post.

Informed School Counseling

At the onset of the COVID-19 outbreak, school counselors quickly learned that the pandemic, political unrest, and social justice reckoning occurring throughout the world brought about a collective trauma that continues to influence nearly all school and community members' personal and professional experiences each day. Compounded by the increase in mental health needs of our youth over the past decade (Meherali et al., 2021; U.S. Surgeon General's Advisory, 2021), these traumas have left school communities with increased levels of anxiety, depression, and stress layered upon individuals' existing trauma histories. As highlighted in the ASCA position statement on trauma-informed practice (ASCA, 2022a), school counselors recognize the impact of trauma on students, teachers, and all school and community partners and create interventions to support a healthy school climate and culture (ASCA, 2020a). This begins with examining and addressing the needs of the school in its entirety and using the results of these interventions to plan for more individualized support thereafter.

According to ASCA (2019a), school counselors are charged with spending 80% of their time in direct and indirect services (see Chapter 6 for more on this). This time is divided among each of the tiers, depending on student needs. When school counselors face high counselor-to-student ratios, there is tremendous benefit in providing meaningful activities to larger groups of school and community partners (e.g., students, staff members, families). Much of this is done in the name of prevention as part of the Tier 1 MTSS framework. Tier 1 activities offer an effective way to address developmentally universal issues in schools such as the issues created by the pandemic (e.g., low student motivation, heightened anxiety, attendance issues, isolation). Many Tier 1 offerings begin with the universal screening of all students to determine critical needs. Following screening and a review of school data, many Tier 1 activities go on to include social and emotional learning activities, large-group developmental counseling lessons, caregiver and teacher programming, and career appraisal. Tier 1 activities also offer meaningful data with respect to planning future interventions at the Tier 2 and Tier 3 levels. More on Tier 2 and Tier 3 activities in Chapters 8 and 9.

Getting Started With Tier 1: The *ASCA Student Standards*

Ideally, the *ASCA Student Standards: Mindsets & Behaviors for Student Success* (hereafter referred to as the *ASCA Student Standards*) are tied to all school counselor interventions (ASCA, 2021). The *ASCA Student Standards* describe the attitudes, knowledge, skills, and behaviors all students should develop in relation to academic development, career and life planning, and social/emotional development. The *ASCA Student Standards* are critical to the holistic development of all students and should be integrated across students' educational experiences using a variety of delivery modalities. They are the foundational standards for each CSCP. Given that the primary focus of a program should be on delivering the standards, this is most often accomplished by offering Tier 1, classroom lessons based on those standards. And, since the developmental counseling curriculum is often the centerpiece of a school counseling program, it is imperative that its delivery be viewed as a shared responsibility between school counselor, staff, and administration. Therefore, all school partners should be made aware of their roles in ensuring that lessons are tied to the *ASCA Student Standards*, as well as other state-mandated standards delivered across developmental levels. Table 7.1 provides information on the appropriate role of the school counselor in the delivery of the *ASCA Student Standards*, as well as other district and state-mandated standards.

TABLE 7.1. **COUNSELOR ROLE IN DELIVERY OF THE *ASCA STUDENT STANDARDS* AND OTHER STATE-MANDATED STANDARDS**

Create learning objectives based on the *ASCA Student Standards*/state-mandated standards. Align these objectives with district and state academic standards.
Coordinate with stakeholders and assist with delivery of appropriate standards throughout the school curriculum.
Provide teachers with crosswalk tools (Where do standards intersect with classroom curricula?)
Plan school-wide climate and culture-building initiatives at each grade level to reinforce standards/competencies (example – Blue Ribbon Week activities, Red Ribbon Week, positive behavioral interventions and supports (PBIS), expanded school mental health).
Document where and how standards were delivered.

Use of Screening Tools to Identify Tier 1 Needs

While the *ASCA Student Standards* outline the foundational rationale for meaningful learning objectives and interventions, school counselors are charged with using school data to identify the standards that are most appropriate for delivery to students in a particular school. In other words, school counselors must ensure that the standards they intend to cover actually meet the needs of their students. To that end, school counselors may conduct and/or become involved with the delivery of certain assessments like universal screenings or UMHSs. Universal screeners provide school and community partners with a clear picture of student needs. UMHSs began gaining significant traction after the Sandy Hook Elementary tragedy in 2012 and have been further emphasized since the onset of the COVID-19 era (Goodman-Scott, et al., 2019). Universal screeners help identify student mental health and internalizing behaviors such as depression, anxiety, and isolation as well as the severity and levels of interventions needed for individual students. UMHSs are often administered school-wide or in classrooms to assess the presence of mental health and/or other behavioral issues that may interfere with a student's success in and outside of the school building. Common UMHSs assess for exposure to trauma, existence of attention deficit hyperactivity, risk for dropping out of school, or a variety of internalizing and externalizing behaviors. Universal screening for behavioral and mental health issues assists with early identification of students who are at risk or in need of intervention related to these concerns, as research suggests that significantly more students require mental health or behavioral services than currently receive them (Villarreal, 2018). Additionally, UMHS may prevent the need for more intensive special education or therapeutic services in the future for some students (Barrett &

Newman, 2018). It should be noted that the results of UMHSs often determine the level of intervention provided to each student; while all students may receive Tier 1 interventions as a result of this data, students with more significant needs are likely to receive interventions at the Tier 2 and Tier 3 levels as well. It is worth noting that post-COVID-19, the National Association of School Psychologists recommends that schools focus on universal supports as opposed to universal screening given that the number of students identified as having needs according to a screening tool would likely be disproportionately high (NASP, 2020).

It is important for schools to analyze existing data before making the determination to engage in additional screening of students. This prevents a duplication of data and staff effort and expenditure of additional resources, as well as unnecessary demands placed upon students to complete surveys. However, the process of "screening" involves far more than simply choosing a tool to use and administering the assessment to students. Careful planning and preparation are required. The Ohio Positive Behavioral and Interventions Support Network has produced "School-Wide Universal Screening for Behavioral and Mental Health Issues: Implementation Guidance." This is an excellent guide for school districts that are developing a screening process. This document is available in the "Helpful Resources" section of this chapter.

Things to Consider

When schools prioritize students' behavioral health and engage in screening as part of their MTSS programs, it is vital to involve families and students from the initial planning phases. Parents and caregivers are partners in the education process and have primary responsibility for the health and well-being of their children. School counselors inform parents and caregivers about screening tools to be used in their children's schools, as well as educate and inform caregivers regarding how information gleaned from a screening tool will be used. Once informed, caregivers can serve as strong community advocates to support this aspect of a school's screening initiative.

School counselors must also understand that the use of tools developed and tested primarily on an English-speaking population from the dominant culture introduces many important considerations related to the linguistic and cultural appropriateness of the tool and interpretation of results. Schools should be aware that the predictive effectiveness of available tools and their accuracy in screening cross-cultural populations may not have been fully researched. Finally, we offer a word of caution to you as a new professional school counselor: because universal screeners are useful in the identification of student mental health needs, many school districts have begun to use them to identify students believed to be at risk of attempting or completing suicide. This can be a dangerous practice when district policies attempt to negate or quantify the risk of any student identified as at risk by a screener that is specifically used with the intent of screening for suicidality. According to ASCA's position statement on suicide screening tools, "If school counselors are required to use assessments, screenings or any type of instrument to determine the suicide risk, they advocate that they are never required to negate any level of risk of harm, as students may tell school counselors what they believe will get them out from under scrutiny." Additionally, "School counselors also advocate that the school district has a policy whereby parents/guardians are always contacted and notified of anything learned through an investigation of potential suicide, or with any instrument, that will guide parents/guardians in efforts to protect their child" (ASCA, 2020b, p. 83). The ethical mandate provided by ASCA (2022b, A.9.b) is clear: The school counselor should never decide that a "low risk" of suicide as determined by an assessment or screener is a reason to not contact parents or caregivers. School counselors contacting parents and/or caregivers is our primary responsibility in any space where the safety of a student is in question (Stone, 2017).

Finally, while the call for use of UMHS is growing, schools must be ready to provide the services and supports for students who demonstrate needs. The use of a UMHS may reveal levels of student needs that are above and beyond what one school counselor or a team of school counselors can provide. Therefore, it is imperative that screening is conducted with a plan to engage clinical mental health support personnel in mind.

Types of Tier 1 Interventions

School counselors design and implement Tier 1 interventions to meet the developmental needs of all students, using school needs assessment data and the *ASCA Student Standards* to guide our efforts. Tier 1 interventions are developmentally appropriate, preventative, and evidence based. In this section, we review several of the components that comprise Tier 1 school counseling interventions.

Developmental Counseling Lessons

School counselors work with other key educational partners to develop and deliver direct instruction to students, according to the Comprehensive School Counseling Curriculum. Tier 1 lessons support youth in a variety of ways, such as teaching knowledge and skills related to identity development, healthy relationships, tools for academic success, and behavioral expectations and strategies. Developmental counseling lessons are designed to support students learning of the key social, emotional, and academic knowledge and skills necessary for educational success and positive functioning in society. Perhaps the most common Tier 1 intervention is an evidence-based social and emotional learning curriculum (SEL), which occurs most commonly in the classroom or large-group settings.

In addition to SEL curricula, classroom lessons offered by school counselors focus on topics that improve academic performance as well as career exploration and preparation. Classroom lessons might include addressing test-taking anxiety, organizational skills, and activities that discuss job skills and resume writing. In alignment with the *ASCA National Model* (ASCA, 2019a), developmental counseling curricula should be provided across grade levels. It is important to note that state policy or state-specific school counseling models may outline other standards to be delivered. Therefore, it is important for school counselors to be aware of their respective state mandates.

School-Wide Programming

School counselors often create and disseminate thematic monthly programming to increase awareness of various topics that impact student well-being. For example, every October, many school counselors take the lead in their schools to deliver programming during Red Ribbon Week (https://www.redribbon.org/). Red Ribbon Week is devoted to keeping kids drug-free. School counselors also devote time each February to help their schools and students celebrate National School Counseling Week (https://www.schoolcounselor.org/Events-Professional-Development/Events/National-School-Counseling-Week). Reflected in Table 7.2 is a list of other commonly celebrated health and well-being initiates.

TABLE 7.2. COMMON MONTHLY HEALTH AND WELL-BEING INITIATIVES

Month	Celebration
September	Suicide Prevention Awareness Month
October	Bullying Prevention Month
November	Adoption Awareness Month
December	International Day of Persons with Disabilities
January	Black Lives Matter at School Week of Action
February	National School Counseling Week
March	Women's History Month
April	Child Abuse Prevention Month
May	Screen Free Week (TV Turnoff Week)
June	LGBTQ Pride Month

This list is by no means exhaustive, and school counselors are encouraged to use additional resources such as those found in the "Helpful Resources" section of this chapter to develop other school-wide programming that advocates for mental health awareness. In doing so, school counselors support universal conversations across grade levels, which are tied to educators' curricula and developmental school counseling lessons.

Parent Workshops and Programming

At the universal, Tier 1 level, school counselors not only serve the needs of the students but also provide workshops and seminars that assist and support parents/caregivers as they strive to help their children navigate the educational system. School counselors either lead or collaborate with other professionals to offer workshops, seminars, or book clubs on parenting strategies, financial aid, learning about race and racism, academic support, postsecondary options, and career information, just to name a few. Building strong partnerships with parents and other caregivers is critical in supporting students. Healthy relationships are necessary to foster trust in the school system and are the cornerstone of an effective working/therapeutic alliance. As school counselors get to know parents and caregivers within a community, they endeavor to learn about and mobilize the profound wisdom and resources that biological, foster, grandparents, and others can offer.

Teacher Workshops

School counselors can have a tremendous impact on improving teacher/student relationships. For example, school counselors work individually with teachers to provide strategies to support student success or insight into student development and behavioral issues. School counselors also offer workshops to school staff on various topics, such as trauma-informed classroom practices, de-escalation strategies, and best classroom practices for working with students from special populations (e.g., LGBTQI+ youth, youth with mixed immigration status, students of color, students with mental health challenges). School counselors can also spearhead bringing programs like Youth Mental Health First Aid (https://www.mentalhealthfirstaid.org/population-focused-modules/youth/) to their teachers and school community.

Appraisal and Advisement

According to the American School Counselor Association (ASCA), "School counselors recognize that each student possesses unique interests, abilities, and goals, which will lead to various future life and career opportunities. Collaborating with students, families, educational staff and the community, the school counselor works to ensure all students develop an academic and career plan reflecting their interests, abilities and goals and including rigorous, relevant coursework and experiences appropriate for the student" (ASCA, 2017, para. 1). To that end, school counselors offer appraisal and provide advisement to students to help them understand and articulate their abilities, values, and career interests. This two-part process, beginning with an evaluation of their interests and abilities, ideally culminates with advisement that supports the establishment of personal goals and the development of academic and career plans. While certain students need more intensive appraisal and advisement that could require Tier 2 and Tier 3 interventions (e.g., small group, individual, crisis counseling), all students should benefit from Tier 1 interventions based on the *ASCA Student Standards* (ASCA, 2021) and any state-mandated standards for student success.

Practically speaking, appraisal is a process in which school counselors use tests (i.e., standard achievement tests), inventories (i.e., interest inventories), screeners, or other existing data to help students plan their career, academic, or social/emotional goals (ASCA, 2019). An example might include examining a student's math scores over time to glean a sense of the student's math abilities. Advisement is a process that takes place following examination of that student's scores. After reviewing a student's scores, the school counselor engages in a discussion with the student to determine if their postsecondary plans align with their strengths and interests in math. In many states, school counselors work with all students to develop personalized educational plans that students follow as they progress through school. This document often guides students' educational paths as they move toward completion of high school.

Consultation Corner: Who You Gonna Call?

After bracketing your thoughts and reading the "Informed School Counseling" section, who would you call in and outside of the school building, and what might you ask them to support your decision-making? Take a moment to document these questions. Now that you have considered your questions for consultation, let's see what professional school counselors from around the world have to say about the case of the school counselor in the social media post and their struggle with students they describe as unmotivated.

Consultation #1

As an experienced school counselor in working with pre-teens and adolescents, there are inevitable challenges that arise. Working with students who have behaviors of resistance and/or lack of compliance with work completion is surely one of them. In order to address this concern, however, there are several strategies that can be used. I would, first, start a conversation with the students (perhaps at the classroom-wide level) and ask them, "Why is it that you are not doing your work?" This can be a discussion-led needs assessment. From my experience, students are transparent about the reasons when provided the opportunity. From sharing reasons such as "I am bored, "I don't get why we need to learn this/that," to "the work is just too hard," kids can (sometimes) be honest to a fault. However, if they are not so open about verbally sharing, you can conduct an anonymous needs assessment (written or electronic survey). Once the data is collected, you can then support the teacher(s) in implementing interventions that target specific behaviors. Additionally, counselors can work with administration and other teachers on modifying his/her pedological approach, as well as classroom management techniques. It's important for teachers to think about questions such as: Can I incentivize work completion? How can I create a classroom community where students are invested?

I truly believe student successes are a result of teamwork. That team should consist of the student, teacher(s), parent/guardian, school counselor, and administration. A parent workshop can discuss the current concerns and stress the importance of their involvement as a member of their child's team. (In order to ensure it is conducive to a family's work schedule it is best practice to schedule workshops for both during the day and the evening.) I have learned that parents/guardians sometimes expect their child(ren) to become autonomous and responsible at this age. However, when an opportunity for discussion among all stakeholders is possible, change in parent and student attitudes and behaviors can occur.

(Jennifer Smith, elementary school counselor, Pennsylvania)

Consultation #2

Hi, my name is Heather Stalnaker, and I am an elementary school counselor at a large school in West Virginia. I have almost 700 students from pre-K to fifth, and I see this issue a lot. Last year, a large number of my fifth graders were having issues completing a speech that all of them had to do. My fifth-grade team was very frustrated, along with many parents. After several students came to me anxious and nervous I decided to try something a little different. I first sat down and talked with my fifth-grade team (I didn't want to overstep). I realized that the speech was not the only area many of the students were having issues with, but I was only going to focus on the speech. I decided to open our distance learning lab up at 7:30 a.m. 3 days a week for students to come in and work on their speeches. They could research, they could type or they could sit with me or peers and discuss their speech content. I realized that many students just didn't understand the directions and how their perspective was so important in coming up with a topic. Initially, I was really just trying to help alleviate some anxiety, but I ended up learning a lot about my fifth graders. I had about 25 students each morning (my fifth-grade teachers couldn't believe we had so many students attending). At first, I was worried because I am not a tutor, but then I realized that I was helping to meet their academic needs. I also realized I was connecting with them and helping them to find their voice. I feel like this can be done for all types of assignments. Many times, we (teachers and counselors) have to shift our focus away from the idea of lack of motivation. We need to examine what is going on for those students and figure out the reason for the motivation issue—in my experience it usually has to do with deficits, lack of encouragement, the student feels like the teacher doesn't like them so why bother, little to no help at home, etc. So, I would spend a little time assessing their needs: belonging, mastery, independence, and generosity. Once we find out where the deficit is, then we can begin to address that need and restore it. I would also look at your Tier 1, especially if it seems like the majority of sixth graders are exhibiting the same behaviors. Maybe it is the delivery of the Tier 1 programming that needs to be adjusted.

(Heather Stalnaker, elementary school counselor, West Virginia)

Consultation #3

Hello, my name is Dave, and I work at an intermediate school in a suburbs, a few miles away from a major city. This is an issue I hear throughout my day from teachers, and even sometimes from the parents of the students. "So and so—I can't get them to do any work, they don't even try, they don't care." If I had a dollar for every time I heard that I would have my own private island or ski resort.

I think this is a universal issue in any school in today's society—what to do about the unmotivated, disinterested student. No matter what you do—no matter how much you praise, reward, maybe even demand or exhort—what can you do as a staff member to convince the student to try to do better?

But true motivation comes from within and is sustained; it is not developed in someone else, no matter how much convincing we try to do. It is not our efforts to be a strong motivator, but it is shifting our mindset from being someone who is convincing, to someone who is inspiring.

Maybe we need to move away from the constant praise, the pep talks, the bribing. Maybe we need to try to get the student to be self-reliant on seeing the rewards of their efforts. In turn, if they feel good about themselves, maybe they will give you more. You still look for any improvement, no matter how small, by only looking for the quality of their work. Instead of praising them for their work, you make an observation about their work. Maybe you give honest feedback about what you observe and make statements like "that is good work," "that is a well-written answer," or " your summary is right on the money."

It is important to be honest, as praise just for the sake of it can seem ingenuine. Maybe just state your observation, and move on. With this very direct approach, maybe something will begin to stir in that student; maybe they will start to feel a sense of pride. Maybe when you truthfully point out quality work, you can spark the student's dormant motivation and "start their engines."

So, I am suggesting when we are struggling to motivate disinterested students, instead of focusing on the student, we focus on their work. I know this is not a specific strategy, as what I am suggesting is a change in our mindset. As maybe this is a long-term approach that brings out the effort in the disinterested student by promoting their creativity and quietly promotes the inner satisfaction of a job well done.

(David Davenport, middle school counselor, New Jersey)

Consultation #4

In my school counseling experience, one of the best ways to instill intrinsic motivation is through career exploration. Once students know what their interests are and how they connect to their future careers, it helps make school relevant. One of the ways that I incorporate career exploration as a school counselor is through a college and career week. During this week, I incorporate a number of activities such as a college fair, a career speaker panel, and have students take a career exploration survey. The website that I use for the career exploration survey is cacareerzone.org, and the survey is called "Interest Profiler."

The second way that I have found helpful to instill intrinsic motivation is through motivational interviewing. The ASCA has a recorded webinar dedicated to this topic. The webinar is called *Enhance Intrinsic Motivation to Change and Achieve*, and it covers how to elicit change talk, listening style used to motivate students to change, open-ended questions to use, and how to summarize change talk.

(Jessica Sandoval, middle school counselor, California)

Consultation #5

School for many students can be a safety net. It can be a means of escape from an otherwise stressful environment. For students in these types of situations where the plan for the day is to make it to the end of the day, it's hard to future plan a month and sometimes even a week ahead of the moment they are in. For students who may not be dealing with overt trauma, we can look to the era we are in. This is a time of very little delayed gratification. We no longer have to listen to the radio all day to catch our favorite song. We no longer have to wait for Blockbuster to get a movie back so we can rent it. We can create a thought and then almost instantaneously have an audience respond to it. Considering both these situations, one of grit and the other of under stimulation, we see school as a long-term investment for which immediate gratification is nonexistent. It is difficult for students to correlate school with success given the range of time in between. To aid in this conundrum, because a counselor trying to take on the role of discovering intrinsic motivation for every individual student would quickly induce burnout, look to the community around the school. Look to those who the students interact with outside the classroom, to be an aid within the classroom. Look to the papi stores that feed the students, the barbershops/beauty salons that cut and style their hair, the recreational facilities where they play, the churches where they worship, the older teenagers/young adults who they interact with, the neighbors who help raise them like family, and even look to the homeless that they pass every day. For in all of these entities, we see yet another person who is invested in that child's future, even though they may not realize they are. Maybe they teach the English lesson for the English teacher one class, or talk about how they have arrived at running a business, or the mistakes they made, or maybe they talk about how painful it is for them to watch societies attempt to ignore them. Now as a counselor, you are beginning to touch on the intrinsic motivation of a number of students through a number of entities. They get to see success and struggle. They get to hear paths to success. The link between school and success becomes more tangible. After which, the counselor can process how it felt to have someone so close to them come in and be a face in the school. Build on this. Just because the school can be a safety net does not mean that we have to keep a net around the school.

(Franklin Hinton, high school counselor, Pennsylvania)

Consultation #6

Well, that is a loaded question, LOL! This is a tough one and definitely something I struggle with too! In middle school, especially sixth grade, they don't have graduation requirements, and being ready for college can seem so far away to the young brain BUT during this time they really, really, REALLY want to be interacting with their peers so that is always a carrot. You will always have those kids who do what they are supposed to because they feel they are supposed to, because they want to, or because their family has instilled it in them, and you also have those who will start because of a relationship with a caring adult. I feel I see this more in our ninth graders coming in with this attitude, and by spring, they have either realized grades do matter or they fall into "acting" like they do not care because they do not feel supported enough or equipped with the tools necessary to move forward in our school systems. One program that was put into place for cultivating the relationship between our ninth graders and teachers was the BARR Program. BARR stands for Building Assets and Reducing Risks and is a model used to build intentional, positive relationships between students and teachers. BARR teachers use "real-time student data to drive instructional change and identify nonacademic supports when needed" (About BARR, 2018, https://barrcenter.org/real-results/). I think that one of the biggest resources is the relationship and feeling part of the community. Discipline That Restores is also a fantastic resource for this (http://restorativejusticediscipline.com/)! With DTR, you can work to increase cooperation, mutual respect, and responsibility among students and staff. DTR can also help empower your students to feel that they have choices and don't need to act out, as that is a huge part of instilling intrinsic motivation. The great thing about DTR is that it can be done school-wide or in a classroom! Finally, focus groups or counselor-generated surveys can be super informative in what is actually going on with the sixth-grade class. If the behavior is more prevalent this year, why? Take a look at discipline data? What are the referrals for? Put this data together, present it to a focus group of sixth-grade students and hear from the voices themselves. Or use the data to drive a lesson being added to next year's core curriculum!

(Kristina Gurganus, high school counselor, California)

#EduCounselor Synthesis

This chapter focuses on the delivery of counseling interventions at the Tier 1 level. Ensuring that school counselors implement school-wide interventions and assessments are important primarily because this sets the stage for the school counselor to move from what Young (2020) refers to as "doer to leader," thus allowing the school counselor to transition from a place of primarily someone who responds to crisis to a leader who proactively plans and delivers a school counseling program (Goodman-Scott et al., 2020).

In our initial post, the author shares concerns that they, along with teacher colleagues, have about the motivation of many of their students. While we are unsure about all the data points collected by our author, we do know that fostering intrinsic motivation seems to be an important goal. Fostering motivation is particularly relevant in the aftermath of the COVID-19 pandemic, where children (kindergarten to adult graduate students), especially those identifying within historically marginalized groups, have suffered from a lack of focus and motivation at higher rates than ever before (U.S. Department of Education, 2021). As such, supporting the "unmotivated" child has been and continues to be an all too familiar challenge for many school counselors as reflected in our consultants' validation of this topic. In this case, our author describes lack of motivation as students not turning in assignments and an overall apathy when it comes to completing work itself. Additionally, it seems as though our social media poster and teachers at the school wish to have support from families but have not been able to connect with them around this issue. Several targeted Tier 1 interventions can begin to address these concerns.

The desire to foster *intrinsic* motivation, as opposed to relying on extrinsic rewards exclusively, is important and is something that many educators and caregivers often think about (Froiland et al., 2012; Rowell & Hong, 2013; Springer, 2014). The question is, how do we address motivation in a world, as our consultant Franklin describes, that is filled with many young students in need of instant gratification? There is no easy answer to this, and aside from instant gratification, there are likely many other reasons for students' lack of motivation. It is always important for school counselors to ask themselves, "what is the function of this behavior?" Many of our consultants call on us to do just this; consider a deeper meaning behind the lack of motivation and support our educators and families in doing the same. In this instance, school counselors are well-served to recall information learned in counseling theory courses and possibly draw on the ideas learned from Adler (2013) and his mistaken goals or the general Adlerian idea that all behavior has a purpose.

It is also important to note that historically, school employees may, often unknowingly, categorize certain students as unmotivated or lazy more frequently than others based on individual bias (Gillen-O'Neel et al., 2011; McMahon et al., 2014). Put simply, here is a place where the diligent school counselor looks to intervene to support the school community while simultaneously acknowledging the possibility of implicit bias as a factor in how students are perceived. Both objectives can be achieved simultaneously by creating school-wide assessments and interventions and collecting data to examine any patterns that might exist around certain populations of students and the categorization of their needs. The truth is, addressing motivation is multifaceted and requires not only school-wide and targeted assessment and intervention for students but also more training and awareness for educators.

Many of our consultants recommended using school-wide activities and programs to address issues surrounding motivation. This is consistent with Tier 1 supports and a good way to address student behavior on a larger level. To plan for these activities, it is important that school counselors understand the pervasiveness of the issue. Jennifer, Heather, and Kristina discuss the value of learning about students' experiences through classroom discussions, surveys, and other assessments and then looking at the data to make decisions. Jennifer suggests that school counselors initiate classroom discussions, and if more insight is needed, school counselors use an anonymous survey. Eliciting student voices, according to Heather, helps students feel heard and seen and supports counselors in understanding the concerns more fully. Certain universal screening tools (e.g., BERS-2) might be used to take the pulse of the school community. Heather also suggests that spending time with educators to learn more about their experiences with students can help teachers feel heard as well. Once school counselors have a clearer picture of students' needs, this information can be shared with school leaders at the annual administrative conference and/or with community partners through the school counseling advisory council. Here, school counselors can advocate for more funding and training to support future interventions.

Upon examining data from students, educators, and families, school counselors look to target various community and school groups individually. Jennifer and Kristina specifically discuss the value of building community to address motivation. Kristina offers two specific programs (BARR and DTR) that help empower student voices; there are several others that target PBIS (e.g., Second Step®) and/ or encourage children to build community through the expression of kindness and good deeds (e.g., see Bucket Filling in "Helpful Resources").

Changing the intent from *convincing* students to *inspiring* students, as Dave suggests, is another interesting perspective to help foster motivation and connects nicely with Franklin's suggestion to bring in community members to share their stories with students. Hearing inspirational stories and focusing on process and effort, rather than content and outcome exclusively can encourage students to develop more intrinsic motivation (Springer, 2014). In addition to Dave's suggested feedback to students, other examples might include the following:

- "I noticed that you communicated directly and kindly with your group to solve that difficult problem."
- "The character details that you added to your story really helped it to come to life for me."
- "All of the time you spent proofreading helped your story to be especially interesting and easy to read."

Providing students with feedback that demonstrates small successes and evidence of our awareness of their efforts is an important way in which we help to motivate students. When school counselors provide this type of feedback publicly, during developmental counseling lessons or grade level events, they also model this language for other educators (and students!). Initiating complementary family programming helps to further this language. Thus, implementing school-wide and community programming affords many opportunities to promote shared language at home and across the school.

Chapter Summary

School counselors working from an MTSS framework recognize the importance of providing interventions to most of their students at the Tier 1 level. That is, interventions that are offered to the whole school and sufficient to meet the needs of 80% of students. Ideally, those interventions are tied to the *ASCA Student Standards* (ASCA, 2021). Often, the use of universal screeners assists school counselors in identifying the nature of needed Tier 1 interventions. Common Tier 1 interventions include classroom lessons, presentations to parents/caregivers and teachers, and activities around appraisal and advisement of students, especially as these activities relate to course selection, career inventories, and planning for the future. These initiatives provide important foundational support and offer meaningful opportunities to meet the needs of all students as well as school and community partners.

Reflective Practitioner Process

School counselors engage in **clinical supervision**, **professional development**, and **self-care** to further develop their knowledge and skills and to help balance professional expectations with personal wellness. All three areas are key to ethical practice and help to mitigate counselor burnout and compassion fatigue (Atici, 2015; Lawson & Myers, 2011; Merriman, 2015; Ohrt et al., 2015).

Clinical Supervision

The *ASCA School Counselor Professional Standards & Competencies* (2019) direct school counselors to "consult with school counselors and other education and counseling professionals when questions of school counseling practice arise" (B-SS 5., p. 5). As a supervisee, it is important to consider the thoughts, feelings, and experiences that come up for you as you work with students, families, and colleagues and seek consultation on difficult issues. The following are some topics for consideration as you react to this chapter.

- What strategies might you use to support teachers with students who are exhibiting disinterest in the classroom?
- How do you begin to think about student behavior from a theoretical framework? What counseling/developmental theory best fits the way you think about child and adolescent behavior?

- What is the potential impact of trauma on student levels of motivation? Consider your own levels of motivation during times of crisis or after some traumatic life event.

Professional Development

According to the *ASCA Ethical Standards for School Counselors* (ASCA, 2022b), professional school counselors engage in professional development and attend trainings in an effort to stay current on the trends and issues that impact students (B.3.e). Many school counselors, novice and seasoned alike, find that there is room for gaining knowledge on using screeners to assess students' needs as well as using the data gleaned from screeners to select appropriate curricula and interventions. Additionally, since many novice school counselors do not have teaching experience, classroom management can be a challenge. Consider finding professional development opportunities on the following topics:

- Validity and Reliability of Universal Screeners
- Ethical Use of Universal Screeners
- Evidence-Based Social Emotional Learning Curricula
- Classroom Management and Instructional Techniques

#PSCSelfCare: Everyday Wellness

When designing, managing, and implementing a CSCP, school and community expectations can tax even the most seasoned school counselor. The *ASCA Ethical Standards for School Counselors* (2022b) require school counselors to recognize the high levels of stress often associated with the job. Therefore, school counselors recognize that self-care must be a priority to maintain health and overall well-being (see ASCA, 2022, B.3.h).

Daily Self-Compassion

Given that we have discussed the use of assessment in this chapter to drive decision-making regarding Tier 1 interventions, it seemed appropriate to discuss assessment regarding your self-care plan. Dr. Kristin Neff is an associate professor of educational psychology and one of the most recognized researchers on self-compassion. Dr. Neff's website (https://self-compassion.org/) provides a number of resources around self-compassion, including a self-assessment. As your self-care activity for this chapter, we encourage you to take the self-assessment (https://self-compassion.org/test-how-self-compassionate-you-are/) and use it as an opportunity to reflect on how you speak to yourself, especially in high-stress moments. This is especially important for school counselors, as this career often comes with high demands and, at times, high stress. In these moments, one of the ways we can work through challenges, our own and others, is to exercise self-compassion. After taking the assessment, spend time working through these exercises and practices and journal your experiences with them (https://self-compassion.org/category/exercises/#guided-meditations). Then go a step further and consider how you might use these to support your school faculty and staff!

Spotlight: School Counseling Advocacy

Here we highlight a practicing school counselor who provides a targeted Tier 1 intervention/program aimed at acknowledging students and staff when they "make a difference" by showing kindness and being inclusive. This is a type of Tier 1 intervention that might be associated with a PBIS program.

Molly Summers

Started something AMAZING at my school inspired by Joe Beckman! Students, Teachers, and staff nominate each other when they notice someone being a Difference Maker. Being a Difference Maker is all about being kind and inclusive. Each morning myself and a student read a nomination slip for our entire school to hear. Every month, I chose a student and staff to be recognized as the Difference Maker of the month! Last month, our school filled out 170 Difference Maker nomination slips.

Image 7.1

Learning Connections

Both professional school counselors in training and seasoned school counselors understand the importance of understanding the connections between the concepts commonly taught in counseling programs and the standards most associated with school counselor training. Therefore, the following table offers broad connections between the material and information in this chapter and the Council for Accreditation of Counseling and Related Educational Programs (CACREP, 2016) standards, The *ASCA School Counselor Professional Standards and Competencies* (ASCA, 2019b), and the *ASCA Ethical Standards for School Counselors* (ASCA, 2022).

Connections to CACREP Core Curricular Areas

Professional Counseling Orientation and Ethical Practice	Social and Cultural Diversity	Human Growth and Development	Career Development	Counseling and Helping Relationships	Group Counseling and Group Work	Assessment and Testing	Research and Program Evaluation
X	X		X	X		X	

Connection to Professional Standards

CACREP	ASCA SC Professional Competencies	Ethical Standards: SC
G.2.a. School counselor roles as leaders, advocates, and systems change agents in P–12 schools	B-SS 1. Design and implement instruction aligned to ASCA Mindsets & Behaviors for Student Success in large-group, classroom, small-group and individual settings.	A.9.b . Recognize the level of suicide risk (e.g., low, medium, high) is difficult to accurately quantify. If required to use a risk assessment, it must be completed with the realization that it is an information-gathering tool and only one element in the risk-assessment process. When reporting risk-assessment results to parents/guardians, school counselors do not negate the risk of students' potential harm to self even if the assessment reveals a low risk, as students may minimize risk to avoid further scrutiny and/or parental/guardian notification. The purpose of reporting any risk-assessment results to parents/guardians is to underscore the need for parents/guardians to act, not to report a judgment of risk.
G.2.c School counselor roles in relation to college and career readiness	B-SS 2. Provide appraisal and advisement in large-group, classroom, small group and individual settings.	A.4.b: Provide and advocate for all students' pre-K–postsecondary career awareness, exploration, and postsecondary planning and decision-making to support students' right to choose from the wide array of career and postsecondary options, including but not limited to college/university, career and technical school, military or workforce.
G.2.g Characteristics, risk factors, and warning signs of students at risk for mental health and behavioral disorders	B-SS 6. Collaborate with families, teachers, administrators, other school staff and education stakeholders for student achievement and success.	A.4.d: Provide opportunities for all students to develop a positive attitude toward learning, effective learning strategies, self management and social skills and an understanding that lifelong learning is part of long-term career success.
G.2.n Legal and ethical considerations specific to school counseling		

CACREP	ASCA SC Professional Competencies	Ethical Standards: SC
G.3.c Core curriculum design, lesson plan development, classroom management strategies, and differentiated instructional strategies		
G.3.e Use of developmentally appropriate career counseling interventions and assessments		

Comprehensive School Counseling Assignments

The following section provides activities that allow for your continued growth as a professional school counselor. Both preservice and practicing school counselors will find it helpful to complete these activities. If you are currently in a graduate training program, your professor might assign these as part of your course. Many of these activities are available with additional details on the active learning platform.

- Prepare, plan, and deliver a classroom lesson for your peers based on the *ASCA Student Standards.*
- Observe a practicing school counselor deliver Tier 1 interventions in their schools. Write a reflection on what you learned from watching. This may include the content of the lesson and behavior management strategies.
- Create an annotated bibliography with a list of books that could be used to create a parent, foster parent, grandparent, or other caregiver book club initiative.
- Create an agenda for a professional development day focused on wellness for educators to support self-care and connectedness with the school counseling program.

Helpful Resources
Web-Based Resources

- 2021–2022 National Educational and Health Awareness Dates:
  - https://www.schoolcounselor.org/getmedia/dd5fdee1-e207-4178-ab42-0c8cfaae9f31/awareness-calendar.pdf?sso=

- PBIS
  - https://www.pbis.org/
- Second Step (SEL curriculum)
  - https://www.secondstep.org/
- SAMHSA Guide to Screening
  - https://www.samhsa.gov/sites/default/files/ready_set_go_review_mh_screening_in_schools_508.pdf
- Best Practices in Social, Emotional, and Behavioral Screening
  - https://www.google.com/url?sa=t&source=web&rct=-j&url=https://smhcollaborative.org/wp-content/uploads/2019/11/universalscreening.pdf&ved=2ahUKEwi3w6Wz9tzvAhUOCM0KHf_HAvIQFjALegQIDBAC&usg=AOvVaw03iDA4xVWATZkxAMpyRq8u
- Georgia Universal Screening Tools
  - https://www.gadoe.org/sites/SearchCenter/Pages/results.aspx?k=universal%20screening

Suggested Readings

- Goodman-Scott, E., Betters-Bubon, J., Olsen, J., & Donohue, P. (2020). *Making MTSS work.* American School Counselor Association.
- Springer, S. I., Mason, E. C. M, Moss, L. J., Pugliese, A., & Colucci, J. (2020). An intervention to support elementary school faculty with meeting the needs of transgender and gender non-conforming students. *Journal of Child and Adolescent Counseling, 6*(3), 181–199. https://doi.org/10.1080/23727810.2019.1689765
- Children's books for potential use at the Tier 1 level:
  - McCloud, C. (2015). *Have you filled a bucket today?: A guide to daily happiness for kids.* Bucket Fillers.
  - Cook, J. (2012). *Wilma Jean the worry machine.* National Center for Youth Issues.
  - Cherry, M. A. (2019). *Hair love.* Penguin.
  - Pett, M., & Rubinstein, G. (2011). *The girl who never made mistakes.* Sourcebooks.
  - Jordan, D., & Jordan, R. M. (2003). *Salt in his shoes.* Simon and Schuster.

References

Adler, A. (2013). *Understanding human nature (psychology revivals).* Routledge.

American School Counselor Association (ASCA). (2017). *The school counselor and individual student planning for postsecondary preparation.* https://www.schoolcounselor.org/Standards-Positions/Position-Statements/ASCA-Position-Statements/The-School-Counselor-and-Individual-Student-Planni

American School Counselor Association (ASCA). (2019a). *ASCA national model: A framework for school counseling programs* (4th ed.).

American School Counselor Association (ASCA). (2019b). *ASCA school counselor professional standards & competencies.* https://www.schoolcounselor.org/asca/media/asca/home/SCCompetencies.pdf

American School Counselor Association (ASCA). (2020a). *The school counselor and student mental health.* https://www.schoolcounselor.org/Standards-Positions/Position-Statements/ASCA-Position-Statements/The-School-Counselor-and-Student-Mental-Health

American School Counselor Association (ASCA). (2020b). *The school counselor and suicide risk assessment.* https://www.schoolcounselor.org/Standards-Positions/Position-Statements/ASCA-Position-Statements/The-School-Counselor-and-Suicide-Risk-Assessment

American School Counselor Association (ASCA). (2021). *ASCA student standards: Mindsets & behaviors for student success.* https://www.schoolcounselor.org/getmedia/7428a787-a452-4abb-afec-d78ec77870cd/Mindsets-Behaviors.pdf

American School Counselor Association (ASCA). (2022a). *The school counselor and trauma-informed practice.* https://www.schoolcounselor.org/Standards-Positions/Position-Statements/ASCA-Position-Statements/The-School-Counselor-and-Trauma-Informed-Practice

American School Counselor Association (ASCA). (2022b). *ASCA ethical standards for school counselors.* https://www.schoolcounselor.org/getmedia/44f30280-ffe8-4b41-9ad8-f15909c3d164/EthicalStandards.pdf

Atici, M. (2015). Professional identity development of counselors-in-training in a school internship program in Turkey. *The Professional Counselor, 5*(1), 137–151. https://doi.org/10.15241/MA.5.1.137

Barrett, C. A., & Newman, D. S. (2018). Examining MTSS implementation across systems for SLD identification: A case study. *School Psychology Forum, 12*(1), 30–43. https://www.nasponline.org/publications/periodicals/spf/volume-12/volume-12-issue-1-(spring-2018)/examining-mtss-implementation-across-systems-for-sld-identification-a-case-study

Froiland, J. M., Oros, E., Smith, L., & Hirchert, T. (2012). Intrinsic motivation to learn: The nexus between psychological health and academic success. *Contemporary School Psychology, 16*(1), 91–100. https://doi.org/10.1007/BF03340978

Gillen-O'Neel, C., Ruble, D. N., & Fuligni, A. J. (2011). Ethnic stigma, academic anxiety, and intrinsic motivation in middle childhood. *Child Development, 82*(5), 1470–1485. https://doi.org/10.1111/j.1467-8624.2011.01621.x

Goodman-Scott, E., Donahue, P., & Betters-Bubon, J. (2019). The case for universal mental health screening in schools. *Counseling Today.* https://ct.counseling.org/2019/09/the-case-for-universal-mental-health-screening-in-schools/

Lawson, G., & Myers, J. E. (2011). Wellness, professional quality of life, and career-sustaining behaviors: What keeps us well? *Journal of Counseling and Development, 89*(2), 163–171. https://doi.org/10.1002/j.1556-6678.2011.tb00074.x

Mason, E., & Lopez-Perry, C. (2019). Tier 1: School counseling core curriculum and classroom management for every student. In E. Goodman-Scott, J. Betters-Bubon, & P. Donohue (Eds.), *A School Counselor's Guide to Multi-tiered Systems of Support.* Routledge.

McMahon, H. G., Mason, E. C. M., Daluga-Guenther, N., & Ruiz, A. (2014). An ecological model of professional school counseling. *Journal of Counseling and Development, 92*(4), 459–471. https://doi.org/10.1002/j.1556-6676.2014.00172.x

Meherali, S., Punjani, N., Louie-Poon, S., Abdul, R. K., Das, J. K., Salam, R.A., & Lassi, Z.S. (2021). Mental health of children and adolescents amidst COVID-19 and past pandemics: A rapid systematic review. *International Journal of Environmental Research and Public Health, 18*(7), 3432. https://doi.org/10.3390/ijerph18073432

Merriman, J. (2015). Enhancing counselor supervision through compassion fatigue education. *Journal of Counseling and Development, 93*(3), 370–378. https://doi.org/10.1002/jcad.12035

National Association of School Psychologists. (NASP). (2020). *Providing effective social–emotional and behavioral supports after COVID-19 closures: Universal screening and Tier 1 interventions* [Handout].

Ohrt, J. H., Prosek, E. A., Ener, E., & Lindo, N. (2015). The effects of a group supervision intervention to promote wellness and prevent burnout. *The Journal of Humanistic Counseling, 54*(1), 41–58. https://doi.org/10.1002/j.2161-1939.2015.00063.x

Rowell, L., & Hong, E. (2013). Academic motivation: Concepts, strategies, and counseling approaches. *Professional School Counseling, 16*(3), 158–171. https://doi.org/10.1177/2156759X1701600301

Springer, S. (2014). Get fit for life: Elementary school group counseling with a twist. *Journal of School Counseling, 12*(17). http://www.jsc.montana.edu/articles/v12n17.pdf

Stone, C. (2017). Appropriate vs. inappropriate duties. *ASCA School Counselor.* https://www.schoolcounselor.org/magazine/blogs/september-october-2017/appropriate-vs-inappropriate-duties

Sugai, G., La Salle, T., Everett, S., & Feinberg, A. B. (2019). Multi-tiered systems of support: The what, why, and how for school counselors. In E. Goodman-Scott, J. Betters-Bubon, & P. Donohue (Eds.), *A School Counselor's Guide to Multi-tiered Systems of Support.* Routledge.

U.S. Department of Education. (2021). *Education in a pandemic: The disparate impacts of COVID-19 on America's students.* https://www2.ed.gov/about/offices/list/ocr/docs/20210608-impacts-of-covid19.pdf

U.S. Surgeon General's Advisory. (2021). *Protecting youth mental health.* https://www.hhs.gov/sites/default/files/surgeon-general-youth-mental-health-advisory.pdf

Villarreal, V. (2018). Mental health referrals: A survey of practicing school psychologists. *School Psychology Forum, 12*(2), 66–77. https://www.nasponline.org/publications/periodicals/spf/volume-12/volume-12-issue-2-(summer-2018)/mental-health-referrals-a-survey-of-practicing-school-psychologists

Young, A. (2020). *From doer to leader.* American School Counselor Association (ASCA). https://www.schoolcounselor.org/newsletters/march-2020/from-doer-to-leader?st=NM

Credit

CHAPTER 8

Multi-Tiered Systems of Support—Tier 2 Interventions

LEARNING OBJECTIVES

#EduCounselors can

- recognize Tier 2 interventions according to the multi-tiered systems of support framework,
- identify the utility and types of small groups led in schools, and
- describe the school counselor's role in providing services to students through intervention teams.

Introduction

Working from a multi-tiered systems framework, school counselors recognize that some students need supports that go beyond whole class/whole school interventions. Within the Multi-Tiered Systems of Support (MTSS) team, roughly 10%–20% of students require Tier 2 interventions in addition to Tier 1 services. School counselors must develop systematic methods of identifying students in need of Tier 2 academic and behavioral support and work with key school and community partners to select evidence-based strategies to meet students' needs. Tier 2 supports may include small-group counseling, mentoring programs, behavioral contracts, and programs that work to foster the school-to-home partnership.

#IRLSchoolCounseling

The following is a social media post from one of the many school counseling groups on Facebook. *Caught in the Middle School Counselors* is a Facebook group primarily hosting topics posed by middle school counselors.

Shelby Beach
March 8, 2019

Help me understand small groups. The way I understand it is that we have small groups, such as a life skills or friendship group, offered to ALL students at the universal level. However we also offer intervention groups at Tier 2 from MTSS behavior referrals that target kids with specific needs, like social skills. Do I have this all wrong? Do you use research based curriculum in all of your lesson plans for groups and interventions?

Bracketing Values for Ethical Practice

It is expected that school counselors continuously reflect on their values, beliefs, worldviews, and cultural norms and how each influences the ways in which they choose to take or not take action. As such, it is important to recognize and set aside any preconceived notions, experiences, and biases to help you respond to this scenario in a culturally sustaining and ethically sound manner. Take a moment to reflect on the previous post and then consider the following questions:

- Think about a time that you started something new and there was a large learning curve. How did you respond when faced with new or conflicting information during this experience? What personal values or previous experiences may influence how you approach the integration of new knowledge?
- What are your preferences between offering a Tier 1 prevention group versus a Tier 2 intervention group for children? Why might you prefer one over the other?
- What reactions do you have to a predesigned small-group curriculum?

Informed School Counseling

When school counselors examine multiple existing data points and identify students with needs beyond those that can be met at the Tier 1 level, it may be time to strategically consider interventions that target specific student concerns. Tier 2 interventions address student concerns that cannot be met in a more traditional classroom setting. Tier 2 interventions should be selected based on their evidence-based status and their ability to reach a diverse population of participants (Goodman-Scott et al., 2020). Examples of Tier 2 interventions include, but certainly are not limited to, targeted large groups, check-in/check-out, mentoring, and small-group counseling. Additionally, at the Tier 2 level, school counselors may provide support to classroom teachers implementing behavioral contracts in classrooms, as well as identify and implement programs that help foster the school-to-home partnership. In the following sections, we focus on what we regard as the most common Tier 2 interventions led by school counselors.

School Counselor Role on Intervention Teams

Each school has a multidisciplinary team responsible for the management of students who need Tier 2 services. This might be the Intervention and Referral Services team, the Response to Intervention team, or the MTSS team. These teams are discussed in greater detail in Chapter 6 of the text. Whatever the name, the Tier 2 team is responsible to identify and suggest interventions to students who need more support than only Tier 1 interventions. Typically, Tier 2 teams are composed of an administrator, school counselor, teacher, special education teacher, and other educational professionals (such as behaviorist and reading specialist).

Students may be identified for Tier 2 support in a variety of ways. Teachers may make a direct referral to the Tier 2 team. The teacher may recognize that students need additional strategies to support their academic needs in the classroom and can ask the team for support and recommendations. Students may also be identified through data, such as students meeting a certain cutoff score in terms of academic, attendance, or disciplinary performance. As discussed in Chapter 7, universal screeners, which have proven reliability and validity for a certain school population, can be helpful tools in identifying students who may need additional academic, behavioral, or social/emotional support. These screeners have set cutoff scores to identify students who are more at-risk and in need of additional interventions.

Prior to a Tier 2 meeting, the coordinator of the student's case collects pertinent information that relates to their performance in school and the identified issue. This can include copies of academic records (grades, standardized test scores); disciplinary records; attendance records; written reports/interviews of teachers, parents, and students; request for assistance form (if applicable); classroom observation; and brief academic/behavioral assessments (Olsen, 2019). The purpose of this data collection is to gain an in-depth and nuanced understanding of the presenting issue, along with the student's strengths and assets. Additionally, this data should also include what interventions have already been implemented.

Based on the data collected and the identified student needs, the team works together to brainstorm possible Tier 2 interventions that may be effective. As stated in Olsen (2019), Tier 2 interventions should include direct instruction of social or academic skills, an opportunity to apply these skills, and frequent feedback to the student. Several potential Tier 2 interventions are discussed in the following sections, starting with targeted large groups.

Targeted Large Groups

When school counselors identify students who need interventions beyond those at the Tier 1 level, targeted large groups may provide a great opportunity to support a smaller subset of students. In many training programs, school counselors receive instruction and direction on how to lead small groups (six to eight members) and how to deliver large classroom guidance or classroom curriculum. However, targeted large-group interventions are often overlooked. We define targeted large groups as a gathering of identified students (10–15 members), pulled together based on common themes or needs, with the purpose of teaching coping skills or strategies that help address the specific challenges these students face. Targeted large groups are larger than small counseling groups (10–15 students vs. 6–8 students, respectively) and often include students identified during the implementation of Tier 1 interventions. Targeted large groups may look different from grade level to grade level. Here are a few examples of what targeted groups might look like:

1. A school counselor who delivers an evidence-based classroom curriculum on reducing stress around graduation notices several students reacting to the material in ways that go beyond the emotionality associated with graduation. Some students offer comments in the group about their personal connections to the material and others mention concerns they are having with high stress levels to the school counselor in private. A targeted group is formed with 12 students to offer early intervention support and universality to these struggling students.

2. During an evidence-based classroom curriculum on anxiety, 10 or more students come forward to report they are struggling with test anxiety. These students indicate that they want to learn more about its impact on them and their academics. During their study hall period, the school counselor creates a targeted group that provides psychoeducation around test taking and test anxiety.

3. A school counselor goes into all the third-grade classrooms on a regular basis to teach conflict resolution skills. As the semester progresses, one of the classroom teachers asks the counselor to come back to address specific concerns in a particular classroom, such as stealing, lying, friendship, or tattle telling. This group targets a particular set of topics and may only be provided to one of the several third-grade classrooms.

Conceptualizing more specific needs of students across these scenarios presents an opportunity to integrate an evidenced-based curriculum with smaller subsets of students outside of large classroom lessons. In these targeted large-group interventions, school counselors recognize that the interactions are not as personal as in small groups and the size of the group limits the amount of processing that will occur.

School-Based Small Groups

Small groups are often initiated when two or more people are struggling with a common issue or experience. Small-group counseling typically refers to six to eight members and may be prevention based (e.g., future leaders group) or intervention based (e.g., divorce group). According to Dahir and Shea (2022), small-group counseling "is an effective and developmentally appropriate school-based intervention used to target specific student needs" (p. 49). Leading small groups in school settings offers many advantages to students and school counselors alike. In comparison to individual counseling, the *ASCA National Model* (ASCA, 2019a) promotes small-group counseling interventions as an important way school counselors address the needs of larger numbers of students in light of high caseloads (Jacobs et al., 2022; Luke & Schimmel, 2022; Springer et al., 2022).

Small-group counseling benefits students of all ages in many ways. Some of the more recognized benefits of small-group counseling for children and adolescents include the ability of members to learn from each other (interpersonal learning), the opportunity for students to understand that they are not alone in their experiences (universality), and the opportunity for children to offer and receive support from someone their own age (instillation of hope; socializing techniques; Jacobs et al., 2022; Luke & Schimmel, 2022; Steen et al., 2022; Yalom & Leszcz, 2020).

Psychoeducation groups, most commonly found in schools, address the academic and career-related concerns of students (Schimmel & Jacobs, 2019; Steen et al., 2022). Specifically, school counselors often lead groups that focus on skills associated with decision-making, new student transitions, improving study skills, and postsecondary decision-making (Jacobs et al., 2022). When personal/social issues interfere with a student's academic success, school counselors may lead groups on topics such as anxiety, anger management, friendship, divorce, grief, bullying, and conflict resolution (Schimmel & Jacobs, 2019; Springer et al., 2022). Within these groups, school counselors use their content expertise and group conceptualization skills to help students connect around shared experiences. These groups may also provide useful data for future Tier 1 or Tier 3 intervention planning. In the "Suggested Readings" section, readers can find several recommendations for more specific information about the utility of small groups in schools.

Check-In/Check-Out and Mentoring

As you get to know students and student needs more intimately via small groups, there may be more ways in which school counselors can support work in small groups by engaging students in check-in/check-out (CICO) and/or maybe assigning a mentor to increase adult attention. According to Mong et al. (2017), CICO is a systematic, behavioral intervention used to assess student behavior at both the beginning and the end of each school day. Typically, in the CICO intervention, identified students follow a structure that includes checking in with an identified adult who outlines expected behaviors for that day. Students can even carry the check-in report with them as they move through their day allowing teachers or other adults to provide written feedback/encouragement to them. At the end of the student's day, a check-out is conducted by the adult assigned to the student who provides additional support and helps graph the feedback in a palatable way for them to understand. The student then takes the report home and a caregiver is expected to sign off, acknowledging their awareness of the student's behavior that day (Martens & Andreen, 2018). Students should be referred to CICO only after it has been determined that they are not responding to Tier 1 interventions. Additionally, students who may pose a threat to others are not appropriate for CICO.

Mentoring programs have a history of assisting students to develop prosocial behaviors, as well as promoting connectedness at school—two factors that lead to improved academic performance (Chan et al., 2013; McQuillen et al., 2015). Many school-based mentoring programs identify adults to serve as mentors to students who are struggling. While this approach has been successful in many schools and should be implemented when feasible, youth mentors offer a potentially more accessible option for mentoring (Herrera & Karcher, 2013). In fact, youth mentors often more accurately "articulate and appreciate others' points of view" (Coyne-Foresi, 2018, p. 69) when compared to adult mentors. Implementing a mentoring program can be a great way to support struggling students, and there are several options that provide leaders with strategies and guidelines for implementation. While recommending specific programs is not aligned with the purpose of this chapter, we offer valuable ideas for getting started in the "Helpful Resources" section.

 ## Consultation Corner: Who You Gonna Call?

After bracketing your thoughts and reading the "Informed School Counseling" section, who would you call in and outside of the school building, and what might you ask them to support your decision-making? Take a moment to document these questions. Now that you have considered your questions for consultation, let's see what professional school counselors from around the world have to say about this case.

Consultation #1

Our groups are two-fold. There are some that are offered to all (i.e., divorce, grief, allergy support) because they are more "needs" based. Then, we run SKILL-BASED, small groups that align with our social and emotional learning curriculum, Second Step. The groups coincide with the units of the program. Our groups are Learning Skills Unit—Ready to Learn Ranchers (my school name is Ridge Ranch ☺), Empathy Unit—Exercise Your Empathy, Emotion Management Unit—Coping Kids, Problem-Solving Unit—Problem-Solving Pals. These groups, while timed with the given units, can certainly be fluid if needed to address MTSS Tier 2 interventions. In addition to these, I usually end up running "social skills" type groups as the need arises. I do not always use research-based curriculum per se, however, more of a compilation of years of work and a whole lot of TPT (Teachers Pay Teachers) ☺. There are so many counselors out there that are producing such amazing things, you really need not look further. In so far as individual needs, I would usually use the solution-focused counseling techniques and styles.

(Laurie Corizzo, elementary school counselor, New Jersey)

Consultation #2

Hi, my name is Heather Stalnaker, and I am an elementary school counselor at a large school in West Virginia. I have almost 700 students pre-K through fifth grade. Small groups are a Tier 2 intervention regarding the MTSS. Tier 1 would involve more whole-group or large-group guidance lessons. So, for my Tier 1 lessons, I address issues such as friendships skills, emotional awareness, emotional regulation, social skills, body safety education, etc. Tier 1 is something that all students will need and benefit from in the classroom. I use small groups at the Tier 2 level. So those students (based on data) who still need more interventions, even after Tier 1 programs are delivered, would be targeted for Tier 2 interventions, such as small groups. Small groups can be whatever topic/issue that the student is struggling with—decision-making, friendship skills, grief, divorce, academics, tardiness, absenteeism, behavior (but be specific), etc. I use a variety of curricula but try to always use an evidence-based, school-wide curriculum for my Tier 1 (example, MindUp). For small groups, sometimes I use an evidence-based curriculum (Centervention, ZooU), but sometimes I use my clinical expertise and develop a group plan. It is also important to remember that small group is one example of Tier 2 Interventions, there are many other interventions that can be used in Tier 2.

(Heather McDonnell Stalnaker, elementary school counselor, West Virginia)

Consultation #3

Hello, my name is Dave and I work at an intermediate school in the suburbs, a few miles away from a major city. This is a great question, as I too have run various topic groups (grief, children of divorced parents, children from substance abusing homes, social skills, etc.) for students throughout my years.

In the past, I have run these groups with a mix of students with various educational abilities, and I have also run the groups based on a student's educational abilities. I have run groups using a research-based curriculum, and I have run groups developed with my own lesson plans. At this point in my career, the groups are based on a blend of the two lessons from a researched-based curriculum and my own plans. This is based on what lessons the students liked, what activities they seemed to enjoy, and my overall impression of what lessons had the most impact.

My overall goal is, hopefully, to encourage the student to be more comfortable with the topic that brought them to the group. What I mean is, if a student is in the grief support group, that has been supported to voice their views on the topic and to share their experiences. They have been given the forum and support, but most importantly, they have felt encouraged to openly share their thoughts and feelings on the topic. They have been given the opportunity to talk about something that maybe they cannot talk about at home or at school. That it is ok to talk about their feelings. That is really the take-home message that I want them to leave with when the group concludes.

That is what I think is most important—the take-home message of being open to talking about feelings and thoughts, as I think that can be difficult to measure or research. I want the students to walk away feeling better about their circumstances, and that the group was meaningful for them.

(David Davenport, middle school counselor, New Jersey)

Consultation #4

Hi, my name is Jen, and I am a middle school counselor in a private American international school in the Middle East. In our middle school, we run some small groups yearly as part of our program. For instance, we always have new student small groups at the beginning of the school year and leaving student small groups at the end of the school year because of the highly transient nature of being overseas. We have about 75 new students for grades six to eight yearly. We base the activities in these groups on the research on third culture kids (TCKs). Using a resource that is evidence based is helpful. However, the most important part of any small-group work is to build positive regard and a safe space for the students to learn and grow. Our other small groups are needs based and come from teacher and/or administrator referrals through our student concern process. These groups are more targeted in terms of the skill(s) being built, like self-regulation, conflict resolution, assertiveness. Again, it is helpful to have an evidenced-based resource to guide you, but in my experience, if the group becomes too scripted, the students disengage, and there is less opportunity to support skill building. Making small groups fun, authentic and safe is what is most important to gain the opportunity to teach any skills.

(Jen Hammonds, middle school counselor, American School of Doha, Qatar)

Consultation #5

First, all small groups should have some kind of screening mechanism as to why the student is a member of the group. An academic issue may be masked as a behavioral issue. You could be providing the wrong intervention. That is why screening is so important. There should also be some way to measure the effectiveness or outcome of the group. If you do not measure, how do you know the intervention worked? Maybe the student needs a different Tier 2 intervention or a Tier 3 intervention, or maybe they can function back at Tier 1? Many times, school counselors use small groups as Tier 1. That is not how MTSS works. School-wide programming or lessons is a better use of universal or Tier 1 supports. Having a student in the same group all year long or every year without measurement is not helpful to the student. A student of divorce does not necessarily need to be in the Banana Splits group every year of their elementary career. The purpose is to teach the necessary skills the first time. Once you see success from the student, the hope is that they have learned strategies to assist them in better decision-making skills or skills that enhance their academic success and then help other children in need. As with all areas of education, the trend is to get to a place where school counselors use as many evidence-based curricula as possible.

(Tracy Jackson, high school counselor, Virginia)

#EduCounselor Synthesis

There are several different interventions that occur at the Tier 2 level; many of these include targeted small groups. Shelby is asking good questions about when to use small groups and for which needs. Shelby is also referencing the importance of evi-denced-based curricula. Unfortunately, small groups are historically challenging to research because of the need to gain consent from all members (and in schools, from a consenting adult). There is an ongoing charge in the field to produce more evidence for the group work interventions used (Luke & Goodrich, 2017; Rubel & Okech, 2017). For now, intentional school counselors either tailor large-group, evidenced-based curricula to small-group interventions or use literature to inform why certain topics and practices should be used in group. You can find samples of small groups based on research in a variety of counseling journals. A couple of examples written by two of our authors specifically include *Get Fit for Life: Elementary School Group Counseling with a Twist* and *Small-Group Counseling Intervention to Support Career Exploration of Rural Middle School Students* (Grant et al., 2021; Springer, 2014). Still others draw from materials they have used for years and that they feel work, based on perceived outcomes. As we continue to discuss throughout this text, advocacy is key, and data speaks loudly! School counselors are regularly challenged to find time to provide interventions, collect data around them, and present them to key school partners. There are a lot of competing priorities, and you as school counselors are encouraged to partner with counselor educators to conduct outcome research studies that ultimately benefit future groups (Springer et al., 2018; Springer et al., 2020). Doing so not only supports the efficacy of your groups, which may impact things like job security, but you may also have the opportunity to publish your results!

Shelby also talks about a few different types of groups. School counselors may run larger (usually Tier 1) prevention psychoeducational groups that reflect the needs of much of a particular population. These large groups can inform smaller "reac-tive" Tier 2 groups based on students who need more intervention. Furthermore, Shelby mentions behavioral referrals for Tier 2 interventions. As discussed earlier in this chapter, these may come out of intervention team meetings. Referrals based on academics and/or social-emotional challenges are also common and can come from families, teachers, and other school partners as well.

Our consultants provide some interesting insights into how they run groups at their schools. We see that there is a great deal of diversity in how they gain materials for their groups. Several of the consultants applaud Shelby for an interest in using evidenced-based curricula. Many of them also provide some examples of curricula that are cataloged in the resources section of this chapter. Most of the consultants share that they mix and match their own experiences with the information gained from other school counselors to create sessions tailored to the specific students at their schools. Networking supports resourcefulness, and school counselors are encouraged to expand their network of colleagues through association memberships and community events. As Laurie points out, school counselors are also encouraged to choose a theoretical orientation and utilize it to conceptualize their groups' progress and to provide techniques that can be processed in the small group itself. The school community looks to school counselors to help conceptualize student issues and plan for appropriate interventions that address their specific needs.

Regarding evidenced-based curricula, the truth is, many of the suggestions provided by our consultants are geared toward large groups. Most of the "programs" can be used as curricula at the Tier 1 level, and adjustments for specific needs should be taken when using them for Tier 2 interventions. Taking ideas and sessions from these curricula and applying them to Tier 2 groups may provide a research-informed group but should not be considered evidenced based, as school counselors are not conducting the curriculum the way it was intended, in its entirety. With that in mind, ensuring that the interventions chosen are based on the literature is a very important step and should be discussed with school partners as school counselors advocate for more small-group opportunities with students. Jen provides a great example of how she uses literature around the needs of TCKs to inform the work she does at her international school.

In addition to the content itself, it is important that school counselors draw upon their group counseling knowledge and skills to use the group process, along with any educational activities chosen. This is how counselors support the therapeutic factors that are so important to group outcomes (Steen et al., 2014; Yalom & Leszcz, 2021). One way in which Dave shares that he helps to draw out these important factors is by encouraging members to hold space for each other. As mentioned by several of our consultants, teaching emotional expression skills as part of small-group sessions is important and can help facilitate meaningful dialogue around many different topics. Setting up the right conditions for groups to be successful is key.

As many of our consultants shared specifically, screening for small groups is important. Consider your "ideal" student for the group. What will this student be able to offer to the group as far as intellectual knowledge, emotional expression skills, behavioral self-control, etc.? Accepting *any* student whose parents have gone through a divorce without screening for fit may render the group unsuccessful. Readiness and preparedness for the group are important, and we encourage school counselors to meet with students individually to engage in this screening process. For instance, there are benefits and drawbacks to having students of different ages, intellectual abilities, and maturity in a group; if the gap is so wide between student needs and abilities, however, the intended goals for the group may be lost (Hines & Fields, 2002; Ritchie & Huss, 2000; Riva et al., 2000). For a divorce group, for instance, consider where the student is in the grieving process; has the student had many years of counseling outside of the schools or have they never spoken to a counselor outside of the large-group classroom lessons? Maybe the student is acting out in class and the behaviors need to be addressed individually before this student can productively give and receive support from other members. School counselors should be very intentional about the content they choose, the size of the group, the members, and the length of each session. For more information about school counseling groups, we encourage readers to check out *A School Counselor's Guide to Small Groups: Coordination, Leadership, and Assessment* (Springer et al., 2022).

Another challenge around running small groups may be a difference in the school district's priorities. Some school leaders and colleagues may encourage (and even try to mandate) that every student who has experienced "X" should have access to a small group. While this sounds ideal, it is important for school counselors to advocate for interventions that provide meaningful outcomes. Not every child is a good fit for a particular group! At the same time, as Tracy shares, a "yearlong" intervention that "checks a box" on an Individualized Education Plan or 504 plan or that offers a particular narrative to the school community, may not provide meaningful interventions to students. Planning for short-term small groups by collecting data through behavioral checklists or after adult or peer mentoring experiences at the Tier 2 level before creating small groups is important, especially within the MTSS framework. We will not know if Tier 3 or outside supports are needed if we do not track student progress in this way.

Chapter Summary

Following the MTSS delivery of services model, typically, 10%–20% of students require targeted support at the Tier 2 level. Many times, these interventions include activities such as targeted large-group activities (between 10 to 15 students), small-group counseling interventions (between six to eight students), and other activities such as CICO, and behavior contracts. School counselors work with intervention teams, teachers, and other partners to collect data, identify students in need of Tier 2 interventions, and work together with those individuals to ensure that these students benefit from the interventions at this level.

Reflective Practitioner Process

School counselors engage in **clinical supervision, professional development**, and **self-care** to further develop their knowledge and skills and to help balance professional expectations with personal wellness. All three areas are key to ethical practice and help to mitigate counselor burnout and compassion fatigue (Atici, 2015; Lawson & Myers, 2011; Merriman, 2015; Ohrt et al., 2015).

Clinical Supervision

The *ASCA School Counselor Professional Standards & Competencies* (ASCA, 2019) direct school counselors to "consult with school counselors and other education and counseling professionals when questions of school counseling practice arise" (B-SS 5., p. 5). As a supervisee, it is important to consider the thoughts, feelings, and experiences that come up for you as you work with students, families, and colleagues and seek consultation on difficult issues. As you begin supervision, it is important to review your initial reactions to the social media post. Unfortunately, receiving supervision specific to small groups, while very important, is not common practice in many schools, and counselors must therefore advocate for it. Ohrt and Gonzales (2022) offer the discrimination model of supervision as an example that can be used for the supervision of small groups. Here are a few things to consider when discussing this scenario with your supervisor:

- Think about your comfort level running small groups with students. What areas of small-group practice (e.g., screening, content knowledge, integrating group process) might be areas in which you'd want more information and/or practice?
- Small groups in schools require time during the day to meet with students. What might advocacy efforts look like with school partners? What do you do if colleagues (e.g., teachers) do not allow you to take students out of class?
- How would you proceed if you felt passionate about leading small groups in your school but your more seasoned colleagues report that there is just no time to run these in your current setting?
- After identifying a gap in discipline issues at your school, your administrator asks you to lead Tier 2 small groups with students of color who are experiencing behavior consequences at higher rates than non-minority students. What is your immediate reaction? What questions arise related to how these students were identified for membership in this group (group composition)?

Professional Development

According to the *ASCA Ethical Standards for School Counselors* (ASCA, 2022), professional school counselors engage in professional development and attend trainings to stay current on the trends and issues that impact students (B.3.e). One factor that commonly impacts the school counselor's ability to lead small groups is training. Oftentimes, school counselors who are trained alongside clinical mental health trainees do not feel adequately prepared to conceptualize, plan, and lead small groups in school settings (Springer & Schimmel, 2016; Finnerty, et al., 2019). To overcome this, school counselors must consider engaging in ongoing supervision, peer consultation, and professional development around leading small groups. Consider finding professional development on the following topics:

- Small-group leadership skills
- Evidenced-based small-group curricula
- Small-group topics for a variety of developmental needs (e.g., mindfulness, test taking, divorce)
- Confidentiality in school-based, small-group counseling

#PSCSelfCare: Everyday Wellness

When designing, managing, and implementing a comprehensive school counseling program, school and community expectations can tax even the most seasoned school counselor. The *ASCA Ethical Standards for School Counselors* (ASCA, 2022) require school counselors to recognize the high levels of stress often associated with the job. Therefore, school counselors recognize that self-care must be a priority to maintain health and overall well-being (see ASCA, 2022, B.3.h).

The School Counselor Support Group

Many school counselors practice in schools where they are the only school counselor. This potentially leads to school counselors feeling greater levels of compassion fatigue compared to those who practice in schools with other colleagues. Bearing the weight of student mental health and well-being independently can take a toll on even the most seasoned school counselors. Self-care is essential to sustaining a career in the field of school counseling. Additionally, the positive effects of small groups for students also hold true for us as adults; feelings of universality and support can be found in school counselor small groups.

For your self-care plan, consider committing to or even forming a self-care small group; the small group can be based on a particular self-care activity (several school counselors who get together each week and take a walk) or perhaps the group can be based on a book that promotes healthy habits (emotional, spiritual, physical, etc.). Given the all too common feelings of isolation that can occur when school counselors are one of few mental health practitioners in their schools or districts, school counselors can benefit greatly from connections to others through a shared activity. Some school districts might even allow monthly peer supervision time during the school day for such activities. We encourage you to advocate for these opportunities within your district.

Spotlight: School Counseling Advocacy

Here we highlight a practicing school counselor who provides targeted Tier 2 interventions for students struggling to adjust to high school. As discussed throughout the chapter, engaging students in Tier 2 interventions such as small-group counseling allows for students to connect around similar struggles. Notably, even the small number of three students in this case allowed students to form a sense of community.

C.A.Tillery
@TilleryCounsols

I love **small group counseling**. It allows me to work with students with similar needs. 3 Freshmen were able to connect today, & learn they are not alone with adjusting to high school. Only day 1 and they have already built their own community and identified some shared struggles

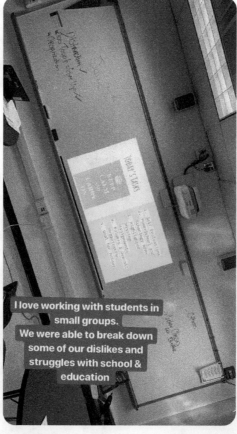

Image 8.1

Jun 16, 2019

Learning Connections

Both professional school counselors in training and seasoned school counselors understand the importance of understanding the connections between the concepts commonly taught in counseling programs and the standards most associated with school counselor training. Therefore, the following table offers broad connections between the material and information in this chapter and the Council for Accreditation of Counseling and Related Educational Programs (CACREP, 2016) standards, the *ASCA School Counselor Professional Standards & Competencies* (ASCA, 2019b), and the *ASCA Ethical Standards for School Counselors* (ASCA, 2022).

Connections to CACREP Core Curricular Areas

Professional Counseling Orientation and Ethical Practice	Social and Cultural Diversity	Human Growth and Development	Career Development	Counseling and Helping Relationships	Group Counseling and Group Work	Assessment and Testing	Research and Program Evaluation
X				X	X		

Connection to Professional Standards

CACREP	ASCA SC Professional Competencies	Ethical Standards: SC
F.6.c. Therapeutic factors and how they contribute to group effectiveness	M 4. Every student should have access to a school counseling program.	A.7.a. Offer culturally sustaining small-group counseling services based on individual student, school and community needs; student data; a referral process; and/or other relevant data.
F.6.f. Types of groups and other considerations that affect conducting groups in varied settings	M 7. School counseling programs promote and enhance student academic, career and social/ emotional outcomes.	A.7.b: Provide equitable access to participation in groups, including alleviating physical, language and other obstacles.
	B-SS 1. Design and implement instruction aligned to ASCA Mindsets & Behaviors for Student Success in large-group, classroom, small-group and individual settings.	A.7.e: Facilitate short-term groups to address students' academic achievement, postsecondary and career exploration, and social/ emotional well-being.
	B-SS 2. Provide appraisal and advisement in large-group, classroom, small-group and individual settings.	A.7.f: Use data to inform group topics, establish well-defined expectations and measure the outcomes of group participation.
	B-SS 3. Provide short-term counseling in small-group and individual settings.	A.7.g: Reflect on group outcomes and determine adjustments that may improve future group interventions.

Comprehensive School Counseling Assignments

The following section provides activities that allow for your continued growth as a professional school counselor. Both preservice and practicing school counselors may find it helpful to complete these activities. If you are currently in a graduate training program, your professor might assign these as part of your course.

- Research evidence-based small-group interventions/curricula and select two to discuss in class.
- Connect with a practicing school counselor, and using their school data, create an outline for a 6-week psychoeducation small-group addressing the needs of a specific population.
- Create an outline for a 4-week psychoeducation leadership group to help students understand and discuss school climate concerns, social justice issues, and advocacy in their school.
- Develop a preliminary plan for a mentoring program in your school.

Helpful Resources
Web-Based Resources

- *Stages of Group Made Fun*:
  - https://www.youtube.com/watch?v=lu1WUe35QEs
- Committee for Children. (n.d.). *Second step:*
  - https://www.secondstep.org/
- Teachers Pay Teachers:
  - https://www.teacherspayteachers.com/
- Mind Up for Life:
  - https://mindup.org/
- Centervention:
  - https://student.centervention.com/
- TCK World: The official home of third culture kids.
  - http://www.tckworld.com/useem/art1.html
- Banana Splits Resource Center. (n.d.). *Banana splits resource center: Support groups for children with divorced/deceased parents.*
  - https://www.bananasplitsresourcecenter.org/

Suggested Readings

Check out these articles on Yalom's curative factors:

- Warming up and therapeutic factors:
  - https://link.springer.com/chapter/10.1007/978-981-33-6342-7_12

- Therapeutic factors and children's groups:
  - https://www.researchgate.net/publication/232481241_An_Investigation_of_Therapeutic_Factors_in_Children's_Groups

Mentoring Programs

For information on a wide variety of mentoring resources, check out the National Mentoring Resource Center at:

- https://nationalmentoringresourcecenter.org/

For the basics involved in school-based mentoring, check out The ABC's of School-Based Mentoring at:

- https://educationnorthwest.org/sites/default/files/abcs-of-mentoring.pdf.

Suggested Readings

- Many school counselors find the following text to be invaluable in their group work:
  - Springer, S. I, Moss, L. J., & Schimmel, C. J. (Eds.). (2022). *A school counselor's guide to small groups: Coordination, leadership, and assessment* (2nd ed.). Cognella.
- For practical group leading skills:
  - Jacobs, E., Schimmel, C. J., Mason, R., & Harvill, R. (2022). *Group counseling: Strategies & skills* (9th ed.). Cognella.

References

American School Counselor Association (ASCA). (2019a). *ASCA national model: A framework for school counseling programs.*

American School Counselor Association (ASCA). (2019b). *ASCA school counselor professional standards & competencies.* https://www.schoolcounselor.org/asca/media/asca/home/SCCompetencies.pdf

American School Counselor Association (ASCA). (2022). *ASCA ethical standards for school counselors.* https://www.schoolcounselor.org/getmedia/44f30280-ffe8-4b41-9ad8-f15909c3d164/EthicalStandards.pdf

Atici, M. (2015). Professional identity development of counselors-in-training in a school internship program in Turkey. *The Professional Counselor, 5*(1), 137–151. https://doi.org/10.15241/MA.5.1.137

Council for Accreditation of Counseling and Related Educational Programs (CACREP). (2016). *2016 CACREP standards.* http://www.cacrep.org/wp-content/uploads/2017/08/2016-Standards-with-citations.pdf

Chan, C. S., Rhodes, J. E., Howard, W. J., Lowe, S. R., Schwartz, S. E. O., & Herrera, C. (2013). Pathways of influence in school-based mentoring: The mediating role of parent and teacher relationships. *Journal of School Psychology, 51*(1), 129–142. https://doi.org/10.1016/j.jsp.2012.10.001

Coyne-Foresi, M. (2018). Wiz kidz: Fostering school connectedness through an in-school student mentoring program (p. 69). *Professional School Counseling, 19*(1), 68–79. https://doi.org/10.5330/1096-2409-19.1.68

Dahir, C., & Shea, M. (2022). Utilizing group facilitation skills to enhance the multitiered systems of support (MTSS) process. In S. I. Springer, J. J. Moss, & C. J. Schimmel (Eds.), *A school counselor's guide to small groups: Coordination, leadership, and assessment* (2nd ed., pp. 28–36). Cognella.

Finnerty, S., Luke, M., & Duffey, J. T. (2019). A grounded theory of experiential group training of school counselors to engage in psychoeducational group lessons with first-in-family students. *Journal for Specialists in Group Work, 44*(2), 99-117. https://doi.org/10.1080/01933922.2019.1599476

Grant, K. L., Springer, S. I., Tuttle, M., & Reno, M. (2021). Small-group counseling intervention to support career exploration of rural middle school students. *The Journal for Specialists in Group Work, 46*(1), 108–127. https://doi.org/10.1080/01933922.2020.1856254

Goodman-Scott, E., Betters-Bubon, J., Olsen, J., & Donohue, P. (2020) *Making MTSS work.* ASCA.

Herrera, C., & Karcher, M. J. (2013). School-based mentoring. In D. L. DuBois & M. J. Karcher (Eds.), *Handbook of youth mentoring* (2nd ed, pp. 203–220). SAGE Publishing.

Hines, P. L. & Fields, T. H. (2002). Pregroup screening issues for school counselors, *The Journal for Specialists in Group Work, 27*(4), 358–376. https://doi.org/10.1080/714860199

Jacobs, E., Schimmel, C. J., Mason, R., & Harvill, R. (2022). *Group counseling: Strategies and skills* (9th ed.). Cognella.

Lawson, G., & Myers, J. E. (2011). Wellness, professional quality of life, and career-sustaining behaviors: What keeps us well? *Journal of Counseling and Development, 89*(2), 163–171. https://doi.org/10.1002/j.1556-6678.2011.tb00074.x

Luke, M., & Goodrich, K. M. (2017). Introduction to research in group work: A renewed focus on exemplary methods. *Journal for Specialists in Group Work, 42*(1), 131–134. https://doi.org/10.1080/01933922.2017.1306415

Luke, C., & Schimmel, C. J. (2022). *Applying neuroscience to counseling children and adolescents: A guide to brain-based, experiential interventions.* Cognella.

Martens, K., & Andreen, K. (2018). School counselors' involvement with a school-wide positive behavior support intervention: Addressing student behavior issues in a proactive and positive manner. *Professional School Counseling, 16*(5), 313–322. https://doi.org/10.1177/2156759X1201600504

McQuillen, S., Strait, G., Smith, B., & Ingram, A. (2015). Brief instrumental school-based mentoring for first- and second-year middle school students: A randomized evaluation. *Journal of Community Psychology, 43*(7), 885–899. https://doi.org/10.1002/jcop.21719

Merriman, J. (2015). Enhancing counselor supervision through compassion fatigue education. *Journal of Counseling and Development, 93*(3), 370–378. https://doi.org/10.1002/jcad.12035

Mong, M. D., Johnson, K. N., & Mong, K. W. (2017). Effects of check-in/checkout on behavioral indices and mathematics generalization. *Behavioral Disorders, 36*(4), 225–240. https://doi.org/10.1177/019874291103600403

Olsen, J. (2019). Tier 2: Providing support for students with elevated needs. In E. Goodman-Scott, J. Betters-Bubon, & P. Donohue (Eds.), *The school counselor's guide to multi-tiered systems of support* (pp. 133–162). Routledge.

Ohrt, J. H., Prosek, E. A., Ener, E., & Lindo, N. (2015). The effects of a group supervision intervention to promote wellness and prevent burnout. *The Journal of Humanistic Counseling, 54*(1), 41–58. https://doi.org/10.1002/j.2161-1939.2015.00063.x

Ohrt, J. H., & Gonzales, S. (2022). Structured feedback to enhance preservice school counselors' group leader skills. In S. I. Springer, J. J. Moss, & C. J. Schimmel (Eds.), *A school counselor's guide to small groups: Coordination, leadership, and assessment* (2nd ed., pp. 89–101). Cognella.

Ritchie, M. H., & Huss, S. N. (2000). Recruitment and screening of minors for group counseling. *The Journal for Specialists in Group Work, 25*(2), 146–156. https://doi.org/10.1080/01933920008411458

Riva, M. T., Lippert, L. & Tackett, M. J. (2000). Selection practices of group leaders: A national survey. *The Journal for Specialists in Group Work, 25*(2), 157–169. https://doi.org/10.1080/01933920008411459

Rubel, D. & Okech, J. A. E. (2017). Qualitative research in group work: Status, synergies, and implementation. *The Journal for Specialists in Group Work, 42*(1), 54–86. https://doi.org/10.1080/01933922.2016.1264522

Schimmel, C. J., & Jacobs, E. (2019). Small group counseling. In A. Vernon & C. J. Schimmel (Eds.), *Counseling children and adolescents* (5th ed., pp. 418–456). Cognella.

Springer, S. (2014). *Get fit for life: Elementary school counseling with a twist.* https://files.eric.ed.gov/fulltext/EJ1034775.pdf

Springer, S. I., & Schimmel, C. J. (2016). Creative strategies to foster pre-service school counselor group leader self-efficacy. *The Journal for Specialists in Group Work, 41*(1), 2–18. https://doi.org/10.1080/01933922.2015.1111486

Springer, S. I., Land, C., Moss, L., & Cinotti, D. (2018). Collecting school counseling group work data: Initiating consensual qualitative research through practitioner-researcher partnerships. *Journal for Specialists in Group Work, 43*(2), 1–16. https://doi.org/10.1080/01933922.2018.1431346.

Springer, S. I., Mason, E. C. M., Moss, L. J., Pugliese, A., & Colucci, J. (2020). An intervention to support elementary school faculty in meeting the needs of transgender and gender non-conforming students. *Journal of Child and Adolescent Counseling, 6*(3), 181–199. https://doi.org/10.1080/23727810.2019.1689765

Springer, S. I., Moss, L. J., & Schimmel, C. J. (2022). *A school counselor's guide to small groups: Coordination, leadership, and assessment* (2nd ed.). Cognella.

Steen, S., Vasserman-Stokes, E. & Vannatta, R. (2014). Group cohesion in experiential growth groups. *The Journal for Specialists in Group Work, 39*(3), 236–256. https://doi.org/10.1080/01933922.2014.924343

Steen, S., Melfie, J., Carro, A., Zhu, L., & Genvese, E. (2022). Introduction: Group leadership considerations for effective facilitation in schools. In S. I. Springer, L. J. Moss, & C. J. Schimmel (Eds.). *A school counselor's guide to small groups: Coordination, leadership, and assessment.* (pp. 1–11). Cognella.

Yalom, I. D., & Leszcz, M. (2020). *Theory and practice of group psychotherapy* (6th ed.). Basic Books.

Credit

CHAPTER 9

Multi-Tiered Systems of Support—Tier 3 Interventions

LEARNING OBJECTIVES

#EduCounselors can

- define Tier 3 interventions aligned with a multi-tiered systems of support framework,
- learn about appropriate types of short-term, individual counseling, and other interventions provided to students, and
- recognize the importance of school counselors assessing for and making decisions about referring students to outside resources.

Introduction

Working from a multi-tiered systems of support (MTSS) model, school counselors recognize that students who are struggling the most require the most in-depth level of intervention. In an MTSS framework, roughly three – 5% of students require Tier 3 interventions. Many professionals enter school counseling training with hopes of providing individual counseling to most of the students they serve. However, school counselors do not necessarily provide those intensive interventions themselves to every student in need of counseling. Tier 3 interventions may take the form of individual counseling by the school counselor with students, but they more frequently require skills associated with school-based consultation and referral of students to outside resources such as community mental health agencies.

#IRLSchoolCounseling

The following is a social media post from one of the many school counseling groups on Facebook. *Caught in the Middle School Counselors* is a Facebook group primarily hosting topics posed by middle school counselors.

Mia Fusco
April 14

Does anyone have any good resources for LGBTQ during this time? I have a student who is really struggling being at home with their family, who is pretty unsupportive of their gender identity. I know it's difficult for them not being able to go to school where they felt accepted. Thank you!!

Bracketing Values for Ethical Practice

It is expected that school counselors continuously reflect on their values, beliefs, worldviews, and cultural norms and how each influences the ways in which they choose to take or not take action. As such, it is important to recognize and set aside any preconceived notions, experiences, and biases to help you respond to this scenario in a culturally sustaining and ethically sound manner. Take a moment to reflect on the previous post and then consider the following questions:

- How do you feel about a student questioning their gender identity?
- What are your perceptions about the student's parents?
- How might you feel toward a student's family if they were unsupportive of their child's experiences?
- What emotions will you need to bracket when parents refuse to listen to you, and your care does not extend to the home?
- How will you respond/react when you feel a student needs outside support, such as counseling, but caregivers fail to follow up with your referrals?

Informed School Counseling

The appropriate duties of school counselors include the delivery of direct services to students. The *ASCA National Model* (ASCA, 2019a) directs school counselors to provide 80% of their time in direct and indirect services to students; direct services include classroom instruction, appraisal and advisement, and counseling (short-term, brief individual, crisis, and small group). Indirect services can include consultation, collaboration, and making referrals of students to more intensive services in cases where brief, short-term interventions are not sufficient for helping students succeed (for more on direct and indirect services, see Chapter 6). Here, we discuss the identification of students for Tier 3 intervention, individual counseling as an intensive intervention, crisis intervention, and community referrals.

Identifying Students for Tier 3 Intervention

Being a student in school is hard. Even on days when a child's life seems perfect, children are navigating evolving physical, emotional, and social dynamics that affect their abilities to cope with challenges. Children and adolescents often face obstacles associated with a variety of "isms" (e.g., racism, ableism, sexism, and sizeism). Often, children and adolescents are treated as less than human and their problems dismissed as insignificant. Additionally, they are often expected to behave and perform in ways that are incongruent with their developmental and cognitive levels (Luke & Schimmel, 2022). For many students, the need for individual counseling to cope with issues associated with anxiety, depression, suicidal ideation, and oppression is exploding. School counselors are uniquely positioned as mental health experts to help students and support them as they navigate school issues related to mental health, trauma, and discrimination (ASCA, 2020; Gallo, 2018; Juhnke et al., 2011).

How do we begin to identify students who need more intensive interventions such as individual counseling, crisis response and management, and outside referrals to community partners? One of the simplest ways to understand who may require Tier 3 interventions is to identify students whose needs are not adequately met by Tier 1 and Tier 2 support. Also, school counselors rely on many forms of data and referrals to identify students who need Tier 3 interventions. For example, in Chapter 7, we introduced you to the concept of using universal screeners as a supplemental data source for beginning to plan and deliver a comprehensive school counseling program. While data gleaned from a universal screener helps you begin to understand what topics and curricula are needed for ALL students, a universal screener can also help to identify students in need of more intensive interventions. Screeners such as the *Difficulties in Emotions Regulations Scale* (Gratz & Roemer, 2004), *The Early Childhood Screening Assessment* (Gleason et al., 2010), and the *Problem Oriented Screening Instrument for Teenagers* (Rahdert, 1991) can be valuable supplemental data tools for identifying students with more significant needs. In case time did not permit you to review *Ready, Set, Go, Review: Screening for Behavioral Health Risk in Schools* (https://www.samhsa.gov/sites/default/files/ready_set_go_review_mh_screening_in_schools_508.pdf) by SAMHSA when reading Chapter 7, we encourage you to do that now. Also, be sure to revisit the *Mental Health, Social-Emotional, and Behavioral Screening and Evaluation Compendium* (2nd ed.) provided by the Ohio Department of Education Center for School-Based Mental Health (http://education.ohio.gov/getattachment/Topics/Other-Resources/School-Safety/Building-Better-Learning-Environments/PBIS-Resources/Project-AWARE-Ohio/Project-AWARE-Ohio-Statewide-Resources/Compendium-Version-2.pdf.aspx) for that expansive list of screening tools, we point you to in Chapter 7.

In addition to universal screening tools, school counselors rely heavily on parent, teacher, and other school and community partner referrals in identifying students through intervention teams (e.g., Positive Behavioral Interventions and Supports team, Child Study team, Response to Intervention team). And while all of these data sources are valuable and assist in identifying students in need of Tier 3 interventions, SAMHSA (2020) reminds us, "It is important for schools to analyze existing data [e.g., attendance, behavior, and academics] before making the determination to engage in additional screening of students" (p. 13). Examining data such as family economic status, school nurse visits, and data gleaned from systems that already exist as part of the school district's data collection tools (e.g., early warning system) also yields rich information that points school personnel toward students in need of more significant interventions.

Common Tier 3 Interventions

The entire scope of intensive interventions is beyond what we can cover here, and many available services to students in need of Tier 3 interventions vary by school district and personnel. In the following, we provide an overview of some of the most common Tier 3 interventions for students. Many Tier 3 interventions are targeted toward learning and academics and delivered by a variety of educators in the building. However, many Tier 3 interventions around social, emotional, and behavioral issues are best provided by school counselors specifically. Some of these include functional behavior assessments, safety plans for students at risk of harming themselves, and collaboration and consultation services. Finally, the most frequently implemented school counselor–delivered interventions for students at the Tier 3 level include individual and crisis counseling and referrals to community partners and providers.

Theory Driven Individual Counseling as a Tier 3 Intervention

While the *ASCA Ethical Standards for School Counselors* clearly state that school counselors do not conduct long-term therapy ("school counselors provide culturally responsive counseling to students in a brief context and support students and families/guardians in obtaining outside services if students need long-term clinical/mental health counseling" ASCA, 2022, A.1.e.), it is common for school counselors to supplement their work with students by providing short-term individual counseling interventions to a smaller number of students; this is often a necessity when there is a lack of resources for students, either based on family income to pay for outside counseling or simply because there are limited mental health counseling options outside of school. Additionally, regardless of income status, many families fail to follow through even with encouragement and financial support when students are referred to outside resources (Kaffenberger & O'Rorke-Trigiani, 2018).

Aligned with the standards embedded in most training programs, school counselors are equipped with the knowledge and skills to provide meaningful short-term individual counseling when more intensive interventions are necessary. In fact, school counselors frequently report a passion for providing individual counseling. When making the decision to provide such services, school counselors select interventions with students that are evidence-based, brief in nature, and have the potential to impact students in as short a timeframe as possible.

According to Vernon and Berry (2013), interventions for children and adolescents should be **creative, hands-on, address a variety of learning styles**, be **culturally responsive,** and be concrete in a way that allows for children and adolescents to apply what is learned in a session. In going further with these recommendations and similar to Vernon and Berry (2013), Singh et al. (2012) suggest that it is important to choose interventions, approaches, and techniques that honor students' cultural and ethnic experiences and translate across languages. Examples include infusing art, drawing, and play to support and enhance communication and connection with our English language learners. School counselors use theory-driven, evidenced-based interventions to assist students in navigating the personal, social, and emotional issues common to this population.

While school counselors in training typically learn a variety of counseling theories throughout their graduate training, there are certain theories that more appropriately lend themselves to the brief nature of school counseling with students and allow for the creativity, diverse expression, and developmental level of young clients. Many of these theories are based on cognitive and behavioral therapies. Here, we include a brief overview of some of the theories and associated strategies and interventions commonly used by school counselors. The resources section includes a variety of readings that provide specific, creative, and practical activities for use with all students in each of the theories covered in the following sections. While we recognize that these theories can be used across all the tiers, they are particularly helpful when providing Tier 3 services in a one-to-one capacity.

Rational Emotive Behavior Therapy

Rational emotive behavior therapy (REBT), a cognitive-behavioral approach, is one of the most researched counseling orientations. Created by Albert Ellis, the general focus of REBT, like most cognitive-behavioral approaches, includes targeting an issue and collaborating with clients to examine their thoughts in connection to feelings and behaviors. According to Vernon (2019), REBT is well suited for work with young clients because it addresses issues immediately and "is generally a briefer form of therapy" (p. 225). Additionally, REBT allows for the use of concrete interventions often based on the use of drawings, writing, and even props (see Jacobs & Schimmel, 2013; Vernon, 2019).

Through psychoeducation, counselors help clients to set goals and change their cognitions (e.g., negative self-talk). School counselors who are guided by REBT help students develop an internal locus of control by addressing common rigid beliefs, irrational statements, or assumptions and often teach them about the A (activating event), B (belief), and C (consequence) that lead to problematic behaviors (thus the 'B' in REBT) resulting from these cognitions. School counselors also address absolutes (e.g., should, always, never) and help students to restructure their thoughts in more rational and constructive ways (Vernon, 2019; Warren & Hale, 2016). Providing psychoeducation around cognitive distortions such as overgeneralization, tunnel vision, and personalization may be especially helpful in supporting students with more self-awareness. REBT and its sibling classroom guidance program, rational emotive education, are evidence-based approaches that help students see the power and value of controlling their beliefs, assumptions, and subsequent self-talk as well as helping students distinguish between facts and assumptions (Vernon, 2019). Additionally, school counselors may integrate more contemporary cognitive behavior approaches such as mindfulness-based therapies and Cognitive Behavioral Intervention for Trauma in Schools (CBITS at a Glance, n.d.). More information about these approaches and a link where readers can complete free CBITS training can be found in the resources section.

Reality Therapy

Reality therapy, developed by William Glasser, MD, is used in many countries and across many delivery approaches (i.e., individual counseling, group counseling, and consultation; Wubbolding, 2019). Reality therapy, rooted in choice theory, centers on connection, personal responsibility, control, and behavior. Glasser postulates that humans have five basic needs (i.e., survival, love and belonging, power, freedom, and fun) that influence behavior. According to Wubbolding (2019), total behaviors are categorized into components; these include physiology (e.g., breathing exercises), thinking, feeling, and actions or behaviors that are controllable (to varying degrees). Additionally, "reality therapy focuses on what clients can control; their own behavioral choices" (Wubbolding, 2019, p. 187). School counselors who use reality therapy collaboratively establish goals based on student needs and develop plans to meet these goals. Many counselors who work from a reality therapy framework rely on the WDEP approach to help students get their needs met.

As school counselors connect with students, they learn about their (W) wants, perceptions, and the quality world, (D) doing, actions, feelings, and self-talk/thoughts, (E) self-evaluation, and ultimately, assist students in developing a (P) plan. Student wants (W), often referred to as their quality world, include desires for connection with school and surrounding community members (e.g., peers, parents, teachers) and are understood in the context of their perceptions. While reality therapy acknowledges systemic concerns that victimize students, Wubbolding (2019) suggests that it is important to help children alter their perceptions from "victimized to victim wise" to empower them through choice (p. 205). Doing (D) refers to counselors examining current behaviors. Self-evaluation (E) is key in this model and helps answer Glasser's (1972) fundamental question, "Is what you're doing/thinking/feeling helping?" The (P) in the plan reflects the need to outline the steps toward action. In essence, reality therapy is grounded in the idea that all actions in life are forms of behaving, and people have substantial amounts of control over these behaviors. School counselors help students examine their thoughts, feelings, and behaviors to determine if they will lead to the student getting their needs met.

Solution-Focused Brief Counseling

Solution-focused brief counseling (SFBC), also known as solution-focused brief therapy, is a strengths-based counseling approach that focuses on students' actions and behaviors over their insights, promotes resilience, and honors students' abilities to solve their own issues (Sabella, 2019; Sabella, 2020; Sklare, 2014). The goal is to find solutions, rather than focus on the problem. School counselors work with students to identify the issue that brings them to counseling, but then refocus the counselor/client relationship not on the issue directly, but instead, on times when the issue was less problematic or not problematic at all. Sabella (2019) outlines the basic guidelines for use of SFBC; these include: "if it works, don't fix it; focus on what is right and is working (solutions); always maintain positive expectations that things will change for the better; and to discover or reach a solution, it is not necessary to analyze or understand the problem" (p. 151). Based in part on these overriding principles, SFBC has much utility for work in schools in that there is less time to focus on actual problems and the root of said problems. Instead, SFBC allows school counselors to focus on just that—solutions!

While SFBC can seem complex to new counselors, the process involves only six basic techniques: detailing, mind fielding, cheerleading, amplifying, reframing, and refocusing (Sabella, 2019; Sabella, 2020; Sklare, 2014). These techniques lend themselves to providing concrete interventions that resonate with young clients. One of the more identifiable techniques used in SFBC is the Miracle Question. The Miracle Question is often framed similarly to this: *If you woke up tomorrow and the problem was gone, what would you notice?* Or, *How would you know the problem wasn't there anymore?* The Miracle Question is often used as a basis for helping the student to set goals and examine progress in conjunction with another popular SFBC technique referred to as scaling. When using the scaling technique, the counselor might say something like, *On a scale of 0–10, how close do you believe you are to getting to a solution?* School counselors who wish to learn more about SFBC are encouraged to read more from Sabella (2019 & 2020) and Sklare (2014).

Play Therapy and Therapeutic Play

For the youngest students in schools, and some older students with developmental delays, school counselors understand that play is the language of children, and toys are their words (Landreth, 2012). Many school counselors find value in seeking advanced training in child-centered play therapy and even working toward certification as a registered play therapist (RPT) through the Association for Play Therapy (https://www.a4pt.org/). Without seeking advanced training in play therapy as a specific intervention, practitioners cannot represent themselves as play therapists. RPTs work from a variety of theoretical models. Many play therapists specialize in a nondirective (child-centered) approach or a combination of nondirective and directive play as represented in Adlerian or cognitive-behavioral approaches. Despite the theoretical orientations, all play therapists recognize the power of play in allowing young clients to access their inner strengths and work through issues with which they are struggling. Play therapists recognize that this model of working with children empowers young people and as a result, children often gain confidence and self-esteem, as well as the ability to process traumatic life events (Dickinson & Kottman, 2019; Landreth, 2012).

While diving into the wide variety of techniques used in play therapy is beyond the scope of this chapter, RPTs become experts in the skills of tracking, encouraging, reflecting, using the whisper technique, and most of all, establishing play spaces where toys are selected with thought given to the common play needs of a variety of children. School counselors interested in engaging in play therapy as a primary mechanism to deliver Tier 3 interventions are ethically called upon to seek training in the field. However, it is noteworthy that not all school counselors will be able to engage in a strict training program or find utility in only providing one form of intervention such as play therapy. Therefore, we offer the concept of therapeutic play as an alternative.

Luke and Schimmel (2022) provide a continuum of play for counselors to consider, and acknowledge that there is value in all forms of play in terms of healthy brain development and recovery from trauma; play-as-play, play-as-therapy, and play therapy, as discussed earlier, all combine to form this continuum. Many school counselors who are not able to seek certification as an RPT find great value in allowing students to engage in and work with students in the play-as-therapy or the therapeutic use of play realm. Oftentimes, the use of therapeutic play involves using therapeutic games designed for therapeutic purposes (i.e., the Talking, Feeling, Doing Game, n.d.). However, therapeutic play may also include using the game of Uno in a creative way to allow a student to express thoughts, concerns, and feelings or improve social skills. Often, playing games such as these allows for more open expression by children and generates increased discussion and sharing versus trying to implement a traditional talk-listen approach to counseling. For older adolescents, there is emerging literature on the therapeutic benefits found in virtual gaming and online tools such as ZooU to enhance social skills (Luke & Schimmel, 2022; Tolliver & Smith, 2022).

Crisis Counseling

An additional Tier 3 direct service provided to students often, unfortunately, comes in the form of crisis counseling or crisis response in times of tragedy or traumatic life and community events. School counselors are often frontline responders when students experience school-wide tragedies, such as the death of a classmate; school violence, such as a school shooting, natural disasters, and community tragedies (i.e., a local mining disaster, a factory explosion, a building collapse, etc.); or even national tragedies such as the events of September 11, 2001, or the social and racial events following the death of George Floyd in 2020. In times such as these, school counselors are called upon to provide short-term grief and supportive counseling.

Grief Counseling

Children and adolescents can experience grief as a result of a variety of events. Most often associated with death and loss, a child's grief can also be associated with a major transition such as a family separation, divorce, or a move to a new city or town. Additionally, a child can find themselves grieving a transition such as leaving elementary school to move to middle school or even graduating high school (Leppma & Schimmel, 2019). Any of these, in addition to other situations that potentially trigger a grief reaction, may require the school counselor to provide short-term, grief counseling as the student processes the event. Grief counseling is often characterized in adults as a long, slow process; however, children and adolescents may experience grief differently, often struggling with intermittent bouts of sadness and/or even physical ailments (Sherner, 2015). Because of this different presentation, school counselors are well positioned to provide the short-term support students need when in crisis. School counselors work to reduce a student's exposure to stress, build protective factors to enhance student resilience, and teach coping skills to assist students in managing times of grief.

Supportive Counseling

As mentioned earlier, there is consensus in the school counseling literature that school counselors refrain from engaging in therapy or long-term counseling (ASCA, 2019a; Erford, 2011; Kolbert et al., 2016). And school-aged children often experience events that trigger feelings of great anxiety, bouts of depressive symptoms, and stress that interferes with a student's ability to succeed academically. In these instances, school counselors can provide supportive interventions that are short-term and developmentally appropriate. School counselors often provide supportive counseling around areas such as academics (i.e., failing an exam and needing to inform parents), relationship issues (i.e., a breakup or getting rejected by a potential partner), family concerns, anger control, and family issues.

School counselors can provide supportive counseling for students who are transitioning out of treatment from a long-term facility such as a substance abuse recovery center or residential behavioral health program. Therefore, it is imperative for school counselors to receive appropriate training in addiction recovery and the signs, symptoms, and treatments of trauma. Students who are transitioning back to school following traumatic events or a long-term placement out of the home need additional support to cope with the emotions they experience that lead them to feel in crisis.

Finally, school counselors should feel equipped to provide appropriate support for students expressing suicidal ideation or who pose a threat of harm to themselves. According to ASCA (2018, 2020), a school counselor's role includes knowing the signs of suicide or suicidal thoughts; being aware of resources available to assist students; preparing students, staff members, colleagues, and parents to recognize warning symptoms of suicidal behavior; and referring students who pose a threat or express suicidal thoughts to local community agencies. School counselors are primarily charged with ensuring that a student who may be considering suicide is returned to the care and custody of the parent or caregiver and that the caregiver is provided options for mental health care outside of the school setting (Stone, 2021).

Community Resources and Referrals

School counselors are trained to address many different concerns throughout their school day. When school counselors determine that students need more intensive interventions that fall outside the scope of their work (through formal and informal student needs assessments), they take appropriate steps to refer families to outside resources. As early as 1994, school counselor literature outlined the importance of the school counselor's role in referring students to outside services. According to Ritchie and Partin (1994), school counselors are in a unique position of both knowing and understanding the needs of their students as well as serving in a position of trust with families, thus allowing them to be well positioned to encourage families to seek outside assistance. School counselors often refer students to outside support for a wide variety of academic, behavioral, physical, and mental health issues. Some of these issues include substance use, self-injury, sexual and physical abuse and trauma, depression, anxiety, suicide ideation, and medical issues to name a few.

The *ASCA Ethical Standards for School Counselors* (ASCA, 2022) devote section A.6 to a thorough discussion on how school counselors proceed when making outside referrals. According to the standards, school counselors are called to provide a variety of referral options to students and families that originate from a list of resources vetted by the school district. Additionally, school counselors refrain from directing students and their families to one referral source over the other by encouraging families to interview providers and make choices based on their own preferences (ASCA, 2022, A.6.b).

Other salient points to consider when referring students to outside resources include the following:

- Students have the right to engage in outside services while also maintaining an appropriate relationship with the school counselor, or students may choose to discontinue services with the school counselor (A.6.d)
- School counselors attempt to gain a release of information to speak to outside providers to ensure that everyone is working on behalf of the student (A.6.f)
- School counselors work to provide outside providers with accurate, meaningful data and information to ensure that students are provided with the best care (A.6.g)
- School counselors refrain from referring their own students to a private practice in which the school counselor works as a provider and refrains from referring students in their school to themselves (A.6.h).

Locating solid referral sources is an essential part of the work of a school counselor. This often includes cultivating relationships with area practitioners and collaborating with them to address students and families with higher needs. School counselors are encouraged to engage with community resources upon first entering a school district and to expand their networks to include practitioners from a variety of backgrounds (e.g., mental health, related services, academic supports).

Consultation Corner: Who You Gonna Call?

After bracketing your thoughts and reading the Informed School Counseling section, who would you call in and outside of the school building, and what might you ask them to support your decision-making? Take a moment to document these questions. Now that you have considered your questions for consultation, let's see what professional school counselors from around the world have to say about this case.

Consultation #1

Hello, Mia:

First, I want to commend you on your advocacy for your student. I appreciate the care and concern you have in working to ensure academic, career, and personal/social success for all your students. Much of your approach will depend upon the identity development of the student in this situation.

According to the preamble of the ASCA ethical code, school counselors should advocate for and affirm students with diverse sexual orientations, gender, and gender identity/expression. As you have stated, this becomes more complex when a student's family does not hold those same values. Even so, our position remains one of advocacy and affirmation.

I want to point you toward the ASCA position statement titled "The School Counselor and LGBTQI+ Youth," which is available for free from the ASCA website. These position statements were created (and are routinely updated) based on "best practices" as advised by experts within the respective fields. One resource within this particular position statement is a guide specific to working with families of LGBTQI+ students titled "A Practitioner's Resource Guide: Helping Families to Support Their LGBTQI+ Children" by Caitlin Ryan, PhD, ACSW, director of the Family Acceptance Project at San Francisco State University.

(Matt Tolliver, elementary school counselor, West Virginia)

Consultation #2

I have discovered many LGBTQI+ online resources for students through local organizations. There are virtual support groups that meet at differing age levels, but it has been difficult to find in-person support groups that accept children as young as 11. Our role as a school counselor is even more important during a mandated quarantine, as we may be the only access to a supportive adult who practices confidentiality. Providing access to request counseling services and maintaining communication with our LGBTQI+ students is extremely important to help them feel less isolated.

(Corinne Arenz, elementary school counselor, New Jersey)

Consultation #3

Hi, my name is Kristina Weiss, and I am a middle school counselor working in a suburban K–8 building. This is a difficult time for our students, particularly our LGBTQI+ students who may be experiencing this time without their safe spaces. The Human Rights Campaign collaborated with the American School Counselor Association to identify ways school counselors can support their LGBTQI+ students during remote learning! It has some wonderful ideas that we were able to use. We have been very intentional to stay in close communication with our LGBTQI+ students during remote learning. We created a Google Classroom where we post daily questions, students can interact with one another, and host biweekly virtual meetings. This has helped the students feel connected to their peers and a space to process their feelings. We also make sure to update weekly different resources for our students. Some of the resources we link our students with are The Trevor Project, The LGBTQI+ National Hotline, Trans Lifeline, National Suicide Prevention Lifeline, Gender Spectrum Lounge, and GLSEN. I cannot stress enough how important it is to thoroughly research any resources that we are providing to our LGBTQI+ students. Unfortunately, students come into contact with sites that are hateful or provide harmful information. Organizations, like the ones listed above, can be great resources for discovering other LGBTQI+ inclusive organizations that provide affirming information and support.

(Kristina Weiss, middle school counselor, New Jersey)

Consultation #4

Hi, Mia! I am a secondary school counselor working in a diverse suburban regional high school of approximately 1,900 students. We have a thriving Gender Sexuality Alliance (GSA) at school; however, students who rely on our GSA, friends at school, or safe spaces created by trusted adults for accepting communities may feel isolated while at home. The Trevor Project is always my go-to! The Trevor Project is the leading national organization providing crisis intervention and suicide prevention services to LGBTQI+ young people under 25. The Trevor Project launched Trevor-Space, a peer-to-peer social media site and an affirming international community for LGBTQI+ young people ages 13–24. Sadly, LGBTQI+ young adults who report high levels of parental rejection are 8 times more likely to report attempting suicide and six times more likely to report high levels of depression (Ryan, 2009). The Trevor Lifeline at 1-866-488-7386 is a great resource to share with your student if they are feeling hopeless. In New Jersey, we also encourage students to use 2ndFloor, a confidentiality and anonymous hotline for youth and young adults. You can text them 24/7 at 1-888-222-2228.

(Teaching Tolerance)

(Claudia Wolf, high school counselor, New Jersey)

Consultation #5

Hi, my name is Joey, I'm a high school counselor at a specialized high school in a major city, and an adjunct instructor of school counseling. As someone who was not "out" until late in my high school career, it's so wonderful that your student felt so safe to share this with you! Because I am out at school, and co-advise our school's queer student organization called Spectrum, I work with many of the LGBTQI+ students. I'm going to share some of my favorite resources you might want to check out, but if you need to chat on the phone, feel free to message me.

- GLSEN (https://www.glsen.org/): Gay Lesbian Straight Education Network has lots of resources specific to education, including recommendations on inclusive curriculum. I frequently share the book list with my school library and curriculum recommendations with the respective department heads.
- The Trevor Project (https://www.thetrevorproject.org/): Amazing organization that continues to expand its outreach and programming over the years. Started as a queer-specific crisis hotline, it now offers text support services (yes, I know, amazing), a monitored social space for young people to connect with one another, and also provides curriculum support as well.
- Trans Student (https://transstudent.org/): This is my favorite trans and gender-expansive resource to use for educational purposes (including your own!). They have info charts and graphics that make things so clear! Also, these are written from within the community, which is really important.
- PFlag (https://pflag.org/): I share this because I know you mentioned that the student was not feeling a great amount of support at home. I have been in similar situations, and let me tell you, the parent groups run by PFlag have really brought some of my families around. Some chapters even offer trans-specific groups, which is super important.

These are some nationwide organizations, but I will say I rely pretty heavily on my community-based organizations here in New York City. If you need some help identifying where those may be in your area, let me know.

(Joseph Feola, high school counselor, New York)

#EduCounselor Synthesis

Within the MTSS framework, Tier 3 supports are focused on more intensive counseling intervention, consultation, and collaboration with school and community partners. While individual counseling is an important part of a school counselor's role, as discussed earlier in the chapter, this work must be short term with referrals to outside supports provided concurrently or thereafter, if needed. This can be especially tricky in schools with lower income families, as outside supports may not be financially possible without assistance. Additionally, many of these schools lack district funding to provide adequate social/emotional/behavioral supports within the school buildings themselves. This can leave school counselors with higher than ideal (over 250:1) caseloads and in positions to provide reactive services almost exclusively. Identifying local resources (e.g., agencies, foodbanks, therapeutic services), sliding scale options, and funding sources (e.g., grants, parent/teacher associations) at the onset of your school counseling career is key, and establishing partnerships with these resources before you "need" them helps to provide your community with well-vetted referrals.

Students who identify within the LGBTQI+ community may be especially at risk for academic and mental health challenges (Crissman et al., 2019; Haas et al., 2011; Reisner et al., 2015); this has a lot to do with a lack of support and community (Graybill & Proctor, 2016; Haas et al., 2011). The *ACA Advocacy Competencies* (Lewis et al., 2002) and the *Multicultural and Social Justice Competencies* (Ratts et al., 2016) speak to the importance of counselors addressing the systems that impact clients with marginalized identities. In our case, Mia is requesting help from colleagues to provide a student, and potentially their family, support around gender identity. Mia appears to understand that the student's unsupportive family in addition to their lack of social supports in school has a significant impact on how they are able to perform. In this case, Mia's student is attending school from home as a result of the COVID-19 pandemic and feeling isolated from resources that might help them to experience more connection. While the school environment can sadly be a place where some gender nonconforming students feel ostracized (Grossman et al., 2009; Grossman et al., 2016; Kosciw et al., 2012; McGuire et al., 2010), it can also be a safe haven for students who are allowed to openly express themselves (Graybill & Proctor, 2016; Ratts et al., 2013). Caring adults, like Mia, can help to address the staggering numbers of gender nonconforming youth who experience academic disruption (e.g., absenteeism, homelessness) and suicide ideation (Crissman et al., 2019; Reisner et al., 2015) by demonstrating allyship and engaging in advocacy efforts to support students in and outside of the schools. This includes counselors examining their own feelings and biases around gender identity, providing culturally responsive interventions, and cultivating relationships with strong referral sources.

As we examine the consultants' responses, it is important to note that school counselors must be aware of how legislation, the political landscape, and societal events shape the supports needed for our most vulnerable students. For instance, in March 2021, the state of Alabama passed a law making hormone therapy and surgery for trans youth a felony. Even if your students do not reside in Alabama or other states that have passed discriminatory legislation (e.g., Tennessee, North Carolina), students in the gender-expansive community are likely to feel unsafe and worried about future lawmaking in their own areas. Thus, school counselors must be aware of federal, state, and local laws that may impact the health and well-being of our students.

After reading the situation, our consultants commend Mia for her efforts to stay in touch with the student during the COVID-19 pandemic. As Matt mentioned, both advocacy and affirmation are important! School counselors must be especially vigilant, as it is easy for some students to hide underneath the radar, even during in-class instruction. Mia clearly developed a relationship with the student pre-pandemic and took opportunities to check in directly during remote instruction. This is likely how Mia discovered that the student was having a particularly difficult time at home.

Each of our consultants provides excellent resources that we encourage readers to explore for themselves. Many of them are listed in the resources section at the end of this chapter. Some of our consultants also mentioned membership in professional organizations. As we have noted throughout this text, it is especially beneficial for school counselors to remain connected to school-based and child-/adolescent-centered organizations. Not only does membership afford school counselors more opportunities for consultation, but it also offers many resources across a variety of topics. For instance, Matt and Kristina discussed the benefit of ASCA's reach and how they paired up with the Human Rights Campaign to provide additional resources for LGBTQI+ youth.

Leadership is another theme that came up in the consultants' responses. Both Claudia and Joey discussed their roles in their schools' GSA and queer student organization, Spectrum, groups. When students see that the school counselor is actively taking on leadership roles in these organizations, they are likely to feel safer and more connected to the school (Beck, 2018; Gonzalez, 2017). Kristina pointed out some innovative ways to use Google Classroom to offer a safe space for LGBTQI+ students to express themselves remotely. Similarly, Corinne mentioned virtual support groups, and Claudia referenced social media platforms and hotlines that exist to help students build community and receive help online. We agree with Kristina: it is important to research these groups before offering them as resources!

Chapter Summary

School counselors are trained to deliver interventions at each of the three tiers in order to meet the needs of all students. Tier 3 represents the most intensive work with and on behalf of students. Guided by their theoretical orientation, school counselors provide behavioral and mental health services for up to 80% of the school-aged children who actually receive support. This includes conducting short-term and crisis counseling for students experiencing grief, loss, and difficult transitions. While school counselors are not called upon to engage in long-term counseling or therapy, they must be skilled and proficient in delivering services by way of short-term counseling, consultation, and appropriate resource referrals to ensure that students are receiving appropriate support both inside and outside of school.

Reflective Practitioner Process

School counselors engage in **clinical supervision, professional development**, and **self-care** in order to further develop their knowledge and skills and to help balance professional expectations with personal wellness. All three areas are key to ethical practice and help to mitigate counselor burnout and compassion fatigue (Atici, 2015; Lawson & Myers, 2011; Merriman, 2015; Ohrt et al., 2015).

Clinical Supervision

The *ASCA School Counselor Professional Standards & Competencies* (2019b) direct school counselors to "consult with school counselors and other education and counseling professionals when questions of school counseling practice arise" (B-SS 5., p. 5). As a supervisee, it is important to consider the thoughts, feelings, and experiences that come up for you as you work with students, families, and colleagues and seek consultation on difficult issues. The following are some topics for consideration as you react to this chapter.

- Which resources can be valuable to learn more about the experiences of gender-expansive youth in the schools?
- How do you apply the theoretical approach of your choice to inform your work with the student and their parents in this case?
- Which advocacy efforts can be used to support this student and their family?
- What actions might be taken if the family dismisses your efforts to support their child?
- What organizational approach can you use to catalog your referral sources?

Professional Development

According to the *ASCA Ethical Standards for School Counselors* (ASCA, 2022), professional school counselors engage in professional development and attend trainings to stay current on the trends and issues that impact students (B.3.e). Relative to the contents of this chapter, consider finding professional development on the following topics:

MTSS – Any training around Tier 3 interventions for school counselors, including the following:

- Counseling theory and techniques specific to short-term work with children and adolescents
- Crisis prevention and intervention
- Community resource networking

#PSCSelfCare: Everyday Wellness

When designing, managing, and implementing a comprehensive school counseling program, school and community expectations can tax even the most seasoned school counselor. The *ASCA Ethical Standards for School Counselors* (ASCA, 2022) require school counselors to recognize the high levels of stress often associated with the job. Therefore, school counselors recognize that self-care must be a priority to maintain health and overall well-being (see ASCA, 2022, B.3.h).

Take Up Yoga

After a long day as a professional school counselor, a day where you have been actively engaged in providing Tier 3 interventions, the need to practice self-care is critical. Failure to attend to the stress and emotional toll that results from dozens of brief individual counseling interventions, group facilitations, conflict resolution calls, and crisis responses can lead to high levels of compassion fatigue and ultimately, school counselor burnout (Coaston, 2017; Holman et al., 2018). Throughout this text, we have provided a variety of strategies to consider when developing your self-care plan. Here we offer the idea of integrating yoga as a piece of the plan!

There is a growing movement that encourages the integration of yoga into a comprehensive school counseling program. As an example, we encourage you to review Taylor et al.'s (2019) findings around its connection to student wellness. While planning wellness activities for children and adolescents is a key focus in any school counseling program, it is equally valuable for counselors to practice what we preach; according to Giovengo-Gurrera (2017), integrating yoga to address counselor self-care and burnout is a good start!

Put very simply, yoga involves the connection between mind, body, and spirit (Monk-Turner & Turner, 2010). Using breathing techniques and mindfulness practices therein has the potential to alleviate anxiety and stress, which are two factors associated with burnout (Coaston, 2017, Monk-Turner & Turner, 2010). According to the website Yogaru (Delahunty, 2020), yoga is most beneficial as part of a self-care plan when users make a commitment to practicing consistently, even if only 10 minutes per day. If you are not familiar with yoga practice, there are simple poses that you can work through each day to help get you started. An article in the *YogaJournal* (https://www.yogajournal.com) may be a good starting place. School counselors can also leverage their positionality in the school to advocate for *eduCounselor* wellness by bringing to school a certified instructor two to three times per week following the end of the school day. In fact, school counselors might even apply for a grant to fund this opportunity for the school community (e.g., teachers, support staff). Initiating adult wellness activities will not only benefit your self-care plan but also support school partners in addressing their own health. Check out a GoatYoga resource in the section below!

Spotlight: School Counseling Advocacy

Here we highlight a practicing school counselor who provides targeted Tier 3 intervention while also making time to advocate for self-care! As discussed throughout the chapter, engaging students in Tier 3 interventions such as individual counseling and suicide referral and safety plans can take a heavy toll on school counselors. Effective school counselors who find long careers in the field commit to caring for themselves and their own mental health.

callslipsandroadtrips . Follow

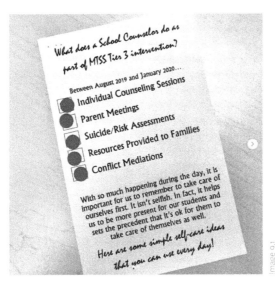

Liked by **twoblondescounseling** and **20 others**

callslipsandroadtrips Sharing data about Tier 3 interventions provided by my School Counseling program this school year (so far), and reminding staff to take care of themselves with these bingo sheets.

Lindsey Morris, "Callslipsandroadtrips Instagram Post." Copyright © by Lindsey Morris. Reprinted with permission.

Learning Connections

Both professional school counselors in training and seasoned school counselors understand the importance of understanding the connections between the concepts commonly taught in counseling programs and the standards most associated with school counselor training. Therefore, the following table offers broad connections between the material and information in this chapter and the Council for Accreditation of Counseling and Related Educational Programs (CACREP, 2016) standards, the *ASCA School Counselor Professional Standards & Competencies* (ASCA, 2019b), and the *ASCA Ethical Standards for School Counselors* (ASCA, 2022).

Connections to CACREP Core Curricular Areas

Professional Counseling Orientation and Ethical Practice	Social and Cultural Diversity	Human Growth and Development	Career Development	Counseling and Helping Relationships	Group Counseling and Group Work	Assessment and Testing	Research and Program Evaluation
X	X			X		X	

Connection to Professional Standards

CACREP	ASCA SC Professional Competencies	Ethical Standards: SC
G.1.d: Models of school-based collaboration and consultation	M 5. Effective school counseling is a collaborative process involving school counselors, students, families, teachers, administrators, other school staff and education stakeholders.	A.1.e: Provide culturally responsive counseling to students in a brief context and support students and families/guardians in obtaining outside services if students need long-term clinical/ mental health counseling.
G.2.e: School counselor roles and responsibilities in relation to the school emergency management plans, and crises, disasters, and trauma	M 7. School counseling programs promote and enhance student academic, career and social/emotional outcomes.	A.1.j: Advocate for equitable, anti-oppressive and anti-bias policies and procedures, systems, and practices, and provide effective, evidence-based and culturally sustaining interventions to address student needs.
G.2.g: Characteristics, risk factors, and warning signs of students at risk for mental health and behavioral disorders	B-SS 3. Provide short-term counseling in small-group and individual settings.	

(Continued)

CACREP	ASCA SC Professional Competencies	Ethical Standards: SC
G.2.k: Community resources and referral sources	B-SS 4. Make referrals to appropriate school and community resources.	A.6.a: Collaborate with all relevant stakeholders, including students, school faculty/staff and parents/guardians, when students need assistance, including when early warning signs of student distress are identified.
G.3.f: Techniques of personal/social counseling in school settings	B-SS 3. Provide short-term counseling in small-group and individual settings.	A.6.b: Provide a list of outside agencies and resources in their community, or the closest available, to students and parents/ guardians when students need or request additional support. School counselors provide multiple referral options or the district-vetted list of referrals options and are careful not to indicate an endorsement or preference for one individual or practice. School counselors encourage parents/guardians to research outside professionals' skills/experience to inform their personal decision regarding the best source of assistance for their student.
		A.6.d: Develop a plan for the transitioning of primary counseling services with minimal interruption of services. Students retain the right for the referred services to be done in coordination with the school counselor or to discontinue counseling services with the school counselor while maintaining an appropriate relationship that may include providing other school support services.
		A.6.e: Refrain from referring students based solely on the school counselor's personal beliefs or values rooted in one's religion, culture, ethnicity or personal worldview. School counselors maintain the highest respect for student cultural identities and worldviews. School counselors pursue additional training and supervision when their values are discriminatory in nature (e.g., sexual orientation, gender identity, gender expression, reproductive rights, race, religion, ability status). School counselors do not impose their values on students and/ or families when making referrals to outside resources for student and/or family support.
		A.6.f.: Attempt to establish a collaborative relationship with outside service providers to best serve students. Request a release of information signed by the student and/ or parents/guardians before attempting to collaborate with the student's external provider.

Comprehensive School Counseling Assignments

The following section provides activities that allow for your continued growth as a professional school counselor. Both preservice and practicing school counselors may find it helpful to complete these activities. If you are currently in a graduate training program, your professor might assign these as part of your course.

1. **DSM-5-TR: Exploring Diagnoses.** Since school counselors are mental health experts in educational settings, we recommend you familiarize yourself with the *Diagnostic and Statistical Manual of Mental Disorders, Text Revision* (*DSM–5-TR*), which contains conditions that children and adolescents may receive as diagnoses in the schools. Pick two diagnoses (e.g., autism spectrum disorder, generalized anxiety, depression.) and research the following:
   a. What are the signs and symptoms? How might these present in school?
   b. Is there a typical onset and age? What might be some development differences in how symptoms manifest?
   c. What are some evidence-based strategies or interventions that have been proven to be successful?
   d. If you were to provide a staff development presentation on one of these disorders, what would you include to help school and community partners understand how students with these diagnoses might present emotionally, behaviorally, and academically in the school setting?

2. **Community Partnership Resources**. Choose a community of interest (e.g., your hometown, current field placement site, a town near your university). Research two community resources within 10 miles of your chosen town. One of these must be a mental health resource and the other should be a non-mental health resource. Non-mental health resources may include tutoring services, college planning and access support, student apprenticeship opportunities, summer programming, employment, occupational/physical/speech therapy resources for children/adolescents, etc.

After locating these resources, make at least one ON-SITE visit to each and report the following information:

- Name of site:
- Location of site:
- Contact information (phone and email if possible)
- Website:
- Credentials of therapists
- Is insurance accepted? If so, which ones?
- Is there a sliding scale?

- Will the site take everyone or are there inclusion/exclusion criteria (e.g., certain counties, age groups, socioeconomic status, documented disability)?
- Is there currently (or usually) a waitlist?
- Transportation options from your school to the site (car, train, bus)
- Describe the space
- What are the steps to make an appointment?

   * If doing this as a group, take the opportunity to share this information with colleagues

3. **Annotated Bibliography.** Find 10 peer-reviewed journal articles specific to the needs of LGBTQI+ youth and create an annotated bibliography, highlighting recommendations for practice. We encourage you to combine this information with the resources provided by our consultants so that you have a comprehensive list of materials to support your work with students and their families.
   a. **Parent/Guardian Presentation.** Using information from the literature, create a parent/guardian presentation around the needs of gender-expansive youth. This presentation may include current statistics regarding students' experiences in school, students' mental health needs, including common at-risk behaviors, and suggestions for how to support students at home.
4. **Theory Presentation.** Choose one of the common theories used with children and adolescents and locate three to five research articles that provide evidence for school-based intervention grounded in that theory. Present this information to your colleagues along with a discussion around specific interventions and concepts that can be used within this theory to support students (e.g., Miracle Question, Tracking, 5 Needs)

Helpful Resources
Web-Based Resources

- Information on Tier 3 interventions:
  - https://www.pbisworld.com/tier-3/
- Information on emerging counseling approaches:
  - https://goatyoga.net/goat-therapy-animal-assisted-therapy/
- Information on rational emotive education:
  - http://www.rebtnetwork.org/library/Rational_Emotive_Education.pdf
- CBITS Training
  - https://cbitsprogram.org

For Working With Students in the LGBTQI+ Community

- ASCA Position Statement on Working with LGBTQ Youth:
  - https://www.schoolcounselor.org/Standards-Positions/Position-Statements/ASCA-Position-Statements/The-School-Counselor-and-LGBTQ-Youth#:~:text=%2C%202014%2C%202016
- GLSEN
  - https://www.glsen.org
- The Trevor Project:
  - https://www.thetrevorproject.org/
- The Trevor Lifeline:
  - 1-866-488-7386
- LGBT National Youth Hotline:
  - 1-800-246-7743
- Trans Student:
  - https://transstudent.org/
- PFlag:
  - https://pflag.org/
- 2nd Floor:
  - https://www.2ndfloor.org/ and hotline 1-888-222-2228
- Gender Spectrum:
  - https://genderspectrum.org/

Model of District Policy re: Suicide Prevention

- https://www.schoolcounselor.org/getmedia/9b28c170-607a-428f-9dae-619850fa531b/Model-School-District-Policy-Suicide-Prevention.pdf

Suggested Readings

Information on Diagnosis of Mental Disorders:

- American Psychiatric Association (Ed.). (2022). *Diagnostic and statistical manual of mental disorders: DSM-5-TR* (5th ed., text revision).

Information Related to Using General Use of REBT and REBT With Underrepresented Students:

- Warren, J. M., & Hale, R. W. (2016). Fostering non-cognitive development of underrepresented students through rational emotive behavior therapy: Recommendations for school counselor practice. *The Professional Counselor, 6*(1), 89–106. https://doi.org/10.15241/jw.6.1.89

Creative Counseling With Children and Adolescents:

- Jacobs, E., & Schimmel, C. J. (2016). *Impact therapy: The courage to counsel.* Impact Therapy Associates.

- Vernon, A. (2002). *What works when with children and adolescents: A handbook of individual counseling techniques.* Research Press.
- Vernon, A. (2009). *More what works when with children and adolescents: A handbook of individual counseling techniques.* Research Press.

Solution Focused Brief Counseling (SFBC)

- Sabella, R. A. (2020). *Solution-focused school counseling: The missing manual.* Sabella & Associates, LLC.

References

American School Counselor Association (ASCA). (2018). *The school counselor and suicide prevention/awareness.* https://www.schoolcounselor.org/Standards-Positions/Position-Statements/ASCA-Positin-Statements/The-School-Counselor-and-Suicide-Prevention-Awaren

American School Counselor Association (ASCA). (2019a). *ASCA national model: A framework for school counseling programs.* (4th ed.).

American School Counselor Association. (ASCA). (2019b). *ASCA school counselor professional standards & competencies.* https://www.schoolcounselor.org/asca/media/asca/home/SCCompetencies.pdf

American School Counselor Association. (ASCA). (2020). *The school counselor and student mental health.* https://www.schoolcounselor.org/Standards-Positions/Position-Statements/ASCA-Positin-Statements/The-School-Counselor-and-Student-Mental-Health

American School Counselor Association (ASCA). (2022). *ASCA ethical standards for school counselors.* https://www.schoolcounselor.org/getmedia/44f30280-ffe8-4b41-9ad8-f15909c3d164/EthicalStandards.pdf

Atici, M. (2015). Professional identity development of counselors-in-training in a school internship program in Turkey. *The Professional Counselor, 5*(1), 137–151. https://doi.org/10.15241/MA.5.1.137

Beck, M. J. (2018). Lead by example. *Professional school counseling, 21*(1), 1–13. https://doi.org/10.1177/2156759X18793838

Council for Accreditation of Counseling and Related Educational Programs (CACREP). (2016). *2016 CACREP standards.* http://www.cacrep.org/wp-content/uploads/2017/08/2016-Standards-with-citations.pdf

CBITS at a Glance. (n.d.). *Cognitive behavioral intervention for trauma in schools.* Retrieved March 30, 2021, from https://cbitsprogram.org/

Coaston, S. C. (2017). Self-Care through self-compassion: A balm for burnout. *The Professional Counselor, 7*(3), 285–297. https://doi.org/10.15241/scc.7.3.285

Crissman H. P., Stroumsa D., Kobernik E. K., & Berger M. B. (2019). Gender and frequent mental distress: Comparing transgender and non-transgender individuals' self-rated mental health. *Journal of Women's Health, 28*(2), 143–151. https://doi.org/10.1089/jwh.2018.7411

Delahunty, R. (2020, September 23). *Yoga for self care.* Yogaru. http://www.yogaru.ie/pause/yoga-for-self-care

Dickinson, R., & Kottman, T. (2019). Play therapy. In A. Vernon & C. J. Schimmel (Eds.), *Counseling children & adolescents* (pp. 111–146). Cognella.

Erford, B. T. (2011). *Transforming the school counseling profession* (3rd ed.). Pearson Education.

Gallo, L. L. (2018). The relationship between high school counselors' self-efficacy and conducting suicide risk assessments. *Journal of Child and Adolescent Counseling, 4*(1), 209–225. https://doi.org/10.1080/23727810.2017.1422646

Giovengo-Gurrera, S. (2017). The lived experiences of school counselors participating in yoga: A hermeneutic phenomenological study of self-care [Doctoral dissertation, Duquesne University]. https://dsc.duq.edu/etd/130

Gleason, M. M., Zeanha, C. H., & Dickstein, S. (2010). Recognizing young children in need of mental health assessment: Development and preliminary validity of the early childhood screening assessment. *Infant Mental Health Journal, 31*(3), 335–257. https://doi.org/10.1002/imhj.20259

Gonzalez, M. (2017). Advocacy for and with LGBT students: An examination of high school counselor experiences. *Professional School Counseling, 20*(1), 38–46. https://doi.org/10.5330/1096-2409-20.18.38

Gratz, K. L., & Roemer, L. (2004). Multidimensional assessment of emotion regulation and dysregulation: Development, factor structure, and initial validation of the difficulties in emotion regulation scale. *Journal of Psychopathology and Behavioral Assessment, 26*(1), 41–54. https://doi.org/10.1023/B:JOBA.0000007455.08539.94

Graybill, E. C., & Proctor, S. L. (2016). Lesbian, gay, bisexual, and transgender youth: Limited representation in school support personnel journals. *Journal of School Psychology, 54*(1), 9–16. https://doi.org/10.1016/j.jsp.2015.11.001

Grossman, A. H., Haney, A. P., Edwards, P., Alessi, E. J., Ardon, M., & Howell, T. J. (2009). Lesbian, gay, bisexual, and transgender youth talk about experiencing and coping with school violence: A qualitative study. *Journal of LGBT Youth, 6*, 24–46. https://doi.org/10.1080/19361650802379748

Grossman, A. H., Park, J. Y., & Russell, S. T. (2016). Transgender youth and suicidal behaviors: Applying the interpersonal psychological theory of suicide. *Journal of Gay & Lesbian Mental Health, 20*(4), 329–349. https://doi.org/10.1080/19359705.2016.1207581

Haas, A. P., Eliason, M., Mays, V. M., Mathy, R. M., Cochran, S. D., D'Augelli, A. R., Silverman, M. M., ... & Clayton, P. J. (2011). Suicide and suicide risk in lesbian, gay, bisexual, and transgender populations: Review and recommendations. *Journal of Homosexuality, 58*(1), 10–51. https://doi.org/10.1080/00918369.2011.534038

Holman, L. F., Watts, R., Robles-Pina, R., & Grubbs, L. (2018). Exploration of potential predictor variables leading to school counselor burnout. *Journal of School Counseling, 16*(9), 1–29. https://files.eric.ed.gov/fulltext/EJ1184754.pdf

Jacobs, E., & Schimmel, C. J. (2013). *Impact therapy: The courage to counsel.* Impact Therapy Associates.

Juhnke, G. A., Granello, D. H., & Granello, P. F. (2011). *Suicide self-injury and violence in the schools.* Wiley & Sons.

Kaffenberger, C. J., & O'Rorke-Trigiani, J. (2018). Addressing student mental health needs by providing direct and indirect services and building alliances in the community. *Professional School Counseling, 16*(5), 323–332. https://doi.org/10.1177/2156759X1201600505

Kolbert, J. B., Morgan, L. M., Crothers, L. M., & Hughes, T. L. (2016). *Introduction to professional school counseling: Advocacy, leadership, and intervention.* Routledge.

Kosciw, J. G., Greytak, E. A., Bartkiewicz, M. J., Boesen, M. J., & Palmer, N. A. (2012). *The 2011 national school climate survey: The experiences of lesbian, gay, bisexual and transgender youth in our nation's schools.* GLSEN.

Landreth, G. L. (2012). *Play therapy: The art of relationship* (3rd ed.). Routledge/Taylor & Francis Group.

Lawson, G., & Myers, J. E. (2011). Wellness, professional quality of life, and career-sustaining behaviors: What keeps us well? *Journal of Counseling and Development*, 89(2), 163–171. https://doi.org/10.1002/j.1556-6678.2011.tb00074.x

Leppma, M., & Schimmel, C. J. (2019). Children and challenges: Counseling from a growth mindset perspective. In A. Vernon, & C. J. Schimmel (Eds.), *Counseling Children & Adolescents* (5th ed., pp. 338–379). Cognella.

Lewis, J. A., Arnold, M. S., House, R., & Toporek, R. L. (2002). *ACA advocacy competencies*. American Counseling Association. http://www.counseling.org/Resources/Competencies/Advocacy_Competencies.pdf

Luke, C., & Schimmel, C. J. (2022). *Applying neuroscience to counseling children and adolescents: A guide to brain-based, experiential interventions.* Cognella.

McGuire, J. K., Anderson, C. R., Toomey, R. B., & Russell, S. T. (2010). School climate for transgender youth: A mixed method investigation of student experiences and school responses. *Journal of Youth and Adolescence*, 39(10), 1175–1188. https://doi.org/10.1007/s10964-010-9540-7

Merriman, J. (2015). Enhancing counselor supervision through compassion fatigue education. *Journal of Counseling and Development*, 93(3), 370–378. https://doi.org/10.1002/jcad.12035

Monk-Turner, E., & Turner, C. (2010). Does yoga shape body, mind and spiritual health and happiness: Differences between yoga practitioners and college students. *International Journal of Yoga*, 3(2), 48–54. https://doi.org/10.4103/0973-6131.72630

Ohrt, J. H., Prosek, E. A., Ener, E., & Lindo, N. (2015). The effects of a group supervision intervention to promote wellness and prevent burnout. *The Journal of Humanistic Counseling*, 54(1), 41–58. https://doi.org/10.1002/j.2161-1939.2015.00063.x

Rahdert, E. H. (1991). Adolescent assessment referral system manual. National Institute on Drug Abuse, 1991. Retrieved July 28, 2021, from http://bit.ly/POSIT_inst

Ratts, M. J., Kaloper, M., McReady, C., Tighe, L., Butler, S. K., Dempsey, K., & McCullough, J. (2013). Safe space programs in K–12 schools: Creating a visible presence of LGBTQ Allies. *Journal of LGBTQ Issues in Counseling*, 7(4), 387–404. https://doi.org/10.1080/15538605.2013.839344

Ratts, M. J., Singh, A. A., Nassar-McMillan, S., Butler, S. K., & McCullough, J. R. (2016). Multicultural and social justice counseling competencies: Guidelines for the counseling profession. *Journal of Multicultural Counseling and Development Special Issue: Hearing Our Elders*, 44(1), 28–48. https://doi.org/10.1002/jmcd.12035

Reisner, S. L., Vetters, R., Leclerc, M., Zaslow, S., Wolfrum, S., Shumer, D., & Mimiaga, M. J. (2015). Mental health of transgender youth in care at an adolescent urban community health center: A matched retrospective cohort study. *The Journal of Adolescent Health*, 56(3), 274–279. https://doi.org/10.1016/j.jadohealth.2014.10.264

Ritchie, M. H., & Partin, R. L. (1994). Parent education and consultation activities of school counselors. *School Counselor*, 41(3), 165–170.

Ryan, C. (2009). Helping families support their lesbian, gay, bisexual, and transgender (LGBT) children. *Washington, DC: National center for cultural competence, Georgetown university center for child and human development.* http://www.eastbaypride.com/LGBT_Brief.pdf

Sabella, R. A. (2019). Solution-focused brief counseling. In A. Vernon, & C. J. Schimmel (Eds.), *Counseling children & adolescents* (5th ed., pp. 111–146). Cognella.

Sabella, R. A. (2020) *Solution-focused school counseling: The missing manual.* Sabella & Associates, LLC

SAMHSA. (2020). *Ready, set, go, review: Screening for behavioral health risk in schools.* https://www.samhsa.gov/sites/default/files/ready_set_go_review_mh_screening_in_schools_508.pdf

Sherner, T. (2015). Help children understand grief and loss. *ONS Connect, 30*(3), 36.

Singh, A. A., Merchant, N., Skuryzk, B., & Ingene, D. (2012). Group worker principles for seeking multicultural and social justice competence. *Journal of Specialists in Group Work, 37*(4), 312–325. https://doi.org/10.1080/01933922.2012.721482

Sklare, G. B. (2014). *Brief counseling that works: A solution-focused therapy approach for school counselors and other mental health professionals* (3rd ed.). Corwin.

Stone, C. (2021, July 12). *Change the narrative on suicide assessments* [Conference presentation]. ASCA Conference, Las Vegas, NV, United States.

Taylor, J. V., Gibson, D. M., & Conley, A. H. (2019). Integrating yoga into a comprehensive school counseling program: A qualitative approach. *Professional School Counseling, 22*(1), 1–13. https://doi.org/10.1177/2156759X19857921

The Talking, Feeling & Doing Board Game. (n.d). *Child therapy toys.* https://www.childtherapytoys.com/products/the-talking-feeling-doing-board-game

Tolliver, M. & Smith, C. (2022). Creative strategies (improvisation and gaming) with school counseling small groups. In S. I. Springer, L. J. Moss, & C. J. Schimmel (Eds.), *A school counselor's guide to small groups: coordination, leadership, and assessment* (2nd ed., pp. 71–80). Cognella.

Vernon, A. (2019). Rational-emotive behavior therapy. In A. Vernon & C. J. Schimmel (Eds.), *Counseling children & adolescents* (5th ed., pp. 222–257). Cognella.

Vernon, A., & Berry, K. L. (2013). *Counseling outside the lines: Individual, small group, and classroom applications: Creative arts interventions for children and adolescents.* Research Press.

Vernon, A., & Schimmel, C. J. (Eds.). (2019). *Counseling children and adolescents* (5th ed.). Cognella.

Warren, J., & Hale, R.W. (2016). The influence of efficacy beliefs on teacher performance and student success: Implications for student support services. *Journal of Rational-Emotive & Cognitive-Behavior Therapy, 34*(1), 187–208. https://doi.org/10.1007/s10942-016-0237-z

Wubbolding, R. E. (2019). Reality therapy. In A. Vernon, & C. J. Schimmel (Eds.), *Counseling children and adolescents* (5th ed., pp. 185–220). Cognella.

Credit

PART IV

The School Counseling Profession

Assess

CHAPTER 10

Assessing School Counselor and Program Impact

LEARNING OBJECTIVES

#EduCounselors can

- discuss the use of an annual comprehensive school counseling program assessment;

- identify the three primary data reports that school counselors complete each year;

- describe the rationale for disaggregating data to ensure that the school counseling program serves all students, especially those students from historically marginalized communities; and

- recognize the elements and use of an annual school counselor performance appraisal.

Introduction

School counselors must be able to identify and communicate how students are different as a result of a comprehensive school counseling program. Twenty-first-century school counselors understand the importance of conducting assessments of the school counseling program and of themselves to provide evidence of the school counselor and program's impact on student success. Engaging in assessments and using data to evidence student impact can feel daunting for many school counselors and, unfortunately, often goes unattended when school counselors are overwhelmed with the day-to-day work of supporting all school and community partners. Furthermore, many school counselors report feeling a lack of confidence when approaching the use of data for any purpose. This chapter provides an overview of program assessment and program evaluation and offers tools to assist in using data to report program results and school counselor effectiveness.

#IRLSchoolCounseling

The following is a social media post from one of the many school counseling groups on Facebook. *Caught in the Middle School Counselors* is a Facebook group primarily hosting topics posed by middle school counselors.

> **Matthew B. Tolliver**
> Posted 17 hours ago
>
> Hello all. A colleague and I were discussing a situation, and I wanted to offer it as a "what would you do in this situation?"
>
> This year, your school hired a new assistant principal who has been assigned to complete your annual evaluation. While discussing this, he frankly admits to never having evaluated a "guidance counselor" before In preparation, he emails you the evaluation from, which (as it turns out) is actually the teacher evaluation, with some of the items not even applicable to your role. Presently, if you were to respond to his email as you are truly feeling, it would probably not go well!
>
> You do not hold him totally responsible for this (it seems as though this was thrown on him too); however, you are also frustrated with the fact that much of your day is spent filling in spaces in the schedule as a rotation teacher (much like art, P.E., music, etc). Any extra time is spent running around the school putting out fires with students in crisis. At this point, you are feeling overwhelmed with being assessed with an evaluation not tied to your job and doing work that is not even what you feel like you should be doing! What would you do?!?

Bracketing Values for Ethical Practice

It is expected that school counselors continuously reflect on our values, beliefs, worldviews, and cultural norms and how each influences the ways in which we choose to take or not take action. As such, it is important to recognize and set aside any preconceived notions, experiences, and biases to help you respond to this scenario in a culturally sustaining and ethically sound manner. Take a moment to reflect on the previous post and then consider the following questions:

- What feelings are immediately generated when you think of an administrator evaluating you or your program?

- How does your cultural identity influence any feelings you might have regarding being 'assessed' by a person in power?
- How comfortable are you organizing and analyzing data to support your role and your program?
- What are your reactions to the possibility of an administrator evaluating you as the school counselor in the same way they would do so for a teacher?

Informed School Counseling

Program assessment, program evaluation, and school counselor self-assessment are interconnected processes and vital to the implementation and sustainability of a comprehensive school counseling program that serves all students. While we cannot possibly cover such critical aspects of school counseling in their entirety in just one chapter, we offer you many supplementary materials in the "Helpful Resources" section that allow you to take a deeper dive into assessment and evaluation and how these apply to your respective school populations. The purpose of this chapter is to familiarize you with common language, concepts, and tools school counselors who align their programs with the *ASCA National Model* (ASCA, 2019a) use to engage in the work of assessment and evaluation.

As discussed in Chapter 1 of this text, it is commonly understood that since the mid-1970s, school counselors coming of age in the educational reform era have felt greater pressure to engage in multiple levels of program evaluation in an effort to be more accountable for the comprehensive school counseling programs they implement (Erford, 2011). Generally speaking, "educational reform" refers to a movement whereby educators attempt to improve teaching by increasing the use of accountability to measure evidence-based curricula and practices (Young & Kaffenberger, 2019). School counseling has also been heavily influenced by the educational reform movement with a call to use evidence-based practices and evaluation mechanisms that demonstrate the effectiveness of interventions. Researchers and school counseling professional organizations alike continue to build evidence for best practice strategies and advocate for methods that measure the impact of interventions, program development, and practitioner effectiveness (Dimmitt et al., 2007; Stone & Dahir, 2016; Young & Kaffenberger, 2019; Zyromski & Marini, 2016).

Collecting data and reporting results is essential for many reasons. First, school counselors who recognize the benefit of a fully implemented comprehensive school counseling program must have some mechanism by which they can assess the level to which their program aligns with either the *ASCA National Model* (ASCA, 2019b) or a state-mandated model. Many programs engage in these processes as they prepare to apply for American School Counselor Association's (ASCA) RAMP (Recognized ASCA Model Program) designation. RAMP is a recognition program for individual comprehensive school counseling programs. It indicates that the program is aligned with the *ASCA National Model* (ASCA, n.d.). To be considered for RAMP, programs must document efforts to assess their programs in terms of design and delivery as well as demonstrate use of evaluation tools like results reports. Second, once a program is more fully aligned with a given model, school counselors must have a structured way to identify areas in need of improvement within their programs. Additionally, professional school counselors understand the need to share the impact of their work with a wide variety of partners (e.g., parents, teachers, administrators, community members). This task is best accomplished through the gathering and dissemination of data that evidences how students have changed, improved, or benefited from the work of the school counselor. It is not simply enough to say, "I just know my students benefit from my program." Finally, once school and community partners are presented with data that demonstrate the impact of the school counseling program, garnering more financial support and advocating for increased resources becomes easier.

Assessing and evaluating the overall impact of a school counseling program begins with assessing the level of implementation of a model that guides the program. For example, school counselors begin evaluating their programs by assessing the degree to which each aligns with the *ASCA National Model* or their state-mandated model.

Program Assessment

Examples of effective school counseling programs are documented in the literature and suggest that students benefit academically when they learn in an environment with a strong comprehensive school counseling program (Parzych et al., 2019; Villares et al., 2011; Wilkerson et al., 2013). According to the *ASCA National Model* (ASCA, 2019a), "the school counseling program assessment is used to analyze progress toward full implementation of a comprehensive school counseling program and to identify program strengths and areas for improvement" (p. 88). By completing an annual program assessment, school counselors demonstrate leadership and a commitment to improving the overall design and delivery of a comprehensive school counseling program. ASCA (2019a) recommends school counselors complete a program assessment toward the end of the school year.

The annual program assessment helps school counselors ensure that their comprehensive school counseling program is aligned with the *ASCA National Model* (ASCA, 2019a). The ASCA School Counseling Program Assessment form helps school counselors track their progress toward full implementation of their programs (ASCA, 2019a). This assessment highlights the following items discussed throughout the text:

- The program vision statement
- The program mission statement
- Data and its use in prioritizing school counseling program initiatives
- Use of time tracking
- Administrative conference use and completed agreement
- Advisory council implementation

- Lesson plans and calendars are used to document interventions
- Classroom and group mindsets and behaviors results reports are completed
- *ASCA School Counselor Professional Standards & Competencies* assessments are completed

These are just a few items on the ASCA School Counseling Program Assessment. When completing the assessment, school counselors simply indicate whether these elements are in place or not and then add any comments or a rationale regarding the lack of implementation. School counseling programs seeking RAMP recognition must complete the ASCA School Counseling Program Assessment as a part of their submission portfolio. However, even if a school is not seeking RAMP, program assessment helps to identify areas of strength and weakness in the comprehensive school counseling program overall.

A template for the ASCA School Counseling Program Assessment is available from ASCA and a link is provided in the "Helpful Resources" section of this chapter.

Program Evaluation

Keeping in mind the importance of school counseling program assessment, CACREP (2016) further highlights the need for accountability in their standards by stating that all school counseling students should be able to engage in the "design and evaluation of school counseling programs" (G.3.b) (see also, Gysbers & Henderson, n.d.). According to Scriven (1991), "program evaluation refers to the process of determining the merit, worth, or value of something, or the product of that process" (p. 139). As stated, prior, to cover the full scope of program evaluation in a single chapter or in a single text would be impossible; many institutions offer full degree programs in program evaluation! However, concepts from the field of program evaluation such as logic models are useful when beginning the process of evaluating school counseling program interventions (Zyromski & Marini, 2016).

Logic models "define and clarify what should be measured and when" (Frechtling, 2007). In many ways, the concept of logic models influenced a commonly accepted strategy used by school counselors globally—Hatch's Flashlight approach (Hatch & Hartline, 2021). Hatch and Hartline's approach represents one example of a manageable way to evaluate a variety of aspects of your school counseling program and to "connect each (activities) with outcomes" (Zyromski & Marini, 2016, p. 5) as opposed to attempting to evaluate all school counseling program interventions. In Chapter 6 of this text, we offer ideas regarding the planning of a comprehensive school counseling program based on issues revealed by examining the data. School counselors must also clearly define what should be measured and why. Attempting to evaluate every single activity and intervention that school counselors deliver would be a heavy lift! Hatch's Flashlight approach (Hatch & Hartline, 2021) offers encouragement to evaluate only the interventions tied to student outcome goals identified in the planning phase. While we would like to present this as a linear process in which the same steps are always followed, the activities involved in planning and managing a school counseling program (the material covered in Chapter 6) and the activities involved in assessing a school counseling program (the material covered in this chapter) are in some ways very circular in nature and require you as the school counselor to be constantly engaging with your school's data.

Reporting Program Evaluation

There are several evaluation models school counselors can use to plan, implement, and report evaluation results to school and community partners (Kolbert et al., 2016). Two popular approaches include the DATA approach and the MEASURE approach.

DATA

Young and Kaffenberger (2019) encourage school counselors to use an approach they call DATA (Design, Ask, Track, Announce). For an extensive and thorough explanation of the DATA approach, please see Young and Kaffenberger's *Making DATA Work* (2019). Here, we only provide a brief explanation:

> **D**ESIGN – identify annual student outcome goals and choose the *ASCA Student Standards* that align with those goals (this step is outlined in Chapter 6 of this text)

> **A**SK – identify the data that demonstrates student needs tied to that annual student outcome goal, identify the interventions and actions to be taken, and plan the time line or calendar of events around this goal (this step is outlined in Chapter 6 of this text)

> **T**RACK – report the results of the work. A portion of this step is required in the planning phase (Chapter 6 content), that is, school counselors plan what data will be most helpful in determining the effectiveness of any intervention(s). However, in the evaluation phase (this chapter content!) school counselors begin to examine "post" intervention data to evaluate the work.

> **A**NNOUNCE – decide who needs to hear about the work, how you will share it, and what exactly the findings and implications of the work are.

MEASURE

Stone and Dahir (2011) offer a commonly implemented approach. For an extensive explanation of their MEASURE approach, see their text, *School Counselor Accountability: A MEASURE for Student Success*. Here, we provide only a brief overview:

> **M**ISSION – school counselors identify student outcome goals that are closely tied to the mission of the school and are tied to student outcome data

> **E**LEMENTS – school counselors work with school improvement committees/administrators to identify data elements toward which the school counselor can work to improve

ANALYZE – begin to disaggregate/break down and analyze data to determine exactly what needs improving; identify gaps in areas related to gender, race, historically marginalized groups, etc.

STAKEHOLDERS UNITE – begin to identify school and community partners that can assist in addressing the needs. Can these needs be met by the school counselor at the Tier I or Tier 2 level? What community agencies or organizations might be able to assist?

RESULTS – based on data analysis, what can be done to further improve outcomes in the identified area

EDUCATE – school counselors create visual representations (e.g., PowerPoints, charts, slides, graphs) to share information with individuals both inside and outside of the school community

Next, we offer an overview of the many templates and strategies provided by ASCA (2019a) that aid in the organization and reporting of data.

Annual Results Report

The *ASCA National Model* (ASCA, 2019a) encourages the use of two distinct types of annual reports: *Classroom and Small Group Results Report* and the *Closing-the-Gap Action Plan/Results Report*. These reports are used to assess the effectiveness of school counseling programs and services and inform plans for improvement.

Classroom and Small Group Results Report

As outlined in the "Deliver" section of this text, school counselors spend significant amounts of time delivering both classroom lessons (Tier 1) and small-group (Tier 2) interventions. Given that school counselors invest a great deal of time at the Tier 1 and Tier 2 levels, assessing the impact of these activities is paramount.

The *Classroom and Small Group Results Report* is a standard template used by school counselors to report on the effectiveness of interventions provided at the classroom and small-group levels. When school counseling programs are applying for RAMP, the *Classroom and Small Group Results Report* is a necessary piece of the submitted portfolio. The *Classroom and Small Group Results Report* includes information regarding the topic and ASCA student standard(s) the intervention addresses, as well as information on participation data, Mindsets and Behavior data, and outcome data on each intervention. Finally, the report calls for the school counselor to outline how data will be analyzed, how the data will inform future practice, and how the school counseling program will adjust to data outcomes. Importantly, the *Classroom and Small Group Results Report* contains a space for the school counselor to indicate if this report is based on classroom or small group intervention(s). A template for the *Classroom and Small Group Results Report* is available from ASCA. A link to all ASCA templates is provided in the "Helpful Resources" section of this chapter.

Closing-the-Gap Action Plan/Results Report

In Chapter 6, we highlighted the use of the *Closing-the-Gap Action Plan/Results Report* regarding planning your program events. Here we focus on the later piece of the report—the results report. Although similar to the *Classroom and Small Group Results Report*, the *Closing-the-Gap Action Plan/Results Report* provides a vital distinction for ensuring that historically marginalized and underserved students' needs are being met. This report specifically asks the school counselor to identify an annual student outcome goal and two distinct ASCA student standards that the program establishes as their focus. Then, the school counselor identifies four services (two direct and two indirect) that will be provided in the attempt to improve the outcome of students who are historically underserved. Most importantly, the *Closing-the-Gap Action Plan/Results Report* asks the school counselor completing the report to consider systemic practices, policies, or procedures that likely contribute to inequalities related to the student outcome goal. For example, a school counselor may review class enrollment data and recognize that Black and Latinx students are under-represented in Advanced Placement classes; as a result, the school counselor creates a goal to increase Black and Latinx student enrollment in these classes. The school counselor creates a range of interventions to help students meet this goal, some of which may be addressing systemic forces that serve to segregate Advanced Placement classes. The closing-the-gap report documents the activities and interventions used, along with how progress toward this goal is assessed. Finally, when completing the report, the school counselor is asked to reflect on all interventions related to closing-the-gap for students who are underserved: Did the intervention(s) help to meet the goal? How could the interventions be improved? Did the goal help meet the identified ASCA student standard? A template for the *Closing-the-Gap Action/Results Report* is available from ASCA. A link to all ASCA templates is provided in the "Helpful Resources" section of this chapter.

Completing results reports can seem like a daunting task, especially for novice school counselors tackling program evaluation for the first time. It is important to lean on existing resources to support your results reporting work and to ensure you write these effectively. We provide a link to a video from ASCA on results reporting in the "Helpful Resources" section of this chapter. Additionally, we encourage you to consider connecting with school counselors whose schools have received RAMP status to see how they successfully created their results reports!

Tech Planning Tools

Now that we have covered a variety of suggested ways in which school counselors can begin to organize the data on which they build their programs and the ways in which they can report the results of program evaluation, you might be asking yourself, how do you actually track all of the data school counselors use? That is, how do you collect the actual numbers, responses to pre- and posttests or surveys, track percentages, and practically deal with and store the numbers involved? Again, there are myriad technology tools, tips, and tricks school counselors use to gather, store, and track data. To attempt to cover all the data technology tools in one place would be daunting. However, it is necessary to outline a few of the common technology tools used in the school counseling world. We challenge you to explore more broadly the world of data management as you continue your journey as a professional school counselor. Technology is constantly evolving, and it is likely that, as you read this sentence, there is a new and more efficient tool emerging in the school counseling data world! Finally, on data technology tools, be sure to continue to seek a tool that works best for you! Not all technology tools are right for everyone. As you progress through your school counseling career, be open to learning new strategies and tools to help you work more effectively and efficiently.

While we have refrained from providing you with a set of "must have" tools in the development of your program, we are compelled to share tools that many school counselors report are extremely useful in their work to plan and report on a variety of program assessment tasks.

Excel

At the risk of stating the obvious, many school counselors find the adage of "keep it simple" to work best for them. According to Zyromski and Marini (2016), Excel spreadsheets can be used to simplify, categorize, and store data you need as a school counselor. The authors recommend narrowing the information you want to capture into three categories: (1) demographic, (2) critical data elements, and (3) interventions. Then, the user must develop a spreadsheet key that allows for the use of a numerical value tied to an intervention to be added for each student entered.

If all of this sounds overwhelming, consider simply using Excel to log the number of students who participate in counseling program activities. That is a great place to begin to get comfortable using Excel! Advanced users of Excel are familiar with the software's ability to take data and turn it into tables and graphs for efficient school and community presentations.

The Auto Closing-the-Gap (AutoCTG) Report Tool
https://schoolcounselor.com/autoctg/

Dr. Russell Sabella offers *Data Boot Camp* classes and resources for using Excel to log your data. See a link to Dr. Sabella's website in the "Helpful Resources" section of this chapter. As part of the resources he suggests, Dr. Sabella's AutoCTG provides a user-friendly option for managing and reporting on closing-the-gap activities. AutoCTG allows school counselors to easily organize data that represents the gap they are attempting to fill (attendance, academics, behavior), documents results, and then automatically creates a PowerPoint presentation that can be saved and shared with school and community partners. Additionally, Dr. Sabella's template allows for the creator to easily complete a "voice over" of the presentation for easy distribution. Dr. Sabella's tool is based on an Excel spreadsheet, but Dr. Sabella has preloaded the formulas for the user, making examining the data simple and easy to do.

Google

The Google suite of applications offers many useful tools for school counselors. Google Forms can be used to gather and track referrals to the school counselor, gather survey data, college information assessments, maintain student visit logs, student rating scales, pre/post assessments, and support other data/information gathering (Oman, n.d.a). Google Sheets function in much the same way Excel spreadsheets do in that they can be used to compile, organize, analyze, and calculate data (Oman, n.d.b). A quick stop on the popular education materials website Teachers Pay Teachers (https://www.teacherspayteachers.com/Browse/Search:google%20forms%20counselors) will yield a multitude of Google Forms for various types of data tracking created by skilled school counselors from around the globe.

Now that we have discussed the need to assess your program and engage in program evaluation to ensure that student outcomes are being met, let us turn our attention to another critical aspect of assessing the impact of your school counseling program: school counselor performance appraisal.

School Counselor Performance Assessment and Appraisal

School counselors also use technology to assess their own performance. ASCA (2021) provides support for ways in which counselors use data from school and community partners to support their performance. School counselors use the process of self-assessment and appraisal to gain understanding of their strengths and areas in need of improvement to ensure they are able to meet the needs of all students and deliver a rigorous comprehensive school counseling program (ASCA, 2019a). The *ASCA School Counselor Professional Standards & Competencies* (ASCA, 2019b) outlines the knowledge, skills, and attitudes school counselors must possess in order to provide a quality comprehensive school counseling program that meets the needs of students P–12. According to ASCA's position statement, "Annually a qualified administrator completes the school counselor performance appraisal to evaluate the school counselor's overall performance. Appraisal documents are often developed in alignment with state or district guidelines and may appear in a variety of frameworks selected by state and district leaders" (ASCA, 2017). ASCA provides two documents to support school counselors in (1) performing a self-assessment of their own mindsets and behaviors related to their professional work and (2) assisting administrators in performing an annual appraisal of the school counselor.

ASCA School Counselor Professional Standards & Competencies Assessment

The *ASCA School Counselor Professional Standards & Competencies Assessment* outlines the key knowledge, skills, attitudes, and behaviors that school counselors should strive to possess. This document serves as a road map for school counselor development, as it highlights an individual's strengths and areas for improvement. This assessment has several uses. First, practicing school counselors use the form as a tool to assess their own mindsets and behaviors and to further develop professional goals. Further, school and district administrators use the form as a tool to aid in formulating evaluations of school counselors as well as to evaluate potential school counselors they intend to hire. Finally, graduate training programs can use the form as a tool to evaluate graduate students in school counseling programs to ensure they are equipped with the knowledge, skills, and attitudes necessary to design and implement a comprehensive school counseling program (ASCA, 2019a). The *ASCA School Counselor Professional Standards & Competencies Assessment* is self-report and based on the mindsets and behaviors found in the *ASCA School Counselor Professional Standards & Competencies* (ASCA, 2019b). A template for the *ASCA School Counselor Professional Standards & Competencies Assessment* is available from ASCA at https://www.schoolcounselor.org/About-School-Counseling/ ASCA-National-Model-for-School-Counseling-Programs/Templates-Resources.

ASCA School Counselor Performance Appraisal

According to ASCA (2019a), school counselors should be evaluated annually by a qualified administrator. The *ASCA School Counselor Performance Appraisal* template is a wonderful tool that can be used, especially in the absence of any appropriate, state-mandated school counselor evaluation. Many states, like those of your authors (West Virginia and New Jersey), have implemented evaluation documents and processes that are required either in addition to or in place of the ASCA performance appraisal.

In states where evaluation metrics specific to school counselors do not exist, there is likely a system that evaluates school counselors according to standard teacher evaluations. Evaluating school counselors the same way in which teachers are assessed can be problematic. Early work in the field of teacher evaluation by Charlotte Danielson outlines the case for school counselor evaluation to be unique to their positions. According to Danielson (2007), "The framework for teaching is just that – a framework for teaching: it is not a framework for school nurses, school psychologists, [and other specialists] ... their positions are essentially different from those of teachers and must be described separately" (p. 109). According to Oliver and Abel (2014), Danielson proposed the model of school counselor evaluation inherent in the *ASCA School Counselor Performance Appraisal* and commonly used across many states and districts. Specifically, Danielson recommends school counselors be evaluated on a scale from "unsatisfactory" to "distinguished" across four domains and 22 components unique to the school counselor position.

The *ASCA School Counselor Performance Appraisal* uses Danielson's scale to evaluate the school counselor according to the *ASCA School Counselor Professional Standards & Competencies* (ASCA, 2019b). The evaluator provides a rating of the school counselor from 0 to 3 (0 = "unsatisfactory"; 3 = "distinguished") on the school counselor's ability to design a comprehensive program; the school counselor's use of data to inform the program and outcome goals; the school counselor's ability to develop data-driven classroom, small-group, and closing-the-gap activities; the school counselor's use of calendars to implement the program; and the school counselor's ability collect and analyze data around interventions (ASCA, 2019a). A template for the *ASCA School Counselor Performance Appraisal* is available from ASCA, and a link is provided in the "Helpful Resources" section of this chapter.

Consultation Corner: Who You Gonna Call?

After bracketing your thoughts and reading the "Informed School Counseling" section, who would you call in and outside of the school building, and what might you ask them to support your decision-making? Take a moment to document these questions. Now that you have considered your questions for consultation, let's see what professional school counselors from around the world have to say about this case.

Consultation #1

Hello, my name is Alex, and I am a K–8 school counselor. Wow, I have to say this exact scenario has happened to me! In my case, I can concur that I did not necessarily blame the administrator, but I was frustrated to be measured by metrics that have no bearing on whether I am doing my job well. I will also confess that during my first year as a school counselor, I actually went ahead and went along with being evaluated on the teacher evaluation. I was the first school counselor at my school site, and I was not huge on making waves (yet!). When these types of evaluations continued to be the case, I was lucky to have a ton of support from my district. I was a part of my district school counseling advisory committee (a leadership group of counselors who met with our lead counselor), and we brought up the idea of creating a counselor-based evaluation. Not everyone has this support and may feel more alone in navigating this dilemma, so I will also say what came to mind in reading this post now as a sixth-year counselor. My first thought is to educate about the *ASCA National Model* and how it exemplifies best practices for school counselors. I would say that these are the standards by which I guide my work, and highlight some specific goals from there, tied to the mindsets and behaviors. I would probably still fill out the teacher evaluation form, as it is probably needed for documentation, but I would want to at least point out all the relevant school counselor activities I am doing for the assistant principal to be aware of how I spend my time. This may just be one small step toward getting a school counselor-geared evaluation, but I would combine assertive advocacy with a balance of patience and recognizing that not all administrators have a background with counselors and may need some education around our role—something I am happy to give!

(Alexandra Todd, elementary school counselor, California)

Consultation #2

Hi, my name is Amy, and I am a school counselor at a career technical high school. At my school, our administrators oversee the evaluations of the school counselors. Some of the evaluations are the same as what is used to evaluate our teachers. It is essential to have an open dialogue between you and your administrators. School counselors play a central role in the school and its students. Having the assistant principal evaluate your performance, I would view it as an opportunity to advocate for your position and the students. Sharing with the vice principal, your expertise and experiences can also benefit your working relationship with them. Given the opportunity, to meet with your vice principal would be a good time to voice your concerns about how filling in as a substitute teacher does not much help the needs of the students and how your role as a school counselor can be best used in creating a healthy school counseling program.

(Amy Lombardo, high school counselor, New Jersey)

Consultation #3

Hi, my name is Dr. Bobby Gueh, and I've had the opportunity to be an elementary, middle, and currently a high school counselor. This situation is what happens a lot to counselors all over, unfortunately. We are constantly working to explain what we do and advocate for what we do, but sometimes is like we are the only ones who appreciate it. Despite that, I think it is extremely critical to train our teachers and administration on what we do, and use ASCA participation agreements at the beginning of each year with the principal to begin that advocacy process. People will only treat you how you allow them to treat you. I feel the same about our profession. We cannot expect admin to automatically "get it," so we have to be extremely intentional and demonstrate what we do and take more leadership roles within the school, which allows even more respect and credibility.

As far as the situation, first, don't respond with an email. Set up a time to speak to that assistant principal, and lay out exactly how you are feeling. This is an opportunity to teach him, especially because of the fact it seems like he is just doing what he was told, but use this opportunity to show all the wonderful things you are doing outside of the "duties as assigned" and start the conversation by letting him know that we are "school counselors." We teach our students how to problem solve and handle these types of situations, therefore we can definitely do it and be effective with it. Lastly, "advocate, advocate, advocate" for what we do. We cannot assume they know and value what we do.

(Bobby Gueh, high school counselor, Georgia)

#EduCounselor Synthesis

Matthew T.'s post is an excellent example of a real-life dilemma faced by many school counselors; in fact, all three of our consultants validated Matthew's experiences immediately and expressed empathy for this situation. The "Informed School Counseling" section of this chapter details the importance of assessing our school counseling programs and the valuable processes involved in assessing the contributions of the school counselor as a member of the school community. Both are essential for advocacy purposes as highlighted by each of our consultants.

Every school district and building operates differently. While some districts employ directors of school counseling with school counseling experience, many other districts employ administrators who are charged with overseeing counselor evaluation that have no background in school counseling. In some school districts, school counselor evaluation may be the responsibility of professionals who possess mental health affiliations such as a school psychologist. However, the role of a mental health affiliated professional can be quite different from that of a school counselor. Unfortunately, this creates a big challenge for school counselors when their evaluators are not familiar with the school counseling profession and are perhaps expected to use teacher evaluations to generalize to school counselors. This can be equally challenging to navigate for administrators who, like in Matthew's case, might be new to their positions as well. Some graduate schools around the country intentionally offer opportunities for preservice school counselors and preservice administrators to take a few courses together to help each understand their respective roles. If you have an opportunity to take a course with future educational leaders, we encourage you to do so! This is a great first step in your advocacy efforts.

Matthew's situation also speaks to the importance of sharing program assessment data with district leadership and, if applicable, the board of education. Many decisions in school systems are made from the top down, and without an appreciation for what school counselors do, systemic changes like the ones necessary in this case cannot happen! Let's take a look at some additional advice from our consultants.

Our initial consultant, Alex, reflects on their first year as a school counselor and acknowledges the importance of an awareness of our positionality within the school. Understanding the lay of the land and the systems that create some of these challenges is important before diving right into these types of advocacy opportunities, especially as a new counselor. As leaders, school counselors must continue to seek and model curiosity as they develop rapport with school and community partners and assess the current school climate. Without solid relationships and a well-informed understanding of the context, well-meaning school counselors may end up distancing themselves from the very people they need on their side.

Alex also shares the value of membership on the advisory council and how this impacted their positionality and ability to advocate for change. This is a great example of school counselors taking advantage of committee work and leadership opportunities and cultivating meaningful relationships that assist with advocacy efforts. Collecting evidence from these committees and from program assessment, and using preexisting ASCA materials, as suggested by Alex and Bobby, is a great way to inform your approach to administrators.

Each of our consultants also talks about the importance of initiating direct conversations with administration. Notably, Bobby encourages face-to-face communication, which allows for more dialogue back and forth. As Amy encourages, using a situation like Matthew's as an opportunity to speak directly with administrators is an important challenge that can create lasting change. These conversations can not only enhance the relationship but also potentially promote confidence in you and your program. During these meetings, Alex suggests that school counselors connect meaningful evaluation to the *ASCA Student Standards*. Bobby indicates that this is also a great time to advocate for your program as a whole, which may mean showing the results of reports (e.g., *Closing-the-Gap*) and other data collection efforts that detail how the program and you as the counselor make a difference in the lives of your students and the greater school community. School counselors may even provide examples of other school counseling-specific evaluation models from other districts or states to reinforce their efforts. New Jersey and West Virginia provide great examples of models and resources that could help to inform these conversations (see links in the "Helpful Resources" section). Several others are also included in the resources section of this chapter. It is important to revisit these resources often, as they are frequently updated with new revisions of the *ASCA National Model* and research-based best practices.

Finally, Bobby punctuates the importance of open communication with administrators as they talk about the importance of modeling. As school counselors, we teach our students how to problem solve, manage conflict, and address situations in a meaningful way; Matthew's situation presents a great opportunity to model the very advice we profess! Using data, resources, professionalism, patience, and advocacy, school counselors have a great opportunity to educate school and community partners about the wonderful things that we bring to our school communities.

Chapter Summary

Program assessment, program evaluation, and school counselor self-assessment are all critical elements of a sustainable and effective comprehensive school counseling program. Program assessment helps school counselors ensure that all key components of a comprehensive school counseling program are in place. Program evaluation answers questions related to the effectiveness of school counseling program initiatives and interventions. Reports commonly used in program evaluation include the *Classroom and Small Group Results Report* as well as the *Closing-the-Gap Results Report.* School counselors often use technology tools such as Excel and the Google suite of tools to collect and analyze data related to program evaluation. Finally, school counselors engage in ongoing self-assessment to identify both areas of strength and areas for improvement to ensure a culturally sustaining school counseling program that works to eliminate barriers to success for all students.

Reflective Practitioner Process

School counselors engage in clinical supervision, professional development, and self-care to further develop their knowledge and skills and to help balance professional expectations with personal wellness. All three areas are key to ethical practice and help to mitigate counselor burnout and compassion fatigue (Atici, 2015; Lawson & Myers, 2011; Merriman, 2015; Ohrt et al., 2015).

Clinical Supervision

The *ASCA School Counselor Professional Standards & Competencies* (ASCA, 2019b) direct school counselors to "consult with school counselors and other education and counseling professionals when questions of school counseling practice arise" (B-SS 5., p. 5). As a supervisee, it is important to consider the thoughts, feelings, and experiences that come up for you as you work with students, families, and colleagues and seek consultation on difficult issues. The following are some topics for consideration as you react to this chapter.

- What are practical considerations for conducting all recommended program assessments? What are practical considerations for conducting evaluations of program interventions tied to student outcomes?
- What are creative venues in which to present the results of program assessments? What are creative venues by which to present results of program evaluation or activities you are "flashlighting" (see Hatch & Hartline, 2021)?
- Where is the best place to begin to share inequities that are uncovered during program evaluation? Do you simply go to administration and report problematic findings?
- How do you navigate program assessment with school counselor colleagues in your school who do not see the value or importance of assessing the overall school counseling program?
- To what degree should a novice school counselor engage in advocacy when it is determined that the person responsible for evaluating the school counselor is not equipped to appropriately complete the evaluation?

Professional Development

According to the *ASCA Ethical Standards for School Counselors* (ASCA, 2022), professional school counselors engage in professional development and attend training to stay current on the trends and issues that impact students (B.3.e). Relative to the contents of this chapter, consider finding professional development on the following topics:

- Technology tools used to streamline program assessment and program evaluation
- Creative ways school counselors disseminate program assessment and program evaluation results
- How to establish a culture in which school counseling program assessment is a priority
- General and advanced approaches to program evaluation
- Simple data analysis and/or statistics made simple (averages, percentages, and change in data over time)

#PSCSelfCare: Everyday Wellness

When designing, managing, and implementing a comprehensive school counseling program, school and community expectations can tax even the most seasoned school counselor. The ASCA *Ethical Standards for School Counselors* (ASCA, 2022) require school counselors to recognize the high levels of stress often associated with the job. Therefore, school counselors recognize that self-care must be a priority to maintain health and overall well-being (see ASCA, 2022, B.3.h).

Meditation

To many, it may seem silly that we have waited until now to offer one of the most common forms of self-care: meditation! According to *Merriam-Webster* (n.d.), the definition of meditate is "to engage in contemplation or reflection." Even further, meditation is defined as a practice in which a person would "engage in mental exercise (such as concentration on one's breathing or repetition of a mantra) for the purpose of reaching a heightened level of spiritual awareness" (Merriam-Webster, n.d.). How fitting to offer the practice of meditation as a form of self-care in a chapter where you have been charged with, as a school counselor, reflecting, contemplating, and working to achieve a heightened understanding of the impact of your work!

There are many benefits of meditation. A few of the more common benefits that potentially meet the needs of school counselors are lower levels of stress, opening the mind and allowing for making better connections, and reducing brain noise that can distract from your work (minful.org, 2022). According to the Mayo Clinic (2022), research on meditation indicates that some medical conditions such as anxiety, asthma, cancer, high blood pressure, and other conditions that are typically made worse by stress can be improved when patients undertake a meditation regiment. Additionally, meditation offers participants a reduction of negative emotions, an increase in imagination and creativity, and an increase in patience and tolerance. What school counselor can't benefit from those outcomes?!

There are many forms and approaches to meditation. If you are new to meditating, we recommend that you begin with the specific approach known as mindfulness meditation. According to Mindful.org, mindfulness meditation occurs "when we pay attention to our breath, we are learning how to return to, and remain in, the present moment—to anchor ourselves in the here and now on purpose, without judgement" (Mindful.org, 2022).

There are many tools to assist you in your meditation journey. Popular apps include Calm, Headspace, Buddhify, and, especially for beginners, The Mindfulness App. A simple search on YouTube will lead users to a wide variety of timed meditation sessions geared to help users improve sleep, stress, being present, and self-soothing. However, as a simple overview, Mindful.org provides the following tips for getting your meditation routine started:

1. Find a quiet, calm, inviting space and then have a seat;
2. Set a time limit; consider starting off small and building up over time;
3. Notice your body, assume a comfortable seating position that can be maintained for a bit;
4. Feel your breath;
5. Begin to notice when your mind wanders and when you notice it wandering, return to your breathing;
6. Forgive yourself for any mind wandering that took place; and
7. Close with kindness—slowly return to your space, notice your surroundings, and notice your emotions and your thoughts.

Many people spend years refining their meditation practice. We are not suggesting that you will be a mindfulness expert by reading our brief introduction to meditation. However, we hope that meditation is something you begin to consider as you reflect and evaluate your own work as a school counselor. Defining, managing, delivering, and assessing your comprehensive school counseling program as well as wearing all of the "hats" and serving all of the partners in your school system can be taxing. Meditation is just one form of self-care we encourage you to explore throughout your school counseling career!

Spotlight: School Counseling Advocacy

In our attempt to honor the importance of the evaluation of both the performance of the school counselor and the overall school counseling program, we chose to highlight two school counseling programs that, by evidence of their social media posts, honor the value of collecting data and working to share the results of program evaluation with school and community partners.

First, we highlight a school counselor who made good use of "minute meetings" (see Counselor1Stop resource in the "Helpful Resources" section) to connect with students around their postsecondary plans. This school counselor collected data that now allows them to see that more than 46% of the students (@ 38 of the 84 students they met with) are uncertain about their postsecondary plans. This data presentation both allows this school counseling team to share the results of their work with school and community partners and provides valuable information for planning future programs and interventions.

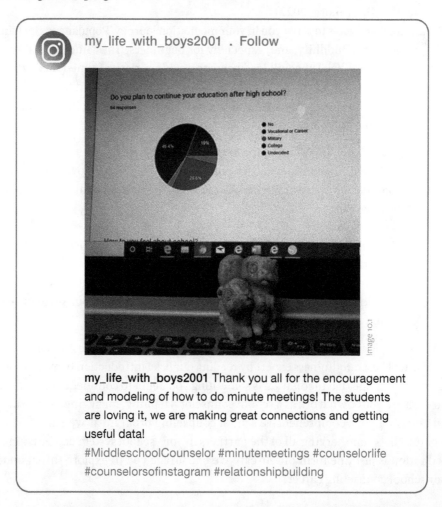

Next, we highlight a shout-out to a school district in Pittsburg, California, as an outstanding example of a school district whose school counseling team understood the importance of not only developing a comprehensive school counseling program but also recognized the importance of sharing their program results in order to garner district level support! Way to go @PittsburgUSD!

Hatching Results
@hatchingresults

We are so incredibly proud of the @PittsburgUSD school counseling team for eloquently & passionately **presenting** an overview of their program & amazing **results** of improved grad & A-G college prep rates!

#scchat #schoolcounselorsrock #schoolcounseloerslead #ReachHigher

Apr 13, 2018

Learning Connections

Both professional school counselors in training and seasoned school counselors understand the importance of understanding the connections between the concepts commonly taught in counseling programs and the standards most associated with school counselor training. Therefore, the following table offers broad connections between the material and information in this chapter and the CACREP (2016) standards, the ASCA *School Counselor Professional Standards & Competencies* (ASCA, 2019b), and the *ASCA Ethical Standards for School Counselors* (ASCA, 2022).

Connections to CACREP Core Curricular Areas

Professional Counseling Orientation and Ethical Practice	Social and Cultural Diversity	Human Growth and Development	Career Development	Counseling and Helping Relationships	Group Counseling and Group Work	Assessment and Testing	Research and Program Evaluation
	X				X	X	X

Connection to Professional Standards

CACREP	ASCA SC Professional Competencies	Ethical Standards: SC
G.1.e: Assessments specific to P-12 education	M 4. Every student should have access to a school counseling program.	A.14.i. Conduct and disseminate the results of school counseling program assessments to determine the effectiveness of activities supporting students' academic, college/career and social/ emotional development through accountability measures, especially examining efforts to close opportunity gaps.
G.3.b: Design and evaluation of school counseling programs	M 7. School counseling programs promote and enhance student academic, career and social/emotional outcomes.	A.7.f. Use data to inform group topics, establish well-defined expectations, and measure the outcomes of group participation.
G.3.n: Use of accountability data to inform decision making	B-PA 5. Assess and report program results to the school community.	A.7.g. Reflect on group outcomes and determine adjustments that may improve future group interventions.
G.3.o: Use of data to advocate for programs and students		A.3.d. Review and use school and student data to assess and address needs, including but not limited to data on strengths and disparities that may exist related to gender, race, ethnicity, socioeconomic status, disability and/or other relevant classifications.
		A.3.f. Collect and analyze participation, ASCA Mindsets & Behaviors and outcome data to determine the progress and effectiveness of the school counseling program.
		A.3.g. Share data outcomes with stakeholders.

Comprehensive School Counseling Assignments

The following section provides activities that allow for your continued growth as a professional school counselor. Both preservice and practicing school counselors may find it helpful to complete these activities. If you are currently in a graduate training program, your professor might assign these as part of your course.

- Access the school counseling program assessment on the ASCA website and complete it for either a school in which you are currently completing field placement or the school in which you currently work.
- Research school counselor evaluation processes in at least two school districts, states, or even international school districts. Compare and contrast your findings, including the following:
  - The person responsible for completing the evaluation

- The forms used to document school counselor goals or performance metrics
- How the evaluation is used once completed
- Rubrics used to determine school counselor performance
- Using either the MEASURE or DATA reporting tools, create a mock data report to share with peers. Then, practice presenting the data in small groups or in front of a classroom of peers.

Helpful Resources
Web-Based Resources

- *ASCA National Model* Assessment Templates:
  - https://www.schoolcounselor.org/About-School-Counseling/ASCA-National-Model-for-School-Counseling-Programs/Templates-Resources
- ASCA Video on Results Reports:
  - https://videos.schoolcounselor.org/results-reports-outcomes-leading-to-systemic-impact
- School Counselors Rubric Example Framework for School Counselors:
  - https://www.k12.wa.us/sites/default/files/public/tpep/frameworks/danielson/schoolcounselorrubric.pdf
- Colorado State Model Evaluation System for Specialized Service Professionals: Practical Ideas Guide for Evaluating School Counselors:
  - https://www.cde.state.co.us/educatoreffectiveness/practical_ideas_guide_schoolcounselors
- New Jersey School Counselor Evaluation Model:
  - https://www.njsca.org/evaluation-model-njsca
- Ohio School Counselor Evaluation Model:
  - https://education.ohio.gov/getattachment/Topics/Career-Tech/Career-Connections/Resources-for-School-Counselors/School-Counselor-Standards-and-Evaluation/OSCES-Model.pdf.aspx
- West Virginia School Counselor Performance Appraisal (and other documents):
  - https://wvde.us/student-support-well-being/wv-school-counselors/school-counselor-evaluation-resources/
- Dr. Trish Hatch's Website, Hatching Results:
  - https://www.hatchingresults.com
- Dr. Russell Sabella's Data Bootcamp:
  - https://www.mydatabootcamp.com/

- Minute Meetings:
    - https://counselor1stop.org/wiki/minute-meetings/#:~:text=The%20 minute%20meeting%20is%20a,school%2C%20friends%2C%20 and%20feelings.

Suggested Readings

- Hatch, T., & Hartline, J. (2021). *The use of data in school counseling: Hatching results for students, programs, and the profession.* (2nd ed.). Corwin.
- Young, A., & Kaffenberger, C. (2019). *Making data work.* (4th ed.). American School Counselor Association.
- Trevisan, M. A., & Carey, J. C. (2020). *Program evaluation in school counseling: Improving comprehensive and developmental programs.* Routledge.
- Zyromski, B., & Mariani, M. A. (2016). *Facilitating evidence-based, data-driven school counseling.* Corwin.

Apps for Practicing Meditation

- Calm
- Headspace
- Buddhify
- The Mindfulness App
- Meditation Studio
- Simple Habit

For more on a variety of meditation apps, check out "The 12 Best Meditation Apps of 2022" at https://www.healthline.com/health/mental-health/top-meditation-iphone-android-apps

References

American School Counselor Association (ASCA). (n.d.). *Recognized ASCA model program.* https://www.schoolcounselor.org/Recognition/RAMP

American School Counselor Association (ASCA). (2017). *The school counselor and school counseling programs.* https://www.schoolcounselor.org/Standards-Positions/Position-Statements/ASCA-Position-Statements/The-School-Counselor-and-School-Counseling-Program

American School Counselor Association (ASCA). (2019a). *ASCA national model: A framework for school counseling programs.* (4th ed.).

American School Counselor Association (ASCA). (2019b). *ASCA school counselor professional standards & competencies.* https://www.schoolcounselor.org/asca/media/asca/home/SCCompetencies.pdf

American School Counselor Association (ASCA). (2021). *ASCA school counselor performance appraisal.* https://videos.schoolcounselor.org/school-counselor-performance-appraisal

American School Counselor Association (ASCA). (2022). *ASCA ethical standards for school counselors.* https://www.schoolcounselor.org/getmedia/44f30280-ffe8-4b41-9ad8-f15909c3d164/EthicalStandards.pdf

Atici, M. (2015). Professional identity development of counselors-in-training in a school internship program in Turkey. *The Professional Counselor, 5*(1), 137–151. https://doi.org/10.15241/MA.5.1.137

Council for Accreditation of Counseling and Related Educational Programs (CACREP). (2016). *2016 CACREP standards.* http://www.cacrep.org/wp-content/uploads/2017/08/2016-Standards-with-citations.pdf

Danielson, C. (2007). *Enhancing professional practice: A framework for teaching* (2nd ed.). Association for Supervision and Curriculum Development.

Dimmitt, C., Carey, J., & Hatch, T. (2007). *Evidence-based school counseling.* Corwin.

Erford, B. T. (2011). *Transforming the school counseling profession.* (3rd ed.). Pearson.

Frechtling, J. A. (2007). *Logic modeling methods in program evaluation.* John Wiley & Sons.

Gysbers, N. C., & Henderson, P. (n.d.). Comprehensive guidance and counseling program evaluation: Program + personnel = results. *ACA Vistas Online, 41.* https://www.counseling.org/docs/default-source/vistas/comprehensive-guidance-and-counseling-program-evaluation-program-personnel-results.pdf?sfvrsn=10#:~:text=Program%20evaluation%20is%20the%20procedure,in%20place%20and%20functioning%20fully

Hatch, T., & Hartline, J. (2021). *The use of data in school counseling: Hatching results for students, programs, and the profession.* (2nd ed.). Corwin.

Kolbert, J. B., Williams, R. L., Morgan, L. M., Crothers, L. M., & Hughes, T. L. (2016). *Introduction to professional school counseling: Advocacy, leadership, and intervention.* Routledge.

Lawson, G., & Myers, J. E. (2011). Wellness, professional quality of life, and career-sustaining behaviors: What keeps us well? *Journal of Counseling and Development, 89*(2), 163–171. https://doi.org/10.1002/j.1556-6678.2011.tb00074.x

Mayo Clinic. (2022). *Meditation: A simple, fast way to reduce stress.* https://www.mayoclinic.org/tests-procedures/meditation/in-depth/meditation/art-20045858

Merriman, J. (2015). Enhancing counselor supervision through compassion fatigue education. *Journal of Counseling and Development, 93*(3), 370–378. https://doi.org/10.1002/jcad.12035

Mindful.org. (2022). *How to meditate.* https://www.mindful.org/how-to-meditate/#what

Ohrt, J. H., Prosek, E. A., Ener, E., & Lindo, N. (2015). The effects of a group supervision intervention to promote wellness and prevent burnout. *The Journal of Humanistic Counseling, 54*(1), 41–58. https://doi.org/10.1002/j.2161-1939.2015.00063.x

Oliver, B. M., & Abel, N. R. (2014). School counselor evaluation: Why it should be different. *Scholarship and Professional Work—Education, 20.* https://digitalcommons.butler.edu/coe_papers/20

Oman, K. R. (n. d.a). *Google forms.* https://sites.google.com/site/schoolcounselingtechnology/forms

Oman, K. R. (n. d.b). *Google sheets.* https://sites.google.com/site/schoolcounselingtechnology/forms

Parzych, J., Donohue, P., Gaesser, A., & Chiu, M. (2019). *Measuring the impact of school counselor ratios on student outcomes.* ASCA Research Report. https://www.schoolcounselor.org/getmedia/5157ef82-d2e8-4b4d-8659-a957f14b7875/Ratios-Student-Outcomes-Research-Report.pdf

Scriven, M. (1991). *Evaluation thesaurus.* SAGE Publications.

Stone, C. B., & Dahir, C. A. (2011). *School counselor accountability: A MEASURE of student success*. Pearson.

Stone, C. B., & Dahir, C. A. (2016). The transformed school counselor. (3rd ed.). Cengage.

Villares, E., Lemberger, M., Brigman, G., & Webb, L. (2011). Student success skills: An evidence-based school counseling program grounded in humanistic theory. *Journal of Humanistic Counseling, 50*, 42–55.

Wilkerson, K., Perusse, R., & Hughes, A. (2013). Comprehensive school counseling programs and student achievement outcomes: A comparative analysis of RAMP versus non-RAMP schools. *Professional School Counseling, 16*(3), 172–184. https://doi.org/10.1177/2156759X1701600302

Young, A., & Kaffenberger, C. (2019). *Making DATA work*. (4th ed.). American Counseling Association.

Zyromski, B., & Mariani, M. A. (2016). *Facilitating evidence-based, data-driven school counseling: A manual for practice*. Corwin.

Credits

Index

A

ACT DISCOVER Career Planning Programs, 101
action plans, 123–124
advisory councils, 79–80, 91–92
American Civil Liberties Union, 11
American Counseling Association (ACA), 5
    Advocacy Competencies, 6, 22, 201
    Counseling Today publication, 17
    Multicultural and Social Justice Counseling Competencies, 6
American Counseling Association Advocacy Competencies, 16
American Personnel and Guidance Association (APGA), 5
American School Counselor Association (ASCA), 5
    annual administrative conference, 120–121
    appraisal and advisement, 153
    classroom and small group results report, 223
    closing-the-gap action plan/results report, 223–224
    effective mission statement, 78
    effective vision statements, 76
    Ethical Standards for School Counselors, xlii, xliv, 19, 30, 33, 38, 46, 53, 61, 74, 86, 111, 136, 162, 180, 197, 232
    National Model for School Counseling, 6–7, 26–28, 44–45, 71, 73, 80, 83, 97, 120, 122–123, 128, 218–219, 222
    National Model Implementation Guide, 120, 122
    position statement on suicide screening tools, 151
    position statement on trauma-informed practice, 148
    RAMP (Recognized ASCA Model Program), 123, 125, 219
    School Counseling Program Assessment, 220–221
    School Counselor Professional Standards and Competencies, xlii, xliv, 18, 29–30, 38, 61, 74–76, 85, 96, 110, 132, 161, 180, 231
    school counselor role, 39
    School Data Profile Template, 102, 112
    student outcome goals, 104
    Student Standards: Mindsets & Behaviors for Student Success, 8, 29, 97–98, 133, 148–149
    Twitter page graphic, 22
annual administrative conference, 120–121
annual calendars, 122–123
Anti-Bullying Bill of Rights Act, 9
Arbery, Ahmaud, 10
Art Therapy, 137
ASCA National Model Assessment Templates, 237
ASCA Video on Results Reports, 237
assessment of counseling program, 216, 218–220
    accountability, 220
    annual, 219
    classroom and small group results report, 223
    closing-the-gap action plan/results report, 223–224
    DATA approach, 221
    logic models, 220
    MEASURE approach, 221–222
    reporting of, 221–222
    tech planning tools, 223–225
Auto Closing-the-Gap (AutoCTG) Report Tool, 224
2020: A Vision for the Future of Counseling, 8

B

Banana Splits Resource Center, 184
behavioral consultation (BC)/conjoint behavioral consultation (CBC), 48
beliefs and mindsets, 73–76
beliefs statement, 75–76, 90–91
Black Lives Matter, xxvii
Bloody Sunday, 11
Bronfenbrenner, Urie, xxv–xxvi
    school counselor at work, xxviii–xxix
    systems and student's experience, xxviii
Brooks, Rayshard, 10
Brown, Jerry, 5

C

CBITS Training, 209
Centervention, 184
check-in/check-out (CICO), 173–174
child maltreatment, 52–53
Child Study team, 190
Choosing a Vocation (Parsons), 4
chronosystem, xxvii, xxix
Civil Rights Act of 1964, 9
classroom and small group results report, 223
classroom lessons, 124–125
clinical supervision, xlii, 35, 85–86, 110, 135–136, 161–162, 180, 203, 231
closing-the-gap action plan/results report, 223–224
collaboration, 50

college and career readiness, 7
Colorado State Model Evaluation System for
  Specialized Service Professionals, 237
Common Core state standards, 8
    State Anti-Bullying Laws and Regulations, 9
community resources and referrals, 197–198
comorbidity, 47
comprehensive school counseling program
  (CSCP), 146
confidentiality, 51–52
consultation models and concepts, xxxviii–xl,
  13–15, 31–33, 49–50, 55–58, 80–83, 105–107,
  130–132, 154–158, 174–177, 198–200, 227–228
contextualization, xxiv
coordination, 51–55
Council for Accreditation of Counseling and
  Related Educational Programs (CACREP), 5, 10,
  37, 44
    core curricular areas, 21, 38, 63, 89, 113, 138,
    164, 183, 206, 235
    professional standards, 64, 89–90, 113–114,
    139, 164–165, 183, 206–207, 236–237
Council for the Accreditation of Educator
  Preparation (CAEP), 10
counseling notes, 54
COVID-19 pandemic, xxiv, 10, 47, 149, 201–202
crisis counseling, 195–197
crisis plans, 129
crisis team, 129
culturally sustaining school counseling, 72

D
data
    behaviors, 97–98
    breaking of data, 104
    collection, 103–104, 109
    mindsets, 97–98
    outcome, 98–99
    participation, 97
    school, 101–103
DATA approach of program evaluation, 221
Deferred Action for Childhood Arrivals, 8
democratic school movement, xxv
developmental counseling lessons, 151–152
Difficulties in Emotions Regulations Scale, 190
Dinkmeyer, Donald, 5
Dr. Levy's *Hip Hop and Spoken Word Therapy*,xliv
Dr. Russell Sabella's Data Bootcamp, 237
Dr. Trish Hatch's Website, 237

E
#EduCounselor Synthesis, 58–60, 83–85, 108–110,
  132–134, 158–161, 177–179, 201, 229–231
The Early Childhood Screening Assessment, 190
Elementary School Counselor Exchange, 118
emancipation, xxxvi
ethical practice of school counselors, xxiv–xxv, 3
exosystem, xxvii, xxix

F
Family Educational Rights and Privacy Act
  (FERPA), 44, 54-55
family systems consultation, 48–49
Floyd, George, xxvii, 10–11, 79
focus groups, 103–104
Forum Guide to Collecting and Using
  Disaggregated Data on Racial/Ethnic Subgroups,
  115

G
Gateway Professional School Counselors, 78
Gender Spectrum, 210
Georgia Universal Screening Tools, 166
Ginsberg, Justice Ruth Bader, 11
GLSEN, 210
Google suite, 225–226
grade point average (GPA), 100
gratitude, 62
grief counseling, 196
guidance counseling, 4, 14–18
Gysbers, Norm, 5

H
HALT, 36–37
Health Insurance Portability and Accountability
  Act (HIPAA), 44, 54–55
    standards for privacy of individually
    identifiable health information, 55
Henderson, Patricia, 5

I
individualism, xxvii
Individualized Education Plans (IEP), 126,
  128–129
Individuals with Disabilities in Education Act
  (IDEA), 129–130
inequities, locating, 99–103
International School Counselor Association
  (ISCA), 26, 28
#IRLSchoolCounseling, xxiv, 2, 27, 33, 35,
  44–45, 71, 95, 118–119, 146–147, 169–170,
  188–189, 215
Irving, Larry, 9

J
Jaffee v. Redmond, 52
21 Jump Street, xxxviii
Johnson, Curly, 5,7
Johnson, Sharon, 5

L
leadership responsibilities, 72–73
Learning for Justice, xxxv
lesson planning
    classroom lessons, 124–125

small-group counseling, 125
Lewis, John, 11
LGBT National Youth Hotline, 210
LGBTQI+ Community, 8–9, 189, 198–199,
    201–202, 209
    web-resources for working with, 210

M

mandala work, 136–137
Matthew S., 108–109
MEASURE approach of program evaluation,
    221–222
meditation, 232–233
mental health collaborator, 50–51
mental health consultant, 47–50
mental health counselor, 46–47
mesosystem, xxvi–xxvii, xxix
Microsoft Excel, 104, 224
microsystem, xxvi, xxviii
Mindfulness App., 233
Mindful.org, 233–234
Mind Up for Life, 184
Minute Meetings, 237
Miss Daisy's Counseling Corner, 140
mission statements, 77–79
Missouri Professional School Counselors and
    Counselor Educators, 65
        moral courage, xxxvii
multi-disciplinary teams (MDTs), 50
multi-tiered systems of support (MTSS), 34,
    50–51, 122–123, 125–126, 136, 146, 188, 201
        screening, 151
        Tier 1 activities, 148
My Hours, 140
Myrick, Don, 5

N

National Board for Certified Counselors, 5
National Defense Education Act (NDEA), 4
National Evidenced-Based School Counseling
    Conference, 109–110
National Vocational Guidance Association, 4
Naviance, 101
2nd Floor, 210
needs assessments, 103
New Jersey School Counselor Evaluation
    Model, 237
No Child Left Behind Act (NCLB), 127

O

Ohio Positive Behavioral and Interventions
    Support Network, 150
Ohio School Counselor Evaluation Model, 237
online instruction, 10
outcome data, 98–99

P

participation data, 97
PBIS, 166–167
perfectionism, xxvii
personal notes, 54
PFlag, 210
Positive Behavioral Interventions and Supports
    team, 190
Powerschool (powerschool.com), 101
privileged communication, 51–52
Privilege Institute, xxxv
Problem Oriented Screening Instrument for
    Teenagers, 190
professional development, xlii, 19, 36, 61, 86, 111,
    136, 162, 180–181, 203–204, 232–233
Professional School Counselors of Color, xxiv
professional standards, xlv–xlvi, 21
program calendars
    annual, 122–123, 139–140
    weekly, 123
Project Implicit, xxxv
psychometric testing, 4

R

ransformational leadership, xxxiii–xxxiv
rational emotive behavior therapy (REBT),
    192–193
rational linear thinking, xxvii
Reach Higher campaign, 8
Ready, Set, Go, Review: Screening for Behavioral
    Health Risk in Schools, 190
reality therapy, 193
reductionism, xxv
registered play therapist (RPT), 194
Rehabilitation Act of 1973, 128
Response to Intervention (RTI) team, 126–127,
    133–134, 190
role-play annual administrative conference, 140

S

SAMHSA Guide to Screening, 165–166
Sandy Hook Elementary tragedy, 2012, 149
school climate and culture team, 129
school counseling advocacy, xliv, 20, 37, 62–63,
    87–88, 112, 137–138, 163, 182, 205, 233–234
school counseling assignments, xlvi, 114–115, 165
    annotated bibliography, 209
    consultation approach comparison, 65
    consumer reports, 114–115
    creating annual calendar, 139–140
    creation of mock advisory council, 91
    designing a brochure, 22
    exploring diagnoses, 208
    identifying professional values, 90
    mandated reporting practice, 65
    parent/guardian presentation, 209
    personal beliefs statement, 90–91

research on community resources, 208–209
role-play annual administrative conference, 140
school counseling program assessment, 236
school data gathering, 114
small-group interventions, 184
state certification and licensure awareness, 22
student outcome goals, 114
time management tools inventory, 140
video/visual social media introduction, 39
writing reflective journal, 39
school counseling profession
  advisory councils, 79–80
  as mental health counselors, 3
  beliefs and mindsets, 73–76
  during pandemic, 10–12
  future of, 12–13
  history of, 3–12
  leadership responsibilities, 72
  locating inequities, 99–103
  middle school, 27
  mission statements, 77–79
  vision statements, 77–78
school counselors, 43–44, 94–95
  as coordinator, 51–55
  as leaders, xxxiii–xxxvi, 33
  as mental health collaborator, 50–51
  as mental health counselors, 46–47
  clinical supervision, 35, 61, 85–86, 110, 135–136, 161–162, 180, 203, 231
  collaborative-process driven model, 48
  committee work, 126–130
  competencies, 30–31
  connection to professional standards, xliv, 20–21, 38, 63, 138, 163, 183, 206, 235
  duties, 28, 33–34
  ethical practice and standards, 30, 45, 71, 95–96, 119, 147, 170, 189, 217
  professional contact, 37
  professional development, 36, 61, 86, 111, 136, 162, 180–181, 203–204, 232–233
  role, 29
  self-care, 36, 61, 86–87, 111–112, 136–137, 162–163, 181, 204–205, 232–233
  tips for, 36–37
  understanding connections between concepts, 37
School Counselors Rubric Example Framework for School Counselors, 237
school counselor support group, 181
The School Data Culture Report, 100
School Improvement/Strategic Plans (SIP), 102
School Information Systems (SIS), 101–102
School Safety Team, 129
screening
  appropriateness of tool and interpretation of results, 150–151
  tools, 149–150
SCUTA, 140
Second Step (SEL curriculum), 166, 184
Section 504 team, 128
self-care, 36, 86–87, 111–112, 136–137, 162–163, 181, 204–205, 232–233
Sharing the Vision: The National Standards for Students (Campbell and Dahir), 6
Simon Sinek Ted Talk, 91
sleep assessment and reflection, 86–87
Sleep Foundation, 87
small-group counseling, 125, 173–174
SMART goals, 104, 115
social-emotional learning, 7
social media cleanses, 111–112
sole possession notes, 54
solution-focused brief counseling (SFBC), 194
solution-focused counseling (SFC) theory, 49–50
Stages of Group Made Fun, 184
standards-based education reform movement, 6
strengths-based counseling, 7
student assistant teams, 50
student outcome goals, 104–105
supportive counseling, 196–197
systems change, xxx–xxxiii
system theory, xxv
  cultural considerations and, xxix–xxx
  equilibrium, xxx

T
targeted large groups, 172–173
Taylor, Breonna, 10
TCK World, 184
teachable moments, 34
Teachers Pay Teachers, 184
Teaching for Change, xxxv
theory driven individual counseling, 191–192
Tier 1 interventions, 127, 148
  appraisal and advisement, 153–154
  developmental counseling lessons, 151–152
  health and well-being initiatives, 152
  parent workshops and programming, 153
  school-wide programming, 152
Tier 2 interventions, 127, 170–171
  check-in/check-out (CICO), 173–174
  mentoring programs, 174
  small-group counseling, 173–174
  targeted large groups, 172–173
Tier 3 interventions, 127
  community resources and referrals, 197–198
  crisis counseling, 195–197
  grief counseling, 196
  identification of students for, 189–191
  play therapy and therapeutic play, 194–195
  rational emotive behavior therapy (REBT), 192–193
  reality therapy, 193

solution-focused brief counseling (SFBC), 194
   supportive counseling, 196–197
   theory driven individual counseling, 191–192
   yoga, 204–205
time logs, 121–122
time management tools inventory, 140
Title IX, 9
Toggl Track, 140
transformational leadership, xxxiii–xxxvii
   critical awareness, xxxvii
   interconnected nature, xxxvii–xxxviii
   moral courage, xxxvii
   principles of democracy, justice, equity, and emancipation, xxxvi
   promotion of equal opportunity, xxxv
   student growth and success, role in, xxxv–xxxvi
   systems perspective, xxxvi–xxxvii
   transformation of conditions, xxxiv
Transforming School Counseling Initiative (TSCI), 6
Trans Student, 210
Trevor Lifeline, 210
Trevor Project, 210
Truss, Joe, xxiv

U

universal screenings (UMHSs), 149, 151, 190
U.S. space exploration program, 4

V

vision statements, 77–78
vocational guidance, 4

W

web-based resources, xlvi–xlvii, 22, 65, 91, 140–141, 165–166, 184
   advocacy competencies, 22
   appropriate vs inappropriate duties, 39
   Bronfenbrenner's ecological systems, xlvi
   for individuals with hidden disabilities, 141
   for information regarding eligibility for 504 accommodations, 141
   for school counseling program assessment, 237–238
   for working with LGBTQI+ Community, 210
   National Educational and Health Awareness Dates, 165
   rational emotive education, 209
   role of school counselor, 39
   school performance indicators, 115
   standards and competencies, 40
   Tier 3 interventions, 209
   yoga, 209
wellness, xlii–xliii, 19–20
   dimensions of, xliii–xliv
West Virginia School Counselor Performance Appraisal, 237
White cultural values, xxvii
White supremacy, xxxiv, xxxv, xliv
Women's Rights Project, 11
WV Balanced Scorecard Dashboard, 115

Y

yoga, 204–205
   web-based resources, 209
Youth Mental Health First Aid, 153

Z

Zoom WV, 115

About the Authors

Dr. Christine J. Schimmel, Ed.D., NCC, LPC is an associate professor and associate director of the School of Counseling and Well-Being at West Virginia University. She received her B.A. in education from Glenville State College, her M.A. in secondary school counseling from West Virginia University, and her Ed.D. from Marshall University. Dr. Schimmel coordinates the counseling program at WVU. She specifically focuses her energies working with and training pre-service school counselors. In that role, Dr. Schimmel provides supervision to students in both practicum and internship experiences. A former school counselor, she has spent the last 20 years providing staff development and conference workshops on topics relevant to school counselors, clinical mental health counselors, and teachers. She has presented on topics such as Impact Therapy, creative counseling techniques, counseling theory, dealing with students who exhibit problematic behaviors, growth mindset, protective factors, group counseling, and Youth Mental Health First Aid. Dr. Schimmel has published more than 10 articles, books, and book chapters on these subjects as well. Along with her colleague, Dr. Ed Jacobs, they have published one of the most widely used group counseling textbooks on the market, *Group Counseling: Strategies and Skills* which is now in its ninth edition. Dr. Schimmel is co-editor of the popular *Counseling Children and Adolescents* text with Dr. Ann Vernon. Along with colleagues at WVU, Dr. Schimmel was recently awarded a Department of Health and Human Services grant to deliver Youth Mental Health First Aid to public school personnel throughout the state of West Virginia.

Dr. Sarah I. Springer, Ph.D., LPC, ACS is an associate professor in the Department of Professional Counseling at Monmouth University. She received her Bachelor of Music Education degree in voice at Mason Gross School of the Arts at Rutgers University and Master of Arts and Master of Education degrees in psychological counseling from Teachers College, Columbia University. She received her Ph.D. in counselor education and supervision from Montclair State University. In addition to her New Jersey School Counselor Certification, she is also certified as a Daring Way™ Facilitator (CDWF) through Dr. Brené Brown's organization and is a Licensed Professional Counselor.

Before moving into higher education, Dr. Springer provided counseling in the high school and elementary settings for nearly a decade, most recently developing an elementary school counseling program from the ground up in Mendham Township, New Jersey. Through her private practice, Dr. Springer has worked as a mental health counselor in a school running groups for children with special needs and provided individual counseling to children, adolescents, and parents, as well as LPC supervision to pre-licensed counselors. She has had the privilege of providing professional development faculty presentations for K-12 educators and presentations around counselor leadership to several area universities. Most recently, Dr. Springer created a graduate counseling course, Courageous Connections, which incorporates the Daring Way™ Curriculum, a highly experiential methodology based on the research of Dr. Brené Brown into pre-service school and mental health training. She regularly researches and publishes on topics specific to school counselor education, counselor supervision, ethics, and group work. Dr. Springer recently released the second edition of a co-edited book titled *A School Counselor's Guide to Small Groups: Coordination, Leadership, and Assessment* (2022).

Kathleen L. Grant, Ph.D., NCC is an assistant professor in the Department of Counselor Education at The College of New Jersey. She earned her Bachelor of Science in biology at Wagner College, her Master of Arts in counselor education at The College of New Jersey, and her Ph.D. in counselor education from Montclair State University. Prior to becoming a counselor educator, Dr. Grant served as both a middle school and high school counselor. Her teaching and research focus on how systems of oppression and domination are upheld and reproduced in K-12 public education and practices that dismantle white supremacy culture within schools. Dr. Grant's current research explores the intersections between white supremacy culture and the climate crisis, particularly examining how youth navigate dominant cultural norms to bring about change. She is also a dedicated mother, climate activist, and runner.

Dr. Kara P. Ieva, Ph.D., NCC, NCSC is an associate professor in the Counseling in Educational Settings program at Rowan University. She received her Bachelor of Arts degree in Spanish secondary education and Master of Education in secondary curriculum and administration from Towson University. Additionally, she earned her Master of Education in school counseling from Loyola College in Maryland and her Ph.D. in counselor education from the University of Central Florida. Dr. Ieva's areas of research interest include counseling children and adolescents of underserved populations regarding college and career readiness, social/emotional development, and group counseling. She focuses on addressing the academic, behavioral, and mental health needs of all students simultaneously in schools. As such, Dr. Ieva provides professional development to K-12 school counselors, teachers, and administrators on how to embed social/emotional development into curricula and strategies for cultivating a safe and welcoming mental health and neurodiverse culture in schools. She has held leadership positions for the Association of Specialists in Group Work (ASGW), the New Jersey School Counselor Association (NJSCA), and the New Jersey Association for Counselor Education and Supervision (NJACES). Dr. Ieva is also on the editorial review board for *Professional School Counselor Journal* published by the American School Counselor Association (ASCA). She was the recipient of the North Atlantic Region of Counselor Education and Supervision (NARACES) Marijane Fall Counselor Educator of the Year Award (2019), the Research Article of the Year Award (2011) from the American Counseling Association (ACA), the NARACES Social Justice Award (2014), and the NARACES Emerging Leader Award (2012). Further, she was the principal investigator and project director for the Rowan University Aim High Science and Technology Academies, a college access program that provided first generation and low-income college students with access to and preparation for post-secondary education in STEM. This grant resulted in her serving as Director of Academic and Student Services for the Rowan University STEAM Academy (2015-present). She also served as a Co-Pi on a grant from the Forman S. Acton Educational Foundation to evaluate funded college access programs. Lastly, Dr. Ieva serves as an evaluator on multiple National Science Foundation (NSF) grants.

Printed in the USA
CPSIA information can be obtained
at www.ICGtesting.com
LVHW071658200124
769095LV00002B/30